SIDREA Series in Accounting and Business Administration

Giovanni Liberatore, University of Florence
Florence, Italy

Andrea Lionzo, Catholic University of the Sacred Heart
Milano, Italy

Rosa Lombardi, University of Rome, Sapienza
Roma, Italy

Davide Maggi, Amedeo Avogadro University of Eastern Piedmont
Novara, Italy

Daniela Mancini, University of Teramo
Teramo, Italy

Francesca Manes Rossi, University of Naples Federico II
Naples, Italy

Luciano Marchi, University of Pisa
Pisa, Italy

Riccardo Mussari, University of Siena
Siena, Italy

Marco Maria Mattei, University of Bologna
Forlì, Italy

Antonella Paolini, University of Macerata
Macerata, Italy

Mauro Paoloni, University of Rome Tor Vergata
Rome, Italy

Paola Paoloni, University of Rome Tor Vergata, Rome, Italy
Sapienza University of Rome
Rome, Italy

Marcantonio Ruisi, University of Palermo
Palermo, Italy

Claudio Teodori, University of Brescia
Brescia, Italy

Simone Terzani, University of Perugia
Perugia, Italy

Stefania Veltri, University of Calabria
Rende, Italy

This is the official book series of SIDREA - the Italian Society of Accounting and Business Administration. This book series is provided with a wide Scientific Committee composed of Academics by SIDREA. It publishes contributions (monographs, edited volumes and proceedings) as a result of the double blind review process by the SIDREA's thematic research groups, operating at the national and international levels. Particularly, the series aims to disseminate specialized findings on several topics – classical and cutting-edge alike – that are currently being discussed by the accounting and business administration communities. The series authors are respected researchers and professors in the fields of business valuation; governance and internal control; financial accounting; public accounting; management control; gender; turnaround predictive models; non-financial disclosure; intellectual capital, smart technologies, and digitalization; and university governance and performance measurement.This book series is indexed in Scopus.

Salvatore Loprevite • Stefano Marasca
Domenico Nicolò • Marcantonio Ruisi
Claudio Teodori
Editors

Startups and Gazelle Enterprises

Insights into the Success and Challenges of High-Growth Firms

Springer

Editors
Salvatore Loprevite
Department of Social and Educational Sciences of the Mediterranean Area
University Dante Alighieri of Reggio Calabria
Reggio Calabria, Italy

Domenico Nicolò
Department of Law, Economics and Human Sciences
University Mediterranea of Reggio Calabria
Reggio Calabria, Italy

Claudio Teodori
Department of Economics and Management
University of Brescia
Brescia, Italy

Stefano Marasca
Department of Management
Marche Polytechnic University
Ancona, Italy

Marcantonio Ruisi
Department of Economics, Business and Statistics
University of Palermo
Palermo, Italy

ISSN 2662-9879 ISSN 2662-9887 (electronic)
SIDREA Series in Accounting and Business Administration
ISBN 978-3-031-90880-4 ISBN 978-3-031-90881-1 (eBook)
https://doi.org/10.1007/978-3-031-90881-1

This Springer imprint is published by the registered company Springer Nature Switzerland AG
The registered company address is: Gewerbestrasse 11, 6330 Cham, Switzerland

Preface

The topic of startups is of relevant interest to academic scholars and policymakers.

For scientific research, startups are a fascinating and complex subject of study. During the first few years of the company's life, the business idea that leads to the creation of the company must be translated into concrete actions aimed at creating the strategic, managerial, financial, and operational conditions for the new venture to survive and develop according to the founders' expectations. This is a critical stage in the entrepreneurial process, as empirical evidence shows a pronounced vulnerability of young firms, which often fail in their first few years. In contrast to the many failures, some young companies grow rapidly, bucking the prevailing trend that leads to failure. On average, only about half survive beyond the first five years. Most survivors remain small, while only a few (about 1%) experience rapid growth, evolving into high-performance companies known as "gazelles" or even scaling up to become "unicorns" in their early years. It should also be noted that even high-growth startups are very fragile, despite having built up a competitive advantage in their early years that has led to rapid growth. This is because they are exposed to a double source of tension: those typical of the startup phase and those resulting from high growth, which puts strain on their human, technical, and financial resources. Understanding the differences between these groups, which may be related to different business factors, is thus a challenge that attracts business scholars, who have long been engaged to explain the causes of startup success and failure.

Startups contribute significantly to job creation and technological development of a socioeconomic system, thereby helping to generate wealth and strengthen the competitiveness of countries. These characteristics also make them of particular interest to policymakers, who are increasingly involved in implementing policies to support innovative startups and startup ecosystems.

Due to the high scientific and practical relevance of startups, SIDREA (Italian Scientific Society of Accounting and Business Professors) organized a specific Study Group on this category of companies. The group was coordinated by Domenico Nicolò, the deputy coordinator, Mara Del Baldo, and the coordinators appointed by SIDREA, Claudio Teodori and Marcantonio Ruisi. Several members of SIDREA, organized into inter-university teams, participated in the research activities, carrying out various scientific research projects on innovative and high-growth startups.

This book is the result of the research activities conducted by the Study Group. It focuses on both startups and gazelles—with a focus on the Italian and European context—believing that understanding their key characteristics and critical success factors can provide a useful reference point for designing startups that can survive and grow. We are pleased to say that it provides contributions to the scientific community that we believe will be useful for advancing knowledge on startups and gazelles.

The book is structured into three parts: "Theoretical and methodological issues," "Performance and resilience," and "Growth and success factors."

The part about "Theoretical and methodological issues" consists of three chapters:

- Chapter 1. It is a study that gathers and synthesizes the extant knowledge on pivoting in the startup development process through a systematic literature review.
- Chapter 2. Adopting an illustrative case study methodology, this chapter presents the example of the impact case study on "Principles, Models, and Financial Accounting Practices for the Startups and the High-Growth Startups (i.e., Gazelles)," promoted by the Gruppo di Studio "Startups" of the Italian academic group of the professors of accounting and business economics (SIDREA) and the Italian Institute of Chartered Accountants (CNDCEC).
- Chapter 3. This chapter discusses the limitations of traditional methodologies and the suitability of alternative methods specifically conceived for valuing startups. To refine the understanding of the intricate valuation process of startups, the chapter also proposes a conceptual model intended to support the fundamental analysis, the selection of models, and the setting of startup valuation methods.

The second part about "Performance and resilience" is in four chapters:

- Chapter 4. This chapter presents an empirical study examining the profitability performance of innovative and social startups across six European countries, comparing pre-COVID (2017–2019) and COVID (2020–2022) periods. By this analysis, the authors investigate the relationship between profitability and several potential drivers, such as financial structure, liquidity, size, and the size of the board of directors. The obtained findings reveal divergent trends for innovative and social startups, highlighting the complex, context-dependent nature of startup performance.
- Chapter 5. Concerning the performance of startups, this chapter presents an empirical study focusing on the performance of profitability and financial structure of Italian innovative startups over the decade 2013–2022. Three hypotheses are tested: profitability is stably positive and high; profitability supports adequate financial statements; performance is influenced by location.
- Chapter 6. This chapter focuses on "gazelle companies" considering the COVID-19 pandemic as a natural experiment. The research shows that the human capital endowment of high-growth startups, indirectly expressed by the

ability of their employees to create added value, positively affects their resilience to external shocks of an exceptional nature and significant, such as the COVID-19 pandemic.
- Chapter 7. It is a study on the role of financial support measures in sustaining business startups. In particular, the chapter focuses on the so-called Credit Guarantee Schemes (CGS) and the role of potential moderating factors that could influence the effectiveness of these financial support measures. Specifically, the chapter examines the potential drawbacks of the "Italian Central Guarantee Fund" and assesses how debt policies affect the survival prospects of new ventures.

The third part about "Growth and success factors" consists of four chapters:

- Chapter 8. The authors of this chapter—by linking together the literature fields on startups, gazelles, innovation, and sustainability—investigate whether firms capable of becoming gazelles at the turn of the COVID-19 crisis show a higher level of attention toward generating social and environmental well-being than their non-gazelle pairs. The study focuses on the Italian context, the first and most affected by the COVID-19 crisis in Europe, finding a significant orientation of gazelles toward sustainability.
- Chapter 9. This chapter conducts a systematic literature review on environmental and social sustainability to examine innovative startups that strongly integrate sustainability principles into their corporate strategies and business models. The authors explore how the sustainability orientation of startups has evolved, identify driving factors and barriers, and assess the tools used to improve sustainability performance accountability. Findings reveal that sustainability orientation is becoming a key factor in evaluating startups, affecting their performance, corporate disclosure quality, and competitiveness in the market.
- Chapter 10. Referring to the Italian healthcare sector, this chapter presents a study of the factors influencing the financial performance of high-growth companies. Results show the critical role of the above factors in the long-term success of healthcare gazelles. The study also provides evidence of specific success factors for healthcare gazelles, such as regulatory compliance, clinical validation and evidence-based practice, patient-centered approach, ethical considerations and social responsibility, and digital health technologies use.
- Chapter 11. The final chapter presents the case study of Widiba (an acronym for Wise Dialogue Bank), a pioneering FinTech company that has achieved remarkable financial and innovative performance within its first decade. Through the lens of the Cultural Entrepreneurship theory to examine the launch of a FinTech venture, the case study analysis highlights the pivotal function of cultural processes in entrepreneurial achievements, focusing on the collective narrative that informs the identity and innovation of new ventures. Specifically, the research identifies pivotal elements of cultural resonance, including cognitive alignment and emotional impact, as essential for strengthening entrepreneurial narratives. Ultimately, the findings of this study offer valuable insights into how cultural

values and processes may drive innovation and contribute to the success of new ventures, even in the financial sector.

The editors would like to thank all the authors of the chapters, who have contributed with professionality and considerable effort to the realization of this book. The editors would also like to thank all the reviewers who, at various stages of the review process, provided valuable suggestions to improve the quality of the chapters. Finally, special thanks are due to the Executive Board of SIDREA, which supported the organization of the Study Group and actively collaborated in the initiative of publishing this book.

Reggio Calabria, Italy — Salvatore Loprevite
Ancona, Italy — Stefano Marasca
Reggio Calabria, Italy — Domenico Nicolò
Palermo, Italy — Marcantonio Ruisi
Brescia, Italy — Claudio Teodori

Contents

Part I
Theoretical and Methodological Issues

Chapter 1
Pivoting and the Startup Development Process: A Systematic Literature Review

Stefano Marasca and Simone Poli

1.1 Introduction

During the planning phase that precedes the launch of new entrepreneurial initiatives, startups are based on a series of hypotheses, including those pertaining to the product/service they intend to offer, the existence and development of a reference market, the creation of adequate production/dispensing processes, etc. Once the business has launched, however, startups may encounter situations or events that manifest in ways that are unexpected or unforeseen.

Some of these situations or events may be adversities that lead to failure caused by a lack of skills, resources, and maturity. Others, however, may present opportunities to be seized.

In the face of both adversities and opportunities, the entrepreneur must decide whether to persevere with or change tack with respect to the decisions taken initially or to wholly abandon the entrepreneurial initiative. Many entrepreneurs, practitioners, and academics refer to this change in terms of pivot.

Ries originated the pivot concept in a blog post entitled "Pivot, do not jump to a new vision" (Ries, 2009) in 2009, and the concept gained traction after it was officially conceptualized in Ries', 2011 book *The Lean Startup* (Ries, 2011). According to Ries (2011), a pivot is a "structured course correction designed to test a new fundamental hypothesis about product, strategy and engine of growth." Despite the rapid spread of the practice among entrepreneurs and practitioners (Blank & Dorf, 2012), this phenomenon has only recently begun to attract the interest of researchers, stimulating scholars to offer additional definitions and conceptualizations, specifying what pivot is and what differentiates pivoting processes from other types of

S. Marasca · S. Poli (✉)
Department of Management, Marche Polytechnic University, Ancona, Italy
e-mail: s.marasca@staff.univpm.it; s.poli@staff.univpm.it

S. Loprevite et al. (eds.), *Startups and Gazelle Enterprises*, SIDREA Series in Accounting and Business Administration,
https://doi.org/10.1007/978-3-031-90881-1_1

strategy and business model changes. While this growing interest yielded a more in-depth understanding of the pivot phenomenon, it has also generated a proliferation of meanings and labels, largely divergent and excessively influenced by the context of the analysis, causing a lack of rigor (Flechas Chaparro & De Vasconcelos Gomes, 2021) and weak generalizability of the provided definitions (Sadeghiani & Anderson, 2023). Moreover, the growing interest in this phenomenon has led to an increase in studies addressing various pivot-related topics and generating new knowledge that requires systematization.

This study provides a systematic literature review (SLR) of papers focused on pivoting in the startup development process published in the last ten years, which corresponds to the time frame that records a notable growth in the number of studies on the topic, with the aim of gathering and synthesizing the extant knowledge on this topic. In so doing, it aims to provide researchers with an updated research landscape and valuable future research directions on pivot decisions in the development process of startups. Meanwhile, it will also provide several useful references for entrepreneurs who should or could make pivot decisions in the startup development process.

This study is organized as follows. The section that follows describes the research methodology. The third section provides a descriptive overview of the papers analyzed, followed by an illustration of the identified thematic areas and the relevant papers. The final section concludes the review and offers some considerations for future research on the topic.

1.2 Research Methodology

An SLR approach was adopted to assemble and summarize the extant literature on pivoting in the startup development process to identify the most widely explored thematic areas and possible directions for future research. Figure 1.1 shows the main research phases.

As argued by Tranfield et al. (2003), LSR allows the extant literature on a certain topic to be analyzed and evaluated in a replicable, transparent, and reliable manner (Cook et al., 1997; Thorpe et al., 2005). In addition, SLR is not limited to a mere description of the extant literature, but it allows the extant literature to be synthesized in an aggregate and integrated manner (Paré et al., 2015).

The research's replicability is guaranteed by the SLR approach's requirement that a research protocol be defined, divided into specific phases (the most important of which is the review protocol) that must be followed and respected (Tranfield et al., 2003).

To the foregoing, it should be added that SLR can be particularly useful when the research topic is characterized by high levels of heterogeneity and fragmentation (Paré et al., 2015; Andreini & Bettinelli, 2017), as in the case of the object of the present study.

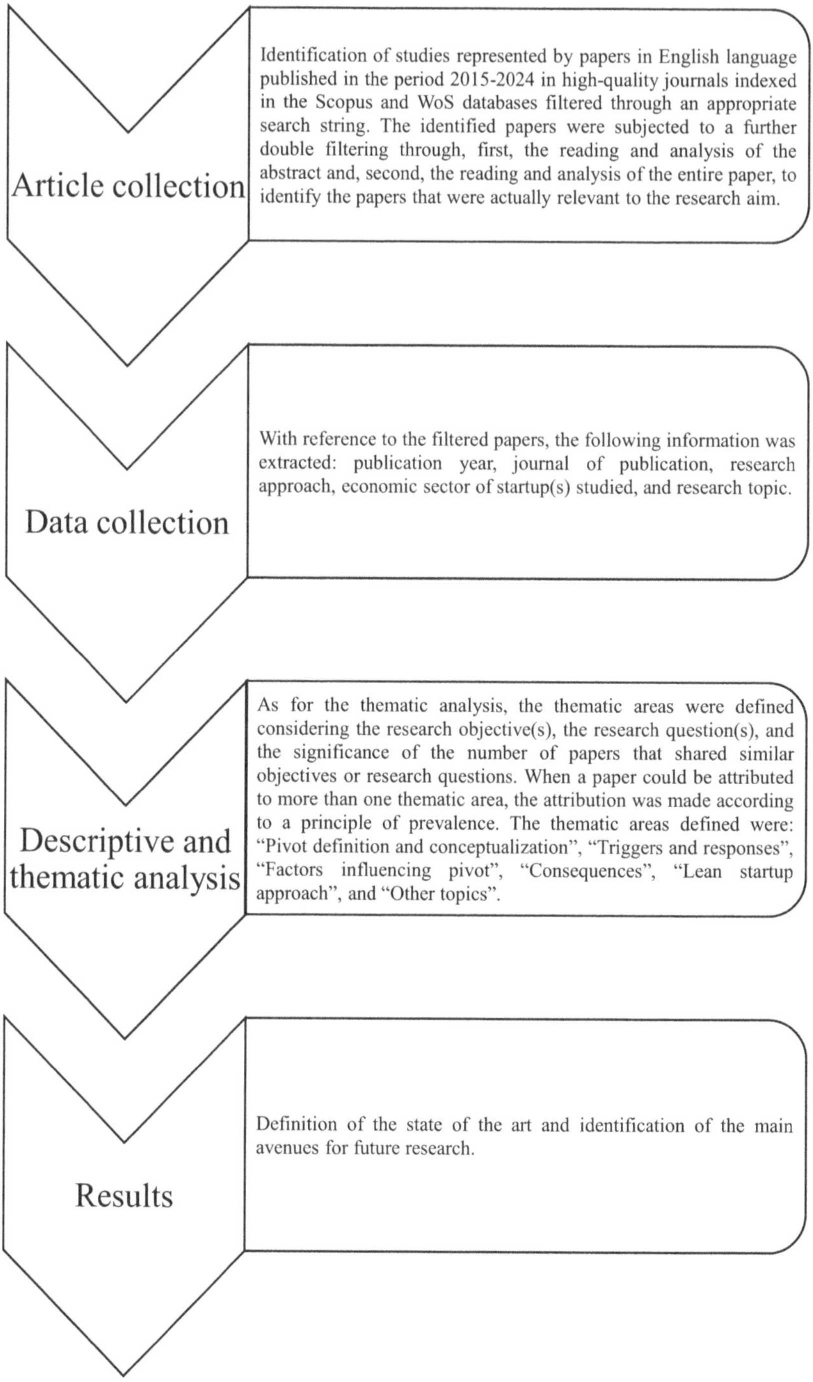

Fig. 1.1 Main research phases

To conduct an SLR, it was necessary to identify suitable databases from which to obtain the papers for analysis. To this end, the authors used Scopus and Web of Science (WoS). The reason that led the authors to select these databases was twofold. The first was the decision to perform an SLR of studies published in high-quality scientific journals. From this perspective, Scopus and WoS guarantee broad coverage of the target journals (Massaro et al., 2015; Secundo et al., 2019). The second reason was the will to guarantee the replicability of the research.

Given the nature of the research object, to minimize the likelihood of finding papers that deal with the concept of pivot but concern irrelevant areas of study, the journals were selected from within the subject areas "Business, Management, and Accounting," "Computer Science," and "Economics, Econometrics, and Finance," with reference to Scopus, and "Business economics" and "Computer science," with reference to WoS.

Two further limitations concerned the type and language of the research product: only papers published in scientific journals in English. The first limitation is consistent with that written above: given the decision to review studies published in high-quality scientific journals, it follows that other research product types, such as books and book chapters, conference proceedings, etc., are excluded. The second limitation was adopted because it favors the replicability of the research.

A final limitation concerned the reference time frame for the papers' publication. The search was limited to the last ten years (2015–2024) because the topic under investigation has attracted the interest of the scientific community relatively recently (Flechas Chaparro & De Vasconcelos Gomes, 2021). Consequently, on the one hand, the time frame limitation minimized the likelihood that the search would identify irrelevant papers; on the other hand, it guaranteed that the time frame corresponding to the greatest number of papers on the topic was observed.

As written, an important aspect in the planning review stage is the definition of the review protocol and, in this context, of the inclusion and exclusion criteria (Tranfield et al., 2003). These criteria were summarized in the search string applied to the databases. The search string was formulated so as not to be excessively stringent so that it might identify the greatest possible number of papers of potential interest to the research.

Considering that the object of the study is the pivoting in the startup development process, the string used is divided into two parts: one that considers the phenomenon under investigation and one that considers the business context in which the phenomenon occurs.

In the first part of the string, the term "pivot" and its possible variations were considered. In addition, considering that the literature has found that scholars often refer to pivot in terms of "business model innovation" and "business model change" (Flechas Chaparro & De Vasconcelos Gomes, 2021), these last two expressions were included in the first part of the string. The inclusion of these two expressions was aimed at extending the potential number of papers of interest.

In the second part of the string, a set of expressions that may refer to the firm in the startup phase and their possible variations were considered.

The search string, therefore, was as follows:

("Pivot*" OR "Business model innovation" OR "Business model change") AND ("Startup*" OR "Start – up*" OR "Start up*" OR "New venture*" OR "New firm*" OR "New company" OR "New companies" OR "entrepreneur*" OR "Early stage*")

The search string was applied to the papers' titles, abstracts, and keywords, yielding 566 papers in Scopus and 160 papers in WoS. The common papers were found to be 146. Consequently, the papers analyzed were 580.[1]

In addition to the definition of the inclusion and exclusion criteria, the definition of the review protocol required the definition of the information that had to be collected for the subsequent analysis phase. Since this subsequent phase consisted in a descriptive and thematic analysis of the papers, the authors collected the following information: publication year, journal of publication, research approach, economic sector of startup(s) studied, and research topic.

Regarding the research topic, the authors have not predefined a coding scheme, but "the authors decided to allow every author to carry out an individual inductive data-driven thematic analysis" (Ancillai et al., 2023).

The analysis phase was conducted in two steps. In the first step, each author read and analyzed the papers' abstracts to exclude those that were not relevant to the research objective. Once the individual analysis phase was completed, the authors compared their respective points of view. The authors analyzed and discussed all cases of divergent results together and treated them uniquely according to the outcome of the analysis and discussion. At the end of this step, the authors excluded 444 papers because they did not deal with or explicitly refer to pivot and retained the others (136).

In the second step, each author read and analyzed the papers retained to exclude those that were not relevant to the research objective and to collect information for the subsequent phase. Information was collected and compiled in an Excel spreadsheet with all information identified in the previous planning phase. Once the individual analysis phase was complete, the authors triangulated the information collected and compared their respective points of view. The triangularization of the information collected and the comparison of their individual perspectives revealed several instances of divergent results with reference to the information that each author had collected. Most instances of divergence concerned the papers' topics and, consequently, the identification of the thematic areas and the placement of the papers within them. All cases of divergent results were analyzed and discussed together by the authors and were treated uniquely according to the outcome of the analysis and discussion.

To identify the thematic areas, the authors considered the objective(s) of the papers, the research question(s), and the number of papers that shared similar objectives or

[1] The original extraction of the papers from the Scopus database was done in March 2024. The extension of the search to the WoS database was done in September 2024. To ensure consistency of the extraction dates from the two databases, the extraction from the WoS database was limited to papers published until 2023, as it was not possible to set a specific date equal to that of the extraction from the Scopus database.

research questions. A specific thematic area was identified when this number appeared relatively significant. In reviewing the papers, the authors found that some papers dealt with multiple aspects of pivot, which might justify their inclusion in more than one of the thematic areas identified. In these cases, the paper's inclusion in a certain thematic area was determined according to a principle of prevalence.

Three different types of papers emerged: (1) papers that had the pivot concept or specific aspects thereof as their main research object (focused papers) (20); (2) papers that did not have the pivot concept or specific aspects thereof as their main research object but that did have as their main research object other topics that dealt with the pivot concept (non-focused papers) (15); (3) papers in which the pivot was mentioned only "incidentally" (101). Papers of the first and second typologies were retained in the sample of papers for analysis and those of the third typology were excluded. Thus, 35 papers altogether were retained in the sample.

Figure 1.2 summarizes the paper selection process. It is inspired by the PRIMA model for SLR (Moher et al., 2009).

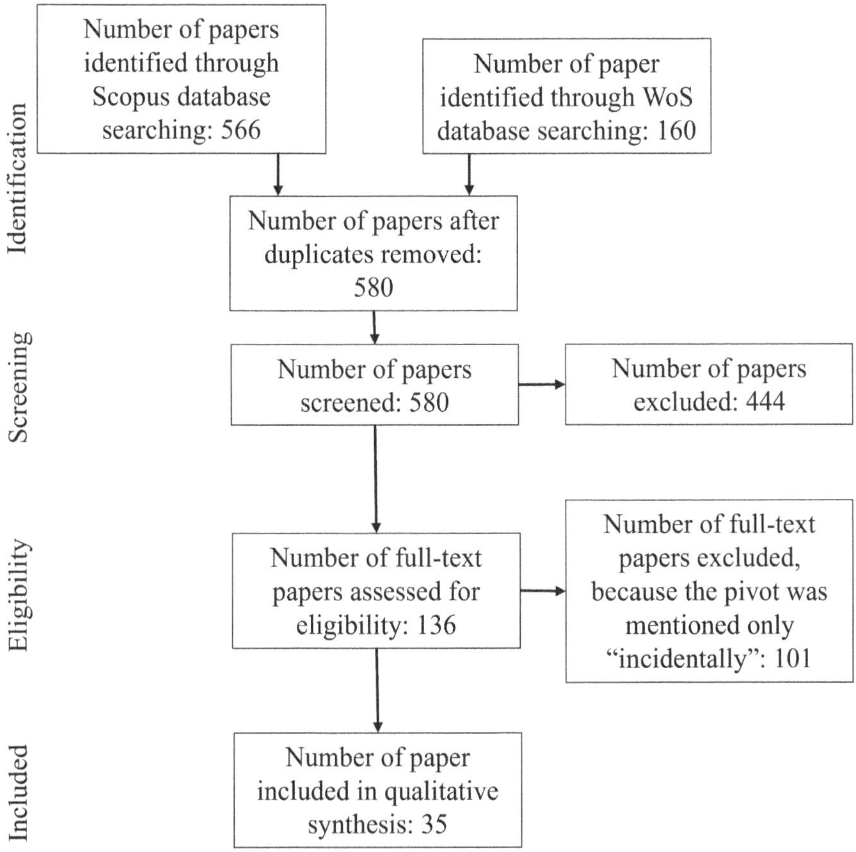

Fig. 1.2 Paper selection process

1.3 Overview of the Selected Papers

The distribution of the papers according to year of publication shows that approximately 89% of them were published in the period 2020–2023, with 51% published in the period 2022–2023 and 38% published in the period 2020–2021. These results are in line with those reported by Flechas Chaparro and De Vasconcelos Gomes (2021) and suggest that pivot is a relatively recent research topic that is attracting rapidly growing interest from academics. It is noteworthy that only one paper was published in 2024, but this is likely attributable to the fact that the sample was assembled in March 2024 (Fig. 1.3).

The papers' distribution according to the journals in which they were published reveals that the 35 selected papers were published in 27 different journals across three different subject areas. One journal published 3 papers, 6 journals published 2 papers, and all other journals published only one paper. The high number of journals and the low concentration of papers per journal suggest that the pivot concept has attracted transversal interest as a research topic (Table 1.1).

The papers' distribution by research approach indicates that an exclusively qualitative approach was used in 66% of the papers, an exclusively quantitative approach in 23% of the papers, and a mixed approach in 6% of the papers. The predominant use of the qualitative research approach may be regarded as secure evidence that the research on pivot is in its infancy (Flechas Chaparro & De Vasconcelos Gomes, 2021) (Fig. 1.4).

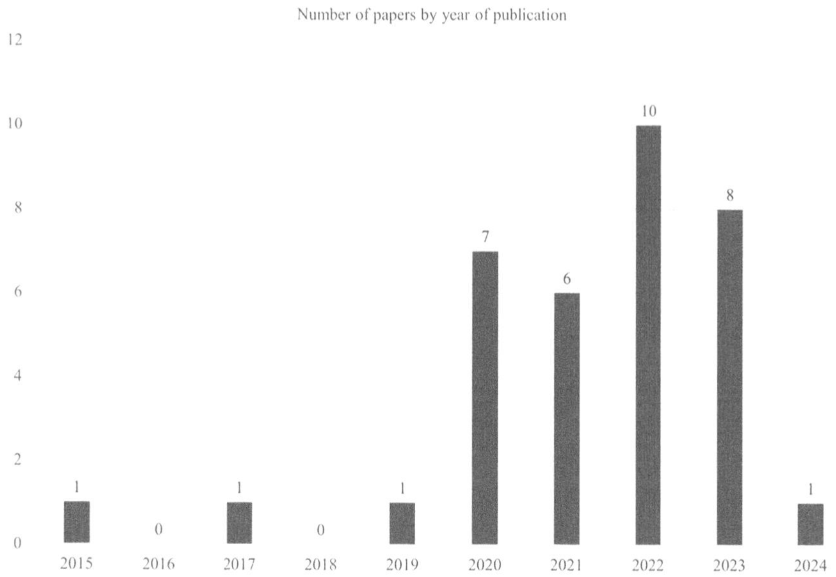

Fig. 1.3 Number of papers by year of publication

Table 1.1 Papers' distribution according to the journals in which they were published

Number of papers per journal	Journals
3	International Small Business Journal: Researching Entrepreneurship
2	Digital Business; International Journal of Entrepreneurial Behaviour and Research; Journal of Business Research; Journal of Business Venturing; Strategic Management Journal; Technological Forecasting and Social Change
1	Academy of Management Journal; Empirical Software Engineering; Entrepreneurship and Regional Development; Entrepreneurship: Theory and Practice; Information and Management; Information Systems Frontiers; International Entrepreneurship and Management Journal; International Journal of Entrepreneurship Behaviour and Research; International Journal of Innovation Management; Journal of Management; Journal of Management Studies; Journal of Small Business and Entrepreneurship; Journal of Small Business Management; Management Decision; Management Science; Managerial and Decision Economics; Marketing Science; New England Journal of Entrepreneurship; Organization Science; Strategic Organization

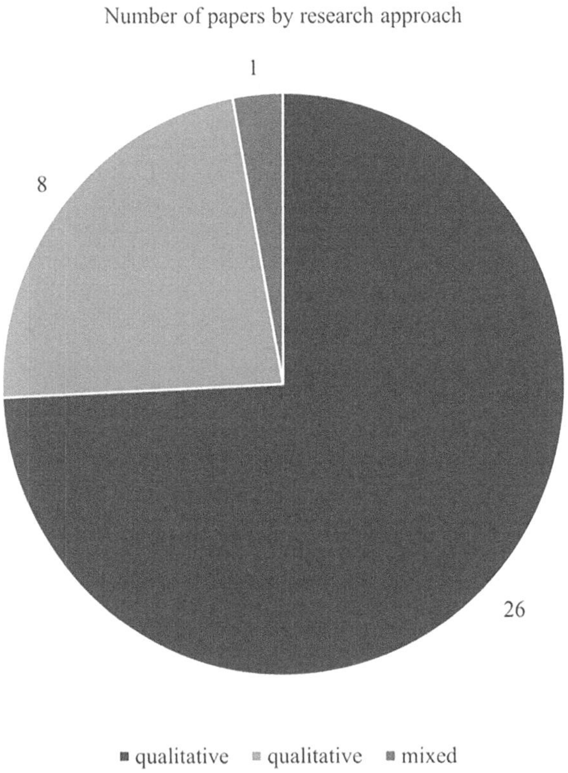

Fig. 1.4 Number of papers by research approach

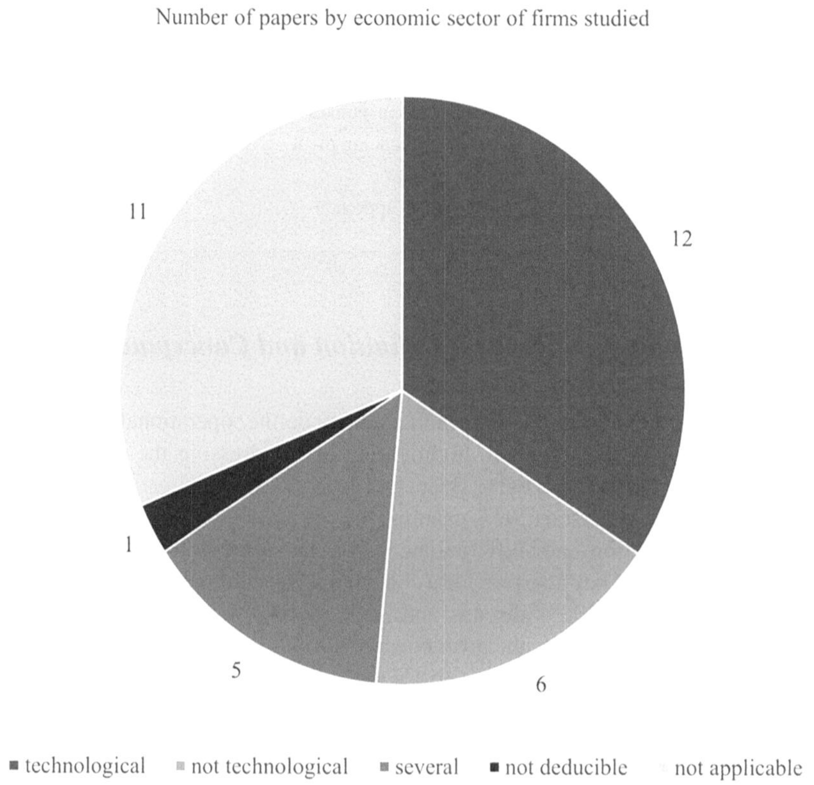

Fig. 1.5 Number of papers by economic sector of firms studied

The papers' distribution according to the economic sectors of the firms studied in them reveals that the technological sector (in a broad sense) features in 50% of the papers in which firms are studied. However, in 25% of cases, the firms studied belong to one or more economic sectors aside from the technological one, while in 21% of cases the firms studied belong to multiple economic sectors. Although the technological sector is prevalent, the excessive focus on it, which was identified as a weakness of the research corpus dealing with the pivot concept, does not emerge in this study (Sadeghiani & Anderson, 2023) (Fig. 1.5).

1.4 Analysis of Thematic Areas

Table 1.2 details the thematic areas identified and the number of articles by thematic area.

Below, the thematic areas identified, and the topics of the papers included in them are described more analytically.

Table 1.2 Number of papers by thematic area

Thematic areas	Number of papers
Pivot definition and conceptualization	6
Triggers and responses	6
Factors influencing pivot	8
Consequences	5
Lean startup approach	5
Other topics	5
Total	35

1.4.1 Thematic Area 1: Pivot Definition and Conceptualization

This thematic area includes the papers that aim to define, operationalize, and conceptualize the pivot phenomenon, highlighting and addressing the problems and critical issues that afflict it (6 out of 35).

Sadeghiani and Anderson (2023) examine the clarity of the pivot concept, reposition it as a "substitution," and differentiate it from another pivoting concept related to its process theory. They also provide a conceptual basis for operationalizing pivot.

Sadeghiani et al. (2023) discuss and seek to resolve the problem of non-generalizability that underlies the pivot concept as both practitioners and academics have intended it. The study suggests that a gap separates that which entrepreneurs claim to do from scholars' interpretations of their actions. The academic community should pay greater attention to what entrepreneurs do and adopt a broader perspective that is informed by neopragmatism. In a longitudinal field study, Kirtley and O'Mahony (2023) examine how startup entrepreneurs determine when and how to change their strategies. Decision-makers changed strategies when new information conflicted with or expanded their beliefs. A pivot was not achieved through a single decision but through the gradual addition or removal of strategy elements over time. Sadeghiani et al. (2021) aimed to understand how pivot practice varies from lean startup context to micro and small business context. The authors emphasize the importance of recognizing pivots in various contexts, as different contexts give rise to different pivots. Bohn and Kundisch (2020) aimed to investigate the underlying interpretations that researchers and practitioners attribute to technology pivots. Their study provides two lists of ranked factors (19 for academics and 22 for practitioners) that conceptualize technology pivot. Flechas Chaparro and De Vasconcelos Gomes (2021) implemented an SLR to identify different conceptualizations, research streams, and theoretical building blocks. They provide a generalizable definition of pivot and a baseline framework. For them, pivot represents a strategic decision that is made after a failure (or the identification of a potential failure) and that manifests itself through a process that entails four different stages: recognition, generation of options, seizing and testing, and reconfiguration.

Although only a few papers focused on pivot definition-related issues, it must be noted that the conceptualization of the pivot phenomenon was a crucial step in all the selected papers, serving as a foundation for their subsequent exploration and analysis. Except for three papers, each selected study defines the pivot phenomenon, underscoring the importance of understanding the pivot phenomenon before attempting to analyze it. Therefore, in the analysis of the definitions provided by the pivot literature, all the selected papers should be taken into consideration.

The definitions provided by the authors highlight a remarkable heterogeneity. In this sense, to achieve a broader understanding of how the pivot phenomenon has been interpreted by the literature, it is essential to deal with this heterogeneity, examining the definitions provided by the reviewed papers through the lens of those aspects that have been characterized by variability across the studies. Coherently, the definitions were analyzed by observing four distinct conceptual blocks of each definition: the concept of pivot; the business elements affected by the pivoting decision; the type of change that derives from pivoting; and, finally, the specific causes that trigger the decision.

Examination of the definitions from the perspective of the first concept (i.e., what a pivot is) reveals that most of the reviewed papers (about 60%) describe the pivot phenomenon as a change involving the reallocation of resources or using words like modification (Ghezzi & Cavallo, 2020; Yoo et al., 2021), alteration (Welter et al., 2021), trajectory shift (Sanasi, 2023), or adaptation (Angus et al., 2024). These definitions classify pivoting decisions as a particular type of change, emphasizing pivot's nature as an "action of transforming and modifying something over time" (Rensink, 2002). Other papers define pivot as a replacement or substitution (Sadeghiani & Anderson, 2023), a course correction (Morgan et al., 2020), or a discontinuity (Sadeghiani et al., 2022), suggesting that the changing decisions are triggered by evidence highlighting the unsustainability and flaws of the firm's current course. Other authors interpret pivot as a strategic decision (Flechas Chaparro & De Vasconcelos Gomes, 2021), strategic reorientation (McDonald & Gao, 2019; Sanasi & Ghezzi, 2022), or strategic change that results from a complex and progressive decision process. Thus, according to the strategic view, pivots do not occur as a single strategic choice in response to new external information but rather as a substantial strategic realignment that develops gradually on the basis of knowledge acquired from smaller strategic decisions implemented over time (Sanasi & Ghezzi, 2022). According to Sadeghiani et al. (2021), a significant difference exists between pivoting and pivot. The former is the process that leads to experimentation and change, while the latter represents the outcome of the process. Pillai et al. (2020) define strategic pivot as a subset of economic experimentation, emphasizing the strong connection between pivoting and hypothesis testing through business experiments. Kirtley and O'Mahony (2023) argue that individual incremental changes, such as strategic additions made to exploit an emerging opportunity, do not constitute a pivot; rather, firms that pivot make numerous incremental decisions that gradually accumulate into a strategic reorientation over time.

Regarding the business model components affected by the pivoting decisions, some definitions specify that the pivot phenomenon can affect both business model components and the firm's strategies (De Oliveira Mota et al., 2022; Sanasi & Ghezzi, 2022; Angus et al., 2024). For instance, Sala et al. (2022) point out that pivot can lead to a change in products, strategy, or, indeed, the entire company.

Similarly, Shepherd and Gruber (2021), referencing Ries' (2011) definition, suggest that pivot affects product, strategy, and growth engine. Other scholars limit the pivot phenomenon to changes in business models or business model components (Flechas Chaparro & De Vasconcelos Gomes, 2021; Yoo et al., 2021; Sanasi, 2023). Nobari and Dehkordi (2023) define "pivoting to keep on the process" as significant changes that are made to one or more components of an innovative service or business model. They also refer to the termination of the process or general changes as "complete pivoting." Sadeghiani and Anderson (2023) specify that pivot represents a substitution of value proposition, target customers, value production, distribution consumption, value promotion, or value capture, while Morgan et al. (2020) specify that business model pivoting implies a change in key partners, key resources, key activities, value proposition, customer relationships, channels, customer segments, cost structure, and revenue streams. Similarly, Sadeghiani et al. (2022) define pivot as a discontinuity in at least one of the three dimensions of the "Business Value Triad": "value protarget," "value prodisumption," or "value procapture."

Regarding the type of change that a pivoting decision should represent, most of the papers examined (approximately 60%) do not specify the manner in which a change or strategic decision should be implemented to earn the label of pivot. By contrast, the remaining studies label the pivot change as fundamental (Burnell et al., 2023), major (Camuffo et al., 2020; Hampel et al., 2020; Sanasi & Ghezzi, 2022; Bruton et al., 2023), radical (Hampel et al., 2020), significant (Sanasi & Ghezzi, 2022), and structured (Morgan et al., 2020; Shepherd & Gruber, 2021; Marvel et al., 2022; Tsionas & Patel, 2022). All these adjectives highlight the profundity of the changes that ensue from pivoting decisions. Additionally, Kirtley and O'Mahony (2023) argue that isolated and discrete strategy changes do not constitute a pivot. Differently, Ye et al. (2024) acknowledge that pivoting ventures can undergo different depth levels of change. In particular, they distinguish "nearby pivots," whereby a venture uses existing resources to move into a related product category, and "distant pivots," whereby a venture seeks out new resources to produce products completely unrelated to their previous outputs.

Finally, examining what the observed definitions say about the specific triggers of the pivot phenomenon, the over-contextualization of the pivot concept appears evident. Silva et al. (2021), Yoo et al. (2021), Zaheer et al. (2022), and De Oliveira Mota et al. (2022) state that pivot changes come from customer feedback. McDonald and Gao (2019) point out that pivot generally comes from discoveries that contradict expectations. Sanasi (2023) states that pivot is derived from the detection of emerging problems. Other papers specify that pivoting decisions come from external shocks (Sadeghiani et al., 2021), the discovery of new business opportunities (Morgan et al., 2020), loss of competitive advantage (Snihur & Clarysse, 2022), failure to validate assumptions regarding customers (Bruton et al., 2023), negative feedback from stakeholders (Burnell et al., 2023), and the belief that the venture's existing business model is flawed (Hampel et al., 2020). According to Angus et al. (2024), pivoting decisions are triggered by "critical" rather than negative, neutral, or positive feedback. Finally, Flechas Chaparro and De Vasconcelos Gomes (2021) state that pivot derives from the identification of failures or potential failures.

1.4.2 Thematic Area 2: Triggers and Responses

This thematic area includes the papers that investigate the factors that pushed startups to pivot ("triggers") and how startups respond to them through pivoting ("responses") (6 out of 35).

It is possible to distinguish two sub-areas in this thematic area. The first includes the papers that aim to validate the triggers and responses suggested by the literature (2 out of 6). Bajwa et al. (2017) conducted a case survey study involving 49 software startups and identified the factors that trigger them to pivot and the types of pivots they undertake. Similarly, Sala et al. (2022) interviewed 30 UK high-tech entrepreneurs and identified the factors that trigger high-tech startups to pivot and the types of pivots they undertake. The authors find that, in several cases, a domino effect ensued from the pivoting action and that the value proposition can be created and sustained through pivoting. The authors also observe the influence of technology entrepreneurship on pivoting.

The second sub-area includes papers investigating how startups behaved when faced with or responding to the COVID-19 pandemic, which is presented as an example of a crisis produced by a major exogenous shock (4 out of 6). Sanasi and Ghezzi (2022) observe that "[t]he COVID-19 pandemic provided an unfortunate, though unique, empirical context for investigating strategic responses to crises."

Morgan et al. (2020) discuss how firms should respond to the opportunities that the crisis produced by major exogenous shocks (such as the COVID-19 pandemic) generate. The authors distinguish these opportunities between "arbitrage opportunities" and "innovative opportunities." Considering the quality (type) of opportunities (arbitrage or innovative opportunities), the degree of adaptation to the current capabilities of the firms (different according to the type of firm) and the cost of carrying out the pivoting, the authors suggest that the "arbitrage opportunities" should prompt business model pivoting by startups, while "innovative opportunities" should prompt business model pivoting on the part of existing SMEs. The authors also suggest that government policies can play an important role in guiding firms to achieve successful pivots.

Manolova et al. (2020) discuss female startups' responses to the crisis produced by major exogenous shocks (such as the COVID-19 pandemic). The authors counter the widespread idea that these responses differ according to the entrepreneur's gender and aim to reduce risks when the entrepreneur is female or to seize opportunities when the entrepreneur is male. The authors argue that: (1) the correct understanding of companies' business models requires adequate consideration of the economic and social structures in which those companies operate and (2) successful business model pivots in response to the crisis produced by major exogenous shocks are those that simultaneously reduce risks and seize opportunities, regardless of the entrepreneur's gender. The authors note that the COVID-19 pandemic has exerted a disproportionately negative impact on female startups. This may be attributable to the fact that female startups tend to be younger, smaller, and more concentrated in industries that were particularly hard-hit by the COVID-19 pandemic. Moreover, women were disproportionately burdened with increased caregiving responsibilities at home as a result of the COVID-19 pandemic, which has diverted their time and energy away from entrepreneurial activities. The authors also note that government support policies for businesses have not taken this last aspect into account, with the result that male-run businesses have derived the greatest benefit from them.

Guckenbieh and Corral de Zubielqui (2022), analyzing the different behaviors of 32 Australian startups operating during the COVID-19 crisis in terms of their emphasis on the opportunities or adversities generated by the pandemic, on the one hand, and the different types and extents of business model changes implemented by startups through pivoting, on the other hand, identify and describe six types of startups (corresponding to six types of behaviors). The authors find that a startup's size influences the type of business model change (adaptation, innovation or a combination of both).

Sanasi and Ghezzi (2022), through a multiple case study design based on four Italian startups that pivoted in response to the crisis produced by the COVID-19 pandemic, develop a "conceptual model of pivots-as-process" for the reorientation of the long-term strategy, divided into three phases: (1) reaction to the shock; (2) response; and (3) retrospection. In so doing, the authors suggest how companies can seek to transform adversities into opportunities by pivoting and reorienting their strategies. The authors argue that their model can support managers and entrepreneurs confronted with crisis situations.

1.4.3 Thematic Area 3: Factors Influencing Pivot

This thematic area includes the papers that investigate the factors influencing pivot (8 out of 35). These factors may be further distinguished depending on whether they influence the decision to implement the pivot or the pivot's method and success.

Six papers aim to investigate those factors that can influence the decision-making process, fostering or hindering the pivoting decision when the manifestation of pivoting triggers has highlighted the necessity of change.

Four of them focus on the effects generated by entrepreneurs' individual, cognitive, and behavioral characteristics on the likelihood of pivoting decisions.

Burnell et al. (2023) observe that, although experimentation and business model pivoting can support early-stage firms in dealing with failure or potential failure when they receive negative feedback, entrepreneurs tend to resist change, thus delaying or inhibiting the pivoting decision. Subsequently, the study theorizes that certain factors may foster pivoting decisions and tests the related hypotheses with a sample of 80 American startups. The results suggest that factors such as startup mentoring, entrepreneurial experience, and team size serve as stimulating factors, broadening startup teams' perspectives and enabling entrepreneurs to overcome their adversity for pivot.

Angus et al. (2024) implement a quantitative analysis based on a sample of 113 participants and demonstrate that low levels of behavioral awareness and constructive cognition are associated with greater propensity to pivot to a new product, while high levels of task motivation are associated with a higher propensity to pivot in response to critical feedback.

Marvel et al. (2022) show that startup founders' experience is linked to prelaunch customer learning and fewer post-launch pivots.

Lastly, Camuffo et al. (2020), analyzing a sample of 116 Italian startups operating in different sectors, find that entrepreneurs who embrace a scientific approach (i.e., deciding on validated business theories and testing their hypotheses through experiments) tend to perform better and are more likely to pivot.

Two of the examined papers seek to understand how specific management processes and tools can affect startups' propensity to undertake business model pivots.

Zaheer et al. (2022) study 50 Australian founders of more than 120 digital startups to explain how characteristics and affordances of digital technologies affect each phase of the entrepreneurial process (i.e., create, pause, abandon, repeat, persist, and pivot). They note that digital technologies act as enablers of these learning activities by providing founders with the unprecedented flexibility to configure, reconfigure, test, and validate their business models and structures. Consequently, thanks to their flexibility and generativity, digital technologies, along with entrepreneurs' passion, positively affect founders' willingness to pivot and foster pivoting decisions.

Sadeghiani et al. (2022) seek to understand how competitive intelligence stimulates startup entrepreneurs to pivot their business models and how startups pivot their business models when exposed to this kind of process. The authors observe that competitive intelligence may affect business model changes and other critical decisions in early-stage ventures, triggering pivoting decisions. Moreover, competitive intelligence helps entrepreneurs to narrow their target markets and value propositions in the initial stages, encouraging them to replace their all-in-one solutions, which target all market segments, with more specific value propositions tailored to particular target markets.

The remaining papers included in this thematic area aim to understand which factors can influence a pivot's success or failure.

Snihur and Clarysse (2022), through a longitudinal single-case study involving a Belgian digital startup, aim to investigate the interplay between organizational identity and pivoting and to understand how a lingering organizational identity can affect pivoting. The qualitative study focuses on two pivoting processes undertaken by the examined startup. The first attempt was successful, while the second failed and was followed by the new venture's demise. Snihur and Clarysse (2022) find that the first attempted pivot was rapidly concluded thanks to a flexible structure, a cognitive restructuring of the team's perceptions about organizational identity, and the presence of venture capitalist investments. However, the first business model change resulted in a rigidification of roles and a decline in organizational adaptability, causing employees and stakeholders to experience some reluctance regarding the second pivot. Thus, the authors observe that organizational identity's rapid formation and crystallization might be a double-edged sword. On the one hand, organizational identity appears to be particularly important for new ventures as it helps to attract resources and employees with the most relevant skills and motivation to expand the venture. On the other hand, the crystallization of organizational members' roles might contribute to structure and identity rigidification, subsequently hindering pivoting processes.

Ye et al. (2024), in an inductive case study of a ride-sharing vehicle venture in China that rapidly became an open service platform during the COVID-19 pandemic, find that digital innovation helped the startup to achieve the mindfulness required to implement the three swift resilience mechanisms known as "data-driven stretching," "collective sharing," and "rapid pivoting." The authors point out that digital innovation can benefit businesses that mindfully engage in strategic addition and exit processes. By leveraging digital innovation, new ventures can effectively reduce the burden of heavy asset investments and seize new opportunities that arise during a crisis while avoiding less successful outcomes. In this manner, the continuous mindfulness process facilitated by digital innovation can streamline the pivoting process, thereby enhancing a venture's ability to adjust its business operations.

1.4.4 Thematic Area 4: Consequences

This thematic area includes the papers that investigate the effects produced by pivot (5 out of 35).

In this thematic area, it is possible to distinguish two sub-areas. The first includes the papers that aim to investigate the impact of pivot on the performance or, more generally, on the success of startups (3 out of 5).

Pillai et al. (2020) explore the relationship between economic experimentation, understood as a learning mechanism, and startup success in the early automobile industry. Pillai et al. (2020) define a particular type of economic experimentation as "strategic pivots" and found that firms that were able to make multiple "strategic pivots" had a greater probability of success. They speculate that this occurred because these companies were able to learn and internalize several interrelated lessons and scale.

De Oliveira Mota et al. (2022) studied the role of resilience with respect to the effects that the crisis produced by the COVID-19 pandemic exerted on startups' performance. They test the following hypotheses: (1) "The COVID-19 crisis increases the short-term performance degradation of startups"; (2) "Startups' resilience-related characteristics positively affect response measures to the COVID-19 pandemic"; and (3) "Startups' response measure moderates the relationship between COVID-19's impact and short-term performance degradation." De Oliveira Mota et al. (2022) include the pivot, understood as strategy change, among the startup's resilience-related characteristics and find that all research hypotheses are supported, in statistically significant terms. As such, the pivot exerts a positive impact on response measures, which, in turn, moderate (decrease) the crisis' negative effect on the startup's performance.

Ilyas et al. (2023) use a meta-analysis to summarize the extant knowledge regarding the relationship between business model innovation and firm performance and find that startups obtain greater profits from a business model innovation (pivot) than incumbent firms do. According to Ilyas et al. (2023), this result may be explained by the fact that startups can more easily innovate their business models thanks to their more agile organizational structures, while incumbent firms must face the structural, strategic, emotional, and cognitive tensions in contrast to radical transformations such as those produced by a business model innovation.

The second sub-area includes the papers that investigate the pivot's consequences in terms of the impact on the existing relationships between startups and key stakeholders (2 out of 5). Given that the pivot represents a radical change in the hypotheses and initial decisions on the basis of which those relationships were established and the key stakeholders decided to give support to the startups (especially in terms of resources), pivots can alter those relationships and leading key stakeholders to withdraw that support initially given. In such circumstances, the startup's initial development and subsequent success may be irremediably compromised. McDonald and Gao (2019) propose a theoretical framework positing that a strategic reorientation (pivoting) that avoids forms of penalization by audiences can depend on how startups anticipate, justify, and stage changes to the various audiences. Hampel et al. (2020), focusing on the relationship between startups and stakeholders who identify with them, utilize the concept of "identification reset work" to explain how startups can address the critical challenge of pivoting. The authors observe that this problem emerges above all or typically when the pivoting takes place at a moment that is not particularly early in the startup's development process because, at this moment, the startup is heavily reliant on external resources, and therefore its relationship with the subjects who provide these resources becomes particularly critical for its survival.

1.4.5 Thematic Area 5: Lean Startup Approach

This thematic area includes the papers that investigate the lean startup approach and consequently investigated the pivot as an element thereof (5 out of 35).

This thematic area encompasses two sub-areas. The first sub-area includes the papers that aim to investigate how the context can impact the adoption of the principles and practices (among which pivoting) of the lean startup approach (2 out of 5). Silva et al. (2021) explore how Brazilian startups in different technological fields adopt the practices of the lean startup approach and whether the latter is suitable for the Brazilian economic context. They identify six contextual limitations that prevent the systematic adoption of the lean startup approach and demonstrate how the firms studied address these limitations by integrating the practices of the lean startup approach with other strategies. Bruton et al. (2023) investigate the lean startup approach in impoverished non-Western contexts. The authors focus their attention on how institutional characteristics and resource constraints, which differentiate the context studied from that of mature economies, impact the implementation of the principles and practices of the lean startup approach (among which pivoting) by entrepreneurs. Bruton et al. (2023) describe how the above characteristics hinder some of the practices of the lean startup approach while encouraging others. In addition, the authors offer suggestions as to how entrepreneurs might adapt the practices of the lean startup approach to make them compatible with the conditions of the contexts they face.

The second sub-area includes the papers that investigate distinct aspects of the lean startup approach (3 out of 5).

Ghezzi and Cavallo (2020) investigate the theoretical and practical relationship between business model innovation and lean startup approaches in dynamic digital environments. They craft a unified framework that can reveal the relationship between business model innovation, lean startup approaches, and "agile development" within the context of "strategic agility." Their findings reveal that lean startup approaches can be employed as agile methods to facilitate business model innovation in digital entrepreneurship.

Welter et al. (2021) verify the existence of relationships between, on the one hand, individual aspects that may be traced back to the "business model method" or the "lean startup method" and, on the other hand, the startup success. Among the aspects linked to the "lean startup method," they consider the pivoting based on customer feedback. They find that the hypothesis of the existence of a relationship between the pivoting based on customer feedback and startup success is not supported when success is measured through "the entrepreneurs' perceived organizational success" (a subjective, not financial measure) and is supported when success is measured through "growth" (an objective, financial measure).

Shepherd and Gruber (2021) review the literature on the five main blocks of the lean startup framework (including what they call "perseverance vs. pivoting") and suggest new trajectories for future research.

1.4.6 Thematic Area 6: Other Topics

This thematic area includes the papers that are not attributable to the previous areas (5 out of 35).

Two of them seek to provide practical advice as to how to pivot optimally. When developing their business opportunities through entrepreneurial action, entrepreneurs must navigate through a series of potential value-creation patterns. During these stages, entrepreneurs engage in stay-search-move-adapt cycles, staying in the opportunity's current version, searching for alternative states to move to, and then adapting. In this sense, entrepreneurs require guidelines that will help them understand when and how to pivot.

Tsionas and Patel (2022) address this topic by seeking to define an optimal stopping rule that could help entrepreneurs understand when to stop pivoting across current versions of their opportunities. The findings indicate that when the gain-to-loss ratio falls below 30% (i.e., when approximately 70% of the potential gains from exploiting the current opportunity or pivoting to future opportunities have been realized), entrepreneurs should consider ceasing to take advantage of the current opportunity or shifting focus to future opportunities.

Yoo et al. (2021) suggest that, given two viable alternative product designs, to maximize the expected profit, entrepreneurs should pivot to a product design represented by a location interior to the two candidate locations. In other words, the final product design should represent a combination of the two potential product designs. Moreover, the usefulness of pivoting may depend on the presence and level of pivoting friction (i.e., the degree of cost associated with experimentation and the pivot itself). When pivoting friction is low, the optimal test products are reduced to a single test product aimed at confirming the most likely design; when pivoting friction is high, it is best not to pivot at all.

Two other papers discuss how pivot appears in specific settings, such as co-creation or early internalization contexts.

In the co-creation setting, Nobari and Dehkordi (2023) explore how digital startups leverage innovation intelligence to gather information for building a value co-creation space and developing collective intelligence. The research applies the Key Intelligence Topics (KITs) concept to the digital domain. It defines "co-creation realization," "co-creation relationship management," and "co-creation pivoting" as specific manifestations of KITs in a digital and co-creation context. For each of these, they propose two different Key Intelligence Capabilities (KICs), which are dynamic capabilities that help create the knowledge required for each topic. Focusing on the co-creation pivoting topic, the authors define it as a strategic decision for reorienting strategy undertaken in the context of co-creation collaboration, generally involving changing or re-evaluating existing collaboration strategies. According to Nobari and Dehkordi (2023), co-creation pivoting requires two different KICs such as "lean agility" and "co-creation performance management."

Tanev et al. (2015) seek to theorize the "Lean Global Startup" (LGS) concept to highlight the problems facing new technology startups in dealing with business development, innovation, and early internalization. The pivot phenomenon represents the final stage of the LGS approach. Regarding the pivot phenomenon, the authors, examining a sample of three Canadian firms and three Danish firms, observe that Danish firms tend to pivot less frequently and with less depth than Canadian firms. They attribute these differences to the specific industries in which the firms operate. Canadian firms operating in the ITC domain benefit from flexibility, enabling swift and in-depth changes to their value proposition and target customers. By contrast, Danish firms developing tangible products operate within a more rigid structure, which limits their ability to pivot.

Finally, Sanasi (2023) aims to provide an overview of the state-of-the-art understanding of business model dynamics. The term "business model dynamics" is used in the literature to identify several phenomena, such as business model innovation, validation, scaling, and pivots. Focusing on the pivot phenomenon, Sanasi (2023) analyzes the different definitions of pivot provided by the literature, emphasizing the existing links between pivoting decisions, experimentation processes, the need to respond to external shock and the new venture context. The study then highlights potential avenues for future research, remarking on the need to understand how constraining conditions and unfolding organizational crises can affect pivot deployment and what performance implications and legitimacy issues can derive from a pivoting decision.

1.5 Main Avenues for Future Research

The SLR revealed a broad heterogeneity of pivot's meanings and conceptualizations. This heterogeneity can represent a critical issue because it may compromise the comparability of study results. In fact, the results of studies that have the same objectives but apply different meanings to pivot may not be comparable. Future studies should seek to identify a single unified meaning that is general in nature and is not affected by the economic sector to which the firm belongs, among other factors.

The SLR also revealed that many papers have studied startup pivot in specific and limited economic sectors and/or geographical areas. Thus, all the thematic areas identified—particularly those labeled "triggers and responses," "factors influencing pivot," and "consequences"—have considerable potential for future development as research topics.

The startup pivot has been studied predominantly in the "technological" sector. On the one hand, this appears consistent with the fact that the concept originates in this sector. On the other hand, this suggests directing research to other economic sectors than the technological one and conducting comparative studies between startups from different economic sectors, to explore whether and how the economic sector can impact the startup pivot.

Among the aforementioned thematic areas, that labeled "consequences" presents the broadest perspective. In the authors' opinion, the analysis of the impacts of pivot on the startup performance/success will require scholarly attention in the future. Closely linked to this is the concept of startup performance/success, a phenomenon that warrants a specific definition, conceptualization, and operationalization in the context of studies seeking to investigate the impacts of pivot on startup performance/success.

Although the term "pivot" was created for application to the phenomenon of change caused by the fact that the hypotheses on which the startup was founded did not find concrete confirmation once the startup's development process began, the analysis highlighted that scholars have extended this denomination to the phenomena of change caused by the opportunities that the startup encounters once the development process has begun. At the same time, although the term pivot was born in the context of startups, the analysis highlighted that academics have broadened the reference context, extending it to existing firms. The extension of studies of the phenomenon of change to cases in which the startup changes for the purpose of seizing opportunities appears fruitful both from the perspective of research and from the perspective of entrepreneurs and practitioners. In fact, any new business idea's path to success passes not only through the ability to respond adequately to situations or factors of crisis or failure but also through the ability to adequately seize any opportunities that may present themselves and that were not initially predictable. Future studies could investigate the causes, implementation methods and consequences of startup pivot that occurs when the startup encounters opportunities.

Finally, the fact that most of the reviewed papers used qualitative research methodologies and that several studies were theoretical seems to align with the stage of the research on the phenomenon. However, this suggests moving toward quantitative studies to test hypotheses and aim for a generalization of the results.

1.6 Conclusions

The SLR led to the identification of only 35 papers on startup pivot, most of which were published in the last years of the considered timeframe. This highlights that the number of papers on startup pivot is limited, but it is steadily increasing, suggesting that the startup pivot is a relatively recent research topic and that it is attracting rapidly growing interest among academics.

The thematic analysis led to the identification of 6 thematic areas and, for 4 of these, 2 thematic sub-areas each. The limited body of literature, on the one hand, and the relatively large number of thematic areas and sub-areas, on the other hand, suggest that the literature on the topic is, at present, quite fragmented.

The thematic analysis also revealed that several relevant aspects of the startup pivot have been explored. However, the limited body of literature suggested valuable future research directions.

This study has some limitations. The first limitation concerns the research products used for the analysis, which were selected based on the criteria illustrated in the research methodology section. By broadening the search for research products across multiple databases and relaxing some inclusion/exclusion criteria, the analysis may encompass a wider range of research products, potentially influencing the results. The second limitation concerns the authors' subjectivity, which characterized several phases of the investigation, particularly the identification of the thematic areas and the inclusion of the papers therein. The third limitation concerns the focus on the papers that investigated startup pivot, therefore addressing the phenomenon underlying this denomination when it is termed as such. However, some academics refer or may refer to this phenomenon using other denominations (for example, "strategic change" or "business model innovation/change," etc.). Thus, for a more complete understanding of this phenomenon, future studies could expand the sample of papers to those that, while refraining from using the term "pivot," refer to the underlying phenomenon using other denominations.

Despite these limitations, the study offers significant contributions to the literature on startup pivot. To the best of the authors' knowledge, it is the first study to make a SLR of the studies addressing this topic with the aim of identifying the thematic areas covered so far by the same and, based on the analysis of these thematic areas, to provide valuable future research directions. At the same time, it provides several useful references for entrepreneurs who should or could make pivot decisions in the startup development process.

References

Ancillai, C., Sabatini, A., Gatti, M., & Perna, A. (2023). Digital technology and business model innovation: A systematic literature review and future research agenda. *Technological Forecasting and Social Change, 188*, 1–43. https://doi.org/10.1016/j.techfore.2022.122307

Andreini, D., & Bettinelli, C. (2017). Business model innovation: From systematic literature review to future research directions. *Journal of Management and Governance, 21*, 785–792. https://doi.org/10.1007/978-3-319-53351-3

Angus, R. W., Houghton, J. D., Neck, C. B., & Kip Holderness, D. (2024). Who responds to critical feedback? The effects of self-leadership on entrepreneurial product pivoting behavior. *Journal of Business Research, 172*, 1–14. https://doi.org/10.1016/j.jbusres.2023.114415

Bajwa, S. S., Wang, X., Duc, A. N., & Abrahamsson, P. (2017). Failures' to be celebrated: An analysis of major pivots of software startups. *Empirical Software Engineering, 22*(5), 2373–2408. https://doi.org/10.1007/s10664-016-9458-0

Blank, S. G., & Dorf, B. (2012). *The Startup owner's manual: The step-by-step guide for building a great company*. K & S Ranch.

Bohn, N., & Kundisch, D. (2020). What are we talking about when we talk about technology pivots?—A Delphi study. *Information & Management, 57*(6), 1–20. https://doi.org/10.1016/j.im.2020.103319

Bruton, G. D., Pryor, C., & Cerecedo Lopez, J. A. (2023). Lean start-up in settings of impoverishment: The implications of the context for theory. *Journal of Management*. https://doi.org/10.1177/01492063231204869

Burnell, D., Stevenson, R., & Fisher, G. (2023). Early-stage business model experimentation and pivoting. *Journal of Business Venturing, 38*(4), 1–19. https://doi.org/10.1016/j.jbusvent.2023.106314

Camuffo, A., Cordova, A., Gambardella, A., & Spina, C. (2020). A scientific approach to entrepreneurial decision making: Evidence from a randomized control trial. *Management Science, 66*(10), 564–586. https://doi.org/10.1287/mnsc.2018.324

Cook, D. J., Mulrow, C. D., & Haynes, R. B. (1997). Systematic reviews: Synthesis of best evidence for clinical decisions. *Annals of Internal Medicine, 126*(5), 376–380. https://doi.org/10.7326/0003-4819-126-5-199703010-00006

De Oliveira Mota, R., Bueno, A., dos Santos Leite Gonella, J., Ganga, G. M. D., Godinho Filho, M., & Latan, H. (2022). The effects of the COVID-19 crisis on startups' performance: The role of resilience. *Management Decision, 60*(12), 3388–3415. https://doi.org/10.1108/MD-07-2021-0998

Flechas Chaparro, X. A., & De Vasconcelos Gomes, L. A. (2021). Pivot decisions in startups: A systematic literature review. *International Journal of Entrepreneurial Behavior & Research, 27*(4), 884–910. https://doi.org/10.1108/IJEBR-12-2019-0699

Ghezzi, A., & Cavallo, A. (2020). Agile business model innovation in digital entrepreneurship: Lean startup approaches. *Journal of Business Research, 110*, 519–537. https://doi.org/10.1016/j.jbusres.2018.06.013

Guckenbieh, P., & Corral de Zubielqui, G. (2022). Start-ups' business model changes during the COVID-19 pandemic: Counteracting adversities and pursuing opportunities. *International Small Business Journal, 40*(2), 150–177. https://doi.org/10.1177/02662426211055447

Hampel, C. E., Tracey, P., & Weber, K. (2020). The art of the pivot: How new ventures manage identification relationships with stakeholders as they change direction. *Academy of Management Journal, 63*(2), 440–471. https://doi.org/10.5465/amj.2017.0460
Ilyas, I. M., Kammerlander, N., Turturea, R., & van Essen, M. (2023). When business model innovation creates value for companies: A meta-analysis on institutional contingencies. *Journal of Management Studies, 61*(5), 1825–1883. https://doi.org/10.1111/joms.12966
Kirtley, J., & O'Mahony, S. (2023). What is a pivot? Explaining when and how entrepreneurial firms decide to make strategic change and pivot. *Strategic Management Journal, 44*(1), 197–230. https://doi.org/10.1002/smj.3131
Manolova, T. S., Brush, C. G., Edelman, L. F., & Elam, A. (2020). Pivoting to stay the course: How women entrepreneurs take advantage of opportunities created by the COVID-19 pandemic. *International Small Business Journal: Researching Entrepreneurship, 38*(6), 481–491. https://doi.org/10.1177/0266242620949136
Marvel, M. R., Wolfe, M. T., Kuratko, D. F., & Fisher, G. (2022). Examining entrepreneurial experience in relation to pre-launch and post-launch learning activities affecting venture performance. *Journal of Small Business Management, 60*(4), 759–785. https://doi.org/10.1080/00472778.2020.1762626
Massaro, M., Dumay, J., & Garlatti, A. (2015). Public sector knowledge management: A structured literature review. *Journal of Knowledge Management, 19*, 530–558. https://doi.org/10.1108/JKM-11-2014-0466
McDonald, R., & Gao, C. (2019). Pivoting isn't enough? Managing strategic reorientation in new ventures. *Organization Science, 30*(6), 1289–1318. https://doi.org/10.1287/orsc.2019.1287
Moher, D., Liberati, A., Tetzlaff, J., Altman, D. G., & The PRISMA Group. (2009). Preferred reporting items for systematic reviews and meta-analyses: The PRISMA statement. *PLoS Medicine, 6*(7), 1–6. https://doi.org/10.1371/journal.pmed.1000097
Morgan, T., Anokhin, S., Ofstein, L., & Friske, W. (2020). SME response to major exogenous shocks: The bright and dark sides of business model pivoting. *International Small Business Journal: Researching Entrepreneurship, 38*(5), 369–379. https://doi.org/10.1177/0266242620936590
Nobari, N., & Dehkordi, A. M. (2023). Innovation intelligence in managing co-creation process between tech-enabled corporations and startups. *Technological Forecasting and Social Change, 186*, 1–20. https://doi.org/10.1016/j.techfore.2022.122107
Paré, G., Trudel, M. C., Jaana, M., & Kitsiou, S. (2015). Synthesizing information systems knowledge: A typology of literature reviews. *Information Management, 52*(2), 183–199. https://doi.org/10.1016/j.im.2014.08.008
Pillai, S. D., Goldfarb, B., & Kirsch, D. A. (2020). The origins of firm strategy: Learning by economic experimentation and strategic pivots in the early automobile industry. *Strategic Management Journal, 41*(3), 369–399. https://doi.org/10.1002/smj.3102
Rensink, R. A. (2002). Change detection. *Annual Review of Psychology, 53*(1), 245–277. https://doi.org/10.1146/annurev.psych.53.100901.135125
Ries, E. (2009) *Pivot, don't jump to a new vision*. Retrieved May 31, 2024, from https://www.startuplessonslearned.com/2009/06/pivot-dont-jump-to-new-vision.html
Ries, E. (2011). *The lean startup: How today's entrepreneurs use continuous innovation to create radically successful businesses*. Crown Currency.
Sadeghiani, A., & Anderson, A. (2023). What pivot is: Touching an elephant in the dark. *Digital Business, 3*(1), 1–16. https://doi.org/10.1016/j.digbus.2023.100056
Sadeghiani, A., Anderson, A., Ahmadi, S., & Shokouhyar, S. (2021). Theorizing 'pivot' in small and micro business. *Journal of Small Business & Entrepreneurship, 36*(3), 411–429. https://doi.org/10.1080/08276331.2021.2014205
Sadeghiani, A., Shokouhyar, S., & Ahmadi, S. (2022). How digital startups use competitive intelligence to pivot. *Digital Business, 2*(2), 1–15. https://doi.org/10.1016/j.digbus.2022.100034
Sadeghiani, A., Anderson, A., Ahmadi, S., Shokouhyar, S., & Hajipour, B. (2023). Sayings and doings become 'practice' through 'practice thirdness': Pivot in recipes for practice. *Entrepreneurship & Regional Development, 35*(9–10), 788–811. https://doi.org/10.1080/08985626.2023.2225044

Sala, P. K., Philbin, S. P., & Barikzai, S. (2022). A qualitative research study of the tech startup journey through entrepreneurial pivoting. *International Journal of Entrepreneurial Behavior & Research, 28*(4), 1050–1074. https://doi.org/10.1108/IJEBR-07-2021-0528

Sanasi, S. (2023). Entrepreneurial experimentation in business model dynamics: Current understanding and future opportunities. *International Entrepreneurship and Management Journal, 19*(2), 805–836. https://doi.org/10.1007/s11365-023-00836-7

Sanasi, S., & Ghezzi, A. (2022). Pivots as strategic responses to crises: Evidence from Italian companies navigating Covid-19. *Strategic Organization*. https://doi.org/10.1177/14761270221122933

Secundo, G., Ndou, V., Del Vecchio, P., & De Pascale, G. (2019). Knowledge management in entrepreneurial universities: A structured literature review and avenue for future research agenda. *Management Decision, 57*(12), 3226–3257. https://doi.org/10.1108/MD-11-2018-1266

Shepherd, D. A., & Gruber, M. (2021). The lean startup framework: Closing the academic–practitioner divide. *Entrepreneurship Theory and Practice, 45*(5), 967–998. https://doi.org/10.1177/1042258719899415

Silva, D. S., Ghezzi, A., Aguiar, R. B., Cortimiglia, M. N., & ten Caten, C. S. (2021). Lean startup for opportunity exploitation: Adoption constraints and strategies in technology new ventures. *International Journal of Entrepreneurial Behavior & Research, 27*(4), 944–969. https://doi.org/10.1108/IJEBR-01-2020-0030

Snihur, Y., & Clarysse, B. (2022). Sowing the seeds of failure: Organizational identity dynamics in new venture pivoting. *Journal of Business Venturing, 37*(1), 1–19. https://doi.org/10.1016/j.jbusvent.2021.106164

Tanev, S., Rasmussen, E. S., Zijdemans, E., Lemminger, R., & Svendsen, L. L. (2015). Lean and global technology start-ups: Linking the two research streams. *International Journal of Innovation Management, 19*(3), 1–41. https://doi.org/10.1142/S1363919615400083

Thorpe, R., Holt, R., Macpherson, A., & Pittaway, L. (2005). Using knowledge within small and medium-sized firms: A systematic review of the evidence. *International Journal of Management Reviews, 7*(4), 257–281. https://doi.org/10.1111/j.1468-2370.2005.00116.x

Tranfield, D., Denyer, D., & Smart, P. (2003). Towards a methodology for developing evidence-informed management knowledge by means of systematic review. *British Journal of Management, 14*(3), 207–222. https://doi.org/10.1111/1467-8551.00375

Tsionas, M. G., & Patel, P. C. (2022). An entrepreneur's dilemma: An optimal stopping rule in pivoting. *Managerial and Decision Economics, 43*(8), 3498–3515. https://doi.org/10.1002/mde.3610

Welter, C., Scrimpshire, A., Tolonen, D., & Obrimah, E. (2021). The road to entrepreneurial success: Business plans, lean startup, or both? *New England Journal of Entrepreneurship, 24*(1), 21–42. https://doi.org/10.1108/NEJE-08-2020-0031

Ye, D., Liu, M. J., Luo, J., & Yannopoulou, N. (2024). How to achieve swift resilience: The role of digital innovation enabled mindfulness. *Information Systems Frontiers, 26*, 551–573. https://doi.org/10.1007/s10796-021-10225-6

Yoo, O. S., Huang, T., & Arifoglu, K. (2021). A theoretical analysis of the lean start-up method. *Marketing Science, 40*(3), 395–412. https://doi.org/10.2139/ssrn.3070613

Zaheer, H., Breyer, Y., Dumay, J., & Enjeti, M. (2022). The entrepreneurial journeys of digital start-up founders. *Technological Forecasting and Social Change, 179*, 1–27. https://doi.org/10.1016/j.techfore.2022.121638

Chapter 2
Designing Impact Case Studies: Lessons from the SIDREA-CNDCEC Joint Project on "High-Growth Startups (Gazelles)"

Massimo Contrafatto, Elbano de Nuccio, Domenico Nicolò, and Matteo Pozzoli

2.1 Introduction

Nowadays, increasing attention has been devoted to the actual and potential role of the academe in shaping businesses, communities, and society. As widely observed by many commentators, academe is expected to contribute, through teaching, research, and knowledge exchange activities, to the development of more responsible and sustainable practices across business and society. Concerning this, a growing interest has been given to the potential and actual "impact" of academic activities and outputs.

At a first approximation, the word "impact" should be understood in its etymological sense as an activity that "drives" and/or "pushes" into something else in a way that determines and/or shapes its original state. From this perspective, impact

M. Contrafatto
Department of Accounting and Finance, Sussex Business School, University of Sussex, Falmer, Brighton, UK
e-mail: massimo.contrafatto@sussex.ac.uk

E. de Nuccio
Department of Management, Finance and Technology, University LUM Giuseppe Degennaro, Bari, Italy
e-mail: denuccio@lum.it

D. Nicolò (✉)
Department of Law, Economics and Human Sciences, University Mediterranea of Reggio Calabria, Reggio Calabria, Italy
e-mail: domenico.nicolo@unirc.it

M. Pozzoli
Department of Law, University of Naples Parthenope, Naples, Italy
e-mail: matteo.pozzoli@uniparthenope.it

S. Loprevite et al. (eds.), *Startups and Gazelle Enterprises*, SIDREA Series in Accounting and Business Administration,
https://doi.org/10.1007/978-3-031-90881-1_2

implies an actual modification of this "original state," i.e., a sort of "imprinting" and/or "legacy." In this context, impact, thus, should be used to refer to the actual and potential possibilities of academe to generate, through its activities, *positive changes* in the existing modes of organizing society, communities, and business. It is clear from these first considerations that impact involves: (a) actual modifications of existing practices and/or modes of organizing; (b) modifications which are regarded as "positive," i.e., which reflect an improvement and/or development; (c) these positive modifications should be related to, and induced by, the scholarly activities, such as teaching, research, and knowledge exchange; (d) the resulting modifications, and activities from which these draw on, should be justified and calculated through rigorous metrics; (e) the metrics for calculating/justifying "impacts" could be ad hoc developed by drawing on the accounting know-how.

Although the growing interests have been devoted to the "impact" and "related projects and/or cases," there is a relative lack of academic literature which has specifically focused on "how" and "why" to undertake, and write about, these projects/cases. In addition, there is not still an overall accepted framework that offers normative, theoretical, and methodological underpinnings for designing, conducting, and assessing "impact case and projects." Finally, though a few examples of good impact case studies do exist,[1] these have not substantially mobilized to develop, as far as we are aware, the *lessons* for wider scholarly dissemination. In sum, there is a gap in the existing academic accounting literature about case studies and projects which could be seen as "impactful."

In this chapter, we seek to fill this gap by providing some theoretical and methodological insights regarding how to design a *successful* impact case study. To this aim, we will first introduce and describe two relevant examples of existing "frameworks," respectively the UK-Research Excellence Framework[2] (hereafter REF) and the Italian "Valutazione della Qualità della Ricerca"–VQR. These two frameworks have been chosen because they represent some of the most notable in the context of "assessing the quality of academic research" in the UK and Italy. In addition, as a further contribution to the main purpose of this chapter, we will report on an example of an "impact case study" that had been designed by the academic group "Start-ups" of the Italian Academic Association of Professors of Accounting and Business Administration (SIDREA) and the Italian National Council of Chartered Accountants CNDCEC (hereafter, SIDREA-CNDCEC case study). This case study, which will be described in the fourth section, is used as an "illustrative example" from which to draw *the lessons* that could offer "practical guidelines" for developing impact case studies.

---

[1] See https://results2021.ref.ac.uk/impact

[2] The UK-Research Excellence Framework (REF) is the formal system for assessing the excellence of research in UK higher education institutions (HEIs). The REF outcomes are used to inform the allocation of public funding for universities' research. It is considered, among others, a mechanism to provide accountability for public investment in research and produce evidence of the benefits of this investment (https://www.ref.ac.uk).

As explained by Hayes et al. (2015), an illustrative case study is adopted when one wants to "*describe a situation or a phenomenon*, what is happening with it, and why it is happening" (p. 8, emphasis added). Hence, illustrative cases are *descriptive* studies that depict an event and its main characteristics to explain the situation/context within which the event has emerged. The use of this methodology is recommended when there is little knowledge, if anything, of the topic and/or issue which is the object of scholarly investigation. Because there is no wide knowledge about the topic/issue, researchers who adopt an illustrative approach to case studies tend to use descriptive, clear, and simple language with the aim of helping readers to familiarize with the topic/issue (Hayes et al., 2015). Drawing on these methodological insights, we illustrate the case of SIDREA-CNDCEC joint project on "high-growth start-ups (Gazelles)" with the aim of providing descriptive details about the context of the project, as well as how the participants involved acted and inter-acted during the design of the project. From this descriptive-illustrative analysis, we intend to *learn* some lessons to draw upon for designing valuable and impactful case studies in the future.

The remainder of this chapter is organized as follows. In the next section, we will briefly introduce the two frameworks mentioned above, the Italian VQR and the UK-REF. In Sects. 2.3 and 2.4, we will provide respectively a theoretical background to the "Startup Gazelle," which represents the scholarly focus of the SIDREA-CNDCEC case study, and the case study per se. Finally, some concluding remarks will be provided.

2.2 Impact Case Study from the Perspectives of the UK-REF and the Italian VQR: A Brief Overview

The Italian VQR framework, designed by the ANVUR (the National Agency for the Evaluation of the University and Research Systems), provides principles, guidelines, and criteria for evaluating the quality of research output of universities and research institutes, mainly through a process of peer review.[3] The VQR-assessment provides an up-to-date evaluation of the state of academic research output in the various scholarly fields, in order to encourage its quality, contribution, and *impact* (see https://www.anvur.it/en/activities/vqr). The impact, from the perspective of VQR, is strictly linked to the activities undertaken under the aegis of "research" and "public engagement" with external stakeholders. The definition of impact, which is quite open and wide, refers to the potential effects that teaching and research activities (may) produce on the policies, activities, practices, and models of organizing of business, society, and the public. This impact must be pertinent and meaningful, that is relevant and significant. In addition, explicit reference is made to the need to

[3]As per Presidential Decree no. 76/2010 (under art. 3, paragraph 1, letter a; and paragraph 2, letter b).

corroborate, that it is to justify and demonstrate, through a set of ad hoc indicators and evidence, the actual and observable differences compared to the starting situations.

The UK-REF framework provides a more structured, articulated, and comprehensive definition and conceptualization of impact and impact case study. From the perspective of REF, impact denotes "an *effect* on, change or benefit to the economy, society, culture, public policy or services, health, the environment, or quality of life" (emphasis added), which goes beyond academia (https://2021.ref.ac.uk/guidance-on-results/impact-case-study-database-faqs/index.html). An impact, thus, represents the outcome generated *through* and *by* any academic activities and related output. This is an important aspect to emphasize: the impact is the *positive outcome* generated through academic *outputs*. When talking about "impact" we need to refer to this positive outcome rather than simply in terms of outputs. In other words, it is not sufficient to produce high-quality research output to achieve a meaningful and positive impact. With regard to this, it is essential to generate, through these outputs, meaningful outcomes. Clearly, however, the starting point for any meaningful outcome is a high-quality, rigorous and credible research output.

The impact is usually evaluated in terms of "reach" and "significance." Reach denotes "the extent and/or diversity of the beneficiaries of the impact," while "significance" refers to "the degree to which the impact has enabled and informed performance, policies, practices, products, services, understanding, awareness or well-being of the beneficiaries" (https://2021.ref.ac.uk/media/1447/ref-2019_01-guidance-on-submissions.pdf) (see Table 2.1 below for a description of the criteria used for assessing the quality of impact case study).

Hence, designing and undertaking an effective "impact case study" has become pivotal. An impact case study requires a constant and constructive engagement between academics and non-academic actors, such as practitioners and policymakers. The center of this constructive and constant engagement is a topic/issue of investigation. This issue, which represents *the core* of any impact case study, should

Table 2.1 Quality levels for assessing impact case study (These are the criteria used by the last REF 2021 to assess the quality of the impact case study (https://2021.ref.ac.uk/guidance-on-results/guidance-on-ref-2021-results/index.html#qualityRatings))

Case study X, Y, Z	Quality level	Description
	4 stars	Outstanding impacts in terms of their reach and significance
	3 stars	Very considerable impacts in terms of their reach and significance
	2 stars	Considerable impacts in terms of their reach and significance
	1 stars	Recognized but modest impacts in terms of their reach and significance
	Unclassified	The impact is of little or no reach and significance; or the impact was not eligible; or the impact was not underpinned by excellent research produced by the submitted unit

Source. Modified from: https://2021.ref.ac.uk/guidance-on-results/guidance-on-ref-2021-results/index.html#qualityRatings

be of interest to academic and non-academic audiences. Identifying this interesting core, however, may be a difficult task per se. This usually requires an iterative and constructive dialogue before any formal engagement starts.

In the next two sections, we will present the example of the impact case study on "Principles, Models, and Accounting Standards for the start-ups and the high growth startups (i.e., Gazelles)," which has been designed by SIDREA and CNDCEC. The SIDREA-CNDCEC case study represents an interesting example that has been developed to promote dialogue and collaboration for jointly designing principles, guidelines, and standards for planning, managing controlling, and evaluating high-growth startups. Hence, the focus of this impact case study is on the "high-growth startups" (Gazelles). In the following section, a brief theoretical background of the "high growth startups" and "gazelle," which are the core of the present impact case study, is provided. The purpose of the following paragraph is to provide the theoretical context within which the impact case was designed.

2.3 High-Growth Startups (Gazelle Enterprises)

Most new firms remain small, while only a few experience high growth during their startup phase (Du & Temouri, 2015; Henrekson & Johansson, 2010; Gilbert et al., 2006; Garnsey & Heffernan, 2005; Mata, 1994). In the United States only 3.5% of new firms become large companies (Acs & Armington, 2006). In Italy, just 1.2% become high-growth enterprises within their first five years of life (ISTAT, 2022). This paragraph focuses on the enterprise gazelle, a specific type of young, high-growth firm. Clarifying this concept of gazelle is very relevant for this impact case study. It is argued that successful startups could be a reference for planning new companies that have good chances to survive the great challenges of the early stage and quickly achieve a lasting competitive advantage that leads them to grow, gaining customers and market shares soon after their foundation. Some startups grow more than gazelles, becoming scale-ups or even unicorns; the latter are rare new businesses that have reached at least 1 billion dollars in market capitalization (Jansen et al., 2023; Kuratko et al., 2020). They have characteristics that are unique and difficult to replicate successfully. For this reason, we only consider gazelles to be a reference for designing startups.

Let's begin by addressing some fundamental questions. What is a startup? What is a gazelle startup? How can we identify a gazelle and distinguish it from other young companies? Why are gazelles considered valuable case studies for establishing guidelines for successful startup design? What should the guidelines be for creating startups??

Regarding the first question (*what is a startup*?), a unique overall accepted definition does not exist. However, this concept is often related to innovative business models developed by friends in a garage, within university departments, or in the research divisions of large companies. Scholars, consultants, and entrepreneurs agree that not all new businesses are startups. According to the well-known definition by Steve Blank, "a startup is a temporary organization in search of a scalable, repeatable, profitable business model" (Blank & Dorf, 2020). The orientation towards growth through a business model that can be replicable (Chliova & Ringov, 2017) and grow in scale, also by reproducing productive systems in different geographical areas by reproducing productive systems in multiple geographical locations (Reuber et al., 2021) and creating social impact (Shepherd & Patzelt, 2022) are fundamental elements of this concept. Another well-known definition has been formulated by Ries (2011). This highlights how startups operate under conditions of extreme uncertainty because of their innovative value proposition. These two definitions, which are the most used, highlight the following characteristics of startups: their vocation to grow through a replicable (in different periods and contests) and scalable business model; the high innovativeness of their value proposition; and the uncertainty about their sustainability and continuity. Graham, founder of Y Combinator, one of the most important startup accelerators, also emphasizes how startups aim to grow fast (http://www.paulgraham.com/growth.html).

Growth is a central aspect of the definition of enterprises gazelle provided by OECD Eurostat (2007). Drawing on this definition, we can answer our second question: *What is a high-growth startup?* According to the OECD Eurostat definition, increasingly spreading in the managerial literature and international statistical reports (Daunfeldt et al., 2015; Coad et al., 2014), gazelles are enterprises up to five years old with an average annualized growth of more than 20 percent per year over three years and with ten or more employees when they start to grow. From this definition, we can infer the following two formulas (2.1) and (2.2) to apply to select each five-year cohort of gazelles.

$$\text{Average annualized growth rate of turnover} = \sqrt[3]{\frac{\text{Turnover}(t)}{\text{Turnover}(t-3)}} - 1 > 0{,}2 \qquad (2.1)$$

$$\begin{aligned}&\text{Average annualized growth}\\&\text{rate of number of employees} = \sqrt[3]{\frac{\text{N.Employees}(t)}{N-\text{Employees}(t-3)}} - 1 > 0{,}2\end{aligned} \qquad (2.2)$$

We come now to the third question: *Why do we consider Gazelles as the focus of a case study for setting guidelines for designing successful startups?* Gazelles are undoubtedly a model of successful startup enterprises. The high growth in their turnover and/or number of employees shows that they have gained customers and achieved a competitive advantage soon after birth. Moreover, these high-growth startups significantly contribute to employment, as highlighted by international literature since the end of the last century (Hölzl, 2014; Henrekson & Johansson, 2010; Acs & Mueller, 2008; Van Praag & Versloot, 2007). Numerous studies have confirmed their role as creators of new jobs in different nations: United States (Kirchhoff, 1994); Canada (Halabisky et al., 2006); Great Britain (Hart et al., 2021); Austria (Hölzl, 2014); Finland (Deschryvere, 2008; Autio et al., 2000); Italy, Spain

(Schreyer, 2000); Holland (Bos & Stam, 2014); Germany (Fritsch & Schindele, 2011); Croatia, Montenegro, Serbia, and Slovenia (Pšeničny et al., 2014); Czech Republic (Krošláková et al., 2015).

These excellent young businesses provide an ideal model for creating a new venture. This is not to say that success can be achieved by simply copying the business model and identity characteristics of these gazelles. There are no definitive "recipes" for building businesses that guarantee lasting competitive success. Achieving entrepreneurial success does not rely on one or a few easily replicable factors; rather, it depends on a combination of unique, valuable, and difficult-to-imitate resources (Barney & Arikan, 2005; Cooper et al., 1994; Barney, 1991; Birley, 1987). However, success stories, such as those of the gazelles, are a useful source of inspiration for those about to start new businesses. This need is emphasized by the fact that there is still little academic literature explaining how certain variables, such as human capital and investment in intangibles, contribute to the growth and performance of these high-growth startups (Cattafi et al., 2023) and enhance their value (Cattafi et al., 2024).

Concerning the fourth question: *What should be the guidelines for the creation of startups?* We just need to focus on principles and analysis tools that allow us to avoid the most common mistakes made in the startup phase and prevent them. By doing so, it is possible to learn the lessons for helping to achieve competitive advantage and sustainability in the first years of life. The guidelines will also have to focus on the main causes of the frequent failures of entrepreneurial projects to mitigate the high vulnerability of startups. Startups are particularly vulnerable, with many failing within their early years (Knaup & Piazza, 2007; Dunne & Hughes, 1994; Venkataraman et al., 1990). On average, only about half of new firms survive until the sixth year. This trend is consistent across countries and periods, highlighting that a high failure rate is a common feature of young firms, regardless of the context and economic cycles (Nicolò, 2019). A key determinant of startups' vulnerability is their lack of reputation. Startups lack a history and financial statements that demonstrate their ability to meet stakeholder expectations. This makes it difficult to build strong trust with investors, lenders, suppliers, strategic partners, and customers. Initial difficulties can easily shatter these fragile bonds of trust, causing stakeholders to lose confidence and withdraw their support for the enterprise, causing it to cease due to a lack of necessary human, technical, and financial resources. In previous research, we have shed light on the strategic relevance of corporate reputation to the survival of startups, highlighting key levers that can facilitate its rapid construction, such as the reputation of the founder (and co-founding team), partners, workers, and the context in which the venture is launched (Bruna & Nicolò, 2020).

Most new companies in Europe and the United States are small. As a result, they often face common small business weaknesses, such as higher costs and lower efficiency compared to larger firms, making them more susceptible to challenges. Additionally, the characteristics of their founders or co-founders—such as risk tolerance, perseverance, education, competence, ability, and experience—can significantly influence their capacity to navigate the startup phase. During their initial stages, startups may encounter issues such as conflicts between co-founders, planning errors like underestimating demand or overestimating production capacity, and decisions regarding sources of financing (Nicolò, 2019).

To achieve this goal, it is essential to clarify the significance of a business plan. It serves as a "laboratory" for testing the competitiveness, economic, financial, social, and environmental sustainability, as well as the volatility and sensitivity of the expected outcomes of business projects before their implementation. This approach helps prevent design errors and identifies any inconsistencies or disharmonies in the strategic direction of emerging companies.

Moreover, even after the business is launched, the business plan remains a valuable tool. It supports the refinement of the strategic approach and facilitates the learning of new strategies. In conjunction with reporting, the business plan can reveal unfavorable trends before they develop into chronic and irreversible issues, allowing for timely and targeted corrective measures.

The guidelines should be aimed at accountants, startuppers, and actors involved in fostering entrepreneurship (universities, entrepreneurship promotion and support agencies, accountants and business consultants, startuppers and entrepreneurs, politicians, etc.).

2.4 The SIDREA-CNDCEC Impact Case Study: An Illustrative Example

The purpose of this section is to introduce our illustrative case study to describe the process followed to constitute the SIDREA-CNDCEC joint group, the organization of the working group, and the short and medium-term development path of the undertaken activities. The SIDREA-CNDCEC impact case study has been modeled taking into consideration the ongoing best practices to date, already considered in the previous section (REF, 2021). However, each project presents unique features that clearly characterize and limit this (Heyeres et al., 2019).

In the example discussed above, the proposal was initiated by the Gruppo di Studio "Start-ups" of SIDREA. SIDREA is a non-profit association with the aim of promoting the development of the economic-business culture and the principles of good governance of all entities, including enterprises, non-profit, and public sector organizations. According to this, SIDREA also intends to provide a contribution to the improvement of methodologies for assessing the quality of scientific research. Ordinary members are essentially full professors, associate professors, and researchers, with permanent and fixed-term contracts, including those in retirement, classified in the scientific sector "Business Economics."

Specifically, the initiative was put in place by the "Startup" research group, which set up an ad hoc Commission, composed of professors Massimo Contrafatto, Mara Del Baldo, Stefano Marasca, Domenico Nicolò, Marcantonio Ruisi, Claudio Teodori. The members reproduced the plan for the project into a policy paper, addressing the research impact of the research, with the intention to create an impact case study involving the Consiglio Nazionale dei Dottori Commercialisti e degli Esperti Contabili (CNDCEC) in drafting guidelines on startups, in particular gazelles. The paper illustrates the main directives of the program and the expected outcomes, highlighting the direct and indirect benefits arising from the research (Reed et al., 2021).

The CNDCEC, constituted as a non-economic public body by Legislative Decree No. 139 of 28 June 2005 and recognized as the institutional representative body of the professional category of accountants, has as its primary purpose the protection of its members and the public interests connected to the exercise of the profession. Among other activities, the National Council, endowed with self-government and self-administration and subject in the exercise of its activities to the supervision of the Ministry of Justice, develops documents of interest to its members, representing the voice of the profession at national and international levels.

The SIDREA "Gruppo di Studio Start-ups" drafted an impact case proposal entitled "Principles, models and accounting principles for high-growth start-ups (i.e. gazelles)" and submitted it to the CNDCEC. SIDREA shared the project with President Elbano de Nuccio in his capacity as delegate for accounting and valuation practices, took the proposal to the National Council, the CNDCEC's executive Board, for approval, appointing a group of accountants, mainly also academics, as members: Elbano de Nuccio, President of the CNDCEC, Francesco De Luca, Francesco Paolone, Matteo Pozzoli and Monica Vettorazzo.

The two institutions opted for a CNDCEC/SIDREA joint group to have equal weight within the Committee and to be able to represent scientific and technical-professional perspectives equally. The equal representation within the Committee was considered a prerequisite for achieving a reasonable equilibrium between the scientific and the professional perspectives.

At the end of this first step of the process, the two components formed the joint academic-professional "Startup" group and met for the first time in February 2024.

The Committee's meetings are managed, on the basis of informal arrangements made in advance, by the CNDCEC Secretariat. Following the provisions of the "Rules of Conduct for Members of National Council Study Committees" they take place online, by adopting the "GoToMeeting" platform. During the first meeting, the Group established, in addition to the presentation of the members, the rules of the engagement, trying to set up the activity of the work in such a way as to define a rigorous path in accordance with the best and well-established procedures developed in other countries (Australian Government, 2020; REF, 2021). Meetings normally take place on a bi-weekly basis and are recorded through a special platform service. Once recorded, the meetings are transcribed, when this is addressed as necessary, using a special software and then rechecked and cleaned up so that there is a record of the main decisions and research developments.

From a methodological point of view, the Committee decided to work with a predefined logical order, given the chance of reviewing and updating what was produced over time in the light of project developments.

The main challenge faced during the initial meetings was to identify the purpose of the analysis and, consequently, the development of the process. About the purpose of the project, some components felt that it would be better to determine, on the basis of past experience and without the ambition of proposing "magic potions," the best practices to be applied, while other components proposed to focus on the main recurring errors, so as to advise practitioners on these risks.

After the initial framing of the topic, it was therefore decided to define the development path of the project, the (potential) beneficiaries of the research and the content of the guidelines.

As far as the expected timing is concerned, the working group has set itself the goal of developing its guidelines over a two-year period. During this period, the working group has also intended to open itself up to the "outside world," confronting itself with the scientific community and the professionals (as the main research users) regarding the project undertaken, the program strategy of the content of the guidelines, and the expected results. This is also due to the fact that, apart from the different backgrounds of the members, the competencies expressed by the Committee mainly concern the economic-business area, while discussions with academics and professionals from different fields could enrich the content of the proposals and structure the considerations in a solid way.

This also makes it possible to monitor the results in the short and medium term and to address the validity of the work done, possibly correcting the approach and program. The main beneficiaries have been more specifically identified in the chartered accountants, although the guidelines can be of use to academics, entrepreneurs, startuppers, policymakers, students, universities, startup incubators, accelerators, and other institutions. The Committee focused, then, its interest on the content of the document. After an interesting debate, the members shared the opinion to focus their interest on business models, principles, and practices for planning, managing, controlling, and evaluating startups.

Furthermore, the guidelines will offer comprehensive support for the modeling, planning, management, control and evaluation of new businesses and startups. The main reference was pointed to the gazelle startups, which, due to their exceptional growth in the early years, represent models of excellence. The working group oriented and detailed the aim of the project on the development of knowledge, skills, and competencies in startups. On the basis of what said above about the purpose of the output, the Committee decided to focus its work on a "mixed approach," considering the main characteristics and issues related to the development of startups and highlighting the most recurring risks that can affect the different phases of the related projects. It was observed that this will allow them to use practices to validate theories and, at the same time, to draw inspiration from good practices to develop new and better theories, principles, and models. Clearly, the Committee repeated its intention to observe, monitor, and detail timing, content, and beneficiaries in order to track the progress and eventually re-program the path of the project.

2.5 Discussion and Conclusion

This chapter has provided some theoretical and methodological insights that may aid in designing and, subsequently implementing, impact case studies. The analysis draws on an illustrative example of an impact case study promoted by the academic group "Start-ups" of the Italian Academic Association of Professors of Accounting and Business Administration (SIDREA) and the Italian National Council of Chartered Accountants CNDCEC (hereafter, SIDREA-CNDCEC case impact). This ongoing case impact, which focuses on specific high-growth startups (gazelles), aims at designing and adopting "Principles, Models, and Accounting Standards" for these types of organizations. The case impact was initiated by the SIDREA "Startup" group and involved the Italian National Council of Chartered Accountants and Experts in Accounting (CNDCEC) (SIDREA-CNDCEC case impact).

From the SIDREA-CNDCEC case impact, which is still in progress, we have drawn some lessons that we hope could provide useful guidelines for designing and implementing other impact case studies in the future: (1) to construct a convergence of interest in defining and considering the focus of the case study, also by investigating the purpose of the project; (2) to implement mechanisms which can continually improve and refine this initial convergence by monitoring the ongoing outcomes and process; (3) to adopt formalized standard procedures, which regulate "when," "how," and "frequency" of the engagement between the members of the case impact; (4) to undertake ongoing dissemination of the achieved outcomes to enlarge the different stakeholders' perspectives; (5) to measure the outcomes which are generated, for each beneficiary, by and through the impact case.

First, the starting point for an impact case study is to create a convergence of interest among the actors involved with regard to the "issue/topic" of analysis. Specifically, the example discussed in this chapter involved a convergence of interest between the SIDREA "Startup" study group and the representatives of the CNDCEC. The convergence was not only about the focus of the project, the "start-ups," but also about the scope, that is to draw "Guidelines, models and Accounting Standards" for managing startups. This allowed the joint group to share different perspectives and opinions, adopting an approach that took into consideration practical issues with a rigorous and methodical *modus operandi*.

Second, the initial convergence needs to be improved and developed over time through frequent dialogue among the members of the joint group. For instance, it was decided to hold bi-weekly meetings. Continuous dialogue was important to design a rational and consolidated approach to be followed.

Third, in addition to being continuous and systematic, the dialogue has to follow formalized standard procedures with measurable outcomes. In our case, the different means of engagement (i.e., meetings, discussions, etc.) were accounted for: for example, transcriptions of the minutes were regularly undertaken. In addition, working papers were regularly prepared where each participant reported their thoughts and ideas. The accounting of the meetings is crucial, as well as considering the views and contributions of each member of the working group. All these metrics allow us to account for how the process of engagement within the impact case study occurs; in particular, these metrics provide information about the number of meetings, their duration, the number of participants, different views and perspectives discussed, etc.

Fourth, another important aspect is to undertake constant dissemination, through conferences, seminars, and workshops, of the working progress. This dissemination is essential for ensuring the improvements of the entire impact case study. The initial results need to be addressed in a wider context, taking into consideration also external opinions, to be confident that the results have taken into appropriate account the diverse interests that somehow can be involved.

Finally, the outcomes generated through impact case studies have to be "measured" by specific metrics designed to "determine" the type and amount of positive benefits produced. In the SIDREA-CNDCEC, the publication of the Guidelines and models for Startups, and their adoption of the different beneficiaries, will be the metrics adopted to "measure" these outcomes.

The implications arising from this project may be varied and geared to the heterogeneous context of the actors involved.

Startup entrepreneurs can reflect on the indications identified in the paper, address whether they encounter the identified evidence and whether they can draw useful advice from the illustrated "lessons from the past," to make their own financial decisions and avoid the critical issues already experienced by others in similar circumstances.

Chartered accountants must be prepared to adopt best practices to support entrepreneurs in their challenges and contribute to the reduction of existing risks and to enable a sustainable development. Indeed, startups are often subject to sudden phases of growth and decline. Stabilization must also be achieved through careful business analyses that professionals must be able to produce.

The (accounting) academia can greatly benefit from the research contained in this chapter, as to date there are no, as far as we are aware, equivalent examples to the one reported in the text. The impact case study presented, with reference to both topic and process, can serve as a reproducible benchmark, possibly revised and improved, to verify whether the path followed can define a process standard.

Finally, the contribution can also serve as a reference for policymakers, who should be ready to verify the possible adoption by startuppers of authoritative guidelines that, by reducing the risk of failure, can bring specific rewards, since the adoption of authoritative management paths is more likely to avoid wasting resources and to provide companies, and the entire community, with a tool for growth.

Some limitations in the discussed impact case study should be considered. First, at present it is not possible to provide evidence of the final step of the process, as it has not come to an end yet; therefore, it is impossible to say whether the project will produce the desired outcomes. Second, another limitation is that the outcome produced by the impact case study can be measured partially; this is because some of the benefits might be related to macroeconomic and market factors that prescind from the publication of future guidelines. In addition, it would be interesting to replicate a similar case study by focusing on specific sectors. The startup world is extremely heterogeneous, and general guidelines could be somewhere more applicable to some business segments than others. Finally, the guidelines, once approved and disseminated, should be repurposed in other geographic areas to assess if the outcomes are applicable and, if it is so, to what extent the local context may have an "impact" on the impact case study. However, we believe that this illustrative case study could provide some insights, theoretically and methodologically, for constructing other similar projects in the future. We hope that other scholars can learn some lessons from our experience; these lessons can provide the coordinates for navigating the complexities of designing and carrying on case studies that are impactful and beneficial to society, economy, and business.

References

Acs, Z. J., & Armington, C. (2006). *Entrepreneurship, geography, and American economic growth*. Cambridge University Press.

Acs, Z. J., & Mueller, P. (2008). Employment effects of business dynamics: Mice, gazelles and elephants. *Small Business Economics, 30*, 85–100.

Australian Government. (2020). *Excellence in research for Australia*. Retrieved from https://www.arc.gov.au/excellence-research-australia

Autio, E., Arenius, P., & Wallenius, H. (2000). *Economic impact of gazelle firms in Finland*. Helsinki University of Technology Working Paper Series.

Barney, J. (1991). Firm resources and sustained competitive advantage. *Journal of Management, 17*(1), 99–120.

Barney, J. B., & Arikan, A. M. (2005). The resource-based view: Origins and implications. In *The Blackwell handbook of strategic management* (pp. 123–182). Wiley.

Birley, S. (1987). New ventures and employment growth. *Journal of Business Venturing, 2*, 155–165.

Blank, S., & Dorf, B. (2020). *The startup owner's manual: The step-by-step guide for building a great company*. Wiley.

Bos, J. W., & Stam, E. (2014). Gazelles and industry growth: A study of young high-growth firms in The Netherlands. *Industrial and Corporate Change, 23*(1), 145–169.

Bruna, M. G., & Nicolò, D. (2020). Corporate reputation and social sustainability in the early stages of start-ups: A theoretical model to match stakeholders' expectations through corporate social commitment. *Finance Research Letters, 35*, 101508.

Cattafi, G., Del Pozzo, A., & Nicolò, D. (2023). People first! Intellectual capital and growth of high-growth social cooperatives (social gazelles) in the startup stage. Evidence from Italy. *Piccola Impresa/Small Business, 1*.

Cattafi, G., Mariani, G., Pistolesi, F., & Nicolò, D. (2024). Cheating in the evaluation. An expedient to estimate the impact of intangibles on the enterprise value of the high-growth start-ups. *Management Control, 2023*(3), 193–218.

Chliova, M., & Ringov, D. (2017). Scaling impact: Template development and replication at the base of the pyramid. *Academy of Management Perspectives, 31*(1), 44–62.

Coad, A., Daunfeldt, S. O., Hölzl, W., Johansson, D., & Nightingale, P. (2014). High-growth firms: Introduction to the special section. *Industrial and Corporate Change, 23*(1), 91–112.

Cooper, A. C., Gimeno-Gascon, F. J., & Woo, C. Y. (1994). Initial human and financial capital as predictors of new venture performance. *Journal of Business Venturing, 9*, 371–395.

Daunfeldt, S. O., Johansson, D., & Halvarsson, D. (2015). Using the Eurostat-OECD definition of high-growth firms: A cautionary note. *Journal of Entrepreneurship and Public Policy, 4*(1), 50–56.

Deschryvere, M. (2008). *High growth firms and job creation in Finland (No. 1144)*. ETLA Discussion Papers.
Du, J., & Temouri, Y. (2015). High-growth firms and productivity: Evidence from the United Kingdom. *Small Business Economics, 44*, 123–143.
Dunne, P., & Hughes, A. (1994). Age, size, growth and survival: UK companies in the 1980s. *The Journal of Industrial Economics, 42*, 115–140.
Eurostat-OECD. (2007). *Manual on business demography statistics*.
Fritsch, M., & Schindele, Y. (2011). The contribution of new businesses to regional employment—An empirical analysis. *Economic Geography, 87*(2), 153–180.
Garnsey, E., & Heffernan, P. (2005). Growth setbacks in new firms. *Futures, 37*(7), 675–697.
Gilbert, B. A., McDougall, P. P., & Audretsch, D. B. (2006). New venture growth: A review and extension. *Journal of Management, 32*(6), 926–950.
Halabisky, D., Dreessen, E., & Parsley, C. (2006). Growth in firms in Canada, 1985–1999. *Journal of Small Business and Entrepreneurship, 19*(3), 255–267.
Hart, M., Prashar, N., & Ri, A. (2021). From the cabinet of curiosities: The misdirection of research and policy debates on small firm growth. *International Small Business Journal, 39*(1), 3–17.
Hayes, R., Kyer, B., & Weber, E. (2015). The case study cookbook. *Worcester Polytechnic Institute, 1*(2), 18–45.
Henrekson, M., & Johansson, D. (2010). Gazelles as job creators: A survey and interpretation of the evidence. *Small Business Economics, 35*, 227–244.
Heyeres, M., Tsey, K., Yang, Y., Yan, L., & Jiang, H. (2019). The characteristics and reporting quality of research impact case studies: A systematic review. *Evaluation and Program Planning, 73*, 10–23.
Hölzl, W. (2014). Persistence, survival, and growth: A closer look at 20 years of fast-growing firms in Austria. *Industrial and Corporate Change, 23*(1), 199–231.
ISTAT. (2022). In ISTAT (Ed.), *Annuario statistico italiano* (pp. 555–591). Rome. https://www.istat.it/storage/ASI/2022/capitoli/C14.pdf
Jansen, J. J., Heavey, C., Mom, T. J., Simsek, Z., & Zahra, S. A. (2023). Scaling-up: Building, leading and sustaining rapid growth over time. *Journal of Management Studies, 60*(3), 581–604.
Kirchhoff, B. (1994). *Entrepreneurship and dynamic capitalism*. Praeger.
Knaup, A. E., & Piazza, M. C. (2007). Business employment dynamics data: Survival and longevity, II. *Monthly Labor Review, 130*, 3.
Krošláková, M., Kubičková, V., Jurkovičová, L., & Kubiniy, N. (2015). Dynamics of high growth enterprises–"gazelles"– In Czech Republic. *Business Perspectives, 2*, 27–35.
Kuratko, D. F., Holt, H. L., & Neubert, E. (2020). Blitzscaling: The good, the bad, and the ugly. *Business Horizons, 63*(1), 109–119.
Mata, J. (1994). Firm growth during infancy. *Small Business Economics, 6*, 27–39.
Nicolò, D. (2019). *La vulnerabilità delle imprese nella fase di start-up. Analisi e interpretazioni delle cause*. Giappichelli.
Pšeničny, V., Jakopin, E., Vukčević, Z., & Čorić, G. (2014). Dynamic entrepreneurship–generator of sustainable economic growth and competitiveness. *Management: Journal of Contemporary Management Issues, 19*(1), 61–92.
Reed, M. S., Ferré, M., Martin-Ortega, J., Blanche, R., Lawford-Rolfe, R., Dallimer, M., & Holden, J. (2021). Evaluating impact from research: A methodological framework. *Research Policy, 50*(4), 104147.
REF. (2021). https://2021.ref.ac.uk/index.html
Reuber, A. R., Tippmann, E., & Monaghan, S. (2021). Global scaling as a logic of multinationalization. *Journal of International Business Studies, 52*, 1031–1046.
Ries, E. (2011). *The lean startup: How today's entrepreneurs use continuous innovation to create radically successful businesses*. Crown Currency.
Schreyer, P. (2000). *High-growth firms and employment*.
Shepherd, D. A., & Patzelt, H. (2022). A call for research on the scaling of organizations and the scaling of social impact. *Entrepreneurship Theory and Practice, 46*(2), 255–268.

Van Praag, C. M., & Versloot, P. H. (2007). What is the value of entrepreneurship? A review of recent research. *Small Business Economics, 29*(4), 351–382.
Venkataraman, S., Van de Ven, A. H., Buckeye, J., & Hudson, R. (1990). Starting up in a turbulent environment: A process model of failure among firms with high customer dependence. *Journal of Business Venturing, 5*(5), 277–295.

Websites

http://www.paulgraham.com/growth.html
https://www.ref.ac.uk
https://results2021.ref.ac.uk/impact
https://2021.ref.ac.uk/guidance-on-results/guidance-on-ref-2021-results/index.html#qualityRatings

Chapter 3
Valuing Startups: Models and Methods in the Face of Criticalities of Newness

Daniela Rupo, Giovanna Centorrino, and Valeria Naciti

3.1 Introduction

Valuing a company is never straightforward, and this complexity is amplified in the case of startups, which inherently carry a high level of entrepreneurial risk (Damodaran, 2024).

The valuation of startups is marked by significant uncertainty, stemming from many factors such as the high likelihood of failure, the unreliability of forecasts due to a lack of historical performance data, and the entrepreneurial dynamics and capabilities of the founders (Miloud et al., 2012). Moreover, valuing startups presents a multifaceted challenge because they usually operate in innovative industries where traditional financial indicators like revenues and profit must be more accurate in capturing their intrinsic worth. This challenge is exacerbated by the absence of comparable firms and the vulnerability of growth, which often shows a low correlation with profitability, consequently making the risk of failure exceptionally high (Köseoğlu, 2023).

Startup valuation strictly depends on several characteristics that influence each phase of the firm's growth. It follows that value estimation can be addressed for specific phases of the startup's growth, from the pre-seed stage to the exit one, with the scope of valuation ranging from the selection among projects to the estimate of the exit price along the firm's life cycle.

Current valuation methods, such as discounted cash flow models and multiples, rely heavily on accounting information, which is often unavailable or unreliable for new ventures. This reliance leads to valuation inconsistencies and subjective estimates by venture capitalists and entrepreneurs, resulting in suboptimal investment

---

D. Rupo (✉) · G. Centorrino · V. Naciti
Department of Economics, University of Messina, Messina, Italy
e-mail: drupo@unime.it; giovanna.centorrino@unime.it; valeria.naciti@unime.it

S. Loprevite et al. (eds.), *Startups and Gazelle Enterprises*, SIDREA Series in Accounting and Business Administration,
https://doi.org/10.1007/978-3-031-90881-1_3

decisions. In their nascent stages, startups may have minimal revenues and profits. Hence, their valuations are based more on assumptions and projections rather than on historical financial data, requiring the adoption of alternative methods to capture the value of qualitative and intangible elements. The domain of startup valuation encompasses an array of methodologies specifically tailored to address the nuances of these emerging enterprises (Usmani et al., 2023). The choice among various methods depends on numerous factors, including the startup's developmental stage, the dynamism of its industry landscape, and the availability and quality of data.

Specific methodologies (i.e., the Venture Capital, Berkus, and Scorecard Methods) adopt different ways to estimate the expectations and probability of generating value. Each model has unique merits and demerits; for instance, the Berkus Method is simple and quick but can be highly subjective. The Scorecard Method has predetermined weightings, adding a degree of objectivity. Financial methods like the Venture Capital Method are reliable for assessing potential investment returns, especially for portfolio diversification, though they may overlook qualitative aspects such as team competence or networks.

In practical application, startup valuations often involve a blend of quantitative methodologies and qualitative assessments of parameters such as market demand, competitive positioning, and the proficiency of the founding team. Acknowledging the inherently subjective nature of startup valuations is crucial; they are subject to significant variance based on the perspectives of investors and other stakeholders (Berre & Le Pendeven, 2023). In this context, uncertainty is a crucial factor, and the precision of valuation methods is essential to prevent the valuation process from contributing to the bursting of the startup bubble and adversely affecting the startup ecosystem.

Therefore, there is room for research to bridge the gap between theoretical frameworks and practical applications in new venture valuation. Accordingly, we address the complexities of startup valuation by adopting a research methodology that involves a comprehensive conceptual analysis of the topic investigated, leveraging the extensive literature available (Fitzgerald, 1996).

This manuscript adds to previous studies on startup valuation methods in that it builds upon traditional startup valuation approaches and novel methodologies that specifically address the limitations identified in previous research. While Montani et al. (2020) provided an extensive review of the most widely used valuation methods, our study goes further by incorporating emerging approaches to startup valuation based on probabilistic scenarios and hybrid models that merge qualitative and quantitative factors, customized to the unique dynamics of modern startups. Moreover, our research provides an interpretative framework deemed suitable to improve predictive accuracy and adaptability of valuations in rapidly evolving markets, effectively filling the gaps noted in Montani et al. (2020) review. The proposed interpretative framework is intended to support the integrated approach to business valuation for startups in the light of two critical dimensions for the success of new ventures: the dimension of intangible and personal key factors.

Critically examining academic papers reveals how conventional financial indicators, such as revenues and profit, often fail to capture the intrinsic worth of startups, particularly those operating in dynamic and high-risk industries. Given such limitations, our approach allows us to dissect and understand the theoretical underpinnings and practical implications of various valuation methodologies tailored to startups.

By exploring different valuation models, we intend to refine our understanding of the intricate valuation process of nascent enterprises (Damodaran, 2009). This exploration underscores the importance of integrating both quantitative and qualitative evaluations, considering factors such as market demand, competitive positioning, and the proficiency of the founding team. Recognizing the subjective nature and inherent uncertainties of startup valuations (Köhn, 2018; Huang & Pearce, 2015), our analysis aims to provide a nuanced perspective that can inform more accurate and reliable valuation practices, ultimately supporting the sustainability and growth of the startup ecosystem.

The chapter critically examines various startup valuation methodologies, exploring their strengths and limitations. Based on the analysis of the literature and adopting the PRISMA protocol for the selection of publications (Shamseer et al., 2015; Kelly et al., 2016), the study aims to focus on the main aspects of business appraisal in a specific setting where the significant sources of uncertainty and complexity of the estimate amplify the risks of errors and biases in valuation. Through this critical lens, we seek to contribute to the broader discourse on startup valuations and propose a conceptual framework for the fundamental analysis and the method setting in the valuation process.

The paper is organized into the following sections: Section 3.2 provides the background; Section 3.3 details the methodology following the PRISMA protocol; Section 3.4 presents the analysis of the literature; Section 3.5 outlines the results; and Sect. 3.6 encompasses the discussion, conclusion, and implications.

3.2 Background

The definition of a startup has evolved, reflecting changes in the business landscape and academic perspectives (Wirtz et al., 2016). Earlier definitions from the 1970s to the late 1990s primarily emphasized the aspect of "newness" in terms of legal existence and operational history. For instance, Keeble (1976) defined a startup as an entirely new enterprise that did not formerly exist as an organization. Gudgin (1978) conceptualized a startup as a new firm that initiates production for the first time. This focus on newness also included the liability associated with being new and small, as noted by Freeman and Reed (1983).

Contemporary definitions from the early 2000s incorporate additional dimensions such as innovation, technology, and growth potential. Modern scholars like Cho and McLean (2009) and Ries (2011) emphasize startups as temporary organizations that create innovative products or services under extreme uncertainty. They highlight the role of high technology and the necessity to operate in uncertain and risky environments. For instance, Paoloni and Modaffari (2018) define a startup as an established young company that focuses on developing social and predominantly innovative products and/or services with high technological value. A relevant definition is given by Blank, who emphasizes that a startup is an organization created to employ a scalable business model (Blank, 2018), i.e., capable of exponentially increasing the size of the business without a proportional increase in the resources used. The firm's success will depend on the market potential, the business model's innovativeness, and the growth's sustainability.

This evolution in the definition underscores the shift from merely being new to being innovative and adaptable in rapidly changing markets, reflecting the dynamic nature of today's entrepreneurial ventures.

In startup valuation, qualitative factors, including industry characteristics and firm-specific attributes, play a significant role. Theories from entrepreneurship and strategic management offer deeper insights into the antecedents of firm performance and valuation. Internal resources, industry conditions, and network relationships determine firm performance and influence valuation outcomes (Lee et al., 2001; Zaheer & Bell, 2005; Dhochak & Doliya, 2020).

The need to take into account the specific features of startups has prompted a transition beyond conventional quantitative metrics such as revenue and market size, embracing qualitative factors that are equally vital (Gonnella & Talarico, 2022). Factors such as the strength and cohesion of the founding team, the uniqueness of the product or service offering, deep market understanding, effective execution strategies, brand reputation, adaptability to change, compliance with legal regulations, and fostering a positive organizational culture are now recognized as essential indicators of a startup's potential and sustainability (Edison et al., 2018; Tripathi et al., 2019).

The valuation of startups has become a crucial focus for venture capitalists due to the growing number of entrepreneurial ventures seeking investment. Mechner (1989) noted that venture capitalists face a high demand for funds and must choose the most suitable valuation approach to make informed investment decisions. Extensive research has aimed to develop effective valuation methods, with early studies (MacMillan & Day, 1987; Zacharakis & Meyer, 1995; Davila & Foster, 2007; Smith et al., 2011; Cambria, 2016; Ali & Khalidi, 2020; Agyare et al., 2022) examining the negotiation process's impact on valuation. Recent research in entrepreneurial finance has delved into the various determinants influencing venture capitalists' investment decisions, highlighting factors such as human capital, market growth, and competitive advantage (Hsu, 2007; Fraser et al., 2015; Bonini & Capizzi, 2019; Seong & Kim, 2021; Wang et al., 2023).

Evaluating startups involves considerable complexity due to the diversity and variability of valuation models and estimation parameters, which heavily depend on the dynamic nature of these companies. Startup valuation cannot be viewed as a single conceptual category because it varies based on the valuation's purpose (investor perspective) and timing (stage of the lifecycle) (Tiscini & Dello Strologo, 2022).

The startup lifecycle consists of several stages (Fig. 3.1), each with unique challenges and objectives. The initial stage, often called the idea or seed stage, focuses on developing a business idea, conducting market research, and creating a viable

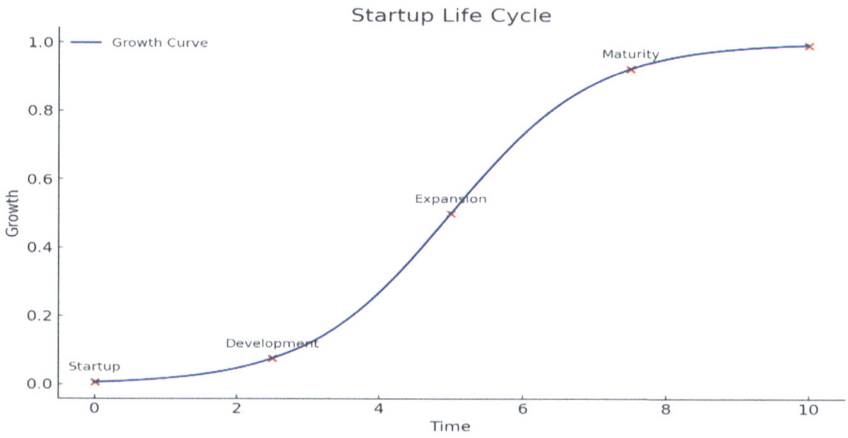

Fig. 3.1 Startup life cycle

business plan. At this stage, forecasts regarding investments and revenues still need to be implemented. The primary aim is to validate the business concept and secure initial funding from angel investors or through "bootstrapping."

The startup stage identifies when the firm officially launches and begins operations. In this stage, the firm is focused on product development, conquering an initial customer base, and refining the business model (Bianchi Martini et al., 2024). This stage often requires additional venture capital (VC) funding to support growth and operations. When the volume of activity grows steadily, the business enters the growth stage, where it manages to expand its market share, increase sales, and take advantage of economies of scale. During this period, companies may seek further rounds of VC funding to support rapid expansion, enhance marketing efforts, and develop new product lines. Valuation methodologies in this stage often emphasize growth potential, market size, and competitive positioning. The final stage is maturity, where the startup has established a stable market presence and consistent revenue streams. At this point, the focus may shift to optimizing operations, maximizing profitability, and exploring exit strategies such as mergers, acquisitions, or initial public offerings (IPOs). Valuation methodologies in this stage are more comprehensive, incorporating qualitative and quantitative factors, such as market conditions, financial performance, and strategic fit with potential acquirers.

The market perspectives are mostly significant in determining the success of a startup since the current level of potential demand and the expected growth of the market are crucial both in determining the profitability of the new venture and the incumbent need to defend the business idea from other competitors.

The graph (Fig. 3.2) elucidates the dynamic lifecycle of startups, characterized by the stages of startup, development, expansion, and maturity, each distinguished by variations in risk levels, funding needs, and revenue growth.

The valuation process should consider specific factors affecting the operating risk. Among them are the managerial experience and entrepreneurial attitude of the

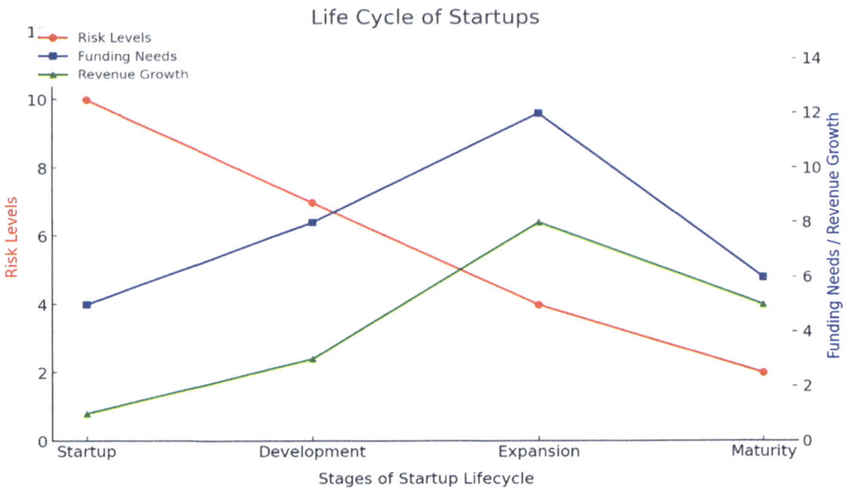

Fig. 3.2 Life cycle of startup by risk level

founders, the viability and profitability of the business idea, the market opportunities, and the competitive strength of the business model against potential entrants. One of the main aspects to consider is the execution risk, expressing the reliability of the timeline of activities envisaged in the business plan and the availability of an alternative plan when the main plan is not satisfactory or practicable (Rey & Agliata, 2022).

The revenue expectations, in terms of price levels, able to compensate all the types of costs—including the cost of capital when the firm has reached the break-even point—depend on assessing all these risk components. From the investors' viewpoint, such valuation is crucial to determine wheteher to support the startup and to what extent financing the business in the various stages of its life cycle.

Initially, the startup phase is marked by elevated risk levels, denoted by the high value of the red curve, reflecting the inherent uncertainties and challenges in establishing a new venture (Mullins, 2017). Risk levels diminish when the startup moves into the Development phase, signifying improved stability and market validation (Tomy & Pardede, 2018). Concurrently, funding needs, represented by the blue line, escalate, particularly peaking in the Expansion phase, where substantial capital is required to scale operations and penetrate new markets (Brown et al., 2019).

Revenue growth, illustrated by the green line, remains modest in the early stages but experiences a significant upsurge during the Expansion phase, indicative of the successful scaling efforts and market acceptance (Appelo, 2019; Horne & Fichter, 2022).

In the final Maturity stage, risk levels and funding need to taper off, reflecting the establishment of a stable market position. At the same time, revenue growth stabilizes, highlighting the shift in focus toward optimization and sustained profitability (Kale, 2024).

The search for funds to sustain the development of startups represents the most critical stage in the value creation. Following the initial stage, when it is common to say that only "fools" can trust the firm's project, given the high rate of failure of startups in the first three years, the need for external funds becomes crucial. Recently, in addition to venture capitalists and business angels, entrepreneurial finance for startups has been enriched by new equity tools, such as crowdfunding platforms, incubators, business angels' groups, and accelerators (Maglio & Rey, 2022). All these actors provide funds and opportunities for startups, contributing to a favorable ecosystem for the creation of new ventures and the pursuit of their growth, particularly in the case of disruptive innovations such as digital technologies (Balcerzak et al., 2023).

The valuation methods reflect the relevance of funding startups, impacting the assumption of the formula adopted and the basis of value (Block et al., 2014; Hidayat, 2022). Thus, among aspects, it is helpful to underline that in a startup appraisal, we distinguish between the pre-money and post-money value. The former is the value of a startup, excluding the investment made by a founder (e.g., business angel or venture capitalist), before starting the first round of financing (Van Osnabrugge & Robinson, 2000; Schmidt, 2014), while the post-money value considers that the financing round has been completed (Botella-Carrubi et al., 2022; Ang et al., 2022). The sum of the pre-money value and external capital contribution, such as from a funding round, gives the post-money value. Some methods belong to the pre-money category (e.g., Berkus Method, Scorecard Method), and others are post-money valuation methods (Venture Capitalist Method).

3.3 Methodology

The systematic review gathers all relevant information needed to answer a research question, which is useful for researchers to summarize existing literature through a gradual, meticulous, explicit, and transparent process (Liberati et al., 2009). A systematic literature review identifies the research question for subsequent studies, helping to fill the gap in the literature, even when the research question involves replicating or developing an existing study (Tranfield et al., 2003).

In this work, we adopted the preferred reporting items for systematic review and meta-analysis (PRISMA) protocol. The PRISMA model is recently spreading in accounting and management (Vale et al., 2022; Kaur et al., 2023; Galletta et al., 2024). The PRISMA flowchart used in this work is based on the following phase sequence:

Identification: In this initial phase, the research question is identified, and relevant studies are searched with clear inclusion and exclusion criteria.

Screening: This phase involves screening the titles and abstracts of studies identified in the first phase, followed by a review of studies meeting the inclusion criteria.

Eligibility: In the third phase, researchers assess the eligibility of the studies reviewed during the screening phase. Studies that meet the paper's aim are included in the systematic review.

The PRISMA protocol enabled us to systematically identify and select the most significant papers that critically examine the topic. By following the PRISMA framework, we meticulously navigated through its phases—identification, screening, and eligibility—to ensure a rigorous selection process. We filtered out outdated or irrelevant studies and focus on contemporary advancements in startup valuation methodologies, thereby providing a comprehensive and up-to-date synthesis of current academic contributions in this field.

Exclusion criteria included conference reports, articles in languages other than English non-academic sector literature. Furthermore, we excluded works that were not aligned with the aim of our paper, studies applying valuation to single case studies or highly specific case studies where the results could not be generalized, and papers that did not provide insights into alternative methodologies. Therefore, we strictly include papers that significantly and critically examine the topic. The inclusion and exclusion criteria are summarized in Fig. 3.3.

To gather the publications, we utilized keywords such as valuation model and startup, valuation method startup, startup valuation, venture capital valuation. Additionally, we conducted a search using the terms value, equity value, and enterprise value. However, the articles identified through these searches were not consistent with our research objectives.

The initial search yielded 130 documents. Following our inclusion and exclusion criteria (see Fig. 3.3), the final sample consists of 13 publications.

3.4 Analysis of the Literature

The literature on startup valuation methods reveals a rich tapestry of approaches, each addressing the unique challenges posed by young companies.

Davila et al. (2003) and Joglekar and Levesque (2009) both explore the impact of VC on startup valuation, albeit from different perspectives. Davila et al. (2003) focus on the prominent role of VC funding in setting the assumption of the valuation process. They argue that the inherent uncertainty and information asymmetry between startups and the market make funding rounds crucial indicators of a startup's potential success. VC backing provides essential capital and validates the startup's viability, reducing perceived risks among potential employees and investors. Their analysis reveals that VC-backed firms typically experience higher growth rates. Such positive results are largely attributed to the comprehensive due diligence conducted by VCs, their active involvement in governance, and their extensive network and reputation, which collectively enhance the startup's growth prospects and market valuation.

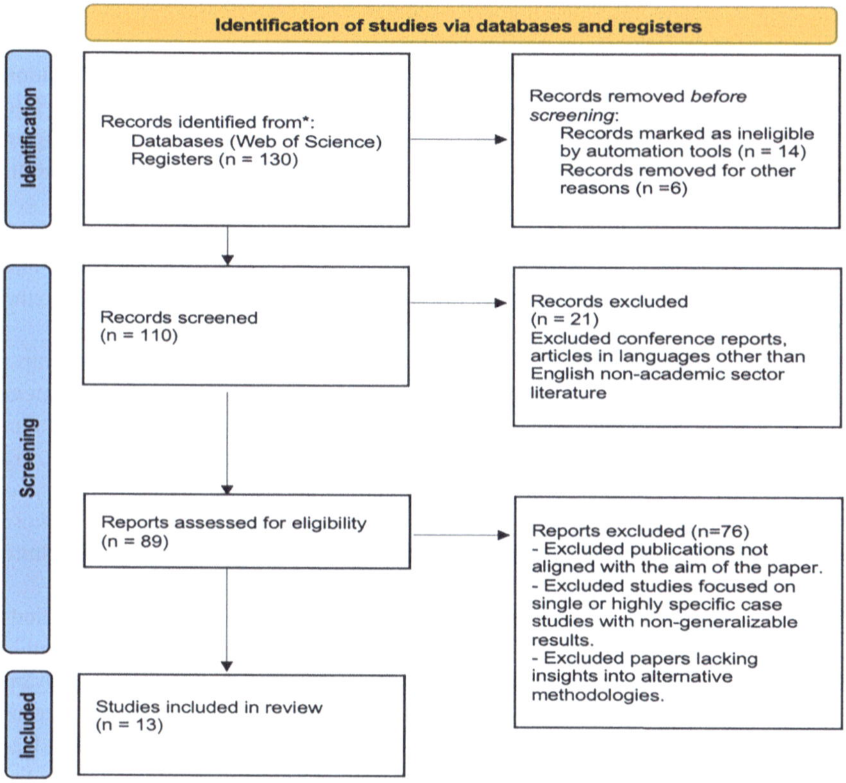

Fig. 3.3 PRISMA protocol

Joglekar and Levesque (2009) focus on venture capital decisions concerning high marketing and R&D expense percentages. They present a resource acquisition and allocation decision model across successive stages of startup growth, considering the funding process aimed at improving product quality and market growth to impact startup valuation positively. The model explores the implications of productivity changes and the evolving payoffs of R&D and marketing investments on essential decisions. It provides insights into best practices for resource acquisition and allocation, showing the optimal limits for marketing and R&D costs as a proportion of sales.

Moreover, Block et al. (2014) and Colombo et al. (2022) contribute to the unique perspectives on startup valuation, highlighting various factors and methodologies. Block et al. (2014) delve into the intricate mechanisms driving startup valuations, emphasizing the role of marketing assets and intellectual property (IP) applications, particularly trademarks. They argue that startup valuation by VCs hinges on a blend of tangible and intangible factors, with trademarks serving as robust indicators of market orientation and growth potential. Unlike patents, trademarks are noted for their higher success rates and immediate applicability in safeguarding brand identity, significantly influencing startup valuation.

Colombo et al. (2022) underscore several critical drivers of startup valuation within the context of Initial Coin Offerings (ICOs). They highlight the pivotal role of the founder CEO's attractiveness, suggesting that investor decision-making in ICO environments, characterized by high information asymmetry, is heavily influenced by perceived personal characteristics.

Instead, the studies by Miloud et al. (2012), Akkaya (2020), Montani et al. (2020), Dhochak and Doliya (2020), Usmani et al. (2023); and Imbierowicz and Rauch (2024) explore diverse approaches to startup valuation, highlighting both the challenges of traditional methods and the potential of alternative frameworks.

Miloud et al. (2012) critique traditional financial valuation methods for startups, such as discounted cash flow and earnings multiples, citing their reliance on extensive accounting data typically lacking in early-stage ventures. They advocate for an alternative approach grounded in strategic management theories, emphasizing industry organization economics, the resource-based view, and network theory as key drivers of startup valuation. This strategic perspective aims to provide a more accurate and defensible valuation method that aligns better with the dynamic nature of startups and reduces conflicts between entrepreneurs and investors.

Akkaya (2020) proposes several tailored valuation methods for startups, including the Berkus Method, Risk Factor Summation, Scorecard Valuation, Comparable Transactions, and the Venture Capital Method. Each method offers distinct advantages and drawbacks, catering to different aspects of startup evaluation. The Berkus Method, for instance, focuses on assigning monetary values to critical success factors like idea strength and market traction, albeit subjectively. In contrast, the Venture Capital Method aligns with startups' high-risk and high-reward nature by underlining potential future returns, albeit relying heavily on speculative financial projections.

Montani et al. (2020) underline the limitations of traditional valuation methods and consider alternative ones: the Real Option Method, the First Chicago Method, and the Venture Capital Method. These approaches aim to accommodate the uncertainties inherent in early-stage companies, with the Real Option Method allowing flexibility in decision-making and the Venture Capital Method focusing on future return potentials. However, they acknowledge the complexities involved, such as the need for extensive market data and the speculative nature of financial projections.

Dhochak and Doliya (2020) contribute to the fuzzy analytic hierarchy process (FAHP) as a strategic evaluation tool for startup valuation. This method integrates internal and external strategic variables to enhance accuracy and transparency in valuation processes. However, its complexity and time-intensive nature pose implementation challenges, particularly in technology-based startups where specific technological variables may still need to be fully captured.

Usmani et al. (2023) propose several alternative valuation methods tailored for startups, including the Venture Capital method, Scorecard method, and Comparable Company analysis. The Venture Capital method focuses on post-money valuation through ROI calculations, reflecting its utility in navigating uncertainties typical of early-stage startups. Meanwhile, the Scorecard method provides a structured assessment framework, albeit with subjectivity, while Comparable Company analysis benchmarks against similar firms, contingent on data availability and comparability.

Imbierowicz and Rauch (2024) propose two main alternative valuation methods for startups: Fundamental Valuation Methods and Relative Valuation Methods. The Fundamental Valuation Methods focus on the intrinsic value of the startup by examining factors such as revenue growth, key performance indicators (KPIs), and net income changes. According to the authors, this method is beneficial for assessing mature startups with stable business models, as it leverages predictable financial data to estimate value. However, it can be less effective for early-stage startups with high uncertainty and limited financial history, leading to potentially inaccurate valuations.

On the other hand, the Relative Valuation Methods involve comparing the startup to similar companies in the same industry. This approach benefits from being more accessible to apply and relies on market-based indicators, making it more practical for early-stage startups with less predictable cash flows. It captures industry trends and external factors, providing a market-oriented perspective on valuation. However, finding comparable companies can be challenging, and the method may not account for the unique aspects of a particular startup, leading to potential over- or under-valuation.

Finally, the studies by Barg et al. (2021), Berre and Le Pendeven (2023), and Chandra and Mazumdar (2024) collectively explore diverse drivers influencing startup valuation, proposing alternative frameworks tailored to specific industry contexts.

The paper by Barg et al. (2021) proposes and empirically validates a reverse-engineering approach to valuing startups using venture capital multiples. The authors introduce a method of calculating venture capital multiples for each financing round by dividing the firm's value at exit by its value at financing. This method corrects for industry trends, dilution, and differing investment durations to provide comparable annualized venture capital multiples for each industry. The study adopts a framework to determine implicit investment multiples from multiples observed within the industry for past venture capital transactions. This method produces reliable valuation multiples specific to industries and financing rounds, and it is easy to implement using readily available public data. The multiples derived through this framework are validated by regression analyses and sanity checks, which show that they accurately describe common valuation characteristics in the real world. The approach considers factors such as investors' experience, the mode of exit (IPO vs. M&A), the stage of financing, and the size of investment consortia.

These methods are positioned as alternatives to traditional approaches like Discounted Cash Flow (DCF) analysis and simple multiple methods, which may need more rigor and accuracy when applied to startups due to their unique characteristics and high early-stage uncertainty.

Berre and Le Pendeven's (2023) systematic literature review comprehensively analyses the drivers influencing startup valuation and explores alternative valuation methods. The study categorizes 36 valuation drivers into five macro-themes: Entrepreneur Characteristics, Firm Characteristics, Investor Characteristics, Market Conditions, and Deal Conditions. Their integrative meta-model combines these drivers and methods into a cohesive framework, emphasizing the importance of internal factors (entrepreneur and firm characteristics) and external influences (market and deal conditions) for realistic valuations.

Chandra and Mazumdar (2024) focus on biotech startups, highlighting key valuation factors such as projected drug sales, development costs, and regulatory risks influenced by market size, growth rates, competition, drug pricing, and clinical efficacy. They note significant valuation disparities due to information gaps between VCs and startup management, with VCs often adopting conservative approaches to mitigate high risks. The study examines three primary valuation methods for biotech startups: the risk-adjusted net present value (rNPV) method, the basic VC valuation formula, and the real options method. The rNPV method adjusts for success probabilities across different drug development stages; the VC valuation formula estimates future value based on projected sales or EBITDA with high discount rates; and the real options method allows for flexible decision-making based on market conditions. Each method provides unique insights into biotech investment risks and opportunities, highlighting the need for a nuanced valuation approach in this complex industry.

Table 3.1 captures the key aspects of each study, outlining the primary issues they address and the results connected to methodological aspect of startup valuation.

3.5 Results

From the literature analysis, it has emerged that traditional valuation methods have significant limitations. Research and practitioners have proposed alternative approaches to capture qualitative and intangible aspects better, significantly impacting startups' equity value. However, these alternative methods also present some critical challenges. In the following sections, we will discuss both aspects, presenting a general overview of traditional and alternative methods, with some insight into their application in the case of startup valuation.

3.5.1 Limitations of Traditional Valuation Methods

Traditional business valuation methodologies often fall short of providing an accurate assessment of the potential value of a startup (Damodaran, 2009a). The Discounted Cash Flow (DCF) method, generally preferred over other listed methods, can be particularly challenging and unreliable when applied to startups due to

Table 3.1 Key aspects of analyzed literature

Study	Issues	Results and methodological aspects
Davila, A., Foster, G., and Gupta, M. (2003)	Uncertainty and information asymmetry in startup valuation: precence of employee growth and VC financing	The study considers the venture capital funding events as key signals, providing necessary capital and validation, reducing perceived risks among stakeholders. Results show that the growth is not a criterion, hence following a growth strategy to attract VC may not be an effective strategy
Joglekar and Levesque (2009)	High percentages of marketing and R&D expenses impacting startup valuation	The paper deals with resource acquisition and allocation decision model to improve product quality and market growth, optimal limits for marketing, and R&D costs as a proportion of sales
Miloud, T., Aspelund, A., and Cabrol, M. (2012)	Traditional financial valuation methods are inadequate for startups due to a lack of extensive accounting information	The study proposes alternative valuation approach integrating strategic perspectives: Industry organization economics, resource-based view, and network theory
Block, J. H., De Vries, G., Schumann, J. H., and Sandner, P. (2014)	Traditional valuation methods are impractical for early-stage startups due to a lack of stable revenue streams	Qualitative assessments and quantitative proxies, including trademarks and patents filed, startup age, and VC experience are suggested. There is an inverted U-shaped relationship between trademark breadth and valuation.
Akkaya, M. (2020)	Limitations of traditional valuation approaches for startups	Alternative valuation methods are considered and referred to the aims of startups' valuation: Berkus Method, Risk Factor Summation, Scorecard Valuation, Comparable Transactions, and Venture Capital Method
Montani, D., Gervasio, D., and Pulcini, A. (2020)	Traditional valuation techniques are inadequate for early-stage companies	The methods investigated are: Real Option Method (ROM), Venture Capital Method (VCM), and First Chicago Method (FCM). Criticalities and lack of accuracy of various methods are discussed
Dhochak, M., and Doliya, P. (2020)	Limitations of traditional financial approaches for startups	The study develops an integrative multicriteria fuzzy decision-making approach to measure the relative importance of the strategic input variables in the methods adopoted by venture capitalist (Fuzzy Analytic Hierarchy Process -FAHP) incorporating strategic input variables
Barg, J. A., Drobetz, W., and Momtaz, P. P. (2021)	Inaccuracies in traditional methods due to industry trends, dilution, and differing investment durations	The study proposes a Reverse-engineering approach using venture capital multiples, validated by regression analyses and sanity checks

(continued)

Table 3.1 (continued)

Study	Issues	Results and methodological aspects
Colombo, M. G., Fisch, C., Momtaz, P. P., and Vismara, S. (2022)	Influence of founder CEO attractiveness and market sentiment on startup valuation in ICOs	The study emphasizes the attractiveness of the founder CEO and the role of market sentiment in investor decision-making. Founder CEO attractiveness serves is relevant in the presence of highly asymmetric information, while its role is weaker in information-richer contexts
Usmani, F., Sarim, M., and Ghayas, A. (2023)	Dependence on projected future revenues and market conditions for traditional methods	The study analyses the various methods for startups' valuation (Venture Capital method, Scorecard method, and Comparable Company analysis) adopting an integrated conceptual framework to examine whether VC' valuation can be driven by factors related to strategy theory crucial for firm performance
Berre, M., and Le Pendeven, B. (2023)	Diverse drivers influencing startup valuation	Based on 87 peer-reviewed studies, the paper proposes an integrative meta-model considering 36 valuation drivers categorized into macro themes (Entrepreneur Characteristics, Firm Characteristics, Investor Characteristics, Market Conditions, and Deal Conditions) placed into appropriate chronological position in the valuation process
Imbierowicz, B., and Rauch, C. (2024)	Inadequacies of traditional methods for early-stage startups with high uncertainty	The study investigates the driver for startup valuation considering both Fundamental Valuation Methods focusing on intrinsic value, and Relative Valuation Methods comparing to similar companies. Results demonstrate the supremacy of external factors as key driver behind valuations, finding that mutual funds are crucial in adjusting the startup share prices in response to changes in the multiples of peers, both in the short- and long-term
Chandra, A., and Mazumdar, S. (2024)	High risks and costs associated with drug development in biotech startups	Risk-adjusted net present value (rNPV), basic VC valuation formula, and real options method are considered within the valuation process for biotech startups. Understanding the key drivers of the alternative methods can help biotech startups in negotiating with VCs and reduce subjectivity in valuation for both parties, in particular in the pre-money valuation phase

the absence of certain necessary factors (Desaché, 2024; Patterson, 2023). Key issues include the high uncertainty characteristic of high-tech initiatives typical of many startups, making it difficult to estimate costs, revenues, and investments. Consequently, cash flows may be unreliable. Additionally, traditional techniques lack the flexibility needed to evaluate inherently flexible startups. A common criticality recurring when using methods based on the DCF concerns the rate calculation. Considering the CAPM as the most common way to determine the expected return on equity, in the case of the startup, it is difficult to get data referred to comparable companies to estimate the stock's volatility, hence the beta of the formula. In addition, the market risk is usually assumed to be constant throughout discounting, which is difficult to sustain here, given the variability of market risk in the different stages of startups. Similar issues arise concerning the capital structure since the weight of equity and debt along the lifecycle of startups is subject to variability, adding complexity to the estimate of WACC.

3.5.1.1 Asset-Based Methods

Asset-based valuation methods are comprised within the "Cost Approach" to valuation and include various types of methods that derive the value of the firm (both the Enterprise Value or the Equity Value) on the adjustment of the accounting values of assets and liabilities to meet their current value (Stowe, 2007). The adjusted book value comes in two types: simple and complex. The simple method considers only the adjusted book value of tangible assets, while the complex method includes intangible assets, such as intellectual property and trademarks.

The Excess Earning Method also relies on this approach. It calculates the enterprise value as the sum of tangible assets and the goodwill, estimated by capitalizing the exceeding returns on capital compared to the normal return (expected return from shareholders or from all people who have claims into the firm).

These methods are fundamentally limited for startups because they focus solely on current values rather than considering future potential. However, some practical applications of this approach, considering the valuation of specific intangibles, could support the estimate of relevant intellectual properties. For instance, in the case of biotech startups, patents, which are often a relevant value driver, can be estimated following the relief from royalties' method (Graham & Sichelman, 2016) to take into account future economic benefits related to their commercial exploitation in terms of specific revenues from sales or from licensing the intangibles to other users.

3.5.1.2 Discounted Cash Flow (DCF)

The Discounted Cash Flow (DCF) method is highly regarded in modern corporate finance for its reliability in correlating a company's value to its ability to generate future cash flows that meet investor return expectations (Bancel & Tierny, 2011;

Cravo, 2023). It calculates the value of a company's equity as the sum of the present values of future net operating cash flows, discounted at the company's weighted average cost of capital (WACC), or future free cash flows to equity investors, discounted at the expected return on equity (Shrieves & Wachowicz, 2001). However, applying this method to startups is challenging due to the difficulty in accurately predicting cash flows, especially since initial cash flows are often negative and the method does not account for future options the company might consider based on current investments (Laitinen, 2019; Akkaya, 2020). Additionally, determining the discount rate for cash flows is problematic, given the lack of historical data to estimate risk parameters like the equity beta of the CAPM model and the absence of long-term averages for benchmarking. In startups, estimable parameters often refer to short periods, making them unreliable. Similar issues arise with income-based methods, which start from an operating result that is often negative, even when expressed in terms of normalized prospective income rather than cash flows.

3.5.1.3 Multiples Method

The multiples method involves applying market multiples to key company financial metrics, such as net income, book value, sales, EBITDA, or EBIT (Lie & Lie, 2002). These multiples are derived from comparable companies. The market approach presents limitations in valuing startups due to the lack of historical data and the volatility of early-stage financial metrics. The need for normalized parameters makes traditional multiples challenging for newly established companies. The absence of comparable companies or the difficulty in identifying them further complicates indirect valuation methods.

Therefore, traditional valuation methodologies must be applied with these considerations in mind, recognizing the unique characteristics of startups (de Oliveira & Zotes, 2018). Traditional models, when adopted in the context of rapidly changing and developing companies, often fail to capture qualitative and intangible elements that impact the firm's intrinsic value.

High-tech startups experience significant uncertainty in estimating costs, revenues, and investments, making it difficult to apply traditional methods that rely on stable and predictable cash flows. Traditional methods may also fail to fully capture qualitative and intangible factors that significantly impact a startup's value, such as innovative potential, management quality, and market opportunities.

3.5.2 Alternative Valuation Methods for Startups

The common logic underlying alternative valuation methods for startups is to focus not on the current results but on a future date when the company is expected to achieve a certain level of economic and financial equilibrium characterized by stable and positive cash flows and earnings. This future value calculation can consider a single scenario or multiple scenarios weighted by specific probabilities of success.

The future value is then discounted back to the present using appropriate discounting techniques. Besides the quantitative variables necessary for applying various methods, these approaches also consider a qualitative analysis of the management team, which can result in an additional premium or a decrease in the obtained value.

3.5.2.1 Venture Capital Valuation Method

This method is generally adopted for highly innovative companies with minimal or nonexistent track records and high expectations for both return and risk. It represents a variant of the financial method based on calculating the cash flow at a future date, usually coinciding with the moment when the venture capitalist plans to exit the investment (Köhn, 2018; Akkaya, 2020; Moro-Visconti & Moro-Visconti, 2021; Maglio et al., 2022). The method involves several steps carefully designed to ensure a comprehensive valuation. The first step is estimating the company's value at the projected exit date. This final value, or Terminal Value, is calculated based on the expected earnings generated by the initiative after a certain number of years, using a market multiple.

The second step is to discount the final value. The Terminal Value is discounted at a rate reflecting the venture capitalist's expected return (Internal Rate of Return, IRR), considering the risk and resources invested. Usually, the model adopts a high measure of discounting rate, ranging from 25% to 60% annually. The third step is to calculate the desired entry stake, which is determined by dividing the planned investment by the discounted final value.

In the last step, the dilution effect is estimated by adjusting the equation to consider the subsequent funding rounds and the impact on the dilution of the venture capitalist's stake. The retention ratio quantifies this dilution, and the required percentage stake is adjusted accordingly.

The main critique of the Venture Capital Method involves using very high discount rates, justified by factors such as the illiquidity of the investment, the significant support provided to the company, and the probability of the company not surviving.

3.5.2.2 First Chicago Model

The First Chicago Model is a realistic approach to startup valuation, accounting for various potential failure scenarios crucial for volatile startups (Trichkova & Kanaryan, 2015; Majercakova & Mittelman, 2018). This method refines traditional methods by combining the Discounted Cash Flow and Venture Capital methods to evaluate three different valuation scenarios: negative, positive, and neutral. Each scenario is assigned a probability percentage multiplied by the startup's value in that specific scenario. A weighted average of these valuations is then calculated.

This model uses lower discount rates than the Venture Capital Valuation Method and replaces the final value with the expected value of the investment, averaging the company's terminal value across three scenarios: best, base, and worst. It also discounts all positive cash flows realized during the investment period. Many investors rely on this method for early-stage startup valuation as it predicts future negative and positive scenarios regarding the startup's development.

3.5.2.3 Real Options Method

This method, which derives from the theory by Bleck and Scholes (1973), values the company not only based on expected cash flows and assets but also considering the pursued strategy and the management's capability to manage the development and pivoting of the business dynamically (Davis & Samis, 2005). The discretionary power of the management in steering the company holds the intrinsic value that must be accounted for. The value of a company is conceived as a portfolio of financial options (put or call). The value consists of the sum of the cash flows generated by the current strategy and the implicit value of future strategic options available to management. However, the expert must carefully avoid double-counting the benefits of these options within the future cash flows.

3.5.2.4 Berkus Method

The Berkus Model is a valuation method for startups developed in 1990 by its namesake creator, Dave Berkus, a well-known angel investor in the California scene of that era (Fabozzi, 2016). The model was created to evaluate pre-revenue startups. Based on a simple structure, it attributes a value to each of five criteria depending on the market size, with typical values ranging from €0 to €500,000 for each: (1) Management team quality (Execution risk); (2) Value proposition (Product risk); (3) Working prototype (Technology risk); (4) Strategic relationships (Market and competitive risk); (5) Product launch and sales (Financial or production risk). A startup that satisfies all criteria can have a pre-money valuation of up to €2.5 million. Despite its effectiveness, this method should be corroborated by at least one other methodology (Akkaya, 2020).

3.5.2.5 Scorecard Method

Developed by the business angel Bill Payne, the Scorecard Method compares the average pre-money valuations of similar startups in the same sector and geographic area. It then adjusts for specific variables such as management team characteristics, product and technology type, market size and competitiveness, need for further investments, and strategic partnerships (Payne, 2011). This method can be used under conditions where there is a substantial reference market from which to derive average startup valuations and the ability to assign evaluation parameters to various startup components (e.g., management team, product type, technology, market competitiveness).

While these alternative valuation methods avoid some pitfalls of traditional models, they still face significant challenges. These include the availability of comparable data, projecting future results, and the highly subjective evaluation of qualitative factors. The difficulty in finding truly comparable companies can lead to significant valuation errors, and the change in the sample of comparables can drastically alter the valuation. Furthermore, the high degree of subjectivity remains a problem, as the comparability of companies is often limited by differences in activities, financial and operational leverage risk profiles, and different development stages.

Table 3.2 reflects the nuances discussed in this section, focusing on each method's effectiveness and limitations in valuing startups.

Table 3.2 Strengths and weaknesses of startup valuation methods

Evaluation method	Strengths	Weaknesses
Discounted cash flow (DCF)	Reliable for companies with stable, predictable cash flows; provides detailed cash flow insights	Unreliable for startups due to unpredictable cash flows and lack of historical data; does not account for future strategic options
Asset-based methods	Considers current assets and liabilities, including intellectual property in some cases (like patents in biotech startups)	Focuses on current values, ignoring future growth potential; limited applicability to intangible asset-driven companies like startups
Multiples method	Easy to apply when comparable companies are available; market-based approach	Difficult to find truly comparable companies for startups; limited by lack of historical data and unstable metrics in early stages
Venture capital valuation method	Focuses on future exit value; useful for high-risk, high-return startups; discounts terminal value based on venture capital returns	High discount rates may overestimate risks; does not consider qualitative factors such as management quality
First Chicago model	Accounts for different future scenarios (positive, neutral, negative); provides a more realistic approach by assigning probabilities to outcomes	Complex to apply and requires scenario-specific market data; speculative nature of assigning probabilities can lead to inaccuracies
Real options method	Recognizes the flexibility in strategic decision-making; evaluates startup as a portfolio of options, useful for high-tech startups	Requires sophisticated modeling and market data; difficult to avoid double-counting future benefits
Berkus method	Simple, quick method focused on early-stage startups; assigns value to intangible factors like management and product risks	Highly subjective and reliant on personal judgment; needs to be supplemented by another method for a more accurate assessment
Scorecard method	Adds objectivity by benchmarking against similar startups; adjusts for specific factors like market size, management quality, and product strength	Depends on the availability of comparable data and subjective weightings; may oversimplify unique factors of the startup

3.6 Discussion, Conclusion, and Implications

Valuing startups is a complex endeavor that requires more than traditional financial metrics, especially given the unique challenges posed by their nascent stages, lack of historical data, and high failure rates (Smith et al., 2011; Griva et al., 2023; Dhochak et al., 2024; Parkinson, 2024).

This study delves into various methodologies tailored for startup valuation, accentuating their individual strengths and limitations. It underscores the pressing need for research to bridge the gap between theoretical approaches and practical applications in this field (Crawford et al., 2022; Nair, 2024). By employing the PRISMA protocol for systematic literature reviews (Abelha et al., 2020; Albhirat et al., 2024), the research explores a diverse array of complementary methodologies for valuing startups.

The critical analysis identifies alternative valuation techniques, highlighting the complex nature of startup valuation that demands a multifaceted approach (Knight et al., 2020). This approach acknowledges both qualitative and quantitative aspects unique to nascent enterprises (Brennan et al., 2005). Traditional methods rely on historical financial data and often fall short for startups that lack such data. Hence, alternative methodologies like the Venture Capital Method, Berkus Method, and Scorecard Method have been developed to capture better the unique characteristics and potential of startups (Akkaya, 2020). These methods consider future growth opportunities, market conditions, and qualitative factors such as the competence of the founding team and market demand.

Due to the specific features of startups, traditional valuation methods often present several limitations when applied in this context. Despite the extensive research on valuation methods and the recognition of the challenges posed by inappropriate valuation due to a lack of proven track records and new market entry, there remains a significant gap in the development and implementation of systematic, reliable valuation approaches specifically tailored for new ventures (Berre & Le Pendeven, 2023; Dhochak & Doliya, 2020; Berk et al., 2004).

Inherent subjectivity and uncertainty in these valuations necessitate continuous refinement and adaptation to ensure their relevance and accuracy. An integrated valuation approach that considers tangible and intangible assets becomes essential.

Recent literature highlights the still existing gap in valuation methodologies for intangible assets, particularly in the context of innovative startups. Emerging technologies like artificial intelligence, big data analytics, and digital branding strategies complement traditional intangible assets such as patents, trademarks, and software, complicating valuation processes (Stein & Maass, 2022). Additionally, machine learning is increasingly integrated into asset valuation models, offering more precise and data-driven insights (Huang, 2023). Digital intellectual assets also present new valuation challenges, requiring tailored approaches that account for their intangible nature and impact on market dynamics (Loseva et al., 2022).

This shift calls for a broadened analytical framework for evaluators that considers both the tangible and intangible elements of a company's value proposition. An integrated valuation approach becomes essential, encompassing an enterprise's ability to generate value through its intellectual capital, the stage of development, and the specific characteristics of its investors. As startups advance through their lifecycle, demonstrating tangible achievements becomes increasingly relevant (Passaro et al., 2016; Becker & Endenich, 2023).

Metrics such as the number and scale of funding rounds, the effectiveness of management control systems, and financial stability become critical indicators of potential and market readiness. Qualitative aspects also play a significant role, complementing quantitative measures in understanding a new venture's full potential and risks. Researchers stress the importance of entrepreneurial skills and the management team's experience in enhancing business performance and increasing investment returns (Pena, 2002; Hsu, 2007; Miloud et al., 2012; Engelen et al., 2015; Olugbola, 2017; Picken, 2017). Therefore, integrating resource-based and network-based valuation methods is crucial for achieving more accurate startup valuations and mitigating investment risks (Garkavenko, 2022; Xu et al., 2024).

At different stages of a startup's lifecycle, the focus and methodology of valuation evolve (de Klerk et al., 2024; Sekliuckiene et al., 2018). In the early stage, valuation primarily aims to identify promising projects for funding by business angels or other potential investors. Qualitative factors such as the entrepreneur's passion, tenacity, and experience are crucial during this phase. These subjective traits often drive investor confidence and significantly influence the perceived value of the startup. The valuation at this stage assesses the viability and potential of the business idea, typically compared to other competing projects, rather than determining the value of stocks. As the startup progresses to the growth stage, the focus of valuation shifts toward securing venture capital funding (Block et al., 2014). While qualitative factors remain important, there is an increased emphasis on quantitative metrics like financial performance, market conditions, and competitive positioning. Investors evaluate the firm's characteristics and external factors, such as macroeconomic conditions and market demand. Constraints related to the CEO's expertise and the team's knowledge in leading growth can be mitigated by the involvement of venture capitalists, who provide organizational support and financial resources.

The valuation process becomes more intricate in the mature stages, particularly when preparing for exit strategies like an IPO or acquisition (Puca, 2020). Investors and stakeholders consider a broader range of factors, including deal-specific conditions and investor characteristics. These qualitative aspects can significantly influence the chosen valuation methodology, making specific approaches more suitable depending on the context. For example, methods incorporating market trends and investor sentiment may provide a more accurate reflection of the startup's worth in a dynamic market environment.

Intangible assets such as patents and ongoing innovation efforts are crucial during the nascent and growth phases, influencing a startup's ability to create sustainable value (Ojaghi et al., 2019; Park et al., 2023). Despite the increasing integration of ESG (Environmental, Social, and Governance) criteria into venture capital valuation models, a significant gap remains in understanding their nuanced impacts on startups. While startups with high ESG scores can achieve higher valuations and attract a broader investor base, there is limited empirical research detailing the long-term performance and survival rates of these startups compared to their non-ESG-focused counterparts.

Moreover, the literature often overlooks startups' challenges in maintaining high ESG standards while scaling operations, affecting their attractiveness to investors over time (Kaddour, 2023; Ylä-Nikkilä, 2024). Additionally, the varying definitions and metrics of ESG across industries and regions add complexity, making it difficult to create a standardized approach for evaluating and comparing ESG impacts on startup success. This gap underscores the need for more comprehensive, longitudinal studies considering both the short-term benefits and long-term implications of ESG integration for startups and their investors.

Based on this discussion, we propose an interpretative framework to support the integrated approach to business valuation for startups.

The evaluation matrix shown in Fig. 3.4 provides a conceptual framework with which it is possible to adopt an integrated approach to the valuation of startup firms in light of two critical dimensions: the dimension of Intangibles and Personal key factors on the y-axis and the dimension of Market Potential on the x-axis.

This matrix functions as a methodological map for appraisal in general and as a strategic tool for stakeholders, such as investors, entrepreneurs, and business developers, who wish to evaluate the potential success and inherent risks associated with different business ventures.

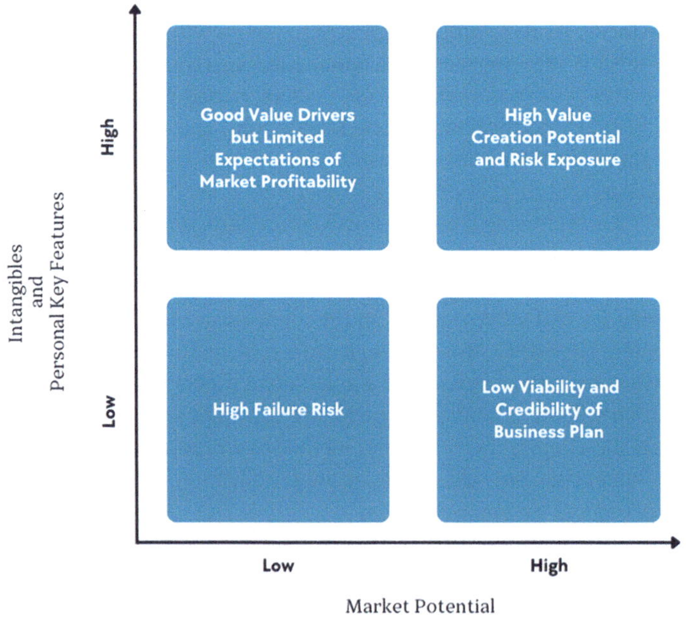

Fig. 3.4 Startup valuation matrix

The vertical axis, relating to intangible assets and personal key features, evaluates success based on these two aspects. Intangible assets, which include copyright, brand equity, customer relationships, the founder's reputation (science star), and core competencies, are critical to competitive advantage and long-term sustainability. Firms located higher on this axis hold vital intangible resources supported by technological expertise, market know-how, or other relevant knowledge bases that give them a strong competitive advantage. Furthermore, everything depends on experience, vision, the management team, and the quality of leadership, factors that substantially influence strategic decisions, operational efficiency, and the overall trajectory of the company.

This axis represents the domain of the so-called intellectual capital, which is undoubtedly a crucial "enabling factor" for the success of a startup, also in light of the commitment of institutions and organizations to sharpen the skills considered relevant for new entrepreneurship. The institutional world is inclined to simplify the rules and create granting incentives, enhancing the intellectual capital of entrepreneurship and promoting accessible financing opportunities, thus creating a favorable business ecosystem where to start a new venture (Rupo et al., 2020).

The horizontal axis, indicating the market potential of growth, represents opportunities to exploit the business idea in terms of market attractiveness. It depends heavily on the degree of novelty relating to the business model, generating therefore variable of innovation, originality, and scalability of the same model. Originality is how unique the value proposition is for the company and how wide the distance is from what they offer in the competition. The companies positioned further to the right on this axis implement very innovative business models, with scalable solutions. It means, therefore, that the same companies will be able to capture and dominate markets more quickly.

The subdivision into the quadrants is given by the intersection of the levels defined based on the dimensions inserted in the matrix.

Upper left quadrant (Good Potential-Limited Profitability). This quadrant includes all those companies that possess high intangibles and leverage the personal characteristics of their owners to achieve business success. It is possible to denote this by aspects such as a strong brand, intellectual property, or a loyal customer base. On the other hand, the business models are not very innovative; therefore they are not fully capable of scaling their current market niche. Growth potential is therefore limited due to disruptive innovations that translate into a larger market barrier. The risk linked to this quadrant lies in the possible difficulty in being able to progress in terms of market positioning over time.

Upper right quadrant (High Potential and Risk). All entrepreneurial initiatives with intangible assets and extremely innovative business models are included in this quadrant. These initiatives materialize strong brand value or special capabilities in terms of intellectual property, linked to those solutions that target significant market demand, while also opening new opportunities. With a high level of profitability and a rapid growth rate, the risks to which these companies are exposed do not disappear this is the case of competitive pressures and the development problems characteristic of rapid growth phases. Within this quadrant, the "unicorn" phenomenon is also included among the success stories of startups. These companies are certainly very interesting in terms of dynamics and growth, but it is considered appropriate to highlight that in situations of rapid expansion, these companies and startups may not be able to sustain the pace, causing failure. On the other hand, if challenges are successfully addressed, companies become industry leaders, and in the particular case of startups, some of them reach “unicorn” status, in its rarity.

Lower left quadrant (High Failure Risk). Entrepreneurial initiatives in this quadrant show little ownership of intangible assets and may be characterized by traditional or non-distinct business models. In this scenario, there is high difficulty in market positioning, as well as the possibility of adapting to changing consumer preferences or market conditions. These initiatives, due to a limited possibility of differentiating themselves from competitive markets, run a greater risk of failure. Unless significant value enhancement opportunities can be recognized in such business ventures, primarily through business model changes or the acquisition of key intangible assets, such ventures may otherwise lack viable means of operating or achieving sustained growth.

The conceptual framework offers a comprehensive approach to selecting the most suitable valuation model, defining growth assumptions, considering alternative valuation scenarios, estimating risks, and more. It emphasizes tailoring the approach based on the startup’s phase, with particular significance during growth stages, whether singular or multiple.

During early growth stages, the company’s value typically lies vertically in the matrix, focusing on the potential of its resources. As the startup progresses to later stages, horizontal dimensions become more prominent, with emphasis shifting to achieve results that support predictions of future cash flows and rational market assessment of growth potential.

In the valuation process, experts must balance traditional and alternative methods, moving between different poles as necessary. They weigh qualitative factors, often translated into scores or proxy indicators of value, alongside financial metrics that require probabilistic projections based on optimistic or conservative scenarios.

This holistic approach enables investors and stakeholders to make informed decisions, supporting startups not solely on financial forecasts but through a comprehensive evaluation of their innovation capabilities, growth prospects, and ability to navigate competitive challenges.

The study holds practical and theoretical implications. For investors, particularly venture capitalists, integrating traditional and alternative valuation methods is essential for informed decision-making. Understanding each method’s strengths and limitations helps choose the most appropriate approach based on the startup’s stage and industry dynamics. Policymakers can leverage these insights to develop frameworks that address the unique complexities of startup valuation, including measures to promote accurate reporting and transparency in financial projections. Entrepreneurs can benefit by using these methodologies to clarify valuations, negotiate effectively with investors, and improve strategic planning and resource allocation.

Furthermore, the study highlights the need for ongoing refinement of startup valuation models, integrating quantitative financial projections with qualitative assessments of market potential and managerial competence to develop more robust frameworks. The gap in systematic, reliable valuation approaches for new ventures presents significant research opportunities. Developing and testing new models incorporating advanced decision-making tools can improve the accuracy of startup valuations. Additionally, incorporating theories from strategic management, entrepreneurship, and finance can provide a more holistic view, bridging theoretical gaps and offering comprehensive models adaptable to the dynamic nature of startups. Uncertainty is often incumbent in valuation; in the case of startups, the accuracy of methods is also needed to protect the startup ecosystem from potential speculative bubbles, and finally, containing the very high risk of failure that characterizes new ventures.

This study has some limitations that can serve as avenues for further research. A primary limitation is the selection and number of studies analyzed, which may impact the generalizability of the findings. Although the PRISMA protocol facilitated a systematic approach to the literature review, the relatively small sample size of selected studies may limit the comprehensiveness of the results, particularly in the fast-evolving domain of startup valuation. Moreover, the emphasis on specific valuation methodologies might have neglected alternative or emerging approaches that could yield additional insights. Acknowledging these limitations contextualizes this research and lays a solid groundwork for future studies to investigate a wider array of valuation techniques, incorporate larger and more diverse datasets, and ultimately enhance the robustness and applicability of the findings in the field of startup valuation.

References

Abelha, M., Fernandes, S., Mesquita, D., Seabra, F., & Ferreira-Oliveira, A. T. (2020). Graduate employability and competence development in higher education—A systematic literature review using PRISMA. *Sustainability, 12*(15), 5900.

Agyare, D., Hahn, D., Minola, T., & Vismara, S. (2022). Non-accounting drivers of start-up valuation by early-stage equity investors: Literature review and future research agenda. *Developments in Entrepreneurial Finance and Technology*, 227–268.

Akkaya, M. (2020). Startup valuation: Theories, models, and future. In *Valuation challenges and solutions in contemporary businesses* (pp. 137–156). IGI Global.

Albhirat, M. M., Rashid, A., Rasheed, R., Rasool, S., Zulkiffli, S. N. A., & Zia-ul-Haq, H. M. (2024). The PRISMA statement in enviropreneurship study: A systematic literature and a research agenda. *Cleaner Engineering and Technology, 100721.*

Ali, S. B., & Khalidi, M. A. (2020). Valuation of equity securities, private firms, and startups. *IBT Journal of Business Studies (JBS), 16*(1).

Ang, Y. Q., Chia, A., & Saghafian, S. (2022). Using machine learning to demystify startups' funding, post-money valuation, and success. In *Innovative technology at the interface of finance and operations* (pp. 271–296). Springer.

Appelo, J. (2019). *Startup, scaleup, screwup: 42 tools to accelerate lean and agile business growth*. Wiley.

Balcerzak, A. P., Zinecker, M., Skalický, R., Rogalska, E., & Doubravský, K. (2023). Technology-oriented start-ups and valuation: A novel approach based on specific contract terms. *Technological Forecasting and Social Change, 197*, 122876.

Bancel, F., & Tierny, J. (2011). Valuing companies with cash-flow@ risk. *Journal of Applied Corporate Finance, 23*(2), 85–93.

Barg, J. A., Drobetz, W., & Momtaz, P. P. (2021). Valuing start-up firms: A reverse-engineering approach for fair-value multiples from venture capital transactions. *Finance Research Letters, 43*, 102008.

Becker, S. D., & Endenich, C. (2023). Entrepreneurial ecosystems as amplifiers of the lean startup philosophy: Management control practices in earliest-stage Startups. *Contemporary Accounting Research, 40*(1), 624–667.

Berk, J. B., Green, R. C., & Naik, V. (2004). Valuation and return dynamics of new ventures. *The Review of Financial Studies, 17*(1), 1–35.

Berre, M., & Le Pendeven, B. (2023). What do we know about startup-valuation drivers? A systematic literature review. *Venture Capital, 25*(4), 385–429.

Bianchi Martini, S., Corvino, A., & Branca, E. (2024). Costruzione e rivisitazione del business model. In S. Bianchi Martini, M. Bonti, & A. Corvino (Eds.), *Startup. Dall'idea all'exit*. McGraw Hill.

Blank, S. (2018). *Why the lean start-up changes everything*.

Bleck, F., & Scholes, M. (1973). The pricing of options and corporate liabilities. *Journal of Political Economy, 81*(3), 637–654.

Block, J. H., De Vries, G., Schumann, J. H., & Sandner, P. (2014). Trademarks and venture capital valuation. *Journal of Business Venturing, 29*(4), 525–542.

Bonini, S., & Capizzi, V. (2019). The role of venture capital in the emerging entrepreneurial finance ecosystem: Future threats and opportunities. *Venture Capital, 21*(2–3), 137–175.

Botella-Carrubi, D., Maqueda-Llongo, A., & Valero-Moya, A. (2022). Financing rounds with private capital. In *Financing startups: Understanding strategic risks, funding sources, and the impact of emerging technologies* (pp. 3–20). Springer.

Brennan, M. C., Wall, A. P., & McGowan, P. (2005). Academic entrepreneurship: Assessing preferences in nascent entrepreneurs. *Journal of Small Business and Enterprise Development, 12*(3), 307–322.

Brown, R., Mawson, S., Lee, N., & Peterson, L. (2019). Start-up factories, transnational entrepreneurs and entrepreneurial ecosystems: Unpacking the lure of start-up accelerator programmes. *European Planning Studies, 27*(5), 885–904.

Cambria, S. L. (2016). *Startup valuation. A descriptive analysis of the Italian market*.

Chandra, A., & Mazumdar, S. (2024). Biotech asset valuation methods: A practitioner's guide. *Journal of Investment Management, 22*(1), 36–57.

Cho, Y., & McLean, G. N. (2009). Successful IT start-ups' HRD practices: Four cases in South Korea. *Journal of European Industrial Training, 33*(2), 125–141.

Colombo, M. G., Fisch, C., Momtaz, P. P., & Vismara, S. (2022). The CEO beauty premium: Founder CEO attractiveness and firm valuation in initial coin offerings. *Strategic Entrepreneurship Journal, 16*(3), 491–521.

Cravo, M. L. G. (2023). *MDCF valuation models: Multi-factor discounted cash flow valuations* (Doctoral dissertation).

Crawford, G. C., Skorodziyevskiy, V., Frid, C. J., Nelson, T. E., Booyavi, Z., Hechavarria, D. M., Li, X., Reynolds, P. D., & Teymourian, E. (2022). Advancing entrepreneurship theory through replication: A case study on contemporary methodological challenges, future best practices, and an entreaty for communality. *Entrepreneurship Theory and Practice, 46*(3), 779–799.

Damodaran, A. (2009). *The dark side of valuation: Valuing young, distressed, and complex businesses*. FT Press.

Damodaran, A. (2009a). *Valuing young, start-up and growth companies: Estimation issues and valuation challenges*. Stern University.

Damodaran, A. (2024). *The little book of valuation: How to value a company, pick a stock, and profit*. Wiley.

Davila, A., & Foster, G. (2007). Management control systems in early-stage startup companies. *The Accounting Review, 82*(4), 907–937.

Davila, A., Foster, G., & Gupta, M. (2003). Venture capital financing and the growth of startup firms. *Journal of Business Venturing, 18*(6), 689–708.

Davis, G. A., & Samis, M. (2005). *Using real options to value and manage exploration*.

de Klerk, S., Miles, M. P., & Bliemel, M. (2024). *A life cycle perspective of startup*.

de Oliveira, F. B., & Zotes, L. P. (2018). Valuation methodologies for business startups: A bibliographical study and survey. *Brazilian Journal of Operations & Production Management, 15*(1), 96–111.

Desaché, G. (2024). The use of options to assess the value of equity in start-ups. *Revista Española de Capital Riesgo, 19*(4).

Dhochak, M., & Doliya, P. (2020). Valuation of a startup: Moving towards strategic approaches. *Journal of Multi-Criteria Decision Analysis, 27*(1–2), 39–49.

Dhochak, M., Pahal, S., & Doliya, P. (2024). Predicting the startup valuation: A deep learning approach. *Venture Capital, 26*(1), 75–99.

Edison, H., Smørsgård, N. M., Wang, X., & Abrahamsson, P. (2018). Lean internal startups for software product innovation in large companies: Enablers and inhibitors. *Journal of Systems and Software, 135*, 69–87.

Engelen, A., Gupta, V., Strenger, L., & Brettel, M. (2015). Entrepreneurial orientation, firm performance, and the moderating role of transformational leadership behaviors. *Journal of Management, 41*(4), 1069–1097.

Fabozzi, F. J. (2016). *Entrepreneurial finance and accounting for high-tech companies*. MIT Press.

Fitzgerald, B. (1996). Formalized systems development methodologies: A critical perspective. *Information Systems Journal, 6*(1), 3–23.

Fraser, S., Bhaumik, S. K., & Wright, M. (2015). What do we know about entrepreneurial finance and its relationship with growth? *International Small Business Journal, 33*(1), 70–88.

Freeman, R. E., & Reed, D. L. (1983). Stockholders and stakeholders: A new perspective on corporate governance. *California Management Review, 25*(3), 88–106.

Galletta, S., Mazzù, S., Naciti, V., & Paltrinieri, A. (2024). A PRISMA systematic review of greenwashing in the banking industry: A call for action. *Research in International Business and Finance, 69*, 102262.

Garkavenko, M. (2022). *Integrated models for predicting start-ups evolution* (Doctoral dissertation, Université Grenoble Alpes [2020–....]).

Gonnella, E., & Talarico, L. (2022). La valutazione delle startup con metodi "qualitativi": il "Berkus Method", lo "Scorecard Method" e il "Risk Factor Summation Method". *Studi di Valutazione D'azienda, 11*, 163–200.

Graham, S. J., & Sichelman, T. S. (2016). Intellectual property and technology startups: What entrepreneurs tell us. In *Technological innovation: Generating economic results* (Vol. 26, pp. 163–199). Emerald Group Publishing.

Griva, A., Kotsopoulos, D., Karagiannaki, A., & Zamani, E. D. (2023). What do growing early-stage digital start-ups look like? A mixed-methods approach. *International Journal of Information Management, 69*, 102427.

Gudgin, G. (1978). *Industrial location processes and regional employment growth*. Saxon House.

Hidayat, W. W. (2022). The effect of leverage and liquidity on the value of the firm with age as a moderating variable on companies in Indonesia. *Jurnal Ekonomi Modernisasi, 18*(2), 264–275.

Horne, J., & Fichter, K. (2022). Growing for sustainability: Enablers for the growth of impact startups–A conceptual framework, taxonomy, and systematic literature review. *Journal of Cleaner Production, 349*, 131163.

Hsu, D. H. (2007). Experienced entrepreneurial founders, organizational capital, and venture capital funding. *Research Policy, 36*(5), 722–741.

Huang, S. (2023). Applied machine learning algorithms for intangible asset value relevance. *Highlights in Business, Economics and Management, 10*, 337–345.

Huang, L., & Pearce, J. L. (2015). Managing the unknowable: The effectiveness of early-stage investor gut feel in entrepreneurial investment decisions. *Administrative Science Quarterly, 60*(4), 634–670.

Imbierowicz, B., & Rauch, C. (2024). What drives startup valuations? *Journal of Banking & Finance, 168*, 107251.

Joglekar, N. R., & Levesque, M. (2009). Marketing, R&D, and startup valuation. *IEEE Transactions on Engineering Management, 56*(2), 229–242.

Kaddour, S. (2023). *Sustainability performance evaluation for start-ups: Defining the characteristics for a tailored ESG assessment tool.*

Kale, V. (2024). *Unleashing the Startup unicorn: Breaking through constraints to the entrepreneurial Spirit.* Business Expert Press.

Kaur, B., Sood, K., & Grima, S. (2023). A systematic review on forensic accounting and its contribution towards fraud detection and prevention. *Journal of Financial Regulation and Compliance, 31*(1), 60–95.

Keeble, D. (1976). *Industrial location and planning in the United Kingdom.*

Kelly, S. E., Moher, D., & Clifford, T. J. (2016). Quality of conduct and reporting in rapid reviews: An exploration of compliance with PRISMA and AMSTAR guidelines. *Systematic Reviews, 5*, 1–19.

Knight, A. P., Greer, L. L., & De Jong, B. (2020). Start-up teams: A multidimensional conceptualization, integrative review of past research, and future research agenda. *Academy of Management Annals, 14*(1), 231–266.

Köhn, A. (2018). The determinants of startup valuation in the venture capital context: A systematic review and avenues for future research. *Management Review Quarterly, 68*(1), 3–36.

Köseoğlu, S. D. (2023). A practical guide for startup valuation: An analytic approach. In *A practical guide for startup valuation: An analytic approach* (pp. 1–6). Springer Nature Switzerland.

Laitinen, E. K. (2019). *Discounted cash flow (DCF) as a measure of startup financial success.*

Lee, C., Lee, K., & Pennings, J. M. (2001). Internal capabilities, external networks, and performance: A study on technology-based ventures. *Strategic Management Journal, 22*(6–7), 615–640.

Liberati, A., Altman, D. G., Tetzlaff, J., Mulrow, C., Gøtzsche, P. C., Ioannidis, J. P., Clarke, M., Devereaux, P. J., Kleijnen, J., & Moher, D. (2009). The PRISMA statement for reporting systematic reviews and meta-analyses of studies that evaluate health care interventions: Explanation and elaboration. *Annals of Internal Medicine, 151*(4), W-65.

Lie, E., & Lie, H. J. (2002). Multiples used to estimate corporate value. *Financial Analysts Journal, 58*(2), 44–54.

Loseva, O. V., Kosorukova, I. V., Fedotova, M. A., Tazikhina, T. V., & Abdikeev, N. M. (2022). Valuation of digital intellectual assets: Principles, factors, approaches and methods. *Finance: Theory and Practice, 26*(4), 6–28.

MacMillan, I. C., & Day, D. L. (1987). Corporate ventures into industrial markets: Dynamics of aggressive entry. *Journal of Business Venturing, 2*(1), 29–39.

Maglio, R., & Rey, A. (2022). Le fonti di finanziamento delle startup. In *La valutazione delle startup*. Giuffré.

Maglio, R., Rey, A., & Roberto, F. (2022). Il venture capital method. In *La valutazione delle startup*. Giuffré.

Majercakova, D., & Mittelman, A. (2018). The analysis of the chosen methods of the evaluation of start-ups on the specific case. *Economic and Social Development: Book of Proceedings, 2018*, 484–490.

Mechner, F. (1989). Present certainty equivalents and weighted scenario valuations. *Journal of Business Venturing, 4*(2), 85–92.

Miloud, T., Aspelund, A., & Cabrol, M. (2012). Startup valuation by venture capitalists: An empirical study. *Venture Capital, 14*(2–3), 151–174.

Montani, D., Gervasio, D., & Pulcini, A. (2020). Startup company valuation: The state of art and future trends. *International Business Research, 13*(9), 31–45.

Moro-Visconti, R., & Moro-Visconti, R. (2021). *Startup valuation* (pp. 213–241). Springer.

Mullins, J. (2017). *The new business road test: What entrepreneurs and investors should do before launching a lean start-up*. Pearson UK.

Nair, M. S. (2024). *Bridging theory and practice: Navigating the success pathways of research productized startups* (Doctoral dissertation, International Institute of Information Technology Hyderabad).

Ojaghi, H., Mohammadi, M., & Yazdani, H. R. (2019). A synthesized framework for the formation of startups' innovation ecosystem: A systematic literature review. *Journal of Science and Technology Policy Management, 10*(5), 1063–1097.

Olugbola, S. A. (2017). Exploring entrepreneurial readiness of youth and startup success components: Entrepreneurship training as a moderator. *Journal of Innovation & Knowledge, 2*(3), 155–171.

Paoloni, P., & Modaffari, G. (2018). Female-owned innovative startups in Italy: Status quo and implications. *Administrative Sciences, 8*(4), 66.

Park, A., Goudarzi, A., Yaghmaie, P., Thomas, V. J., & Maine, E. (2023). The role of pre-formation intangible assets in the endowment of science-based university spinoffs. *International Journal of Technology Management.*

Parkinson, R. (2024). *Decision-making criteria and challenges: An analysis of business angels and venture capitalists in Sweden's life science Startup ecosystem* (Doctoral dissertation, ResearchSpace@ Auckland).

Passaro, R., Quinto, I., Rippa, P., & Thomas, A. (2016). The start-up lifecycle: An interpretative framework proposal. In *RSA AiIG*, pp. 1–25.

Patterson, A. (2023). Valuation versus pricing: A conceptual and practical guide to estimate economic value for early-stage companies via DCF. In *A practical guide for startup valuation: An analytic approach* (pp. 67–102). Springer Nature Switzerland.

Payne, B. (2011). *Scorecard valuation methodology. Establishing the valuation of prerevenue.*

Pena, I. (2002). Intellectual capital and business start-up success. *Journal of Intellectual Capital, 3*(2), 180–198.

Picken, J. C. (2017). From startup to scalable enterprise: Laying the foundation. *Business Horizons, 60*(5), 587–595.

Puca, A. (2020). *Early stage valuation: A fair value perspective*. Wiley.

Rey, A., & Agliata, F. (2022). I fattori di rischio da considerare nella valutazione delle startup. In *La valutazione delle startup*. Giuffré.

Ries, E. (2011). *The lean startup*. Crown Business.

Rupo, D., Accordino, P., La Rocca, E. T., & Abbate, T. (2020). Intellectual capital and enabling factors for Startups in a business ecosystem. In Y. Weber, D. Vrontis, E. Tsoukatos, & S. M. Riad Shams (Eds.), *The cross-disciplinary perspectives of management: Challenges and opportunities*. Emerald.

Schmidt, D. (2014). *Entrepreneur's choice between venture capitalist and business angel for start-up financing*. Anchor Academic Publishing

Sekliuckiene, J., Vaitkiene, R., & Vainauskiene, V. (2018). Organisational learning in startup development and international growth. *Entrepreneurial Business & Economics Review, 6*(4).

Seong, H. E., & Kim, B. Y. (2021). Critical factors affecting venture capital investment decision on innovative startups: A case of South Korea. *International Journal of Management (IJM), 12*(3), 768–781.

Shamseer, L., Moher, D., Clarke, M., Ghersi, D., Liberati, A., Petticrew, M., Shekelle, P., & Stewart, L. A. (2015). Preferred reporting items for systematic review and meta-analysis protocols (PRISMA-P) 2015: Elaboration and explanation. *BMJ, 2015*, 349.

Shrieves, R. E., & Wachowicz, J. M., Jr. (2001). Free cash flow (FCF), economic value added (EVA™), and net present value (NPV):. A reconciliation of variations of discounted-cash-flow (DCF) valuation. *The Engineering Economist, 46*(1), 33–52.

Smith, J., Smith, R. L., Smith, R., & Bliss, R. (2011). *Entrepreneurial finance: strategy, valuation, and deal structure*. Stanford University Press.
Stein, H., & Maass, W. (2022). Requirements for data valuation methods. In *Proceedings of 55th HICSS*, Hawaii, pp. 6155–6164.
Stowe, J. D. (2007). *Equity asset valuation* (Vol. 4). Wiley.
Tiscini, R., & Dello Strologo, A. (2022). Metodi di valutazione e fasi del ciclo di vita delle startup. In *La valutazione delle startup*. Giuffré.
Tomy, S., & Pardede, E. (2018). From uncertainties to successful start ups: A data analytic approach to predict success in technological entrepreneurship. *Sustainability, 10*(3), 602.
Tranfield, D., Denyer, D., & Smart, P. (2003). Towards a methodology for developing evidence-informed management knowledge by means of systematic review. *British Journal of Management, 14*(3), 207–222.
Trichkova, R., & Kanaryan, N. (2015). *Startups valuation: Approaches and methods*.
Tripathi, N., Oivo, M., Liukkunen, K., & Markkula, J. (2019). Startup ecosystem effect on minimum viable product development in software startups. *Information and Software Technology, 114*, 77–91.
Usmani, F., Sarim, M., & Ghayas, A. (2023). Analysis of startup valuation methods: Understanding the investor's perspective. In *A practical guide for Startup valuation: An analytic approach* (pp. 129–145). Springer Nature Switzerland.
Vale, J., Amaral, J., Abrantes, L., Leal, C., & Silva, R. (2022). Management accounting and control in higher education institutions: A systematic literature review. *Administrative Sciences, 12*(1), 1.
Van Osnabrugge, M., & Robinson, R. J. (2000). *Angel investing: Matching startup funds with startup companies--The guide for entrepreneurs and individual investors*. Wiley.
Wang, S., Wareewanich, T., & Chankoson, T. (2023). Factors influencing venture capital performance in emerging technology: The case of China. *International Journal of Innovation Studies, 7*(1), 18–31.
Wirtz, B. W., Pistoia, A., Ullrich, S., & Göttel, V. (2016). Business models: Origin, development and future research perspectives. *Long Range Planning, 49*(1), 36–54.
Xu, S., Wu, X., He, J., Zhu, R., Morrison, A. M., & Xie, C. (2024). Turning entrepreneurial networks into business model innovation for start-ups. *Management Decision, 62*(4), 1395–1423.
Ylä-Nikkilä, H. (2024). *Strategically leveraging sustainability-integration in early-stage venture capital investing*.
Zacharakis, A. L., & Meyer, G. D. (1995). The venture capitalist decision: Understanding process versus outcome. *Frontiers of Entrepreneurship Research, 1995*, 465–478.
Zaheer, A., & Bell, G. G. (2005). Benefiting from network position: Firm capabilities, structural holes, and performance. *Strategic Management Journal, 26*(9), 809–825.

Part II
Performance and Resilience

Chapter 4
A Comparative Study on the Profitability Performance of European Innovative and Social Startups in Pre-Covid and Covid Periods

Salvatore Loprevite, Roberto Mavilia, Domenico Raucci, and Bruno Ricca

4.1 Introduction

This study presents the results of research examining the profitability performance of startups and some of its conceivable drivers, with a comparative analysis between the pre-Covid and Covid periods.

The chapter refers to the European Union (EU), focusing on the continental and Mediterranean contexts of Europe.

Concerning the startup concept, in line with Audretsch et al. (2020) we assume that a startup is a young venture in the early stage of its life cycle, engaged in activities related to the development of new products, services, or processes to scale the market and achieve economic sustainability. This definition allows us to examine startups at the critical moment when they face initial challenges and adapt to market conditions. As for the sample of startups, to balance the need for representativeness of the broad territorial context of reference with the practical difficulties of studying too many countries, we analyze a sample of 7179 startups from France, Germany, Greece, Italy, Portugal, and Spain. The choice aligns with previous studies (Colombo et al., 2019; Defourny & Nyssens, 2008; Dimelis et al., 2017; Grilli & Murtinu,

S. Loprevite · R. Mavilia
Department of Social and Educational Sciences of the Mediterranean Area, University Dante Alighieri of Reggio Calabria, Reggio Calabria, Italy
e-mail: s.loprevite@unidarc.it; r.mavilia@unidarc.it

D. Raucci (✉)
Department of Economics, University G. d'Annunzio of Chieti-Pescara, Pescara, Italy
e-mail: domenico.raucci@unich.it

B. Ricca
Department of Economics, University of Messina, Messina, Italy
e-mail: bricca@unime.it

S. Loprevite et al. (eds.), *Startups and Gazelle Enterprises*, SIDREA Series in Accounting and Business Administration,
https://doi.org/10.1007/978-3-031-90881-1_4

2014), which considered countries like these to represent the continental and Mediterranean context of Europe, capturing the variety of economic-cultural conditions, different dimensions of economies (from larger ones such as Germany and France, to medium-sized ones such as Italy and Spain, to smaller ones such as Portugal and Greece) and the diversity of startup ecosystems.

The Covid-19 pandemic was a relevant impact factor for all companies, but particularly for the new ventures (Chundakkadan et al., 2022; Dimelis et al., 2017; Fairlie, 2020). For this reason, some studies have investigated its effects on European young companies and agreed on the significant decrease in profitability for most startups in the pandemic years compared to previous years (Kuckertz et al., 2020; Newman et al., 2022). However, these studies observe the same companies at two different points in time. In contrast, no studies have compared cohorts of early-stage startups—specifically, ventures founded before the pandemic, which were not expected to face such a crisis, with those that were established after the pandemic began or had to contend with its impact shortly after their founding.

By adopting this approach, which we believe offers a different useful perspective for adding to the literature, we concentrate our analysis on the first three years after the company's foundation, a critical period for startup development. This is especially important considering how certain financial and other variables observable in the early stages relate to profitability outcome (Blank & Dorf, 2020; Fuertes-Callén et al., 2022; Ziakis et al., 2022), and distinguishing for the pre-Covid and Covid periods. Therefore, for the empirical analysis, we use two distinct samples from the six European countries mentioned above: a cohort of companies founded in 2016 and observed in the 2017–2019 triennium (pre-Covid period) and a cohort of companies founded in 2019 and observed in the 2020–2022 triennium (Covid period). The analysis of these two periods enables us to capture significant changes induced by the pandemic on startups, which are critical drivers of innovation and technological development (Audretsch et al., 2020).

As previously mentioned, our research hypotheses focus on startups' profitability and some of its conceivable drivers. In addition to comparing different time periods, we also take a second comparative approach by examining two types of startups: innovative startups operating in the high-tech sector and social startups.

Several studies have shown that startups in the technology sector have a higher probability of surviving and performing economically and financially compared to other new companies (Audretsch et al., 2020; Skawińska & Zalewski, 2020). In contrast, it has been demonstrated that startups active in social entrepreneurship can also show significant performance development capabilities, even in conditions of high environmental uncertainty (Hoogendoorn, 2016). The recent Covid-19 pandemic had a significant impact on both types of startups.

While some innovative startups have experienced accelerated growth, many social startups have had to adapt quickly to address the new social needs that emerged during the COVID-19 pandemic (Kuckertz et al., 2020). However, there is a lack of studies that comparatively examine the ability of these different types of startups to respond to significant external shocks, such as the COVID-19 pandemic. Therefore, from this comparative perspective, the chapter contributes to the literature on innovative and social startups, by addressing gaps in the understanding of the key drivers of their performance in crisis contexts, such as the COVID-19 pandemic. It also provides valuable insights into the adaptability of these startups both during periods of normal business activity and in times of crisis.

The chapter is organized as follows: Section 4.2 provides a review of the relevant literature on innovative and social startups, along with the research hypotheses. Section 4.3 details the sample and methodology. Section 4.4 presents the analysis results and their discussion. Finally, Sect. 4.5 offers the conclusions.

4.2 Literature Review and Research Hypotheses

4.2.1 Innovative and Social Startups

Since the late 1970s—a period when startups emerged in Western countries as small, highly innovative enterprises primarily active in the high-technology, electronics, and information technology sectors (Skawińska & Zalewski, 2020)—startups have developed by challenging the established business theories of the time. From the outset, they have been viewed as a dynamic entrepreneurial model for new employment opportunities and territorial economic development. Consequently, over time, policymakers have introduced various forms of support for the development of startup ecosystems in specific local or national contexts (Viscusi & Moore, 1993). In line with this trend, the EU and various member states have issued a series of legislative measures aimed at promoting the creation and growth of startups, emphasizing in recent years particularly those expressly defined as "innovative," which are deemed more capable of promoting technological progress, employment, and territorial economic development (Audretsch et al., 2020; European Commission, 2014, 2016; Rossetti et al., 2018).

This has also led to different notions of innovative startups as delineated by the laws of various European countries, [1] which, as highlighted in the literature, can generate interpretative risks in the perceptions of investors, financiers, and stakeholders regarding the survival and growth potential of these enterprises (Audretsch et al., 2020; Biancalani et al., 2022). The legal definitions of "innovative startups" present risks for scientific research, not only because the concept varies across different legislations and makes it difficult to construct homogeneous samples, but also because the actual capacity to innovate, although fundamental, represents only one of the dimensions of analysis (Onesti et al., 2022; Rocha & Grilli, 2024; Skawińska & Zalewski, 2020).

[1] In Italy, for example, Legislative Decree 179/2012, known as the "Italian Startup Act," regulates the creation of innovative startups by analytically outlining funding opportunities to promote their implementation in various sectors. This law has defined precise identification criteria for innovative startups that can operate in any sector, including agricultural, industrial, artisanal, commercial, or services, including social sectors, and can benefit from targeted incentive schemes.

Beyond legal definitions, it is evident that startups are inherently characterized by high levels of innovativeness and business uncertainty, which require flexible responses to environmental dynamics. These characteristics are closely linked to their critical success or failure factors, variously delineated in the literature and generally categorized within two macro-categories of variables: those attributable to the entrepreneur or the new venture; and those attributable to the geographical context, operational sector, or the more specific social and support network of the startups (Abou-Moghli & Al-Kasasbeh, 2012; Skawińska & Zalewski, 2020). The intrinsic innovative nature of startups is referenced in a vast body of literature (Skawińska & Zalewski, 2020) in connection with various aspects such as the function of disruptive innovation (Christensen, 2013), the visionary and entrepreneurial characteristics of the founders' personalities (Bergset & Fichter, 2015), the ability to create new solutions for markets or new products/services (Ries, 2011; Thiel & Masters, 2014), the orientation toward technological innovations (Breschi et al., 2018), and the inception phase (seed stage), which is characterized by a particular emphasis on innovation (Skawińska & Zalewski, 2020). Innovative startups are generally defined as young enterprises with a strong orientation toward technology and innovation, aiming to develop and commercialize new products, services, or business models (Bailetti, 2012). These enterprises are characterized by high growth potential, but also by high levels of risk and uncertainty (Ries, 2011). Blank and Dorf (2020) emphasize that innovative startups pursue scalable and repeatable business models, thereby distinguishing themselves from traditional small businesses.

Although numerous elements have been highlighted in the literature to emphasize the intrinsic innovative nature of startups, the distinctive character of innovation is more traditionally and commonly associated with the sector in which startups operate, namely the high-tech sector. This association has been further reinforced recently due to the proliferation of Industry 4.0 tools, 5G, ICT, and, especially, Artificial Intelligence. Indeed, significant market presence of startups within this technological sector has facilitated their identification with innovative startups, capable of generating better performance in growth and profitability, accelerating recovery processes after the Covid-19 pandemic crisis (Coad et al., 2023; Guerzoni et al., 2021; Zhang et al., 2020).

Therefore, although this approach has certain limitations, there have long been studies in the literature that considered high-tech startups as a benchmark for innovative startups (Bertoni et al., 2011; Colombo et al., 2019). In line with this literature, this chapter also uses the high-tech sector as a proxy for innovative startup.

For social startups, multiple criteria have been employed to circumscribe social entrepreneurship, and there is no full consensus regarding its delimitation.

Despite this, there is a general agreement that it encompasses organizations engaged in entrepreneurial activities with the primary objective of serving a social mission (Hoogendoorn, 2016; Stephan et al., 2015). Moreover, the concept of social entrepreneurship can be derived, as seen in some legislations such as the Italian one, from the "nature" of the business activity itself, which leads to qualifying as social those enterprises engaged in specific sectors of activity (social assistance, socio-health care, protection of the environment and ecosystem, etc.).

Based on the above, we adopt the nature of the activity as a reference for constructing the sample of social startups. With the same logic followed for innovative startups to delimit the object of analysis, we consider from among the multiple activities with social content the social assistance, using companies with this activity as a proxy for social startups.

We also point out that the commitment to a social mission related to the activity of social assistance implies that social entities do not necessarily prioritize a market orientation or income generation (profit) as their primary objectives. Due to this possible absence of a market orientation, both non-profit and for-profit organizations may be included in the social startups used for our study. To prevent any potential distortions in our empirical analysis regarding the profitability of startups, as we explain in Sect. 4.3.1, the social startups included in our sample are exclusively profit-oriented companies.

There is no doubt that differences exist between innovative startups and social startups:

- Innovative startups are often associated with specific entrepreneurial ecosystems, such as technological clusters or areas with high concentrations of venture capital (Spigel, 2017). On the other hand, social startups tend to emerge in contexts where significant unresolved social or environmental problems exist, often in response to market or state failures (Zahra et al., 2009);
- in terms of performance, innovative startups are generally evaluated based on traditional financial metrics and their ability to scale rapidly; social startups, on the other hand, must balance the creation of social value with financial sustainability (Smith et al., 2013). This dual objective can present unique challenges for social startups in terms of measuring success and attracting investments (Battilana & Lee, 2014).

Despite these differences, some elements offer the possibility of conducting a fruitful comparison between innovative startups and social startups from the perspective followed in this chapter:

- Albeit with differences in their primary objectives, both innovative and social startups share some common characteristics. Both tend to be driven by a strong sense of mission and a desire for change (Austin et al., 2006). Moreover, both often operate in contexts of high uncertainty and must be highly adaptable in order to survive and thrive (Dacin et al., 2010);
- despite differences in their fields of activity and business models, they share the common goal of creating value through unconventional approaches;
- both the literature on innovative startups (Audretsch et al., 2020; Skawińska & Zalewski, 2020) and that on social startups (Defourny & Nyssens, 2008) have highlighted that such startups have a higher probability of survival compared to others, as they are able to generate improvements in performance even under conditions of strong environmental uncertainty;
- as previously mentioned, the recent Covid-19 pandemic had a significant impact on both types of startups.

4.2.2 Hypotheses Development

The relationships between financial structure, company size, board size, and performance have been studied in recent decades for both mature companies and startups.

Key factors characterizing startups include the limited financial and human resources, business scalability, flexibility to environmental dynamics, and significant growth potential in the market (Blank & Dorf, 2020; Damodaran, 2009; Ries, 2011). These characteristics make the evaluation of startup performance and the identification of its potential drivers particularly complex, both in an ordinary environmental context and in a situation of exogenous shocks, such as the Covid-19 pandemic, when one wants to estimate their ability to adapt and respond to adverse events.

The evaluation of startup performance, as a field of research, has primarily been explored in studies on factors contributing to success or failure (Azeem & Khanna, 2024). These studies have examined various sectors (Cantamessa et al., 2018) as well as different geographical contexts, including European countries and beyond (Skawińska & Zalewski, 2020), and more specific local settings (Onesti et al., 2022). Concerning explanatory variables, or those otherwise connected to performance levels, some studies have emphasized the measures concerning employees, such as the employment growth rate and staff productivity (Brüderl & Preisendörfer, 1998; Ouimet & Zarutskie, 2014). Other research has focused on commercial indicators such as sales volume, business stability, customer acceptance, and overall entrepreneur satisfaction (Sebora et al., 2009). Additional studies have concentrated on efficiency measures, such as the learning curve, customer acquisition costs, or customer lifetime value (Ripsas et al., 2018).

Accounting information and ratios derived from financial statements (liquidity, margin analysis, ROI, ROE, etc.) have also been used to assess performance from a financial perspective, focusing on financial structure, profitability, and survival (Cotei & Farhat, 2017; Migliaccio & Pavone, 2021; Reid & Smith, 2000). Although part of the literature has highlighted that the complex dynamics of the early stage are likely reflected in their financial statements and the prospective reliability of the first accounting data on performance (Maurya, 2016; Miloud et al., 2012), many authors acknowledge the signaling role of startups' early financial statements for predictions on their survival and their economic and financial performance capabilities. In this perspective, it has been empirically demonstrated that financial ratios derived from balance sheet data can predict, to a certain extent, the failure of a startup as early as the first year after its establishment (Fuertes-Callén et al., 2022; Laitinen, 1992, 2017).

Profitability ratios are among the most commonly used accounting measures for performance evaluation, as they reflect the potential for economic sustainability over time. Even though not all startups achieve profitability in their early stages, reaching a certain level of sales and profitability in their initial financial statements can be seen as an important milestone, increasing the likelihood of survival and making it more predictable (Coad et al., 2016; Fuertes-Callén et al., 2022). In this context, several studies have empirically emphasized the significance of positive profitability ratios (ROE, ROA, ROS) in the financial statements of the first years and their positive impacts on the probabilities of future survival (Delmar et al., 2013; Laitinen, 1992, 2017; Migliaccio & Pavone, 2021; Reid & Smith, 2000; Wiklund et al., 2010). As specific measure of profitability, we utilize the Return of Assets (ROA), for several reasons outlined in previous studies. First, it is a more effective measure for analyzing the economic performance of European startups because they are more debt-dependent than startups in other countries (such as US startups), and it can be better compared with ROA which is a measure not influenced by capital structure (Altman et al., 2017; Cotei & Farhat, 2017; Laitinen, 2017). Second, due to the fragmentation of the European context, ROA enables more accurate comparisons of the profitability performance of startups operating in markets of different sizes in their countries (Delmar et al., 2013; Lukason et al., 2016; Wang & Guedes, 2024). Third, during the pandemic crisis, some studies used ROA to compare the resilience of various sectors of the European economy, showing that it is best suited to capture differences in impacts between traditional and innovative sectors and to measure the efficiency of resource utilization (Audretsch et al., 2014; Fuertes-Callén et al., 2022).

While existing literature provides valuable insights into startup performance metrics and factors influencing their success, there is a significant gap in understanding how these dynamics evolve during periods of major external shocks, such as the global Covid-19 pandemic. The unprecedented nature of this crisis presents a unique opportunity to examine how startups' profitability reacts to extreme environmental volatility.

The Covid-19 pandemic has disrupted global markets, supply chains, and consumer behaviors in ways that particularly challenge startups, given their limited resources and nascent market positions. However, their inherent flexibility and adaptability may enable them to navigate such crises more effectively than larger, more established firms. Our study aims to contribute to the literature by focusing the impact of the Covid-19 pandemic on startup profitability.

By studying profitability performance and its conceivable drivers in the pre-Covid and Covid periods, we can gain insights into not only the immediate effects of the pandemic but also the ability of startups to adapt and respond in the face of major economic disruptions.

We consider ROA as a composite measure of performance trends from the pre-Covid period to the Covid period, and we test the following research hypothesis:

H1 The profitability performance of startups declined in the Covid period compared to the pre-Covid period.

Regarding the accounting variables associated with performance levels, first, we take as reference the two following ratios of financial structure:

- debt ratio, calculated as equity/total assets;
- current ratio, which is the ratio between current assets and current liabilities.

Startups must satisfy their need for capital from the early stages of life with a balanced structure of sources and uses of funds. In this regard, firstly, they must have a balanced debt ratio. Although startups aiming to grow in the early years seem more inclined to seek bank financing (Cassar, 2004), it is essential to maintain a balanced ratio of external sources to equity, as demonstrated by empirical evidence indicating that startups with higher levels of debt have a higher probability of failure (Cotei & Farhat, 2017; Robb & Robinson, 2014). Conversely, startups with a greater weight of equity capital and profits realized but not distributed in the early years tend to have a more balanced debt ratio, which is an important indicator of their distance from failure (Fuertes-Callén et al., 2022).

The relationship between financial structure and profitability becomes particularly crucial in times of economic uncertainty, such as the Covid-19 pandemic. During such periods, startups with a more robust financial structure may be better positioned to weather the storm and maintain their profitability. The degree of capitalization can serve as a buffer against external shocks and provide startups with the financial flexibility needed to adapt to rapidly changing market conditions. Furthermore, in the context of the pandemic, traditional sources of financing may become less accessible or more costly for startups. Those with a higher degree of capitalization may be less reliant on external financing, potentially providing them a competitive advantage. While both the debt ratio and current ratio are important indicators of financial structure, we focus our next hypothesis on the degree of capitalization. This choice is motivated by the long-term implications of equity financing for startup resilience and growth potential, which may be particularly salient in the face of prolonged economic uncertainty. Thus, by examining the relationship between capitalization and profitability performance, we aim to provide insights into the financial dynamics of startups during times of crisis and their connection to profitability performance.

Building on the above, and consistent with our aim of exploring the effects of financial structure on profitability performance, we test the following hypothesis:

H2 The degree of capitalization of startups (increase in equity over total assets) is positively associated with profitability performance in both the pre-Covid and Covid periods.

Alongside the degree of capitalization, from a financial perspective, the balance between the financial structure and the related liquidity plays a significant role, namely, the ability to meet short-term obligations with current assets. Even startups with low levels of debt may see their survival capabilities and economic performance compromised due to an imbalance between short-term investments and short-term sources, and a resulting lack of liquidity (Oliveira & Fortunato, 2006). These critical issues can accentuate their negative effects on startup performance, especially in periods of environmental uncertainty, such as the recent Covid-19 lockdown and the years immediately following. During this period, companies' ability to meet payment obligations using their liquidity and other current assets were hindered by operational challenges, including difficulties in generating and collecting sales revenue, as well as in securing supplies due to logistical disruptions

(Chundakkadan et al., 2022; Fairlie, 2020). These challenges become even more severe in the case of negative liquidity situations. The few studies focused on the role of startup liquidity (Fuertes-Callén et al., 2022; Wiklund et al., 2010) have shown that those with greater liquid availability and better liquidity ratios have lower probabilities of failure, also because greater financial capabilities make startups more agile in changes of product/service, technology, etc., and more capable of adapting to changes in market demand (Santisteban & Mauricio, 2017). There is, however, a lack of studies on the role played by liquidity in the periods before and during the Covid-19 lockdown in various European countries.

The exploration of liquidity's role in startup performance, particularly in the context of the Covid-19 pandemic, presents a unique opportunity to understand how the availability of financial resources may shift in importance during times of crisis. While our previous hypothesis focused on the long-term aspect of financial structure through capitalization, examining liquidity enables us to examine the role of the short-term financial health of startups during times of crisis. While higher liquidity generally provides a safety net, it could also represent missed opportunities for investment in growth during periods of stability. However, during a crisis like the Covid-19 pandemic, the security provided by high liquidity might outweigh the opportunity costs, potentially leading to better performance relative to less liquid peers.

On this basis, we test the additional research hypothesis:

H3 The degree of company liquidity is positively associated with profitability performance, and this association becomes more pronounced in periods of uncertainty and environmental crisis (Covid period).

To strengthen our research, we control for some additional dimensional factors potentially linked to the performance capabilities of startups.

The relationship between company size and performance has been investigated in numerous studies, often with conflicting results. For mature companies, some studies have found a positive relationship between size and profitability (Doğan, 2013). Other researchers have highlighted non-linear or even negative relationships in some contexts (Pervan & Višić, 2012). Ventures in the early stage are certainly smaller compared to successful mature companies and enjoy greater flexibility and ability to adapt to changing market conditions compared to the latter (Dean et al., 1998). Even in the field of new ventures, however, initial size can have a significant impact on survival prospects and performance, as demonstrated by the literature that has found the initial size of innovative startups to be positively correlated with their subsequent growth, thus underlining the importance of initial resources and scale (Colombo et al., 2010).

Examining the size of startups in connection with performance, particularly in the context of the Covid-19 pandemic, provides an opportunity to investigate the role of this corporate variable in case of unexpected external shocks. While our previous hypotheses focused on financial structure and liquidity, controlling for size allows us to address a fundamental structural characteristic that may influence a startup's ability to navigate through crises. The existing literature's conflicting findings on the relationship between size and performance in various contexts highlight the complexity of this issue. For startups, this relationship may be even more intricate due to their unique position in the business lifecycle. On one hand, a larger startup's size might indicate more resources and a potentially stronger market position, which could be beneficial during economic downturns. On the other hand, the flexibility and adaptability associated with smaller dimension of startups might prove advantageous in rapidly changing environments, such as those precipitated by the Covid-19 pandemic. In this regard, a variation in the size-performance relationship from the pre-Covid to Covid period could reveal important insights. If smaller startups demonstrate a relative performance advantage during the crisis, it might suggest that agility and adaptability are more crucial factors for success during times of extreme uncertainty. Conversely, if larger startups show greater resilience, it could indicate the importance of resource buffers in weathering economic shocks.

Since it is reasonable to assume that during environmental crises (such as the period of the Covid-19 pandemic) smaller size, with its associated higher levels of flexibility, may have been a factor that enabled startups to better adapt to shifting needs and, consequently, to experience less negative impact of the crisis on profitability, we test the following additional research hypothesis:

H4 The size of startups is positively associated with profitability performance, but this association becomes less relevant in periods of uncertainty and environmental crisis (Covid period).

A variable directly related to company size, or at least one that should reasonably be, is the governance size (here referring to the number of board directors). The literature has analyzed governance structures in dimensional terms, demonstrating their links to performance. The composition and size of the board of directors have been extensively studied as factors influencing company performance. According to agency theory, a larger board of directors can provide more effective monitoring of management (Jensen & Meckling, 1976). However, excessively large board may suffer from coordination problems and inefficient decision-making (Yermack, 1996). In this context, Eisenberg et al. (1998) found a negative relationship between board size and profitability in a sample of small and medium-sized Finnish companies. The conflicting results may depend on specific company factors, as illustrated by Coles et al. (2008), who demonstrated that the relationship between board size and company value can be non-monotonic and dependent on the specific characteristics of the company. In the case of startups, it is reasonable to believe that governance size, when balanced with the company size, can serve as a strategic safeguard to navigate the challenges of the initial phase of life, and even more so when the early stage coincides with an external environmental shock such as in the case of the Covid-19 pandemic. Therefore, the examination of this variable adds a crucial dimension to our analysis concerning the profitability performance of startups and its conceivable drivers, addressing the human capital aspect of startup management, which may be critical during times of crisis.

In the context of startups, the impact of board size may differ substantially from that observed in mature companies. A larger managerial team could represent a broader pool of skills, experiences, and networks, potentially crucial for navigating both the challenges of early-stage growth and unexpected external shocks such as the Covid-19 pandemic. However, it is important to consider that a larger team might also lead to higher overhead costs and potential decision-making complexities, challenges that could be particularly pronounced during resource-constrained periods.

In this regard, the Covid-19 pandemic provides a unique opportunity to examine how the relationship between board size and performance may shift during times of extreme uncertainty. If a broader managerial base proves more beneficial during the crisis, it could suggest that diverse expertise and collaborative decision-making become more crucial in navigating unprecedented challenges. Conversely, if leaner management structures show an advantage, it might indicate the importance of agility and streamlined decision-making processes during crises.

This analysis complements our previous hypotheses by addressing the impact of board size on profitability performance.

On this basis, we test the following final research hypothesis:

H5 The number of directors is positively associated with profitability performance, and this association becomes more relevant in periods of uncertainty and environmental crisis (Covid period).

4.3 Research Design

4.3.1 Sample

Our analysis is conducted on two distinct sample sets corresponding to the pre-Covid (2017–2019) and Covid (2020–2022) periods. As clarified in the introduction, in line with previous studies (Colombo et al., 2019; Defourny & Nyssens, 2008; Dimelis et al., 2017; Grilli & Murtinu, 2014), we consider startups from six European countries (France, Germany, Greece, Italy, Portugal, and Spain) which are representative of both the continental and Mediterranean context of Europe.

We retrieved our samples from the Orbis Database, provided by Bureau van Dijk. For the pre-Covid period (2017–2019 triennium), we selected companies founded in 2016, while for the Covid period (2020–2022 triennium), we focused on those founded in 2019. As explained in Sect. 4.2, the differentiation between innovative and social startups was based on their respective fields of activity. Specifically, we utilized the following NACE Rev. 2 codes from the database:

- For innovative startups, code 5415 (Computer Systems Design and Related Services) and code 54171 (Research and Development in the Physical, Engineering, and Life Sciences).
- For social startups, code 624 (Social Assistance).

Subsequently, we excluded all entities with missing data during the analysis period, thereby deriving our two primary samples for the pre-Covid and Covid periods, each comprising two unbalanced sub-samples. The selection process and the resulting sample sizes are presented in Table 4.1.

The use of the NACE codes for categorizing innovative and social startups aligns with established practices in the literature and reflects the core activities commonly associated with these types of enterprises. The selection of companies established in 2016 for the pre-Covid sample and 2019 for the Covid sample allows us to focus on startups in their early stages of development, typically considered to be the first three years of operation.

It is important to note that while these NACE codes provide a standardized method for classification, they may not capture all innovative or social startups, as some may operate in different or multiple sectors. Nevertheless, this approach offers a consistent and replicable method for sample selection across different countries and periods.

The exclusion of companies with missing data, while necessary for maintaining the integrity of our analysis, may introduce some selection bias. Companies that have ceased operations or failed to report data might be systematically different from those included in our sample. We acknowledge this limitation and will account for its implications when interpreting our results.

Table 4.1 Samples selection

		Cohort 2016		Cohort 2019	
Search step		Step result	Search result	Step result	Search result
1. NACE Rev. 2	5415—Computer systems design and related services, 54,171—Research and development in the physical, engineering, and life sciences, 624—Social assistance	7,650,815	7,650,815	7,650,815	7,650,815
2. Geographical area/country/region	France (FR), Germany (DE), Greece (GR), Italy (IT), Portugal PT), Spain (ES)	45,052,354	1,039,701	45,052,354	1,039,701
3. Foundation year	From 2016 to 2016	17,993,659	38,034	16,635,268	44,175
4. Years with available financial statements	2017, 2018, 2019	18,782,928	5637	22,474,081	7321
5. Companies with missing data on one or more of the analysis variables			2327		3452
Total			3310		3869

Table 4.2 presents the final composition of the samples categorized by country and startup type.

To assess the comparability between the cohorts, we conducted two types of tests on each pair of variables. The *t*-test for two independent samples tests for equality of means (H0), and Levene's test evaluates for equality of variances (H0). In most cases, it was possible to retain the null hypothesis (H0) at the 5% significance level.

4.3.2 Variables

Our analysis models utilize the following five key variables sourced from the Orbis Database by Bureau van Dijk:

- Dependent Variable.
  - Return on Assets (ROA), calculated as the ratio of Earnings Before Interest and Taxes (EBIT) to Total Assets. This metric serves as our primary indicator of profitability and overall financial performance because it offers a comprehensive gauge of how efficiently a company utilizes its assets to generate earnings. This makes it particularly suitable for comparing different types of startups.
- Independent Variables.
  - Debt Ratio (R_I), computed as Equity divided by Total Assets. This measure provides insight into the company's capitalization and financial leverage, allowing us to examine the impact of capital structure on performance, a relevant issue since startups often have limited access to external financing;
  - Current Ratio (C_R), defined as the ratio of Total Current Assets to Total Current Liabilities. This liquidity indicator assesses the company's short-term solvency and the startup's ability to manage its liquidity, which can be very challenging during the early stage or in times of economic uncertainty;
  - Size (SZ), expressed through Total Assets, is a variable that reflects the scale of the company's operations and resource base. This variable enables us to

Table 4.2 Samples by startup type and country

	Cohort 2016			Cohort 2019		
	Innovative	Social	Total	Innovative	Social	Total
France (FR)	345	70	415	212	30	242
Germany (DE)	8	4	12	8	27	35
Greece (GR)	72	4	76	78	5	83
Italy (IT)	1385	281	1666	1946	216	2162
Portugal (PT)	446	32	478	713	36	749
Spain (ES)	620	43	663	552	46	598
Total	2876	434	3310	3509	360	3869

control for scale effects and investigate whether larger resource bases offer advantages in terms of performance. To normalize the distribution, we use the natural log of the variable;

- Board size (Dim_B), represented by the total number of directors in each year of the analysis. This variable aims to quantify the breadth of the company's top management structure and allows us to control the role of managerial skills;
- NACE, the statistical classification of economic activities in the European Community, which we use to categorize innovative and social startups;
- Country, for controls variables on the six selected European countries.

It is worth noting that while these variables provide a robust framework for our analysis, they may not capture all factors influencing startup performance. Intangible factors such as innovation capacity, market positioning, or team dynamics are not directly measured but may be partially reflected in the overall performance metrics.

4.3.3 Methodology

To examine the relationships between our dependent variable (ROA) and the independent variables, we utilize panel data regression models.

The panel data are obtained from the original values through an operation of "pooling" so that the observations can be considered two-dimensional, with variation across both countries and years. This approach allows us to capture both cross-sectional and temporal variations in our analysis. Thus, we apply a "two-way" (fixed and time effect) regression model on our panel data, formulated as follows:

$$y_{it} = \alpha + \beta x_{it}^{(j)} + \vartheta_i + \omega_t + \varepsilon_{it}$$

where:
the effects vary between countries and over year;
y = ROA (Return On Assets);
$x(j)$ are the continuous and dummy independent variables: R_I, C_R, SZ, DIM_B, NACE, and Country;
α is the intercept;
β are the partial regression coefficients;
ϑ_i is the individual error term which is constant over time and varies from country to country;
ω_t is the time error term which is invariant between countries but variable over years;
ε_{it} represents the pure component of error.

This model enables us to account for unobserved heterogeneity across both countries and time periods. We will estimate this model separately for the pre-Covid and Covid periods, enabling us to compare how the relationships among variables may have shifted due to the pandemic. This approach will offer insights into the factors shaping startup performance during periods of economic stability and disruption.

4.4 Data Processing, Results, and Discussion

4.4.1 Descriptive Analysis

In this section, we present the results of our empirical analysis, beginning with a comprehensive examination of the descriptive statistics for our key variables.

Table 4.3 presents the mean values and standard deviations for the variables, categorized by the two overall cohorts (2016 and 2019) and distinguished by NACE classification.

The data exhibits relatively low variability across most parameters, indicating a certain level of homogeneity within the sample, which facilitates more reliable comparisons between the pre-Covid and Covid periods.

Although the median values are positive, the mean ROA values remain consistently negative, suggesting a skewed distribution. This skewness suggests that while many startups may be performing moderately well, a subset of underperforming startups is significantly influencing the overall average. At the aggregate sample level, we observe a deterioration from the pre-Covid period (−8.2%) to the Covid period (−9.6%), supporting our first hypothesis (H1). This overall decline aligns with the anticipated negative economic impact of the pandemic. However, a disaggregation by NACE classification reveals divergent trends. Innovative startups demonstrate a marked improvement, with mean ROA increasing from −8.3% (pre-Covid) to −2.2% (Covid). This unexpected positive shift warrants further investigation and may suggest that innovative startups were better positioned to adapt to the challenges posed by the pandemic. Conversely, social startups exhibit a slight decline, with mean ROA decreasing from −7.3% (pre-Covid) to −8.19% (Covid). This slight deterioration, while in line with the overall trend, is less severe than might have been anticipated given the social startup sector's challenges during the pandemic. The variability of ROA within the samples, as measured by standard deviation, has increased substantially for social startups while remaining low, and even decreasing, for innovative startups. This divergence in performance consistency is noteworthy and suggests that innovative startups may have more consistent business models or strategies compared to their social counterparts.

Our analysis of structural characteristics highlights clear distinctions between innovative and social startups. On average, social startups in the sample are smaller in size compared to innovative startups. The mean value of the size variable remains relatively consistent between the two cohorts for both startup categories, suggesting that the pandemic did not significantly alter the overall scale of operations for either group. In terms of board size, social startups exhibit a lower average number of

Table 4.3 Descriptive statistics

Total sample										
	Cohort 2016					Cohort 2019				
Statistic	ROA	R_I	C_R	SZ	Dim_B	ROA	R_I	C_R	SZ	Dim_B
No. of observations	9930	9930	9930	9930	9930	11,607	11,607	11,607	11,607	11,607
No. of missing values	0	0	0	0	0	0	0	0	0	0
1st Quartile	−0.044	0.081	0.959	1.537	1.000	−0.049	0.099	1.028	1.525	0.000
Median	0.062	0.293	1.427	1.972	1.000	0.061	0.340	1.645	1.999	1.000
3rd Quartile	0.227	0.587	2.644	2.442	3.000	0.248	0.634	3.177	2.481	2.000
Mean	−0.082	0.092	12.052	2.004	2.019	−0.096	0.028	3.950	2.016	1.219
Standard deviation (*n*)	4.447	3.236	362.018	0.757	2.258	7.004	7.685	10.282	0.774	1.868

Cohort 2016										
	Social startups					Innovative startups				
Statistic	ROA	R_I	C_R	SZ	Dim_B	ROA	R_I	C_R	SZ	Dim_B
No. of observations	1302	1302	1302	1302	1302	8628	8628	8628	8628	8628
No. of missing values	0	0	0	0	0	0	0	0	0	0
1st Quartile	−0.065	0.020	0.798	1.420	1.000	−0.042	0.095	0.985	1.552	1.000
Median	0.038	0.156	1.199	1.825	3.000	0.066	0.318	1.474	1.991	1.000
3rd Quartile	0.173	0.408	1.979	2.281	4.000	0.238	0.608	2.750	2.468	2.000
Mean	−0.073	−0.020	14.446	1.833	3.055	−0.083	0.109	11.691	2.030	1.862
Standard deviation (*n*)	0.813	1.626	349.259	0.762	2.428	4.760	3.414	363.904	0.753	2.189

Cohort 2019										
	Social startups					Innovative startups				
Statistic	ROA	R_I	C_R	SZ	Dim_B	ROA	R_I	C_R	SZ	Dim_B
No. of observations	1080	1080	1080	1080	1080	10,527	10,527	10,527	10,527	10,527
No. of missing values	0	0	0	0	0	0	0	0	0	0
1st Quartile	−0.077	0.004	0.878	1.352	1.000	−0.047	0.119	1.044	1.541	0.000
Median	0.041	0.141	1.281	1.861	2.000	0.064	0.363	1.689	2.015	1.000
3rd Quartile	0.206	0.441	2.171	2.291	3.000	0.253	0.650	3.302	2.499	1.000
Mean	−0.819	−0.314	3.116	1.835	2.158	−0.022	0.063	4.035	2.035	1.123
Standard deviation (n)	22.041	5.923	11.262	0.760	1.815	2.047	7.842	10.173	0.774	1.846

directors. Interestingly, there was a significant decrease in the average number of directors from the pre-Covid to Covid period for both innovative and social startups. This reduction occurred despite relatively stable average sizes for innovative startups, potentially indicating a streamlining of management structures in response to the pandemic.

The analysis of financial ratios reveals differences between innovative and social startups. All startups exhibit a low R_I, indicating high leverage. However, the social startups present negative average values of R_I, indicating a state of asset shortfall. This situation deteriorated markedly from the pre-Covid (−2.0%) to the Covid period (−31.4%), suggesting severe financial strain. In contrast, innovative startups maintain positive, albeit low, R_I values across both periods, indicating a more stable financial structure.

C_R values are notably high in the pre-Covid period for both categories of startups. While there is a substantial contraction in the Covid period, the values remain good for both startup types. This suggests maintained short-term solvency despite the economic disruption, though the decrease may indicate a greater utilization of liquid assets to navigate the crisis.

These descriptive statistics provide a foundational understanding of the financial and structural characteristics of innovative and social startups in our sample, as well as how these characteristics evolved from the pre-Covid to Covid period. The differing trends observed between innovative and social startups, particularly in terms of ROA and financial structure, highlight the importance of sector-specific analyses in understanding startup resilience during economic shocks. The insights gathered from this descriptive analysis will inform our subsequent regression analyses and contribute to a better interpretation of our research hypotheses.

Building upon our descriptive analysis, we now focus our attention to the correlation matrices presented in Table 4.4, which provide key insights into the relationships among our variables of interest. These matrices represent an essential preliminary step in our analysis, aiding in the identification of potential multicollinearity concerns and offering initial indications of the strength and direction of the relationships between the dependent and independent variables.

An interesting observation emerges from the pre-Covid period cohort, where we observe a high correlation between ROA and R_I for both social and innovative startups. This strong association suggests that the capital structure, as represented by R_I, played a crucial role in determining profitability during this period. Such a connection aligns with established financial theories that posit a link between a firm's capital structure and its performance.

Interestingly, this relationship undergoes a marked transformation in the Covid period cohort. For social startups, the correlation between ROA and R_I strengthens considerably, reaching a remarkably high value of 0.917. This strengthening suggests that the capital structure became an even more critical factor influencing profitability for social startups during the pandemic, potentially reflecting the increased importance of financial stability in times of economic turbulence.

Conversely, for innovative startups, we observe a dramatic shift in the opposite direction. The correlation between ROA and R_I in the Covid period diminishes

Table 4.4 Correlation matrices

	Cohort 2016—total sample					Cohort 2019—total sample				
Variables	ROA	R_I	C_R	SZ	Dim_B	ROA	R_I	C_R	SZ	Dim_B
ROA	**1**					**1**				
R_I	**0.824**	**1**				**0.200**	**1**			
C_R	0.001	0.006	**1**			0.010	**0.027**	**1**		
SZ	**0.107**	**0.169**	0.006	**1**		**0.080**	**0.130**	0.015	**1**	
Dim_B	−0.008	0.004	0.009	**0.324**	**1**	0.002	0.011	0.005	**0.322**	**1**

	Cohort 2016—social startups					Cohort 2016—innovative startups				
Variables	ROA	R_I	C_R	SZ	Dim_B	ROA	R_I	C_R	SZ	Dim_B
ROA	**1**					**1**				
R_I	**0.780**	**1**				**0.831**	**1**			
C_R	0.007	0.007	**1**			0.001	0.006	**1**		
SZ	**0.283**	**0.233**	0.017	**1**		**0.109**	0.167	0.005	**1**	
Dim_B	0.039	**0.074**	−0.016	**0.110**	**1**	−0.010	0.002	0.013	0.387	**1**

	Cohort 2019—social startups					Cohort 2019—innovative startups				
Variables	ROA	R_I	C_R	SZ	Dim_B	ROA	R_I	C_R	SZ	Dim_B
ROA	**1**					**1**				
R_I	**0.917**	**1**				**−0.029**	**1**			
C_R	0.013	0.041	**1**			0.018	**0.026**	**1**		
SZ	**0.177**	**0.258**	0.023	**1**		**0.103**	**0.120**	0.012	**1**	
Dim_B	0.036	0.040	0.011	**0.096**	**1**	−0.010	0.012	0.009	**0.364**	**1**

Values in bold are different from 0 with a significance level of alpha = 0.05

substantially, almost disappearing with a value of 0.029. This striking contrast to the pre-Covid period suggests a fundamental change in the dynamics governing innovative startups' performance during the pandemic. It raises intriguing questions about the factors that superseded capital structure in importance for these firms during the crisis.

Crucially, our examination of the correlation matrices reveals no high correlations among the independent variables themselves. This absence of strong inter-variable correlations is a positive indicator for our subsequent regression analysis, as it suggests that multicollinearity is unlikely to be a significant concern in our models.

The patterns observed in these correlation matrices provide a foundation for our more sophisticated regression analyses and offer preliminary support for some of our hypotheses. They also highlight the differential impacts of the Covid-19 pandemic on social and innovative startups, underscoring the importance of disaggregated analysis in understanding the nuanced effects of economic shocks on different types of entrepreneurial ventures.

As we proceed to our regression models, these insights from the correlation analysis will inform our interpretation of the results and help contextualize the evolving dynamics of startup performance amid unparalleled economic disruption.

4.4.2 Main Analysis

We now turn to the results of our panel regression models presented in Tables A1 and A2 in the Appendix, where we examine the relationships between our variables of interest, controlling for various factors and exploring potential interaction effects.

The first model (Table A1) presents a straightforward analysis without interaction terms, while the second model (Table A2) incorporates interactions between the NACE classification and continuous variables. This approach allows us to discern whether the effects of our independent variables differ significantly between innovative and social startups.

Notably, all variables demonstrate statistical significance at the $p < 0.05$ level, except for C_R in the second model for the 2019 cohort which does not reach statistical significance. This broad pattern of significance lends credence to the relevance of our chosen variables in explaining startup performance.

To aid in interpreting our regression results, we have employed the "marginsplot" command in STATA to generate predictive margins. These graphical representations provide a clear visual representation into the relationships between our variables, allowing for a more accessible understanding of complex interactions.

Our findings offer partial support for hypothesis H2, which proposed a positive link between the degree of capitalization (as expressed by R_I) and profitability. Figure 4.1 illustrates this relationship, revealing interesting temporal and sectoral dynamics. During the pre-Covid period, both innovative and social startups exhibited a similar relationship between R_I and ROA, with higher equity levels relative to total assets being positively correlated with profitability. However, this relationship showed divergence during the Covid period. For social startups, the positive link between R_I and ROA not only persists but strengthens, suggesting that a solid capital structure remained vital for profitability even amid economic disruption. In contrast, innovative startups display a notably different pattern in the Covid era. The relationship between R_I and ROA for these firms becomes relatively flat, indicating that the level of capitalization had a diminished impact on profitability during

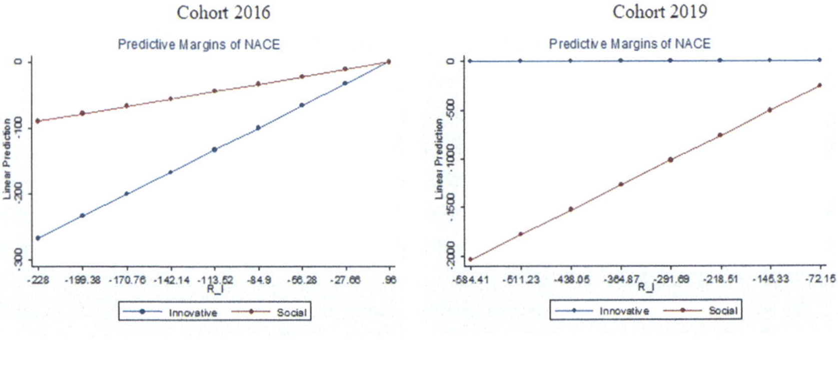

Fig. 4.1 Predictive margins of debt ratio by NACE

this period. This divergence in the Covid period is particularly intriguing and warrants further investigation. This may imply that innovative startups were able to capitalize other factors—such as their technological capabilities or adaptive business models—to sustain profitability regardless of their capital structure. On the other hand, social startups might have grown more dependent on their financial stability to navigate the economic turbulence. These findings not only reinforce our hypothesis but also emphasize the importance of considering sectoral differences and temporal changes when analyzing startup performance. The contrasting patterns observed between innovative and social startups, as well as the pre-Covid and Covid periods, highlight the complex and evolving nature of the factors that drive startup profitability amid major economic disruptions.

Concerning the relationship between liquidity and profitability performance as hypothesized in H3, our findings uncover a nuanced and context-sensitive connection between liquidity and profitability in startups, only partially supporting our initial expectations.

Figure 4.2 illustrates the association between the C_R and ROA, revealing distinct patterns across startup types and periods. The association varies differently for innovative and social startups and undergoes significant modifications when comparing the pre-Covid and Covid periods.

In the pre-Covid period, social startups exhibit a positive, albeit weak, statistical correlation between C_R and ROA. This suggests that for these ventures higher levels of liquidity were modestly associated with improved profitability. In contrast, innovative startups during the same period exhibit a more pronounced negative relationship between C_R and ROA. This unexpected inverse relationship may indicate excessive liquidity related to inefficient use of resources, potentially reducing profitability. However, the Covid period marks a striking reversal of these trends. Innovative startups shift to a weak positive relationship between C_R and ROA, suggesting that liquidity became a more valuable asset for these firms during the economic turbulence. This shift may reflect the heightened importance of financial flexibility and cash reserves in navigating the uncertainties caused by the pandemic.

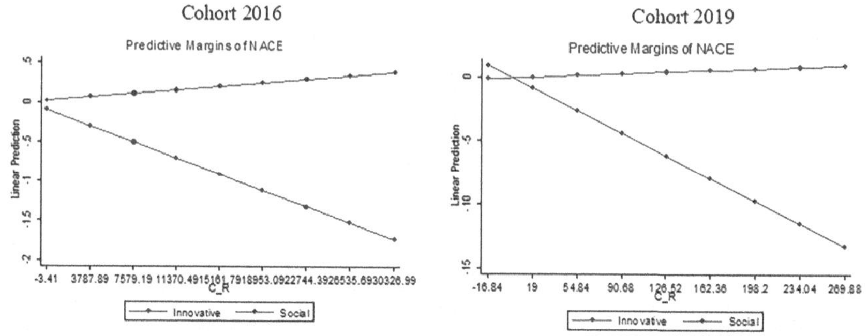

margins NACE, at(C_R =(-3.41(3791.3)30327))

Fig. 4.2 Predictive margins of the current ratio by NACE

On the other hand, social startups in the Covid period display a marked negative relationship between C_R and ROA, similar to the pattern observed for innovative startups in the pre-Covid period. This may again suggest that excessive liquidity, associated with inefficient resource use, negatively affected profitability.

The observed differences between innovative and social startups, as well as the temporal shifts from pre- to Covid periods, emphasize the need for sector-specific approaches to liquidity management in entrepreneurial ventures. Moreover, they underscore the importance of adaptive financial strategies when facing significant economic disruptions. The changing dynamics of the liquidity–profitability relationship suggest that startups may need to reconsider and possibly adjust their liquidity management practices in response to major external shocks. These insights contribute to a more refined understanding of startup financial management and highlight the need for additional research into the factors that influence the relationship between liquidity and profitability in different startup types and economic contexts.

Our regression models yield differentiated patterns for the two types of startups regarding the relationship between company size and profitability performance, providing partial confirmation of our fourth hypothesis (H4). As illustrated in Fig. 4.2, the pre-Covid period displays a clear dichotomy in the relationship between size and profitability across our startup categories. Social startups exhibit a positive association, suggesting that larger scale corresponded with enhanced profitability for these enterprises. This alignment may reflect economies of scale or increased resource availability that benefited social startups before the pandemic.

Conversely, innovative startups in the pre-Covid period showed a negative relationship between size and profitability. This counterintuitive finding might indicate that smaller, more agile innovative firms were better positioned to capitalize on market opportunities or maintain operational efficiency, thereby achieving superior profitability relative to their larger counterparts. The Covid period, however, presents a striking reversal of these trends. Social startups transition to a negative relationship between size and profitability, implying that larger scale became a potential liability during the economic turbulence induced by the pandemic. This shift may reflect increased operational challenges or reduced flexibility in adapting to rapidly changing market conditions for larger social enterprises. In contrast, innovative startups in the Covid period exhibit a positive, albeit weak, association between size and profitability. This shift suggests that larger innovative firms may have been better positioned to withstand the economic challenges, possibly due to more substantial resource reserves.

These findings provide only partial support for our hypothesis H4, which predicted a generally positive relationship between size and profitability, with a diminished effect during the crisis period. The sector-specific reversals observed in the size-profitability relationship from pre-Covid to Covid periods highlight the differential impacts of the pandemic on various types of startups. Furthermore, these results highlight the context-dependent nature of the size-performance relationship in startups. They suggest that the optimal organizational scale may vary not only between sectors but also across different economic environments (Fig. 4.3).

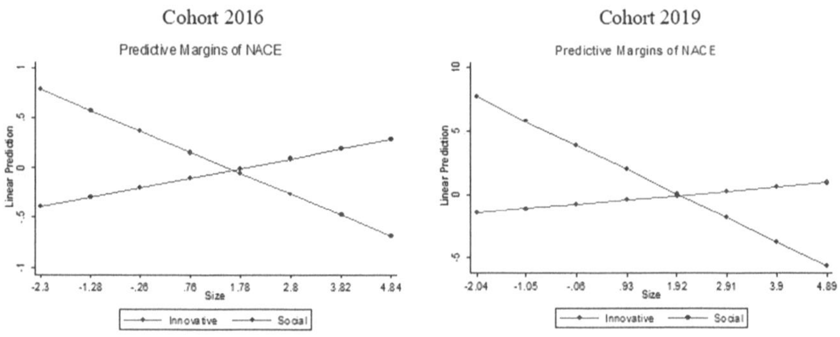

Fig. 4.3 Predictive margins of size by NACE

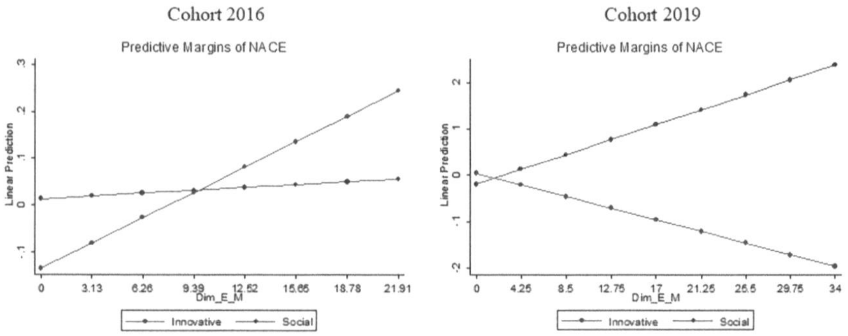

Fig. 4.4 Predictive margins of board size by NACE

Our H5 proposed a positive statistical association between the board size and profitability, and that this relationship would become more pronounced during the Covid-19 crisis period. The results from our analysis, however, offer only partial confirmation of this research hypothesis, revealing a more complex relationship between board size and startup performance.

As illustrated in Fig. 4.4, our sample reveals a positive relationship between the board size and profitability for both types of startups in the pre-Covid period. This finding supports traditional views on corporate governance, which suggest that a larger leadership team may enhance decision-making, bring diverse expertise, and ultimately lead to better financial performance. The consistency of this positive association across both innovative and social startups in the pre-pandemic era indicates a generalized benefit of expanded managerial capacity in stable economic conditions. However, the Covid period reveals a divergent trend that challenges our initial expectations. For social startups, the positive relationship between board size and profitability not only persists but intensifies. This increase indicates that a broader managerial base became even more crucial for social enterprises as they navigated the complexities and uncertainties of the pandemic-driven economic environment. The enhanced positive association may reflect the value of diverse perspectives and expanded networks in adapting to rapidly changing social needs and operational challenges during the crisis. Conversely, innovative startups exhibit a striking reversal in the Covid period, with the relationship between the number of directors and profitability turning negative. Unexpected reversal raises intriguing questions about the optimal governance structure for innovative firms during times of severe economic disruption. The negative association could suggest that more streamlined, agile decision-making structures were better suited for innovative startups in responding quickly to the unprecedented challenges and opportunities presented by the pandemic.

In conclusion, while our hypothesis H5 is only partially confirmed, the findings provide valuable insights into the complex relationship between board size and performance in startups. They emphasize the importance of adaptive governance strategies during major economic disruptions and reinforce the need for sector-specific approaches to startup management and policy support.

Although we did not include a specific research hypothesis on the point, it is worth noting that even the country controls did not yield meaningful results to capture specific trends, which could have been expected given the distinct characteristic of the countries examined (large, medium, and small-medium size).

Overall, there are notable differences in average performance levels at the country level between the Covid and pre-Covid periods for both social and innovative startups (Fig. 4.5). Innovative startups generally have lower profitability in the pre-Covid period, except in the smallest economies (Greece and Portugal). This situation is not reflected in the Covid period cohort, in which the average performance levels of innovative startups are very similar across countries, except for Germany where they are lower. The differences for social startups in the second period compared to the first period vary significantly by country, with a trend of decreasing average levels, except for Portugal, for which the value increases significantly in the Covid period. Thus, the pandemic appears to have affected countries differently for both types of startups. A noticeable trend is that, compared to the pre-Covid period, profitability performance among innovative startups appears to level out across countries during the Covid period.

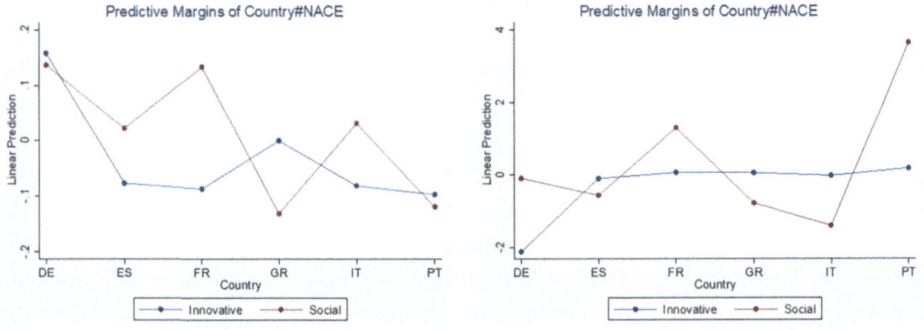

Fig. 4.5 Predictive margins of country by NACE

4.5 Conclusions

In this study, we have introduced an innovative approach to the analysis of startup performance. While the existing literature has extensively explored the role of profitability, capital structure, and liquidity for startups (Fuertes-Callén et al., 2022; Robb & Robinson, 2014), our research distinguishes itself through two fundamental aspects: the comparative analysis between two different types of startups, innovative startups and social startups; the comparative analysis between the pre-Covid period and the Covid period, which offers a unique perspective on the adaptability of different types of startups in response to a global exogenous shock.

Our findings validate the anticipated overall decline in profitability levels from the pre-Covid to Covid period for both startup types. However, the relationships between profitability performance and some of its potential drivers undergo notable and sector-specific changes across startup types during the Covid period. This divergence suggests distinct crisis response strategies for innovative and social startups.

The complex dynamics revealed in the relationships among our analyzed variables underscore the need for a more articulated understanding of how these factors interrelate to influence startup performance.

As evidenced from the results exposed in Sect. 4.4, our analysis demonstrates that the impact of financial structure, liquidity, size, and governance on profitability is not consistent across startup types or external economic conditions.

Building on this empirical evidence, our chapter contributes to the literature on innovative and social startups by providing valuable insights into understanding the key drivers (already detailed in Sect. 4.4) that influence their performance in periods of normal business activity (pre-Covid) and crisis situations (Covid period). In this regard, the findings also carry important implications for practice and policymakers.

From a practical perspective, our results offer valuable insights for startup management strategies during crises. They indicate that a universal approach to startup management is inadequate, particularly during economic shocks. Instead, startups may need to tailor their financial, operational, and governance strategies based on their specific type (innovative or social) and the prevailing economic conditions.

For policy makers, our findings highlight the importance of developing targeted support measures for different types of startups during economic crises. The varied impacts of the Covid-19 pandemic on innovative and social startups imply that policy interventions may need to be customized to address the specific challenges faced by each startup category.

While our study provides important insights, it is not without limitations highlighting the need for further research.

The main limitations stem from the use of a non-probabilistic sample, which represents only a subset of European countries, and from using high-tech startups and startups focused on social assistance as proxies for the broader categories of innovative and social startups. Additionally, there is a need for a deeper exploration of the specific mechanisms that influence the relationships between financial structure, size variables, and profitability in various types of startups. Moreover, investigating how these interaction mechanisms are moderated by external economic conditions (such as institutional and regulatory factors in each country) could provide a more comprehensive understanding of startup resilience. Moreover, longitudinal studies that track startups over extended periods, encompassing multiple economic cycles, could offer further insights into the long-term dynamics of startup performance and adaptability. This type of research could contribute to the development of more reliable predictive models for startup success and failure in different economic environments. As the global economy encounters ongoing uncertainties, gaining a deeper understanding of these dynamics will be essential for building resilient and adaptable startup ecosystems.

Appendix

Table A1 Panel regression model 1

Cohort 2016					Cohort 2019				
No. of obs.	=	9930			No. of obs.	=	11,607		
F(15; 9912)	=	1424.42			F(10; 11,594)	=	52.87		
Prob > F	=	0			Prob > F	=	0		
R-squared	=	0.68			R-squared	=	0.44		
Adj R-squared	=	0.68			Adj R-squared	=	0.43		
Root MSE	=	2.51			Root MSE	=	6.85		
ROA (Dep. Var.)	Coef.	Std. Err.	t	P > t	ROA (Dep. Var.)	Coef.	Std. Err.	t	P > t
R_I	1.145	0.008	144.308	0.000	R_I	0.175	0.008	20.893	0.000
C_R	0.000	0.000	−1.916	0.055	C_R	0.002	0.001	3.987	0.000
SZ	−0.189	0.037	−5.082	0.000	SZ	0.496	0.093	5.356	0.000
Dim_B	0.011	0.005	2.148	0.032	Dim_B	−0.056	0.024	−2.354	0.019
Social. NACE	0.152	0.078	1.963	0.050	Social. NACE	−0.594	0.232	−2.565	0.010
Country					Country				
ES	−0.077	0.043	−1.812	0.070	ES	−0.124	0.071	−1.745	0.081
FR	−0.041	0.023	−1.804	0.071	FR	−0.088	0.037	−2.366	0.018
GR	0.780	0.396	1.972	0.049	GR	−0.020	0.008	−2.454	0.014
IT	−0.115	0.042	−2.710	0.007	IT	−0.031	0.014	−2.189	0.029
PT	0.257	0.123	2.085	0.037	PT	−0.201	0.072	−2.796	0.005
Year					Year				
2018	0.071	0.018	3.947	0.059	2021	0.171	0.030	5.780	0.029
2019	0.185	0.019	9.990	0.010	2022	0.179	0.042	4.290	0.050
_cons	0.088	0.013	6.590	0.022	_cons	−1.022	0.145	−7.060	0.019

Table A2 Panel regression model 2

	No. of obs.	=	9930		No. of obs.	=	11,607	
	F(14; 9913)	=	1593.2		F(14; 11,590)	=	2962.17	
	Prob > F	=	0		Prob > F	=	0	
	R-squared	=	0.6924		R-squared	=	0.7817	
	Adj R-squared	=	0.6919		Adj R-squared	=	0.7814	
	Root MSE	=	2.4687		Root MSE	=	3.2752	
	Cohort 2016				Cohort 2019			
ROA (Dep. Var.)	Coef.	Std. Err.	t	P > t	Coef.	Std. Err.	t	P > t
NACE.Social	−0.380	0.212	−1.795	0.073	4.449	0.306	14.530	0.000
R_I	1.170	0.008	147.247	0.000	−0.011	0.004	−2.710	0.007
C_R	0.000	0.000	−3.108	0.002	0.004	0.003	1.129	0.259
SZ	−0.205	0.040	−5.145	0.000	0.346	0.046	7.481	0.000
Dim_B	0.017	0.001	12.851	0.000	−0.059	0.019	−3.108	0.002
NACE. Social#c.R_I	−0.778	0.044	−17.626	0.000	3.491	0.018	194.591	0.000
NACE. Social#c.C_R	0.000	0.000	2.128	0.033	−0.053	0.009	−5.575	0.000
NACE. Social#c.SZ	0.299	0.101	2.952	0.003	−2.269	0.151	−15.038	0.000
NACE. Social#c. Dim_B	−0.015	0.005	−2.877	0.004	0.134	0.059	2.278	0.023
Country								
ES	−0.066	0.022	−2.970	0.003	−0.436	0.136	−3.205	0.001
FR	−0.040	0.024	−1.711	0.087	−0.218	0.137	−1.592	0.111
GR	0.817	0.451	1.812	0.070	−0.444	0.041	−10.827	0.000
IT	−0.085	0.042	−2.027	0.043	−0.429	0.136	−3.168	0.002
PT	0.201	0.043	4.716	0.000	−0.257	0.136	−1.884	0.060
_cons	0.182	0.043	4.192	0.000	−0.292	0.037	−7.856	0.000

References

Abou-Moghli, A. A., & Al-Kasasbeh, M. M. (2012). Social network and the success of business start-up. *International Journal of Business and Management, 7*(9), 134.

Altman, E. I., Iwanicz-Drozdowska, M., Laitinen, E. K., & Suvas, A. (2017). Financial distress prediction in an international context: A review and empirical analysis of Altman's Z-Score model. *Journal of International Financial Management & Accounting, 28*(2), 131–171. https://doi.org/10.1111/jifm.12053

Audretsch, D., Colombelli, A., Grilli, L., Minola, T., & Rasmussen, E. (2020). Innovative start-ups and policy initiatives. *Research Policy, 49*(10), 104027. https://doi.org/10.1016/j.respol.2020.104027

Audretsch, D., Segarra, A., & Teruel, M. (2014). Why don't all young firms invest in R&D? *Small Business Economics, 43*(4), 751–766. https://doi.org/10.1007/s11187-014-9561-9

Austin, J., Stevenson, H., & Wei-Skillern, J. (2006). Social and commercial entrepreneurship: Same, different, or both? *Entrepreneurship Theory and Practice, 30*(1), 1–22.
Azeem, M., & Khanna, A. (2024). A systematic literature review of startup survival and future research agenda. *Journal of Research in Marketing and Entrepreneurship, 26*(1), 111–139. https://doi.org/10.1108/JRME-03-2022-0040
Bailetti, T. (2012). Technology entrepreneurship: Overview, definition, and distinctive aspects. *Technology Innovation Management Review, 2*(2).
Battilana, J., & Lee, M. (2014). Advancing research on hybrid organizing—Insights from the study of social enterprises. *Academy of Management Annals, 8*(1), 397–441.
Bergset, L., & Fichter, K. (2015). Green start-ups—A new typology for sustainable entrepreneurship and innovation research. *Journal of Innovation Management, 3*(3), 118–144.
Bertoni, F., Colombo, M. G., & Grilli, L. (2011). Venture capital financing and the growth of high-tech start-ups: Disentangling treatment from selection effects. *Research Policy, 40*(7), 1028–1043. https://doi.org/10.1016/j.respol.2011.03.008
Biancalani, F., Czarnitzki, D., & Riccaboni, M. (2022). The Italian Start Up Act: A microeconometric program evaluation. *Small Business Economics, 58*(3), 1699–1720. https://doi.org/10.1007/s11187-021-00468-7
Blank, S., & Dorf, B. (2020). *The startup owner's manual: The step-by-step guide for building a great company*. Wiley.
Breschi, S., Lassébie, J., & Menon, C. (2018). *A portrait of innovative start-ups across countries*.
Brüderl, J., & Preisendörfer, P. (1998). Network support and the success of newly founded business. *Small Business Economics, 10*(3), 213–225. https://doi.org/10.1023/A:1007997102930
Cantamessa, M., Gatteschi, V., Perboli, G., & Rosano, M. (2018). Startups' roads to failure. In *Sustainability* (Vol. 10, Issue 7). https://doi.org/10.3390/su10072346
Cassar, G. (2004). The financing of business start-ups. *Journal of Business Venturing, 19*(2), 261–283. https://doi.org/10.1016/S0883-9026(03)00029-6
Christensen, C. M. (2013). *The innovator's dilemma: When new technologies cause great firms to fail*. Harvard Business Review Press.
Chundakkadan, R., Natarajan, R. R., & Sasidharan, S. (2022). Small firms amidst COVID-19: Financial constraints and role of government support. *Economic Notes, 51*(3), e12206. https://doi.org/10.1111/ecno.12206
Coad, A., Amaral-Garcia, S., Bauer, P., Domnick, C., Harasztosi, P., Pál, R., & Teruel, M. (2023). Investment expectations by vulnerable European firms in times of COVID. *Eurasian Business Review, 13*(1), 193–220. https://doi.org/10.1007/s40821-022-00218-z
Coad, A., Segarra, A., & Teruel, M. (2016). Innovation and firm growth: Does firm age play a role? *Research Policy, 45*(2), 387–400. https://doi.org/10.1016/j.respol.2015.10.015
Coles, J. L., Daniel, N. D., & Naveen, L. (2008). Boards: Does one size fit all? *Journal of Financial Economics, 87*(2), 329–356. https://doi.org/10.1016/j.jfineco.2006.08.008
Colombo, M. G., D'Adda, D., & Piva, E. (2010). The contribution of university research to the growth of academic start-ups: An empirical analysis. *The Journal of Technology Transfer, 35*(1), 113–140. https://doi.org/10.1007/s10961-009-9111-9
Colombo, M. G., D'Adda, D., & Quas, A. (2019). The geography of venture capital and entrepreneurial ventures' demand for external equity. *Research Policy, 48*(5), 1150–1170. https://doi.org/10.1016/j.respol.2018.12.004
Cotei, C., & Farhat, J. (2017). The evolution of financing structure in US startups. *The Journal of Entrepreneurial Finance, 19*(1), 4.
Dacin, P. A., Dacin, M. T., & Matear, M. (2010). Social entrepreneurship: Why we don't need a new theory and how we move forward from here. *Academy of Management Perspectives, 24*(3), 37–57. https://doi.org/10.5465/amp.24.3.37
Damodaran, A. (2009). *Valuing young, start-up and growth companies: Estimation issues and valuation challenges*. Available at SSRN, 1418687.
Dean, T. J., Brown, R. L., & Bamford, C. E. (1998). Differences in large and small firm responses to environmental context: Strategic implications from a comparative analysis of business

formations. *Strategic Management Journal, 19*(8), 709–728. https://doi.org/10.1002/(SICI)1097-0266(199808)19:8<709::AID-SMJ966>3.0.CO;2-9

Defourny, J., & Nyssens, M. (2008). Social enterprise in Europe: Recent trends and developments. *Social Enterprise Journal, 4*(3), 202–228. https://doi.org/10.1108/17508610810922703

Delmar, F., McKelvie, A., & Wennberg, K. (2013). Untangling the relationships among growth, profitability and survival in new firms. *Technovation, 33*(8), 276–291. https://doi.org/10.1016/j.technovation.2013.02.003

Dimelis, S., Giotopoulos, I., & Louri, H. (2017). Can firms grow without credit? A quantile panel analysis in the Euro area. *Journal of Industry, Competition and Trade, 17*(2), 153–183. https://doi.org/10.1007/s10842-016-0216-1

Doğan, M. (2013). Does firm size affect the firm profitability? Evidence from Turkey. *Research Journal of Finance and Accounting, 4*(4), 53–59.

Eisenberg, T., Sundgren, S., & Wells, M. T. (1998). Larger board size and decreasing firm value in small firms1We wish to thank Asiakastieto Oy for furnishing us with the data analyzed here, Clas Bergström, Jonathan Macey, David Yermack, and an anonymous referee for helpful comments, and Linda Bölling for. *Journal of Financial Economics, 48*(1), 35–54. https://doi.org/10.1016/S0304-405X(98)00003-8

European Commission. (2014). *European competitiveness report 2014 – Helping firms grow*. Publications Office. https://doi.org/10.2769/28020

European Commission. (2016). *Europe's next leaders: The start-up and scale-up initiative*. https://eur-lex.europa.eu/legal-content/EN/TXT/?uri=COM:2016:733:FIN

Fairlie, R. (2020). The impact of COVID-19 on small business owners: Evidence from the first three months after widespread social-distancing restrictions. *Journal of Economics & Management Strategy, 29*(4), 727–740. https://doi.org/10.1111/jems.12400

Fuertes-Callén, Y., Cuellar-Fernández, B., & Serrano-Cinca, C. (2022). Predicting startup survival using first years financial statements. *Journal of Small Business Management, 60*(6), 1314–1350. https://doi.org/10.1080/00472778.2020.1750302

Grilli, L., & Murtinu, S. (2014). Government, venture capital and the growth of European high-tech entrepreneurial firms. *Research Policy, 43*(9), 1523–1543. https://doi.org/10.1016/j.respol.2014.04.002

Guerzoni, M., Nava, C. R., & Nuccio, M. (2021). Start-ups survival through a crisis. Combining machine learning with econometrics to measure innovation. *Economics of Innovation and New Technology, 30*(5), 468–493. https://doi.org/10.1080/10438599.2020.1769810

Hoogendoorn, B. (2016). The prevalence and determinants of social entrepreneurship at the macro level. *Journal of Small Business Management, 54*(S1), 278–296. https://doi.org/10.1111/jsbm.12301

Jensen, M. C., & Meckling, W. H. (1976). Theory of the firm: Managerial behavior, agency costs and ownership structure. *Journal of Financial Economics, 3*(4), 305–360. https://doi.org/10.1016/0304-405X(76)90026-X

Kuckertz, A., Brändle, L., Gaudig, A., Hinderer, S., Morales Reyes, C. A., Prochotta, A., Steinbrink, K. M., & Berger, E. S. C. (2020). Startups in times of crisis – A rapid response to the COVID-19 pandemic. *Journal of Business Venturing Insights, 13*, e00169. https://doi.org/10.1016/j.jbvi.2020.e00169

Laitinen, E. K. (1992). Prediction of failure of a newly founded firm. *Journal of Business Venturing, 7*(4), 323–340. https://doi.org/10.1016/0883-9026(92)90005-C

Laitinen, E. K. (2017). Profitability ratios in the early stages of a startup. *The Journal of Entrepreneurial Finance, 19*(2), 1–28.

Lukason, O., Laitinen, E. K., & Suvas, A. (2016). Failure processes of young manufacturing micro firms in Europe. *Management Decision, 54*(8), 1966–1985. https://doi.org/10.1108/MD-07-2015-0294

Maurya, A. (2016). *Scaling lean: Mastering the key metrics for startup growth*. Penguin.

Migliaccio, G., & Pavone, P. (2021). In C. Bevilacqua, F. Calabrò, & L. Della Spina (Eds.), *Italian innovative start-up cohorts: An empirical survey on profitability BT – New Metropolitan perspectives* (pp. 834–843). Springer.

Miloud, T., Aspelund, A., & Cabrol, M. (2012). Startup valuation by venture capitalists: An empirical study. *Venture Capital, 14*(2–3), 151–174. https://doi.org/10.1080/13691066.2012.667907

Newman, A., Obschonka, M., & Block, J. (2022). Small businesses and entrepreneurship in times of crises: The renaissance of entrepreneur-focused micro perspectives. *International Small Business Journal, 40*(2), 119–129.

Oliveira, B., & Fortunato, A. (2006). Firm growth and liquidity constraints: A dynamic analysis. *Small Business Economics, 27*(2), 139–156. https://doi.org/10.1007/s11187-006-0006-y

Onesti, G., Monaco, E., & Palumbo, R. (2022). Assessing the Italian innovative start-ups performance with a composite index. In *Administrative sciences* (Vol. 12, Issue 4). https://doi.org/10.3390/admsci12040189

Ouimet, P., & Zarutskie, R. (2014). Who works for startups? The relation between firm age, employee age, and growth. *Journal of Financial Economics, 112*(3), 386–407. https://doi.org/10.1016/j.jfineco.2014.03.003

Pervan, M., & Višić, J. (2012). Influence of firm size on its business success. *Croatian Operational Research Review, 3*(1), 213–223.

Reid, G. C., & Smith, J. A. (2000). What makes a new business start-up successful? *Small Business Economics, 14*(3), 165–182. https://doi.org/10.1023/A:1008168226739

Ries, E. (2011). *The lean startup: How today's entrepreneurs use continuous innovation to create radically successful businesses*. Crown Currency.

Ripsas, S., Schaper, B., & Tröger, S. (2018). In G. Faltin (Ed.), *A startup cockpit for the proof-of-concept BT – Handbuch entrepreneurship* (pp. 263–279). Springer Fachmedien Wiesbaden. https://doi.org/10.1007/978-3-658-04994-2_21

Robb, A. M., & Robinson, D. T. (2014). The capital structure decisions of new firms. *The Review of Financial Studies, 27*(1), 153–179. https://doi.org/10.1093/rfs/hhs072

Rocha, V., & Grilli, L. (2024). Early-stage start-up hiring: The interplay between start-ups' initial resources and innovation orientation. *Small Business Economics, 62*(4), 1641–1668. https://doi.org/10.1007/s11187-023-00818-7

Rossetti, F., Nepelski, D., & Cardona, M. (2018). *The startup Europe ecosystem. Analysis of the startup Europe projects and of their beneficiaries*. Publications Office of the European Union. https://doi.org/10.2760/78946

Santisteban, J., & Mauricio, D. (2017). Systematic literature review of critical success factors of information technology startups. *Academy of Entrepreneurship Journal, 23*(2), 1–23.

Sebora, T. C., Lee, S. M., & Sukasame, N. (2009). Critical success factors for e-commerce entrepreneurship: An empirical study of Thailand. *Small Business Economics, 32*(3), 303–316. https://doi.org/10.1007/s11187-007-9091-9

Skawińska, E., & Zalewski, R. I. (2020). Success factors of startups in the EU—A comparative study. In *Sustainability* (Vol. 12, Issue 19). https://doi.org/10.3390/su12198200

Smith, W. K., Gonin, M., & Besharov, M. L. (2013). Managing social-business tensions: A review and research agenda for social enterprise. *Business Ethics Quarterly, 23*(3), 407–442. https://doi.org/10.5840/beq201323327

Spigel, B. (2017). The relational organization of entrepreneurial ecosystems. *Entrepreneurship Theory and Practice, 41*(1), 49–72. https://doi.org/10.1111/etap.12167

Stephan, U., Uhlaner, L. M., & Stride, C. (2015). Institutions and social entrepreneurship: The role of institutional voids, institutional support, and institutional configurations. *Journal of International Business Studies, 46*, 308–331.

Thiel, P., & Masters, B. (2014). *Zero to one: Notes on startups, or how to build the future*. Crown Currency.

Viscusi, K. W., & Moore, M. J. (1993). Product liability, research and development, and innovation. *Journal of Political Economy, 101*(1), 161–184.

Wang, W., & Guedes, M. J. (2024). Firm failure prediction for small and medium-sized enterprises and new ventures. *Review of Managerial Science*, 1–34.

Wiklund, J., Baker, T., & Shepherd, D. (2010). The age-effect of financial indicators as buffers against the liability of newness. *Journal of Business Venturing, 25*(4), 423–437. https://doi.org/10.1016/j.jbusvent.2008.10.011

Yermack, D. (1996). Higher market valuation of companies with a small board of directors. *Journal of Financial Economics, 40*(2), 185–211. https://doi.org/10.1016/0304-405X(95)00844-5

Zahra, S. A., Gedajlovic, E., Neubaum, D. O., & Shulman, J. M. (2009). A typology of social entrepreneurs: Motives, search processes and ethical challenges. *Journal of Business Venturing, 24*(5), 519–532. https://doi.org/10.1016/j.jbusvent.2008.04.007

Zhang, D., Zhuge, L., & Freeman, R. B. (2020). Firm dynamics of hi-tech start-ups: Does innovation matter? *China Economic Review, 59*, 101370. https://doi.org/10.1016/j.chieco.2019.101370

Ziakis, C., Vlachopoulou, M., & Petridis, K. (2022). Start-Up Ecosystem (StUpEco): A conceptual framework and empirical research. In *Journal of open innovation: Technology, market, and complexity* (Vol. 8, Issue 1). https://doi.org/10.3390/joitmc8010035

Chapter 5
Performance and Resilience of Italian Startups: A Quantitative Approach

Guido Migliaccio

5.1 Introduction

Numerous innovative startups are driving the support and revitalization of the Italian economy. This trend aligns with recent "neoliberalism" ideas (Dodaro, 2023), which view these startups as a valuable new form of entrepreneurship (Draebye, 2019).

Since 2012, the year of their regulation in Italy, there has been frequent reflection in the doctrine to refine the norm continuously and the facilitated modes of financing (Giraudo et al., 2019; De Stefanis, 2017).

Top political bodies also require annual reporting, especially since the innovative startup appears to be an instrument that seems to provide very positive outcomes, although not without criticism (Confimprenditori – Centro Studi, 2016; Cassandro, 2016).

According to Urso's most recent data (2023), innovative startups and innovative small and medium-sized enterprises (SMEs) (which arise from startups after a few years) have shown steady growth since 2012. They are mainly located in north-western Italy (35%), especially in Lombardy, although there is a significant presence in the South of Italy. A proportion of 17.6% consists of young individuals, with a rising prevalence among females. These companies, especially the large ones, have favored a considerable increase in employment, almost in parallel with the positive evolution of the value of their production.

Innovative ways of financing (Pais et al., 2018), incubators (Lukeš et al., 2019), accelerators (Del Sarto et al., 2019; Rippa et al., 2019; Greco & Tregua, 2022), and

G. Migliaccio (✉)
Department of Law, Economics, Management and Quantitative Methods (DEMM), University of Sannio, Benevento, Italy
e-mail: guido.migliaccio@unisannio.it

S. Loprevite et al. (eds.), *Startups and Gazelle Enterprises*, SIDREA Series in Accounting and Business Administration,
https://doi.org/10.1007/978-3-031-90881-1_5

business angels (Grilli, 2019) have contributed to the success of this entrepreneurial model.

In Italy, numerous statistical and econometric data are available from various sources.

Instead, research focusing on financial and economic performance based on financial statements, which this study aims to enrich and update, is rarer (Migliaccio & Pavone, 2021a, 2021b, 2024).

The study first frames some defining aspects of "startups" concerning the leading national and international bibliography. It then proceeds to illustrate the research methodology that uses static analysis of annual financial statements, selecting the leading ratios, verifying their trend, and subjecting the results to statistical processing that favors temporal and spatial comparisons. They are necessary because some studies on the subject (Capozza et al., 2018; Ghio et al., 2016; Fini et al., 2009) have shown that economies of location and diversification seem to be among the prevailing factors favoring the emergence of such firms. This is especially true in Italy due to the economic imbalances between the macro-areas of the country (North, Centre, and South).

After analyzing the data, we present and discuss our findings. We then conclude by considering the limitations of our study and the broader implications of what we discovered.

5.2 Theory and Hypothesis Development

Numerous local publications have focused on the phenomenon in Italy, seeking a balance between theoretical, scientific, and operational aspects. We therefore refer to Rosapepe (2023), Capone and Innocenti (2023), Bianchi et al. (2021). References to financing are instead proposed by Nadotti et al. (2023). In his 2024 book, Mauro focuses on management within the primary sector.

The international publications, identifying above all those relating to the Italian situation, can be distinguished based on the subject matter into different groups analyzing the sectors in which the companies operate, their location, the prevailing skills, the financial dimension, and the need for assistance and performance monitoring in management evolution. These six aspects are relevant to provide a relatively exhaustive picture of current dynamics and verify the impacts on the management of internal components, primarily managerial and technological, and external components (state, territory, universities, large companies, financiers, etc.). A comprehensive overview of the contributions on the subject also helps better define the hypotheses underlying this study.

5.2.1 The Sector

In Italy, innovative startups can operate in all sectors, provided the business project has a significant technological innovation component (Mise, 2019). Some have a prevalent "social vocation" (Ricci, 2015), thus also enjoying the benefits typical of "social enterprises" (Marasà, 2019; Smeriglio, 2019) with a good reputation (Bruna & Nicolò, 2020), which are closer to the underprivileged population and therefore considered "hybrid enterprises" (Venturi & Zandonai, 2016).

Service-based startups were initially investigated by Santarelli and Piergiovanni (1995) and, more recently, by Nosella et al. (2006), who analyzed innovation development in biopharmaceutical startup firms.

Characteristic Made in Italy products are also produced by innovative startups, such as pizza (Franceschelli et al., 2018), craft beer (Cardoni et al., 2019), and cosmetics (D'Epiro, 2018). Such companies can also be found in the cultural (Campagnoli, 2019) and music (Brownlees, 2017) sectors.

In the Italian biopharmaceutical sphere, the factors for a positive start were distinctive competencies, excellence in quality, relational, technical, and managerial skills (Nosella et al., 2006). In biotechnology, they were, instead, the importance of knowledge creation and management (Merlino & Testa, 2011) and internationalization strategies (Delerue & Lejeune, 2011).

Tourism uses such enterprises even before the enactment of the 2012 law: thus Santarelli (1998). Manufacturing enterprises also have previous experience (Audretsch et al., 1999). More recently, Iazzolino et al. (2019) evaluated the knowledge-based strategies of Italian energy innovative startups.

Italian entrepreneurs have also launched innovative startups abroad (Filion et al., 2003).

Generally, the norm and available statistics favor initiatives concentrated in business services, notably IT consulting, R&D, and information services.

The sectoral diversification of Italian startups affects their performance and resilience. Skills, knowledge management, and specific aspects of each economic sphere condition their ability to adapt and grow and thus may be the determining causes of the variable trends in the summary determinations derived from their financial statements.

5.2.2 Localization

The local activity of large firms (Corvello et al., 2024) and urbanization build a local ecosystem favorable to startups, generating practical osmosis (Capozza et al., 2018). The propulsive role of universities is also helpful (Visconti, 2016; Minola et al., 2021): some alumni sometimes become first promoters of spin-offs (Corsi, 2018) and then of innovative startups, continuing the productive collaboration with their universities of origin (Bikse et al., 2018; Matricano, 2020). Academic spin-offs are essential for the technology transfer of basic academic research to firms (Fini et al., 2009; Ghio et al., 2016).

Innovative startups are, therefore, the natural place to conceive and implement innovation, not only technical but also social, for which a productive and constant relationship with the surrounding community (Colombelli, 2016) and with the related "technological environment" (Matricano, 2024) is still necessary.

Always and everywhere, therefore, the territory influences business management and vice versa. Italy's stark regional differences, traditionally divided into North, Centre, and South (Bergamante, 2016), make spatial comparative analyses particularly relevant. Therefore, analysis of trends in ratios expressive of economic and financial performance must necessarily be split, with the national figure as the benchmarking parameter.

5.2.3 Skills

As with other types of businesses, innovative startups also depend on the skills of the founders (Peruffo et al., 2018), which are a necessary condition: specialized skills of the board of directors and funding received seem to be necessary conditions for the success of any such initiative (Errico et al., 2024).

Especially in Italy, however, they are accompanied by relational and friendly values that foster cohesion and reduce conflict (Marrapodi, 2023), limiting the risks of manipulative narcissism on the part of some entrepreneurs (Leonelli & Jalal, In Press). Psychological well-being is a condition for hoping for better success, including economic success (Tognazzo & Mazzurana, 2017; Zhou & Verburg, 2020). Startup entrepreneurs' personality traits (extraversion, agreeableness, conscientiousness, neuroticism, openness to experience) (Presenza et al., 2019; Hand et al., 2020) and women's resourcefulness (Shinnar et al., 2017; D'Epiro, 2018) certainly contribute to it.

The skills and abilities of the founding partners also sometimes make up, albeit to a limited extent, for the lack of venture capital (Colombo et al., 2004), identifying the best financing, and helping to determine the optimal startup size of enterprises.

Skills growth must be considered physiologically during day-to-day operations, especially by accommodating stakeholder demands: it is a necessary condition that prevents closure (De Massis et al., 2012; Innocenti & Zampi, 2019). Growth, development, market specialization, technological diversification, and enhancement of the local culture can represent permanent success (Ulijn et al., 2011), favoring the transition from "startup to scale-up" (Caselli, 2018).

Optimal financial statement results serve as desirable evidence of competent and forward-looking management. Therefore, growing profitability trends and progressive asset balance improvements can be precise indicators of strong managerial and organizational capabilities.

5.2.4 Capital

The need for "financial well-being" is typical of all enterprises, including those under analysis. The lack of capital can be provided for by public authorities, considering the potential desirable economic benefits, the prevention of the "brain drain" abroad and the obsolescence of the national production system.

Building on prior economic studies on public funding (Del Monte & Scalera, 2001), researchers conducted empirical and econometric analyses to assess public funds' efficiency and proper allocation (Fregonara, 2013). The possible interrelation between firms' access to a government-guaranteed bank loan program and tax incentives for venture capital investments has also been analyzed (Giraudo et al., 2019). There are, however, alternative ways to the traditional ones, such as using insurance contracts that make capital available in case of default (Casagrande & Spallone, 2005).

Much also depends on the legislative framework and the support of local public bodies, including, in Italy, the regions (Corsi et al., 2019).

Analysts should conduct financial statement analyses focusing on the relationship between debt and equity capital, particularly in the industrial sector, to quickly understand the current situation. Here, the focus should be on the "financial coverage" capacity of tangible fixed assets, which are crucial for industrial companies. Nothing better than spatial and temporal comparisons of dedicated ratios can, therefore, measure the needs and modalities of the necessary coverage right from the first years of activity.

5.2.5 Assistance

Often, the initiative of companies of this kind stems from strong technological skills without the necessary managerial elements for the durability of the nascent productive organism. Hence, there is a need for external assistance, especially in the initial stages. Business incubators and accelerators are expected to offer such support (Lukeš et al., 2019; Rippa et al., 2019; Greco & Tregua, 2022), often in collaboration with universities (Scagnelli et al., 2019) or chartered accountants specialized in assisting small and medium-sized enterprises (Blackburn et al., 2018).

The productivity of innovative startups should, therefore, be attributed to the capacities of internal bodies but also, in part, to external inputs. The effectiveness of all inputs can easily be assessed over time by looking at trends in the summary determinations obtained from financial statements.

5.2.6 Control

To be evaluated and ensure the successful implementation of their deliberate strategies, innovative startups must leverage management control tools to monitor their economic and financial performance. This is crucial considering the unique characteristics of each startup (Blackburn et al., 2013). Appropriately, Meyssonnier (2015) distinguished the information needs about the company's age: specific information on which to focus becomes relevant at each stage. Control instruments also change according to sector and size.

Adopting the different tools is thus neither coeval nor similar in all startups: their activation seems to depend on antecedent factors such as country-based cultural context, strategy, organizational structure, and performance (Crespo et al., 2019; Davila et al., 2015).

They are necessary (Carraro et al., 2019) to achieve set goals, as recent experiences also show (Taylor et al., 2019). Furthermore, financial statement analyses may also play a relevant role among these tools, contributing to the construction of a composite indicator—the Startups Performance Score (SP-score) (Onesti et al., 2022)—which assesses a company's performance by synthesizing general profitability and employee productivity, also concerning company size.

This study is part of this framework, using traditional analysis tools and enhancing the comparability of financial statements prepared.

The literature review highlights some salient aspects of Italian innovative startups, noting their sectoral diversification and the necessary conditions for success. These firms operate in various sectors, from services to handicrafts to biotechnology and tourism, favoring those with a significant technological component. The territorial context and the possible support of universities and large companies can be crucial in creating a favorable ecosystem for their growth. Fundamental, however, are the founders' skills, especially in the technical and managerial spheres, often complemented by personal relationships that foster internal cohesion and external relations. Startups often need funding, which may come from public or private investment. External assistance from incubators or specialized consultants can fill the possible lack of internal managerial skills. Finally, to ensure sustainability, these enterprises need to implement management control tools, which help monitor economic and financial performance. For this study, the framework that emerged facilitates the planned analysis.

The Chambers of Commerce, Industry, and Handicrafts maintain company registers nationwide. This data provides readily available statistical evidence to identify the presence of these companies in various sectors. Similarly, it is easy to obtain location data. Analysis of financial statements data can reveal insights into the effectiveness of internal skills and external consultancy, the quality of managerial decisions, and the fairness of the relationship between internal and external capital. These are also useful in highlighting the impact of relations with territories.

A quick literature review shows a lack of empirical studies evaluating innovative Italian startups' equity, economic, and financial statements. These studies are essential for assessing the phenomenon based on financial statement data, which has been examined by only a few authors (Migliaccio & Pavone, 2021a, 2021b, 2024). Moreover, the existing analyses were conducted during different periods, not reflecting the current context of the post-pandemic economic rebound and the conflicts in Ukraine and Palestine.

This study aims to contribute to a current assessment of the phenomenon by verifying the temporal evolution of the most representative asset and income relations ratios, using rigorous statistical techniques that favor geographical comparisons.

In summary, therefore, we wish to verify the following hypotheses:

H1 Profitability is permanently positive and high.

Indeed, literature and official statistical data point to highly innovative entrepreneurial projects induced by applying existing regulations. Innovativeness is a fundamental element of enterprises with a "social vocation." The sectors investigated by the scholars are dynamic and often of high added value (management consulting, research and development, innovative energies, biopharmaceuticals, biotechnology, "Made in Italy" handicrafts, culture, leisure, etc.). Facilitating legislation and finance, external support with incubators and accelerators, frequent iterations with universities and public institutions proposed for development, and high internal and external skills justify the expectation of high profits in the first years after startup.

H2 Positive profitability favors an adequate financial and equity balance.

This assumption is the natural consequence of the first. If management skills were also drawn from outside the company, appropriate policies for setting aside net and gross profits should be implemented in companies that are assumed to have recorded high profitability. Such financial statement policies should have been carried out primarily in the first years of operation to foster continuous and systematic self-enhancement for the benefit of future years in which some or all public subsidies might end.

H3 Financial statement outcomes are affected by the location of production processes.

For all business ventures, relations with the surrounding environment are a prerequisite for success. This is even more so for innovative startups that often rely on relationships with public bodies, public and private research centers, and universities. The Italian territory, however, is not homogeneous. Economic and social structural differences are atavistic and the result of a problematic reconstruction of national unity that is still unfinished. While it is true that the new technologies of globalization have reduced the physical distances between places, there are, unfortunately, still disadvantages that predominantly characterize the southern areas. There are, moreover, significant differences concerning the prevailing sectors between the different regions. For these reasons, different trends can be expected in the main ratios of financial statements to be compared with the national average value.

5.3 Methodology and Sample Characteristics

After precisely delineating the sample's characteristics, this research outlines the trend of the most representative income (Roe and Roi) and financial (Leverage and Capital coverage of tangible fixed assets) ratios for 2013–2022.

The size of the 9860 innovative startups surveyed in 2024 is measured by data points, including the number of employees, turnover, and total assets. We employed the column-wise method to analyze all available observations for each variable.

Their legal status and legal form are also specified, as well as the sector in which they operate.

Descriptive statistics that facilitate a detailed analysis of the phenomenon are arithmetic average, standard error, median, mode, standard deviation, sample variance, kurtosis, skewness, range, minimum, maximum, and sum.

However, data from the Moody's database (formerly Bureau van Dijk) may not always be available. To address this, we have included indications of missing observations for reference.

The absence of values in earlier years is unsurprising, as the legislation was enacted only briefly ago. Moreover, after a few years, companies lose their status as innovative startups and transition into innovative small and medium-sized enterprises.

The evolution of the annual average value of each ratio is represented graphically with broken straight lines and interpolating curves obtained from sixth-degree polynomial equations that maximize R^2.

Alongside the national average data, a disaggregated analysis by geographic macro-areas (North, Central and South Italy) is proposed, with descriptive statistics and the "one-way ANOVA" (Gu, 2013; Ross & Willson, 2017; Liao & Li, 2018) and Tukey Kramer (Tukey, 1949, 1953, 1993; Kramer, 1956) tests, which have already proven their validity in several similar analyses (Migliaccio & De Blasio, 2024; Migliaccio & De Palma, 2024; De Blasio et al., 2022).

Thus, the sample consists of 9860 innovative startups, most of which will be in the whole operation in 2024: 9595 (97.31%). Non-active companies are a minority: 261 (2.65%). Only four are active companies but with insolvency proceedings in place.

The predominant legal form is the "Limited Liability Company": 9302, 94.34% of the total, followed by the "Limited Liability Company simplified," adopted by 426 enterprises, 4.32%. The other legal forms are much less used (Table 5.1).

The areas of operation are very diverse and heterogeneous. The decisively predominant sector is "Computer programming, consultancy and related activities," where 3965 companies operate. One thousand four hundred sixty-three operate in "Scientific research and development." Eight hundred and twenty-one characterize the "Information service activities." All other activities have less than 300 enterprises (Table 5.2).

The preferred location is Northern Italy, which gathers more than half of the innovative startups (50.87%). This is followed by the southern macro-region with

Table 5.1 The legal form

	N.	%
Public limited company	75	0.76%
Public limited company single member	0	0.00%
Limited Liability Company	9302	94.34%
Single-member limited liability company	0	0.00%
Limited Liability Company simplified	426	4.32%
Limited partnership	0	0.00%
Joint-stock consortium	0	0.00%
Limited liability cooperative joint-stock company	52	0.53%
Limited liability consortium company	5	0.05%
Total	9860	100%

Source: our elaboration

the major islands (28.50%) and then by Central Italy (20.63%). Lombardy is the region with the most companies (2564), followed by Campania (1138) and Lazio (1204) (Table 5.3).

The size of the analyzed companies is measured first concerning the number of employees, which is not always available. Those that were silent averaged around 7298 over the decade but steadily declined from 9856 to 992. More than 1500 companies still operate without employees. Employment, however, is steadily increasing, as is evident in Fig. 5.1, which records the trend of innovative startups that reported several employees other than zero.

The higher employment presumably also stems from the steadily increasing turnover, as shown in Fig. 5.2.

Recent pandemics and wars do not seem to have dented the decidedly favorable trend.

The excellent market performance may also have positively impacted investment, which is growing everywhere, albeit much slower (Fig. 5.3).

5.4 Results

5.4.1 ROE—Return on Equity

The ratio relates net profit to equity and measures the overall percentage profitability of the company. Table 5.4 presents the primary statistical evidence concerning Italy and its three macro-regions.

The striking fact in the above table is the absence of information in the decade's early years, immediately following the enactment of the specific regulations on innovative startups. Our records show only a handful of residual experiences from Southern Italy. All the others established at the beginning of the decade should have

Table 5.2 The areas of operation

Section	Division	Description	N.
J	62	Computer programming, consultancy and related activities	3965
M	72	Scientific research and development	1463
J	63	Information service activities	821
M	70	Activities of head offices; management consultancy activities	293
C	28	Manufacture of machinery and equipment n.e.c.	282
M	74	Other professional, scientific, and technical activities	250
M	71	Architectural and engineering activities; technical testing and analysis	221
C	26	Manufacture of computer, electronic, and optical products	216
G	47	Retail trade, except for motor vehicles and motorcycles	178
J	58	Publishing activities	156
C.	32	Other manufacturing	147
N	82	Office administrative, office support, and other business support activities	115
M	73	Advertising and market research	113
C	27	Manufacture of electrical equipment	111
P	85	Education	95
G	46	Wholesale trade, except for motor vehicles and motorcycles	90
C	10	Manufacture of food products	87
D	35	Electricity, gas, steam, and air conditioning supply	78
C	20	Manufacture of chemicals and chemical products	77
C	25	Manufacture of fabricated metal products, except machinery and equipment	77
A	1	Crop and animal production, hunting and related service activities	69
C	30	Manufacture of other transport equipment	66
N	79	Travel agency, tour operator, and other reservation service and related activities	63
J	59	Motion picture, video and television program production, sound recording and music publishing activities	57
F	43	Specialized construction activities	48
C	22	Manufacture of rubber and plastic products	47
F	41	Construction of buildings	43
C	14	Manufacture of apparel	42
Q	86	Human health activities	38
C	29	Manufacture of motor vehicles, trailers, and semi-trailers	35
C	23	Manufacture of other non-metallic mineral products	32
I	56	Food and beverage service activities	32
C	31	Manufacture of furniture	30
N	77	Rental and leasing activities	28
C	15	Manufacture of leather and related products	28
S	96	Other personal service activities	27
J	61	Telecommunications	25

(continued)

Table 5.2 (continued)

Section	Division	Description	N.
C	33	Repair and installation of machinery and equipment	25
C	13	Manufacture of textiles	24
C	11	Manufacture of beverages	20
K	66	Activities auxiliary to financial services and insurance activities	20
L	68	Real estate activities	20
R	90	Creative, arts, and entertainment activities	19
C	17	Manufacture of paper and paper products	15
R	93	Sports activities and amusement and recreation activities	15
H	52	Warehousing and support activities for transportation	15
C	16	Manufacture of wood and products of wood and cork, except for furniture, manufacture of articles of straw and plaiting materials	13
C	21	Manufacture of primary pharmaceutical products and pharmaceutical preparations	12
E	38	Waste collection, treatment, and disposal activities; materials recovery	11
C	18	Printing and reproduction of recorded media	11
K	64	Financial service activities, except insurance and pension funding	10
I	55	Accommodation	9
F	42	Civil engineering	7
N	78	Employment activities	7
G	45	Wholesale and retail trade and repair of motor vehicles and motorcycles	6
M	69	Legal and accounting activities	6
M	75	Veterinary activities	6
N	81	Services to buildings and landscape activities	6
Q	88	Social work activities without accommodation	6
Q	87	Residential care activities	5
C	24	Manufacture of basic metals	4
R	91	Libraries, archives, museums, and other cultural activities	4
A	3	Fishing and aquaculture	3
N	80	Security and investigation activities	3
A	2	Forestry and logging	2
E	36	Water collection, treatment, and supply	2
E	39	Remediation activities and other waste management services	2
H	53	Postal and courier activities	2
E	37	Sewerage	1
H	49	Land transport and transport via pipelines	1
J	60	Programming and broadcasting activities	1
S	95	Repair of computers and personal and household goods	1
	–	No code indicated	1
		Total	9860

Source: our elaboration

Table 5.3 Geographical distribution

North		Centre		South and Islands	
Aosta Valley	15	Tuscany	445	Campania	1138
Piedmont	546	Umbria	160	Abruzzo	234
Liguria	178	Marche	225	Molise	73
Emilia-Romagna	701	Latium	1204	Apulia	423
Lombardy	2564			Basilicata	103
Trentino-Alto Adige	191			Calabria	190
Veneto	642			Sicily	521
Friuli-Venezia Giulia	179			Sardinia	128
Total	5016	Total	2034	Total	2810

Source: our elaboration

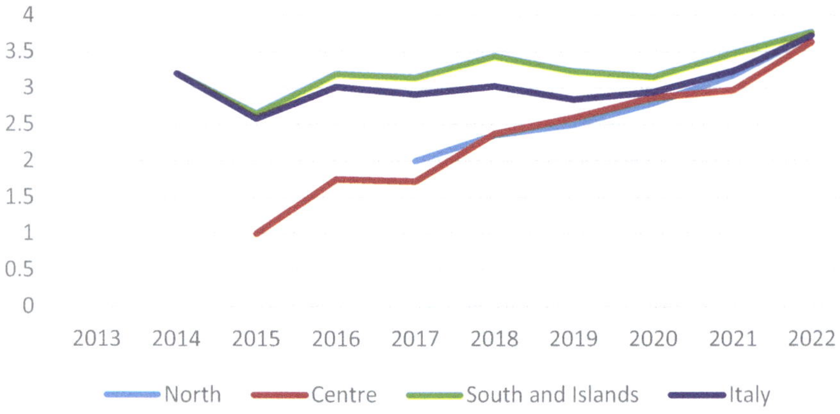

Fig. 5.1 Employee development (Source: our elaboration)

already transformed into innovative small and medium-sized enterprises, as required by law, barring possible closures.

Despite this, the phenomenon's growth is undoubtedly evidenced by the number of observations increasing exponentially everywhere: for the nation, the number of available data has risen from 4 to 7638, representing 77.43% of the sample identified in 2024.

A striking disparity emerges in profitability across regions. Despite hosting many initiatives, the North exhibits concerning shallow average profitability ratios, often negative.

An interpolating curve will be employed to visualize the trend of the average ratio value over the decade, plotted alongside the actual data points. A sixth-degree polynomial function will maximize the *R*-squared value (Table 5.5).

Among the possible functions, the choice of the sixth-degree polynomial is the one that maximizes the value of R^2, which is excellent for the South and Italy as a whole, sufficient for the North, extremely deficient, on the other hand, for the Centre.

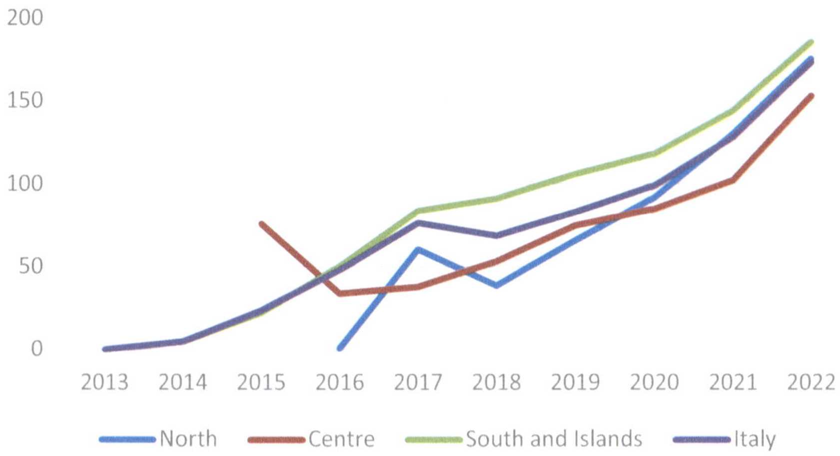

Fig. 5.2 Turnover development (Source: our elaboration)

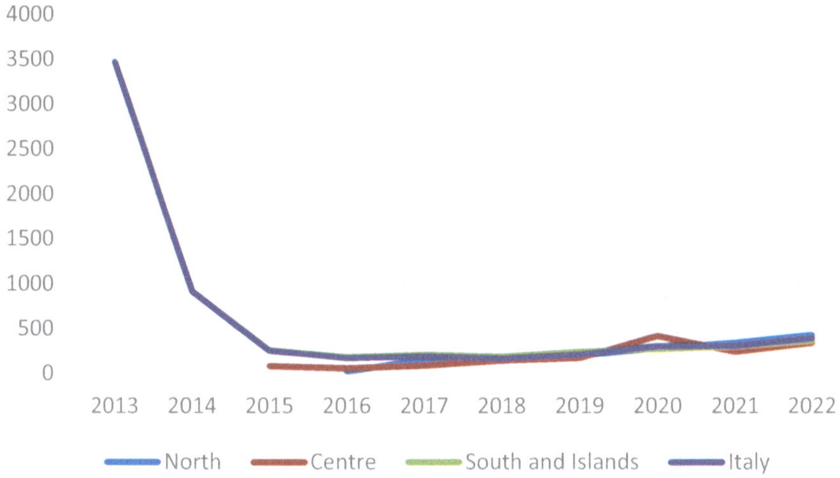

Fig. 5.3 Evolution of total assets

The graphical representation that provides an immediate perception of the trend follows (Fig. 5.4).

The trends in the early years are not very significant, considering the small number of observations. However, differences between the different geographical areas seem to emerge, which will be verified later with rigorous statistical methods.

Relative parallelism between the curves can be seen in recent years, with a relative decrease in 2020 and a more marked one in 2022, presumably due to the residual effects of the pandemic crisis and the advance of those wars in areas not far from Italy.

Table 5.4 ROE—Descriptive statistics

Year	2013	2014	2015	2016	2017	2018	2019	2020	2021	2022
Italy										
Average	−9.157	−2.9	1.7702	−1.599	0.5415	4.0922	3.0922	2.6171	4.9965	−2.763
Standard error	5.3247	8.6491	4.1923	3.2358	2.1104	1.2756	0.8882	0.6734	0.5269	0.4961
Median	−8.45	−5.865	−2.84	−1.28	0	0	0	0.385	1.5	0.01
Mode	–	–	0	0	0	0	0	0	0	0
Standard deviation	10.649	29.962	33.799	42.806	41.787	43.088	44.622	43.467	42.487	43.358
Sample variance	113.41	897.69	1142.4	1832.3	1745.9	1856.6	1991.1	1889.4	1805.1	1879.9
Kurtosis	−5.645	5.6436	2.3491	1.8271	1.4463	1.1361	1.0694	1.3609	1.2661	1.2726
Asymmetry	−0.062	2.0836	1.1226	−0.085	−0.441	−0.156	−0.353	−0.451	−0.32	−0.515
Range	19.77	115.22	182.54	275.05	249.56	294.37	290.35	289.19	299.09	299.7
Minimum	−19.75	−35.02	−75.44	−140.8	−149.6	−149.9	−149.9	−149.7	−149.5	−150
Maximum	0.02	80.2	107.1	134.28	99.98	144.5	140.51	139.5	149.59	149.7
Sum	−36.63	−34.8	115.06	−279.9	212.25	4669.2	7804.6	10,902	32,482	−21,106
Observations	4	12	65	175	392	1141	2524	4166	6501	7638
North										
Average	–	–	–	−8.257	−10.51	−0.683	−2.365	−3.307	−0.106	−7.387
Standard error	–	–	–	6.3671	8.7825	2.3572	1.4461	1.0009	0.7721	0.7097
Median	–	–	–	−9.08	−11.19	−1.9	−1.72	−0.93	0	−2.03
Mode	–	–	–	–	–	0	0	0	0	0
Standard deviation	–	–	–	11.02807	40.24631	42.42873	46.56897	44.03782	43.444	44.31885
Sample variance	–	–	–	121.6184	1619.765	1800.197	2168.669	1939.33	1887.381	1964.161
Kurtosis	–	–	–	–	0.8484	1.0645	1.0034	1.2285	1.1846	1.1034
Asymmetry	–	–	–	0.3341	0.2175	0.0044	−0.274	−0.39	−0.272	−0.49
Range	0	0	0	22.01	170.31	246.55	290.35	281.83	297.48	299.7
Minimum	0	0	0	−18.85	−95.08	−146.6	−149.8	−149.7	−147.9	−150

Maximum	0	0	0	3.16	75.23	99.95	140.51	132.14	149.59	149.7
Sum	0	0	0	−24.77	−220.6	−221.4	−2453	−6412	−336.1	−28,795
Observations	0	0	0	3	21	324	1037	1939	3166	3900
Centre										
Average	–	–	28.425	−2.625	−1.893	4.8528	4.0012	1.7981	5.3346	−2.362
Standard error	–	–	12.565	14.348	5.6399	2.7477	1.9301	1.506	1.1122	1.0705
Median	–	–	28.425	−3.665	−3.54	0	0.6	0.55	1.42	0.31
Mode	–	–	–	–	0	0	0	0	0	0
Standard deviation	–	–	17.77	53.685	40.67	41.032	42.986	43.15	41.422	42.914
Sample variance	–	–	315.76	2882.1	1654	1683.6	1847.8	1861.9	1715.8	1841.6
Kurtosis	–	–	–	0.2697	1.9285	1.2677	1.19	1.63	1.5698	1.2845
Asymmetry	–	–	–	−0.118	0.0153	−0.022	−0.297	−0.504	−0.346	−0.439
Range	0	0	25.13	200.86	214.82	223.21	249.46	288.77	296.13	286.58
Minimum	0	0	15.86	−108.3	−114.8	−123.3	−145.1	−149.3	−149.5	−146.3
Maximum	0	0	40.99	92.58	99.98	99.96	104.32	139.5	146.63	140.26
Sum	0	0	56.85	−36.75	−98.44	1082.2	1984.6	1476.2	7399.1	−3796
Observations	0	0	2	14	52	223	496	821	1387	1607
South and Islands										
Average	−9.157	−2.9	0.924	−1.382	1.6655	6.4114	8.3480	11.265	13.049	5.3898
Standard error	5.3247	8.6491	4.2734	3.3654	2.3551	1.8073	1.3558	1.1046	0.9146	0.8801
Median	−8.45	−5.865	−2.85	−1.025	0	0.06	2.27	4.705	8.095	3.01
Mode	–	–	0	0	0	0	0	0	0	0
Standard deviation	10.65	29.962	33.919	42.303	42.063	44.048	42.681	41.419	40.368	40.629
Sample variance	113.41	897.69	1150.5	1789.5	1769.3	1940.2	1821.6	1715.5	1629.6	1650.7
Kurtosis	−5.646	5.6436	2.5498	2.0553	1.5591	1.2263	1.1497	1.6202	1.3437	1.7730

(continued)

Table 5.4 (continued)

Year	2013	2014	2015	2016	2017	2018	2019	2020	2021	2022
Asymmetry	−0.062	2.0836	1.1981	−0.085	−0.553	−0.286	−0.427	−0.485	−0.339	−0.582
Range	19.77	115.22	182.54	275.05	245.58	294.37	276.64	284.21	289.83	285.37
Minimum	−19.75	−35.02	−75.44	−140.8	−149.6	−149.9	−147.7	−147.8	−141.5	−148.3
Maximum	0.02	80.2	107.1	134.28	96	144.5	128.95	136.39	148.31	137.11
Sum	−36.63	−34.8	58.21	−218.3	531.3	3808.4	8272.9	15,838	25,419	11,486
Observations	4	12	63	158	319	594	991	1406	1948	2131

Source: our elaboration

Table 5.5 ROE—Interpolating equation and R^2

Zone	Interpolating equation	R^2
North	$y = -0.002x^6 + 23.778x^5 - 119{,}980x^4 + 3E{+}08x^3 - 5E{+}11x^2 + 4E{+}14x - 1E{+}17$	0.6225
Centre	$y = 0.0154x^6 - 185.81x^5 + 937{,}198x^4 - 3E{+}09x^3 + 4E{+}12x^2 - 3E{+}15x + 1E{+}18$	0.3662
South	$y = -0.0017x^6 + 20.069x^5 - 101{,}230x^4 + 3E{+}08x^3 - 4E{+}11x^2 + 3E{+}14x - 1E{+}17$	0.9805
Italy	$y = -0.003x^6 + 36.2x^5 - 182{,}586x^4 + 5E{+}08x^3 - 7E{+}11x^2 + 6E{+}14x - 2E{+}17$	0.9001

Source: our elaboration

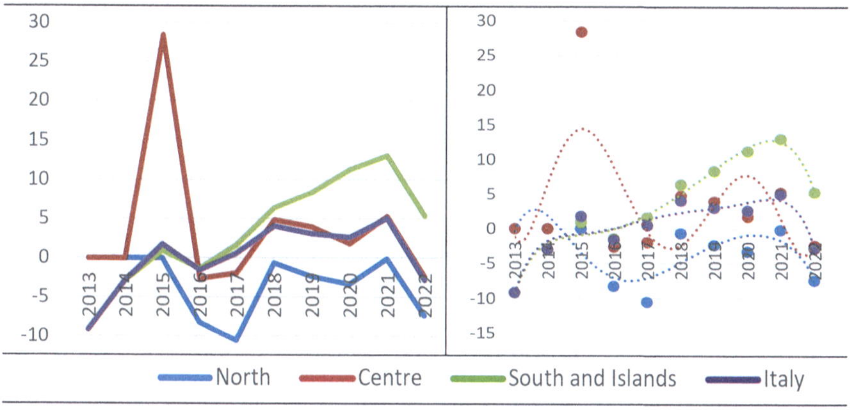

Fig. 5.4 ROE—the 10-year trend

The value of the ratio remains, on average, low and, unfortunately, negative for northern companies, which are the most numerous, as already highlighted in the descriptive statistics table. A one-way ANOVA test will assess potential differences in the average profitability ratio between the three macro-regions. The chosen significance level is alpha = 0.05 (Table 5.6).

The value of F is lower than the critical F: there are, therefore, no statistically significant differences between the three groups, which, on average, evolve according to similar logic. The final figure, therefore, contradicts the first observation of the comparative graphs. The subsequently proposed Tukey Kramer test confirms this first conclusion, which is quite surprising because the economic and social contexts are considerably different: the statistically significant diversity between regions confirms our expectation that disparate economic environments would lead to varying profitability outcomes.

Table 5.6 ROE—One-way ANOVA test

Summary				
Groups	Count	Sum	Media	Variance
North	7	−32.6068	−4.65811	16.3614
Centre	8	37.53112	4.69139	102.7447
South and Islands	10	33.61303	3.361303	46.87101

Analysis of variance						
Origin of the variation	SQ	Dof*	MQ	*F*	Significance value	*F* crit
Between groups	381.5377	2	190.7689	3.386737	0.052208	3.443357
Within groups	1239.221	22	56.32821			
Total	1620.758	24				

Source: our elaboration. (*Degrees of Freedom)

5.4.2 ROI—Return on Investment

This ratio measures the percentage profitability of the core business alone. It relates the operating result to a summation expressing the capital invested in that management area, calculated by the database with the following summation: shareholders' equity + bonds within 12 months + bonds over 12 months + banks within 12 months + banks over 12 months + other lenders within 12 months + shareholders for loans within 12 months + shareholders for loans over 12 months + other lenders over 12 months.

Table 5.7 summarizes the national and macro-regional statistics.

The number of observations of this second profitability ratio allows for similar reflections to the first one: It starts with a few residual companies that have strangely retained the title of an innovative startup and then witnessed a more than proportional increase. However, information availability is less than Roe's over time.

This population of frequencies shows a surprisingly reduced range (difference between minimum and maximum value); the data is, therefore, more homogeneous and more significant than a common trend. The variance values, being significantly lower than Roe, reinforce the observation of lower variability in the data compared to Return on Equity.

However, negative average values are much more frequent, a worrying element considering that the ratio measures the profitability of companies' core business: If harmful, it calls for significant reflection on broader company strategies.

Similarly to Roe, we first identify the function that allows us to draw the interpolating curve next to the broken line. Again, the choice falls on the sixth-degree polynomial that maximizes R^2 (Table 5.8).

While maximizing R-squared identified a suitable function, a visual comparison of the graphical representations revealed that the equations accurately represent the data only for Italy and the South. This suggests that additional methods alongside R-squared are needed to ensure model generalizability across different regions (Fig. 5.5).

The figure tends to stabilize after the first few years. Only a slight decrease is seen, not everywhere, in the worst year of the pandemic. The analysis reveals a

Table 5.7 ROI—Descriptive statistics

Year	2013	2014	2015	2016	2017	2018	2019	2020	2021	2022
Italy										
Average	−5.03	−5.268	−2.555	−3.066	−0.237	−0.075	−0.082	−0.121	0.9256	0.5183
Standard error	4.9683	3.5478	1.5755	1.5189	1.0378	0.7624	0.535	0.4078	0.3539	0.336
Median	−1.11	−1.45	−2.26	−0.57	−0.655	0	0	0	0.43	0.47
Mode	–	–	0	0	0	0	0	0	0	0
Standard deviation	9.9366	10.643	10.686	11.667	11.463	12.982	12.536	12.31	12.835	13.54
Sample variance	98.736	113.28	114.18	136.13	131.40	168.54	157.14	151.53	164.74	183.32
Kurtosis	3.4496	0.6376	2.4891	0.7795	0.6495	−0.136	0.0035	0.1014	−0.178	−0.415
Asymmetry	−1.837	−0.358	0.8746	0.3749	0.1453	0.0482	0.003	−0.027	−0.013	−0.002
Range	21.55	37.05	53.34	56.21	59.71	58.83	59.41	59.79	59.52	59.94
Minimum	−19.73	−25	−23.99	−27.88	−29.82	−29.2	−29.79	−29.96	−29.57	−29.98
Maximum	1.82	12.05	29.35	28.33	29.89	29.63	29.62	29.83	29.95	29.96
Sum	−20.13	−47.41	−117.6	−180.9	−28.88	−21.86	−45.24	−110.7	1217.2	841.7
Observations	4	9	46	59	122	290	549	911	1315	1624
North										
Average	–	–	–	−8.36	−2.545	−2.689	−2.514	−2.75	−0.852	−0.766
Standard error	–	–	–	–	4.7529	1.5283	0.8215	0.6146	0.5171	0.4874
Median	–	–	–	−8.36	−5.345	−2.815	−1.68	−1.81	−0.09	0
Mode	–	–	–	–	–	−11.26	0	0	0	0
Standard deviation	–	–	–	–	13.443	13.498	11.734	12.369	12.834	13.622
Sample variance	–	–	–	–	180.72	182.19	137.68	152.98	164.70	185.57

(continued)

Table 5.7 (continued)

Year	2013	2014	2015	2016	2017	2018	2019	2020	2021	2022
Kurtosis	–	–	–	–	3.6224	0.0683	0.2	−0.098	−0.131	−0.467
Asymmetry	–	–	–	–	1.7564	0.4653	0.1183	−0.049	0.0348	0.0426
Range	0	0	0	0	42.18	58.12	59	59.03	59.52	59.77
Minimum	0	0	0	−8.36	−15.08	−28.49	−29.38	−29.96	−29.57	−29.81
Maximum	0	0	0	−8.36	27.1	29.63	29.62	29.07	29.95	29.96
Sum	0	0	0	−8.36	−20.36	−209.7	−513.9	−1114	−525	−598
Observations	0	0	0	1	8	78	204	405	616	781
Centre										
Average	–	–	16.02	−0.808	0.8289	−0.045	0.5689	1.927	1.4227	0.6265
Standard error	–	–	–	7.4369	2.9791	1.7741	1.3415	0.9175	0.746	0.7010
Median	–	–	16.02	−3.22	−0.03	0	0	0.5	0.575	0.815
Mode	–	–	–	–	–	0	0	0	0	2.33
Standard deviation	–	–	–	16.629	12.283	12.915	13.746	11.998	12.348	13.040
Sample variance	–	–	–	276.54	150.88	166.81	188.96	143.96	152.47	170.04
Kurtosis	–	–	–	2.3344	1.1189	0.0001	−0.354	−0.007	−0.028	−0.27
Asymmetry	–	–	–	1.2863	1.0349	−0.154	0.0982	0.0369	0.029	−0.059
Range	0	0	0	44.34	47.29	53.88	56.63	55.64	59.28	59.34
Minimum	0	0	16.02	−18.05	−17.4	−28.22	−28.17	−26.19	−29.54	−29.72
Maximum	0	0	16.02	26.29	29.89	25.66	28.46	29.45	29.74	29.62
Sum	0	0	16.02	−4.04	14.09	−2.4	59.73	329.51	389.81	216.77
Observations	0	0	1	5	17	53	105	171	274	346

South and Islands										
Average	−5.033	−5.268	−2.968	−3.179	−0.233	1.1967	1.704	2.0102	3.1811	2.4616
Standard error	4.9683	3.5478	1.5546	1.5632	1.1427	1.0019	0.7976	0.6452	0.6205	0.6074
Median	−1.11	−1.45	−2.38	−0.49	−0.7	0	0	0.14	1.99	1.05
Mode	–	–	0	0	0	0	0	0	0	0
Standard deviation	9.9366	10.643	10.429	11.381	11.254	12.633	12.356	11.809	12.792	13.542
Sample variance	98.736	113.28	108.76	129.52	126.65	159.59	152.68	139.46	163.64	183.38
Kurtosis	3.4496	0.6376	3.1210	0.7174	0.6614	−0.0004	0.2572	0.3945	−0.24	−0.398
Asymmetry	−1.837	−0.358	0.9531	0.1905	−0.167	−0.079	−0.2	0.041	−0.102	−0.031
Range	21.55	37.05	53.34	56.21	56.56	58.46	59.35	59.01	55.63	59.85
Minimum	−19.73	−25	−23.99	−27.88	−29.82	−29.2	−29.79	−29.18	−25.71	−29.98
Maximum	1.82	12.05	29.35	28.33	26.74	29.26	29.56	29.83	29.92	29.87
Sum	−20.13	−47.41	−133.6	−168.5	−22.61	190.28	408.96	673.42	1356	1223.4
Observations	4	9	45	53	97	159	240	335	425	497

Source: our elaboration

Table 5.8 ROI—Interpolating equation and R^2

Zone	Interpolating equation	R^2
North	$y = -0.003x^6 + 36.855x^5 - 185{,}929x^4 + 5E{+}08x^3 - 8E{+}11x^2 + 6E{+}14x - 2E{+}17$	0.5498
Centre	$y = 0.011x^6 - 132.82x^5 + 66{,}9916x^4 - 2E{+}09x^3 + 3E{+}12x^2 - 2E{+}15x + 7E{+}17$	0.4828
South	$y = -0.0008x^6 + 9.1597x^5 - 46{,}195x^4 + 1E{+}08x^3 - 2E{+}11x^2 + 2E{+}14x - 5E{+}16$	0.9754
Italy	$y = -0.0006x^6 + 7.5131x^5 - 37{,}883x^4 + 1E{+}08x^3 - 2E{+}11x^2 + 1E{+}14x - 4E{+}16$	0.9411

Source: our elaboration

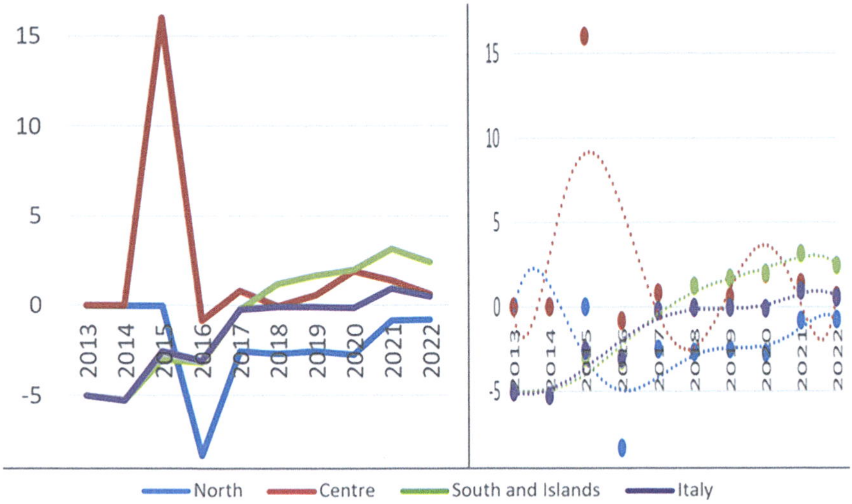

Fig. 5.5 Roi—the 10-year trend (Source: our elaboration)

surprising slight decrease in profitability in 2022. This calls for a more thorough investigation into the causes behind this decline. Following this, we will conduct a one-way ANOVA test with a significance level 0.05 to assess whether these profitability differences between the macro-regions are statistically significant (Table 5.9).

This time, the value of F is greater than the critical F-value. This results in significant differences. The subsequent Tukey Kramer test identifies areas that deviate from the others.

5.4.3 *Leverage*

Italian innovative startups enjoy public financial support. It is, therefore, useful to study the ten-year evolution of the leverage ratio, calculated by dividend total assets to net worth. Table 5.10 presents a comprehensive breakdown of profitability ratio statistics, including a further categorization by geographic area.

Table 5.9 ROI—One-way ANOVA test

Summary				
Groups	Count	Sum	Media	Variance
North	7	−20.4808	−2.92582	6.482277
Centre	8	20.54052	2.567565	30.24234
South and Islands	10	−6.12685	−0.61269	10.31633

Analysis of variance						
Origin of the variation	SQ	Dof*	MQ	*F*	Significance value	*F* crit
Between groups	114.9437	2	57.47187	3.681552	0.041766	3.443357
In the groups	343.437	22	15.61077			
Total	458.3807	24				

Source: our elaboration. (*Degrees of Freedom)

There is more wealth data than income data. A similar upward trend can be seen at a more than proportional rate, reaching 9282 observations in the last year of the decade, representing 94.09% of the total sample identified in 2024.

Considering the evident indebtedness, if one accepts an optimal average reference value of 2, an initial data reading reveals a significant concern. One also notes a very high interval between the minimum and the maximum, the first indication of a considerable heterogeneity of data, confirmed by a very high sample variance that shows data within the sample significantly dispersed concerning their average. The observations are, therefore, very different; there is a great deal of uncertainty about individual values, and therefore, the average is less reliable, which may be poorly representative.

The function for drawing the interpolating curve is as follows: polynomial equations of the sixth degree that maximize R^2 are helpful for this purpose (Table 5.11).

Although we have chosen the equation that produces better R^2 values, we note a modest representation for Southern and Italy. Indeed, it is better for the Centre and optimal for the North. Paradoxically, the exact opposite characterized the two profitability ratios.

The graphical representation follows (Fig. 5.6).

The spatial and temporal comparison immediately shows an upward trend. Debt is increasing everywhere, with a temporary reduction in 2021. It is indeed difficult to identify common and constant elements in such a heterogeneous situation that, unfortunately, are united only by evidence of a worsening of the average financial structure of companies.

The heterogeneity between the macro-regions, however, seems to be compensating. Therefore, the one-way ANOVA test with a tolerance of 0.05 is necessary to determine whether there are any statistically significant differences between the macro-regions (Table 5.12).

F is less than critical *F*. Therefore, there are no significant statistical differences despite first appearances.

Table 5.10 Leverage—Descriptive statistics

Year	2013	2014	2015	2016	2017	2018	2019	2020	2021	2022
Italy										
Average	2.863	2.609	8.747	3.083	4.860	7.050	7.228	5.338	5.769	6.976
Standard error	1.583	1.380	4.842	1.597	2.107	1.871	1.806	1.315	0.875	1.281
Median	1.425	1,31	1,35	1575	1,95	1,8	1,92	1,89	1,85	1,9
Mode	–	1,73	1	1	1	1	1	1	1	1
Standard deviation	3.17	5.69	41.66	22.82	45.00	68.22	98.39	91.91	76.31	123.44
Sample variance	10.02	32.40	1735.2	520.56	2025.2	4653.6	9679.8	8447	5822.8	15,236
Kurtosis	3.90	3.33	68.54	108.72	178.15	709.48	655.66	808.74	2129.6	4727.2
Asymmetry	1.97	1.49	8.15	−8.33	−6.53	23.65	14.14	21.30	37.43	62.44
Range	6.6	24.92	368.71	365.18	1156.7	2538.2	5455.3	5330.1	5939.3	10,555
Minimum	1	−6.12	−12.92	−273.6	−726.6	−418.7	−1929	−1773	−1195	−579.7
Maximum	7.6	18.8	355.79	91.57	430.17	2119.6	3526.4	3557	4744.7	9975.7
Sum	11.45	44.36	647.29	628.99	2216.3	9369.4	21,444	26,064	43,904	64,754
Observations	4	17	74	204	456	1329	2967	4883	7610	9282
North										
Average	–	–	–	2.967	2.093	6.575	4.316	5.073	5.826	7.932
Standard error	–	–	–	1.441	0.432	2.362	1.968	2.234	1.037	2.315
Median	–	–	–	1.95	1.525	1.605	1.735	1.77	1.8	1.79
Mode	–	–	–	–	1	1.02	1	1	1	1.01
Standard deviation	–	–	–	2.495	2.025	46.400	69.901	107.56	63.962	162.45
Sample variance	–	–	–	6.227	4.101	2153	4886.1	11,569	4091.1	26,390
Kurtosis	–	–	–	–	3.340	114.2	481.84	712.64	642.5	2960.5
Asymmetry	–	–	–	1.529	1.552	5.808	−15.64	19.432	21.049	50.891
Range	0	0	0	4.67	9.7	1060.7	2624	5330	30,705	10,555
Minimum	0	0	0	1.14	−1.58	−418.7	−1929	−1773	−887.2	−579.7

Maximum	0	0	0	5.81	8.12	642.09	695.14	3557	2183	9976
Sum	0	0	0	8.9	46.04	2537.8	5446.8	11,759	22,184	39,067
Observations	0	0	0	3	22	386	1262	2318	3808	4925
Centre										
Average	–	–	5.15	0.985	5.569	3.275	6.771	7.790	6.197	5.211
Standard error	–	–	3.59	1.602	1.974	0.912	1.657	3.624	3.165	1.223
Median	–	–	5.15	1.49	1.94	1.645	1.96	2.02	1.83	1.94
Mode	–	–	–	1	1.06	1	1	1	1	1
Standard deviation	–	–	5.077	6.604	15.541	14.471	39.287	112.6	126.9	53.76
Sample variance	–	–	25.776	43.608	241.5	209.42	1543.5	12,675	16,103	2890
Kurtosis	–	–	–	12.909	19.784	83.821	155.2	389.85	1220.1	1276.8
Asymmetry	–	–	–	−3.294	3.375	−4.116	8.910	17.917	32.195	31.854
Range	0	0	7.18	31.49	134.56	273.58	983.66	3299.3	5939.3	2649
Minimum	0	0	1.56	−23.18	−38.75	−164.2	−343.1	−783.7	−1195	−517.1
Maximum	0	0	8.74	8.31	95.81	109.41	640.57	2515.6	4744.7	2132.2
Sum	0	0	10.3	16.75	345.29	825.25	3805	7518	9959	10,068
Observations	0	0	2	17	62	252	562	965	1607	1932
South and Islands										
Average	2.863	2.609	8.847	3.279	4.906	8.692	10.667	4.242	5.358	6.441
Standard error	1.583	1.380	4.977	1.765	2.563	3.332	4.073	0.928	0.772	1.000
Median	1.425	1.31	1.285	1.575	2.065	2.09	2.2	2.02	1.96	2.11
Mode	–	1	1	1	1	1	1	1	1	1
Standard deviation	3.166	5.692	42.229	23.940	49.429	87.584	137.72	37.137	36.167	49.229
Sample variance	10.024	32.397	1783.3	573.13	2443.2	7671	18,965	1379.1	1308	2423.5
Kurtosis	3.904	3.326	66.707	99.821	150.08	497.04	406.25	128.62	275.55	729.79

(continued)

Table 5.10 (continued)

Year	2013	2014	2015	2016	2017	2018	2019	2020	2021	2022
Asymmetry	1.971	1.491	8.037	−8.028	−6.073	21.007	15.508	0.917	0.024	20.81
Range	6.600	24.920	368.71	365.18	1156.7	2512.8	4817.6	1206.6	1597.3	2328.4
Minimum	1.000	−6.120	−12.92	−273.6	−726.6	−393.3	−1291	−558.7	−813.8	−547.8
Maximum	7.600	18.800	355.8	91.57	430.17	2119.6	3526.4	647.96	783.43	1780.6
Sum	11.450	44.360	636.99	603.34	1825	6006.3	12,192	6786.7	11,761	1560
Observations	4	17	72	184	372	691	1143	1600	2195	2425

Source: our elaboration

Table 5.11 Leverage—Interpolating equation and R^2

Zone	Interpolating equation	R^2
North	$y = -0.0011x^6 + 12.777x^5 - 64{,}453x^4 + 2E{+}08x^3 - 3E{+}11x^2 + 2E{+}14x - 7E{+}16$	0.9034
Centre	$y = 0.0037x^6 - 44.258x^5 + 223{,}227x^4 - 6E{+}08x^3 + 9E{+}11x^2 - 7E{+}14x + 2E{+}17$	0.7659
South	$y = 0.0032x^6 - 38.699x^5 + 195{,}133x^4 - 5E{+}08x^3 + 8E{+}11x^2 - 6E{+}14x + 2E{+}17$	0.4644
Italy	$y = 0.0031x^6 - 37.64x^5 + 189{,}824x^4 - 5E{+}08x^3 + 8E{+}11x^2 - 6E{+}14x + 2E{+}17$	0.4426

Source: our elaboration

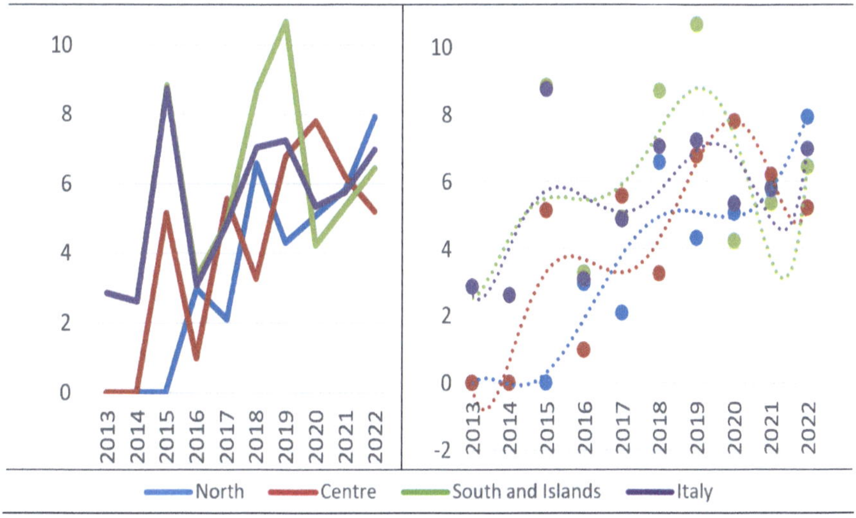

Fig. 5.6 Leverage—The ten-year trend (Source: our elaboration)

Table 5.12 Leverage—One-way ANOVA test

Summary				
Groups	Count	Sum	Media	Variance
North	7	34.781	4.968714	4.135472
Centre	8	40.94855	5.118568	4.532442
South and Islands	10	57.90398	5.790398	7.814915

Analysis of variance						
Origin of the variation	SQ	Dof*	MQ	*F*	Significance value	*F* crit
Between groups	3.385097	2	1.692549	0.293488	0.748532	3.443357
In the groups	126.8742	22	5.767007			
Total	130.2593	24				

Source: our elaboration. (*Degrees of Freedom)

5.4.4 Coverage Ratio of Tangible Fixed Assets

It is calculated using the following ratio: tangible fixed assets/shareholders' equity. With the analysis of capital strength, one studies the possibilities of tendential maintenance of financial equilibrium in the non-short term. Table 5.13 proposes the statistical data.

As with the other ratios, few innovative startups have survived the first years of the law. This confirms that the remaining companies have transitioned into innovative small and medium-sized enterprises (SMEs). The data are increasingly homogeneous, consistent, and compact. The variance is significantly lower compared to our previous findings. After the first few years of insignificant residual values, observations increase, and there is a significant convergence toward common values for all groups considered. This makes the average genuinely expressive of the standard trend toward acceptable values.

We proceed with identifying the best interpolating equations (Table 5.14).

Except for the Central Italy macro-region, the chosen and subsequently represented equations express a suitable interpolating curve that is correct to compare with the spline from which it is derived (Fig. 5.7).

It is evident that in the middle of the decade considered, the curves converge toward common values when the numerosity of the observations makes the arithmetic average more significant. An abstract reference value of the ratio could be 1 when equity is the same amount as tangible fixed assets, assuming the absence or rapid amortization of intangible fixed assets and the absence of financial fixed assets. Instead, there is a tendency toward values below 0.5. Probably in the first years of activity, prudent management limits lasting tangible investments.

Across the country's macro-regions, the graphs reveal broadly consistent trends over the past five years, with some notable variations in the initial period. An objective determination requires the ANOVA test (Table 5.15).

A significant F-statistic (more remarkable than the critical F-value) suggests rejection of the null hypothesis in the ANOVA test. We will proceed with a Tukey Kramer test to determine which macro-regions exhibit statistically different profitability ratios.

5.5 The Tukey Kramer Test

The one-way ANOVA test used for the four ratios indicates whether there are statistically significant differences when comparing the macro-areas of the country. It does not, however, specify which differences are statistically significant. This requires the subsequent test, which thus completes the spatial comparisons (Table 5.16).

The test identified a few significant differences. Only one is for the Roi, and two are for the tangible fixed assets coverage ratio. In these three cases, the differences

Table 5.13 Coverage ratio of tangible fixed assets—Descriptive statistics

Year	2013	2014	2015	2016	2017	2018	2019	2020	2021	2022
Italy										
Average	1.69	0.83	0.91	0.63	0.37	0.36	0.33	0.26	0.26	0.25
Standard error	1.31	0.50	0.32	0.16	0.08	0.04	0.03	0.02	0.01	0.01
Median	0.63	0.00	0.00	0.00	0.00	0.00	0.00	0.00	0.00	0.00
Mode	0.00	0.00	0.00	0.00	0.00	0.00	0.00	0.00	0.00	0.00
Standard deviation	2.61	2.05	2.73	2.24	1.79	1.52	1.56	1.24	1.23	1.27
Sample variance	6.83	4.21	7.48	5.03	3.20	2.32	2.44	1.55	1.51	1.61
Kurtosis	2.87	7.57	10.41	13.92	19.72	31.13	36.77	42.14	43.86	41.26
Asymmetry	1.72	2.80	3.20	3.36	2.42	4.24	4.72	4.21	4.44	3.72
Range	5.51	7.52	15.78	18.97	22.25	24.21	24.32	24.86	24.75	24.64
Minimum	0.00	0.00	−2.89	−5.17	−9.87	−9.86	−9.79	−9.94	−9.77	−9.80
Maximum	5.51	7.52	12.89	13.80	12.38	14.35	14.53	14.92	14.98	14.84
Sum	6.76	14.17	66.18	125.47	167.69	470.67	962.16	1253.64	1935.35	2315.53
Observations	4	17	73	200	450	1318	2930	4812	7542	9199
North										
Average				0.00	0.07	0.16	0.26	0.22	0.22	0.19
Standard error				0.00	0.04	0.05	0.04	0.02	0.02	0.02
Median				0.00	0.00	0.00	0.00	0.00	0.00	0.00
Mode				0.00	0.00	0.00	0.00	0.00	0.00	0.00
Standard deviation				0.00	0.18	1.05	1.37	1.18	1.11	1.19
Sample variance				0.00	0.03	1.10	1.87	1.39	1.23	1.42

(continued)

Table 5.13 (continued)

Year	2013	2014	2015	2016	2017	2018	2019	2020	2021	2022
Kurtosis					17.72	42.25	53.43	61.61	48.83	47.19
Asymmetry					4.08	3.00	6.07	5.71	4.75	3.12
Range	0.00	0.00	0.00	0.00	0.84	17.46	21.85	24.86	22.69	24.64
Minimum	0.00	0.00	0.00	0.00	0.00	−8.23	−7.32	−9.94	−9.32	−9.80
Maximum	0.00	0.00	0.00	0.00	0.84	9.23	14.53	14.92	13.37	14.84
Sum	0.00	0.00	0.00	0.00	1.43	60.53	324.12	509.34	826.21	952.01
Observations	0	0	0	3	22	383	1250	2288	3780	4887
Centre										
Average			0.00	−0.14	0.39	0.12	0.20	0.20	0.16	0.24
Standard error			0.00	0.35	0.16	0.03	0.04	0.03	0.02	0.03
Median			0.00	0.00	0.00	0.00	0.00	0.00	0.00	0.00
Mode			0.00	0.00	0.00	0.00	0.00	0.00	0.00	0.00
Standard deviation			0.00	1.43	1.28	0.48	1.00	0.97	0.94	1.16
Sample variance			0.00	2.04	1.63	0.23	1.01	0.95	0.89	1.35
Kurtosis				11.38	20.86	41.26	90.22	48.46	56.09	46.56
Asymmetry				−2.64	4.36	4.91	8.22	5.29	1.66	5.32
Range	0.00	0.00	0.00	7.67	7.76	6.85	17.54	16.49	22.72	20.65
Minimum	0.00	0.00	0.00	−5.17	0.00	−2.19	−4.03	−6.49	−9.77	−6.43
Maximum	0.00	0.00	0.00	2.50	7.76	4.66	13.51	10.00	12.95	14.22
Sum	0.00	0.00	0.00	−2.44	24.28	29.52	114.54	196.51	250.30	464.67
Observations	0	0	2	17	62	252	562	964	1598	1922
South and Islands										

Average	1.69	0.83	0.93	0.71	0.39	0.56	0.47	0.35	0.40	0.38
Standard error	1.31	0.50	0.33	0.17	0.10	0.07	0.06	0.04	0.03	0.03
Median	0.63	0.00	0.00	0.00	0.00	0.00	0.00	0.00	0.00	0.01
Mode	0.00	0.00	0.00	0.00	0.00	0.00	0.00	0.00	0.00	0.00
Standard deviation	2.61	2.05	2.77	2.31	1.91	1.92	1.94	1.46	1.55	1.48
Sample variance	6.83	4.21	7.67	5.34	3.66	3.69	3.76	2.14	2.42	2.20
Kurtosis	2.87	7.57	10.02	13.00	17.66	19.37	21.45	23.73	30.00	30.33
Asymmetry	1.72	2.80	3.14	3.40	2.20	3.53	3.37	2.56	4.18	3.55
Range	5.51	7.52	15.78	17.55	22.25	24.21	23.96	23.12	22.82	23.81
Minimum	0.00	0.00	−2.89	−3.75	−9.87	−9.86	−9.79	−9.80	−7.84	−9.79
Maximum	5.51	7.52	12.89	13.80	12.38	14.35	14.17	13.32	14.98	14.02
Sum	6.76	14.17	66.18	127.91	141.98	380.62	523.50	547.79	858.84	898.85
Observations	4	17	71	180	366	683	1118	1560	2164	2390

Source: our elaboration

Table 5.14 Coverage ratio of tangible fixed assets—Interpolating equation and R^2

Zone	Interpolating equation	R^2
North	$y = 1E{-}05x^6{-}0.1491x^5 + 751.08x^4 - 2E{+}06x^3 + 3E{+}09x^2 - 2E{+}12x + 8E{+}14$	0.9841
Centre	$y = -0.0002x^6 + 2.2426x^5{-}11{,}312x^4 + 3E{+}07x^3 - 5E{+}10x^2 + 4E{+}13x - 1E{+}16$	0.5368
South	$y = 0.0003x^6{-}4.2103x^5 + 21{,}238x^4 - 6E{+}07x^3 + 9E{+}10x^2 - 7E{+}13x + 2E{+}16$	0.9558
Italy	$y = 0.0004x^6{-}4.5408x^5 + 22{,}906x^4 - 6E{+}07x^3 + 9E{+}10x^2 - 8E{+}13x + 3E{+}16$	0.9853

Source: our elaboration

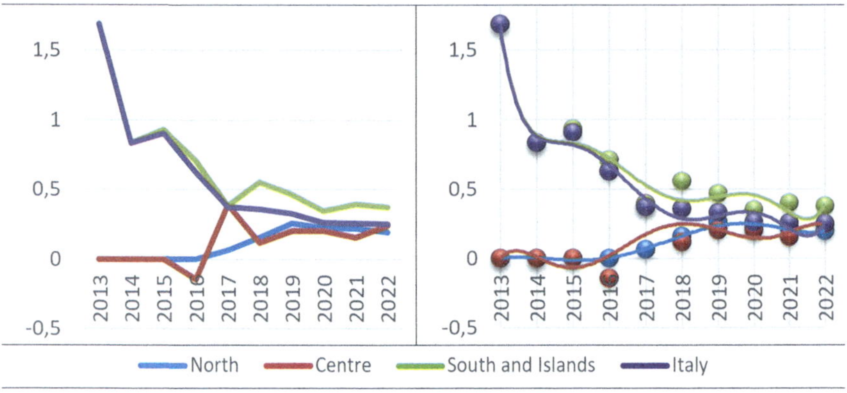

Fig. 5.7 Coverage ratio of tangible fixed assets—The ten-year trend (Source: our elaboration)

Table 5.15 Coverage ratio of tangible fixed assets—One-way ANOVA test

Summary				
Groups	Count	Sum	Media	Variance
North	7	1.11833	0.159761	0.008842
Centre	8	1.17128	0.14641	0.026039
South and Islands	10	6.703812	0.670381	0.170347

Analysis of variance						
Origin of the variation	SQ	DoF*	MQ	*F*	Significance value	*F* crit
Between groups	1.608997	2	0.804498	10.00823	0.000811	3.443357
In groups	1.768442	22	0.080384			
Total	3.377439	24				

Source: our elaboration. (*Degrees of Freedom)

are realistically attributable to values located in the first years of the decade when the observations are numerically modest and the average insignificant. It is, therefore, possible to conclude that the trends of the averages of the analyzed ratios are substantially similar everywhere.

Table 5.16 Tukey Kramer test

	Roe	Roi	Leverage	Coverage ratio of tangible fixed assets
Media North	−4.65811344	−2.925824575	4.968713984	0.159761438
Variance North	16.36139816	6.482276928	4.135472145	0.008841813
n Group North	7	7	7	7
Media Centre	4.691389898	2.56756548	5.118568127	0.146409976
Variance Centre	102.7447362	30.24233887	4.532441716	0.026038905
n Centre	8	8	8	8
South and Island Media	3.361303045	−0.61268537	5.790397645	0.670381174
South and Island Variance	46.87101222	10.31632856	7.814914928	0.17034652
n South and Island	10	10	10	10
N (total number)	25	25	25	25
Group size smallest	7	7	7	7
Number of groups	3	3	3	3
Pooled variance (common)	56.32821147	15.61077231	5.767007238	0.080383723
Degrees of Freedom	22	22	22	22
Q	3.55	3.55	3.55	3.55
Comparison North and Centre				
The average difference between North and Centre	9.349503338	5.493390055	0.149854142	0.013351463
Critical value	10.0702978	5.301411645	3.222215491	0.380420044
	Difference NOT significant	Difference significant	Difference NOT significant	Difference NOT significant
Comparison of North and South and Island				
The average difference between North and South and Island	8.019416485	2.313139204	0.821683661	0.510619736
Critical value	10.0702978	5.301411645	3.222215491	0.380420044
	Difference NOT significant	Difference NOT significant	Difference NOT significant	Difference significant
Comparison Centre and South and Island				
The average difference between Centre and South and Island	1.330086853	3.180250851	0.671829518	0.523971199
Critical value	10.0702978	5.301411645	3.222215491	0.380420044
	Difference NOT significant	Difference NOT significant	Difference NOT significant	Difference significant

Source: our elaboration

5.6 Discussion and Conclusions

The detailed analysis of the evolution of four financial statement ratios of a large sample of Italian innovative startups, supplemented by numerous statistical elaborations, allows us to assess this study's assumptions.

H1 Profitability is permanently positive and high because innovative startups operate in sectors with high added value.

Hypothesis partially confirmed

Despite operating in high value-added sectors, which typically generate substantial profits, many companies exhibit only modest, and sometimes hostile, profitability. This considers both profitability ratios, referring to core and total operations.

Table 5.17 offers a quick comparison of the average trends recorded in the nation.

The Roe fluctuates between an annual average minimum value of around −9.2% in 2013, with only 4 data available to a maximum of just under 5% in 2021 out of 6501 observations. The simple average for the decade is positive but slightly above zero (0.07%). The one weighed with observations is about 1.5%, better but still small. Even worse are the results of the profitability of ordinary operations, which nevertheless have a negative minimum value (−5.3%) in 2013 on similar observations, higher than the minimum value of Roe. On the contrary, the maximum value is only close to 1% in 2021 out of 1315 observations. However, the few observations in the first years of the decade under consideration must be emphasized. However, mitigating the negativity of the judgment does not reduce the disappointment, considering that the weighted average with observations is only 0.3%, positive but derisory. Some favorable notes can be found in the disaggregated and comparative analysis of the macro-regions. Surprisingly, there is a generally positive trend in southern initiatives in an area ordinarily disadvantaged. Only the 2022 result seems to halt a constant and significant trend growth that starts from a minimum of −9.2% in 2013 with only 4 data available to a maximum of about 13% in 2021 with almost 2000 observations recorded for the Roe. In parallel, the Roe is still increasing, albeit with much lower values, becoming positive in 2018. The maximum recorded in 2021 is only 3.2%, with 425 data available. Diametrically opposite results are recorded in Northern Italy, characterized by a consistently negative Roe, with a minimum of −10.5% in 2017 with only 21 data available and a maximum of −0.1% in 2021 with 3166 observations. On the other hand, one can guess that northern innovative startups are more likely to turn into innovative SMEs.

The necessary connection with the dramatic contextual events (pandemics and wars), generating modest and temporary downturns, does not mitigate the judgment.

Table 5.17 Income ratios comparison—Italy

	2013	2014	2015	2016	2017	2018	2019	2020	2021	2022	SA*	WA**
Roe	−9.16	−2.90	1.77	−1.60	0.54	4.09	3.09	2.62	5.00	−2.76	0.069	1.535
Roi	−5.03	−5.27	−2.56	−3.07	−0.24	−0.08	−0.08	−0.12	0.93	−5.03	−1.5	0.302

Source: our elaboration. *SA = Simplified average; **WA = Weighted average

The figure can only be partially justified considering that these are companies in their early years. The assessment should be deepened in continuing their activities after their transformation into innovative small and medium-sized enterprises: only in the medium to long term can the judgment be more articulate and complete.

Interestingly, although these companies' employees, revenue, and total assets have grown over the past ten years, they are still relatively small businesses on average.

Articulated evaluations concerning the sectors could allow comparisons with management outcomes measured by other studies, such as those concerning services (Santarelli & Piergiovanni, 1995), the biopharmaceutical sector (Nosella et al., 2006), or biotechnology (Merlino & Testa, 2011). Future developments of this research are possible.

H2 Positive profitability supports adequate financial and asset balance.

Hypothesis not confirmed

The relationship between internal and external sources worsens over time, almost everywhere.

Table 5.18 offers a quick comparison of the average trends recorded in the nation.

The debt ratio ranges from an annual average of about 2.6 in 2014, with only 4 data available to a high of over 7% in 2019 on 2967 observations. The simple average for the decade is about 5.5; the one weighted with observations is about 6.3, thus worse. No comfort comes from the disaggregated and comparative analysis of the macro-regions because the trend is increasing everywhere, albeit oscillating.

After all, the negativity or modest positivity of incomes could hardly have triggered the beneficial self-financing process in young and, on average, small companies, which takes a long time.

The outcome is surprising, especially since this type of company enjoys numerous benefits that should have favored more balanced assets and financial structures.

The negative assessment is tempered by the results of the last ratio analyzed, suggesting a potential improvement in profitability. It appears that internal sources are more than adequate compared to permanent structures.

The second ratio analyzed records the lowest value in the last year of the decade, 2022, with a value of just over 0.2 out of 9199 observations: the highest in 2015, around 0.9 out of 73 observations. The simple average for ten years is about 0.6, and the weighted average is close to 0.3. However, it must be considered that the ratio refers to tangible assets only, without considering intangible and financial assets. Additional analysis would, therefore, be necessary, even though innovative startups

Table 5.18 Asset ratios comparison—Italy

	2013	2014	2015	2016	2017	2018	2019	2020	2021	2022	SA*	WA**
Leverage	2.86	2.61	8.75	3.08	4.86	7.05	7.23	5.34	5.77	6.98	5.45	6.3
CRTFA***	1.69	0.83	0.91	0.63	0.37	0.36	0.33	0.26	0.26	0.25	0.59	0.28

*SA = Simplified average; **WA = Weighted average; ***Coverage ratio of tangible fixed assets
Source: our elaboration

should be set up to exploit their patentable insights rather than acquire know-how from third parties by incurring depreciable multi-year costs.

The trend assessment should also distinguish the sectors of operation because investments are different in terms of the production processes required. Tangible fixed assets are likely to be small in the first few years, hoping for growth in proportion to the increase in turnover.

Thus, this research seems to confirm some of the perplexities from previous scientific contributions (Briolini, 2016; Del Monte & Scalera, 2001; Colombo & Grilli, 2006). Facilitated financing induced a reduction in equity injections. Facilitated tax policy may also have contributed to this outcome (Giraudo et al., 2019). To be hoped, therefore, is the expansion of microcredit initiatives in the future, making use of past experiences (Shahriar et al., 2015) and insurance contracts that make capital available in case of default (Casagrande & Spallone, 2005).

H3 Financial statement outcomes are affected by the location of production processes.

Hypothesis not confirmed

There is a significant geographic disparity in the distribution of innovative startups across Italy. Over half of them are concentrated in the North (5016). The rest are distributed almost equally between the Centre (2034) and the South (2810), with a slight predominance in the South.

The disaggregated and comparative analysis by regional macro-areas has only occasionally revealed significant differences, mainly due to the few observations in the early years of the decade.

Table 5.19 provides a summary of the quantitative elaborations for spatial comparisons.

The North differs from the Centre and the South and Islands regarding Roi and the coverage ratio of tangible assets. A significant difference between the Centre and the South is also noticeable for this last ratio. There were only three statistically significant differences out of twelve pairwise comparisons.

It would thus seem that geographic location has little impact on the economic-financial performance of innovative startups, presumably because the concentrated sectors are relatively independent of the socio-economic context close to the registered office.

Table 5.19 Spatial comparisons

	ANOVA			Tukey Kramer	
Ratio	*F*	*F* Critic	Differences	First difference	Second difference
Roe	3.386737	3.443357	No	None	None
Roi	3.681552	3.443357	Yes	North and Centre	None
Leverage	0.293488	3.443357	No	None	None
Coverage of tangible fixed assets	10.00823	3.443357	Yes	North and South and Island	Centre and South and Island

Source: our elaboration

However, it must also be considered that many company services or products are often placed in areas other than production areas. In such a case, the corporate legal residence is an insignificant parameter concerning the proposed analyses. Except for a more in-depth analysis disaggregated by sectors, this general assessment would seem to contrast with studies that have emphasized, on the contrary, the importance of the external macro context (already Powell et al., 1996), at least for some production segments. Limited to the profiles investigated in this study, the prominence of local factors associated with the emergence of innovative startups, such as the activity of large companies, the presence of universities (Ghio et al., 2016; Bikse et al., 2018), local politics (Capozza et al., 2018), etc., seems relatively reduced. Managers should be assigned the task of exploring possible areas of enhancement of local relationships, perhaps excessively sacrificed, by enhancing access to immediately accessible resources such as support networks and infrastructures that could be useful for improving internal and external efficiency (Feldman & Francis, 2004; Audretsch & Keilbach, 2007).

A comparison with similar analyses referring to 2014–2017 (Migliaccio & Pavone, 2021a) is possible and valuable. This prior study utilized a considerably smaller sample size of 3821 innovative startups, representing just over a third of the current dataset. The prior study identified a trend of rising profitability, which is at odds with the findings of this research. This discrepancy could be due to the inclusion of smaller companies in the current, more comprehensive data set. However, the North showed a low and sometimes negative Roi. The internal and external resource relationship analysis yielded results like those of the previous study, revealing modest company capitalization. However, this research identified a more significant deterioration in capitalization than in earlier findings.

The main limitation of this study is its almost exclusively quantitative nature, based on data from financial statements. Another significant limitation is that the analysis independent of the sector uses only location as a disaggregation parameter.

Incorporating a more comprehensive range of financial ratios would be beneficial to gain a more comprehensive understanding of company performance. Additionally, following the approach suggested by Nicolò (2017), Nicolò and Nania (2017), and Nicolò and Ricca (2019), a trend analysis of these ratios by company cohorts would provide valuable insights. This methodology aligns with the work of Migliaccio and Pavone (2021b).

In addition to accounting data, qualitative parameters should be incorporated to facilitate interdisciplinary evaluations, particularly concerning employment and social development. This approach aligns with Piccarozzi (2017), who analyzed the relationship between social innovation and sustainability.

Everywhere, it would indeed be necessary to integrate sustainability issues into corporate strategies (Elkington, 1997; Schaltegger et al., 2016) to improve the startup's reputation and attract investors sensitive to ESG (Environmental, Social, and Governance) issues. Sustainable and circular economy choices could also facilitate partnerships with institutional actors, especially public institutions and trade associations that advocate sustainable growth logic.

Furthermore, in-depth studies examining the potential correlations between quantitative financial data and the quality of human capital (Grajkowska, 2011; Furlan, 2019) would be valuable. Such analyses should also consider evaluations linking profitability, financial stability, organizational well-being (Tognazzo & Mazzurana, 2017; Presenza et al., 2019), and physical health (Lee, 2016).

The proposed method, however, has the merit of being rigorous and interdisciplinary. It also facilitates valid temporal and spatial comparisons of the individual production unit to assess its distance from the sector average according to the benchmarking logic, identifying improvement areas and innovation opportunities. The data collected can thus serve as a helpful reference for revising corporate strategies, setting growth targets, and evaluating performance (Camp, 1989; Latham & Locke, 2007; Hunold et al., 2024). In an environment characterized by economic volatility and uncertainty, this study also provides adequate stimuli to address the challenge of growth and scalability in a competitive market (Ries, 2011; Blank & Dorf, 2012). Indeed, the research shows a significant increase in company size in terms of employees and turnover, but with modest profitability and excessive debt. Companies should, therefore, focus on new hypotheses for sustainable growth strategies, balancing rapid expansion with profitability and rebalancing external and internal sources, mitigating plausible financial strains. Therefore, leadership must emphasize managerial guidelines and those related to production assets without neglecting the ability to manage more significant and complex teams. Greater attention to capital balances should be focused everywhere on the efficient use of working capital to reduce dependence on external financing and strengthen financial resilience. Diversification of capital sources, exploring alternatives such as venture capital, crowdfunding, etc., can be helpful for this purpose (Kaplan & Strömberg, 2009; Cumming & Zambelli, 2013). Pandemic crises and wars have had little effect. Startups, therefore, seem to have an appreciable capacity to adapt to adversity (Teece et al., 1997; Hamel & Välikangas, 2003). Managers should enhance this natural aptitude by internalizing it in their strategies and planning to reshape their ability to adapt to new economic or political crises. To this end, business continuity plans, diversification of target markets, and adoption of even more innovative technologies, including digital and artificial intelligence technologies, could be helpful.

It is, however, above all, public authorities that draw helpful information from studies concerning possible policies for promoting social forms of this kind.

Furthermore, it is crucial to consider the potential for exporting these innovative startups. These Italian entrepreneurial models hold significant promise for successful replication in international markets.

References

Audretsch, D. B., & Keilbach, M. (2007). The theory of knowledge spillover entrepreneurship. *Journal of Management Studies, 44*(7), 1242–1254. https://doi.org/10.1111/j.1467-6486.2007.00722.x

Audretsch, D. B., Santarelli, E., & Vivarelli, M. (1999). Startup size and industrial dynamics: Some evidence from Italian manufacturing. *International Journal of Industrial Organization, 17*(7), 965–983. https://doi.org/10.1016/s0167-7187(98)00002-2

Bergamante, F. (Ed.). (2016). *Crisi economica e squilibri territoriali una lettura multidimensionale dei contesti regionali*. Isfol-Istituto per lo sviluppo della formazione professionale dei lavoratori.

Bianchi, R., Favretto, C., & Ragno, M. (2021). *Le start up innovative*. Maggioli, Sant'Arcangelo di Romagna.

Bikse, V., Lusena-Ezera, I., & Rivza, B. (2018). Innovative startups: Challenges and development opportunities in Latvia. *International Journal of Innovation Science, 10*(2), 261–273. https://doi.org/10.1108/ijis-05-2017-0044

Blackburn, R., Carey, P., & Tanewski, G. (2018). Business advice by accountants to SMEs: Relationships and trust. *Qualitative Research in Accounting and Management, 15*(3), 358–384. https://doi.org/10.1108/qram-04-2017-0022

Blackburn, R. A., Hart, M., & Wainwright, T. (2013). Small business performance: Business, strategy and owner manager characteristics. *Journal of Small Business and Enterprise Development, 20*(1), 8–27. https://doi.org/10.1108/14626001311298394

Blank, S., & Dorf, B. (2012). *The startup owner's manual: The step-by-step guide for building a great company*. K & S Ranch.

Briolini, F. (2016). Patent ownership, sale of the company and cof the enterprise in the Italian «startup innovative» and «pMI innovative» decrees. *Osservatorio del Diritto Civile e Commerciale, 5*(2), 465–482.

Brownlees, T. (2017). *La tua band è una start up. Quando fare musica significa fare impresa*. Phasar.

Bruna, M. G., & Nicolò, D. (2020). Corporate reputation and social sustainability in the early stages of startups: A theoretical model to match stakeholders' expectations through corporate social commitment. *Finance Research Letters, 35*, 101508. https://doi.org/10.1016/j.frl.2020.101508

Camp, R. C. (1989). *Benchmarking: The search for industry best practices that lead to superior performance*. ASQC Quality Press.

Campagnoli, G. (2019). *Riusiamo l'Italia. Da spazi vuoti a start-up culturali e sociali*. Il Sole 24 Ore, Milano.

Capone, F., & Innocenti, N. (2023). *Innovazione, Startup Innovative e Industria 4.0. Aspetti teorici ed evidenze empiriche*. Franco Angeli, Milano.

Capozza, C., Salomone, S., & Somma, E. (2018). Local industrial structure, agglomeration economies and the creation of innovative startups: Evidence from the Italian case. *Entrepreneurship and Regional Development, 30*(7–8), 749–775. https://doi.org/10.1080/08985626.2018.1457087

Cardoni, A., Dumay, J., Palmaccio, M., & Celenza, D. (2019). Knowledge transfer in a startup craft brewery. *Business Process Management Journal, 25*(1), 219–243. https://doi.org/10.1108/bpmj-07-2017-0205

Carraro, W. B. W. H., Meneses, R., & Brito, C. (2019). Combining categories of management control tools for high performance of startups. *Review of Business Management, 21*(4), 861–868. https://doi.org/10.7819/rbgn.v21i5.4022

Casagrande, A., & Spallone, M. (2005). Relaxing liquidity constraints for startups: A welfare analysis over the Italian revised corporate law. *European Journal of Law and Economics, 20*(3), 339–357. https://doi.org/10.1007/s10657-005-4200-1

Caselli, S. (2018). Da start-up a scale-up: è tempo di cambiare narrative. *Economia & Management, 2*, 85–90.

Cassandro, D. (2016). *Il latinorum delle startup*. From the site: internazionale.it (accessed 13 June 2019).

Colombelli, A. (2016). The impact of local knowledge bases on the creation of innovative start-ups in Italy. *Small Business Economics, 47*(2), 383–396. https://doi.org/10.1007/s11187-016-9722-0

Colombo, M. G., Delmastro, M., & Grilli, L. (2004). Entrepreneurs' human capital and the startup size of new technology-based firms. *International Journal of Industrial Organization, 22*(8–9), 1183–1211. https://doi.org/10.1016/j.ijindorg.2004.06.006

Colombo, M. G., & Grilli, L. (2006). Supporting high-tech startups: Lessons from Italian technology policy. *International Entrepreneurship and Management Journal, 2*(2), 189–209. https://doi.org/10.1007/s11365-006-8684-0

Confimprenditori – Centro Studi. (2016). *Startup: Tanto rumore per nulla?* From the site: su confimprenditori.it (accessed 13 June 2019).
Corsi, C. (2018). *Il trasferimento tecnologico tramite gli spin-off universitari. Caratteri, modelli e approcci manageriali*. Giappichelli.
Corsi, C., De Luca, F., & Prencipe, A. (2019). What startup firms are more likely to obtain public funding support? A systematic analysis of the funding program promoted by the Abruzzo Region in Italy. *Contributions to Management Science*, 291–312. https://doi.org/10.1007/978-3-030-19685-1_13.
Corvello, V., Felicetti, A. M., Ammirato, S., Troise, C., & Ključnikov, A. (2024). The rules of courtship: What drives a startup to collaborate with a large company? *Technological Forecasting and Social Change, 200*, 123092. https://doi.org/10.1016/j.techfore.2023.123092
Crespo, N. F., Rodrigues, R., Samagaio, A., & Silva, G. M. (2019). The adoption of management control systems by startups: Internal factors and context as determinants. *Journal of Business Research, 101*, 875–884. https://doi.org/10.1016/j.jbusres.2018.11.020
Cumming, D. J., & Zambelli, S. (2013). *Private equity and venture capital in Europe: Markets, techniques, and deals*. Elsevier.
D'Epiro, A. (2018). *Donne che creano impresa. Il mondo «beauty»: scopri come realizzare la tua start-up attraverso la storia di chi ce l'ha fatta*. Infinito, Formigine.
Davila, A., Foster, G., & Jia, N. (2015). The valuation of management control systems in startup companies: International field-based evidence. *European Accounting Review, 24*(2), 207–239. https://doi.org/10.1080/09638180.2014.965720
De Blasio, V., Pavone, P., & Migliaccio, G. (2022). Cosmetics companies: Income developments in time of crisis. *Journal of Small Business and Enterprise Development, 29*(7), 1017–1048. https://doi.org/10.1108/JSBED-11-2019-0369
De Massis, A., Minola, T., & Viviani, D. (2012). Entrepreneurial learning in Italian high-tech startups: An exploratory study. *International Journal of Innovation and Learning, 11*(1), 94–114. https://doi.org/10.1504/ijil.2012.044331
De Stefanis, C. (2017). *Startup innovative. Come costituire e modificare on line un atto costitutivo di start-up srl senza notaio*. Fisco e Tasse – Maggioli, Sant'Arcangelo di Romagna, Italia.
Del Monte, A., & Scalera, D. (2001). The life duration of small firms born within a startup programme: Evidence from Italy. *Regional Studies, 35*(1), 11–21. https://doi.org/10.1080/00343400120025646
Del Sarto, N., Isabelle, D. A., & Di Minin, A. (2019). The role of accelerators in firm survival: An fsQCA analysis of Italian startups. *Technovation*, 102102. https://doi.org/10.1016/j.technovation.2019.102102
Delerue, H., & Lejeune, A. (2011). Internationalisation of biotechnology startups: Geographic location and mimetic behaviour. *International Small Business Journal, 30*(4), 388–405. https://doi.org/10.1177/0266242611402565
Dodaro, M. (2023). *Unpacking the 'startup city'. Entrepreneurship, neoliberal governance and local actors agency*. Palgrave Macmillan. https://doi.org/10.1007/978-3-031-50212-5
Draebye, M. (2019). *Startup entrepreneurship. The smart way*. Bocconi University Press, Milano.
Elkington, J. (1997). *Cannibals with forks: The triple bottom line of 21st century business*. Capstone.
Errico, F., Messeni Petruzzelli, A., Panniello, U., & Scialpi, A. (2024). Source of funding and specialised competences: The impact on the innovative performance of startups. *Journal of Knowledge Management, 28*(2), 564–589. https://doi.org/10.1108/jkm-11-2022-0928
Feldman, M. P., & Francis, J. (2004). Homegrown solutions: Fostering cluster formation. *Economic Development Quarterly, 18*(2), 127–137. https://doi.org/10.1177/0891242403262556
Filion, L. J., Brenner, G. A., Ramangalahy, C., & Menzies, T. V. (2003). Démarrage d'entreprises par les chinois, italiens et sikhs au Canada: Quelques résultats empiriques. *Journal of Small Business and Entrepreneurship, 16*(3–4), 41–65. https://doi.org/10.1080/08276331.2003.10593307

Fini, R., Grimaldi, R., & Sobrero, M. (2009). Factors fostering academics to start up new ventures: An assessment of Italian founders' incentives. *Journal of Technology Transfer, 34*(4), 380–402. https://doi.org/10.1007/s10961-008-9093-z

Franceschelli, M. V., Santoro, G., & Candelo, E. (2018). Business model innovation for sustainability: A food startup case study. *British Food Journal, 120*(10), 2483–2494. https://doi.org/10.1108/bfj-01-2018-0049

Fregonara, E. (2013). *La start up innovativa. Uno sguardo all'evoluzione del sistema societario e delle forme di finanziamento*. Giuffrè, Milano.

Furlan, A. (2019). Startup size and pre-entry experience: New evidence from Italian new manufacturing ventures. *Journal of Small Business Management, 57*(2), 679–692. https://doi.org/10.1111/jsbm.12427

Ghio, N., Guerini, M., & Rossi-Lamastra, C. (2016). University knowledge and the creation of innovative startups: An analysis of the Italian case. *Small Business Economics, 47*(2), 293–311. https://doi.org/10.1007/s11187-016-9720-2

Giraudo, E., Giudici, G., & Grilli, L. (2019). Entrepreneurship policy and the financing of young innovative companies: Evidence from the Italian Startup Act. *Research Policy, 48*(9), 103801. https://doi.org/10.1016/j.respol.2019.05.010

Grajkowska, A. (2011). Valuing intellectual capital of innovative startups. *Journal of Intellectual Capital, 12*(2), 179–201. https://doi.org/10.1108/14691931111123386

Greco, F., & Tregua, M. (2022). It gives you wheels: The university-based accelerators in startup ecosystems. *International Journal of Entrepreneurship and Small Business, 45*(2), 235–257. https://doi.org/10.1504/ijesb.2022.10045152

Grilli, L. (2019). There must be an angel? Local financial markets, business angels and the financing of innovative startups. *Regional Studies, 53*(5), 620–629. https://doi.org/10.1080/00343404.2018.1479524

Gu, C. (2013). *Smoothing spline ANOVA models* (2nd ed.). Springer.

Hamel, G., & Välikangas, L. (2003). The quest for resilience. *Harvard Business Review, 81*(9), 52–63.

Hand, C., Iskandarova, M., & Blackburn, R. (2020). Founders' social identity and entrepreneurial self-efficacy amongst nascent entrepreneurs: A configurational perspective. *Journal of Business Venturing Insights, 13*, e00160. https://doi.org/10.1016/j.jbvi.2020.e00160

Hunold, S., Xie, B., & Shu, K. (Eds.). (2024). *Benchmarking, measuring, and optimising*. Springer Nature. https://doi.org/10.1007/978-981-97-0316-6

Iazzolino, G., De Carolis, M., & Clemeno, P. (2019). Energy innovative startups and knowledge-based strategies: The Italian case. *International Journal of Energy Economics and Policy, 9*(5), 88–102. https://doi.org/10.32479/ijeep.7926

Innocenti, N., & Zampi, V. (2019). What does a startup need to grow? An empirical approach for Italian innovative startups. *International Journal of Entrepreneurial Behavior & Research, 25*(2), 376–393. https://doi.org/10.1108/ijebr-04-2018-0194

Kaplan, S. N., & Strömberg, P. (2009). Leveraged buyouts and private equity. *Journal of Economic Perspectives, 23*(1), 121–146. https://doi.org/10.1257/jep.23.1.121

Kramer, C. Y. (1956). Extension of multiple range tests to group means with unequal numbers of replications. *Biometrics, 12*(3), 307–310. https://doi.org/10.2307/3001469

Latham, G. P., & Locke, E. A. (2007). *New developments in goal setting and task performance*. Routledge.

Lee, Y. S. (2016). Creative workplace characteristics and innovative startup companies. *Facilities, 34*(7/8), 413–432. https://doi.org/10.1108/f-06-2014-0054

Leonelli, S., & Jalal, R.N.-U.-D. (In Press). Will my startup survive? The effect of entrepreneurs' manipulative narcissism and cultural factors on startups' survival. *Global Business Review*. https://doi.org/10.1177/09721509231219082

Liao, Q., & Li, J. (2018). *An adaptive reduced basis ANOVA method for high-dimensional Bayesian inverse problems*. arXiv:1811.05151 [math.NA].

Lukeš, M., Longo, M. C., & Zouhar, J. (2019). Do business incubators really enhance entrepreneurial growth? Evidence from a large sample of innovative Italian startups. *Technovation, 82–83*, 25–34. https://doi.org/10.1016/j.technovation.2018.07.008

Marasà, G. (2019). *Imprese sociali, altri enti del terzo settore, società benefit*. Giappichelli.

Marrapodi, R. (2023). 8 Managing conflicts to improve performance in start-ups: A theoretical analysis. In D. Matricano, L. Castaldi, W. Jackson III, & L. Marino (Eds.), *Entrepreneurial processes in the era of digital transformation* (pp. 129–144). De Gruyter. https://doi.org/10.1515/9783110790313-009

Matricano, D. (2020). Higher education and startup intentions: The role of intellectual capital in entrepreneurial processes. *Industry and Higher Education, 34*(1), 48–59. https://doi.org/10.1177/0950422219886259

Matricano, D. (2024). The influence of the technological regime on the performance of Italian innovative startups. *Technology Analysis and Strategic Management, 36*(5), 902–915. https://doi.org/10.1080/09537325.2022.2065978

Mauro, M. (2024). *Start-up e PMI innovative in agricoltura. Imprese agricole tra innovazione e sostenibilità*. Cedam, Padova.

Merlino, M., & Testa, S. (2011). Knowledge creation and management in an Italian Biotech Startup. In A. Fayolle & K. Todorov (Eds.), *European entrepreneurship in the globalizing economy* (pp. 143–155). Edward Elgar. https://doi.org/10.4337/9781849808224.00014

Meyssonnier, F. (2015). Quel contrôle de gestion pour les start-ups? *Comptabilité Contrôle Audit, 21*(2), 33–61. https://doi.org/10.3917/cca.212.0033

Migliaccio, G., & De Blasio, V. (2024). The Italian plastics industries toward a plastic-free society: What possible strategies? *World Review of Entrepreneurship, Management and Sustainable Development, 20*(2), 179–218. https://doi.org/10.1504/wremsd.2024.10061683

Migliaccio, G., & De Palma, A. (2024). Profitability and financial performance of Italian real estate companies: Quantitative profiles. *International Journal of Productivity and Performance Management, 73*(11), 122–160. https://doi.org/10.1108/IJPPM-02-2023-0075

Migliaccio, G., & Pavone, P. (2021a). Innovative small startups in Italy: A successful business model? *International Journal of Management and Enterprise Development, 20*(4), 405–455. https://doi.org/10.1504/ijmed.2021.119525

Migliaccio, G., & Pavone, P. (2021b). Italian innovative startup cohorts: An empirical survey on profitability. In C. Bevilacqua, F. Calabrò, & L. D. Spina (Eds.), *New metropolitan perspectives – Knowledge dynamics and innovation-driven policies towards urban and regional transition* (Vol. 2, pp. 834–843). Springer Nature. https://doi.org/10.1007/978-3-030-48279-4_78

Migliaccio, G., & Pavone, P. (2024). Innovativeness in the economic system: The Italian experience. *International Journal of Business Innovation and Research, 34*(1), 109–138. https://doi.org/10.1504/ijbir.2024.138141

Minola, T., Hahn, D., & Cassia, L. (2021). The relationship between origin and performance of innovative startups: The role of technological knowledge at founding. *Small Business Economics, 56*(2), 553–569. https://doi.org/10.1007/s11187-019-00189-y

Mise. (2019). *Ministero dello Sviluppo Economico. La policy del Governo a sostegno delle startup innovative*. Ministero dello Sviluppo Economico, Roma.

Nadotti, L. L. M., Gallo, M., & Martelli, D. (2023). *Il finanziamento delle start-up innovative*. Isedi.

Nicolò, D. (2017). Young firms sustainability and corporate reputation: A comparison of the survival rates in the US and EU. In A. J. Vasile & D. Nicolò (Eds.), *Sustainable entrepreneurship and investments in the green economy* (pp. 1–27). IGI Global. https://doi.org/10.4018/978-1-5225-2075-7.ch001

Nicolò, D., & Nania, I. (2017). Risk, capitalisation and survival of young firms: Empirical survey on Italian companies. *Diem – Dubrovnik International Economic Meeting, 3*(1), 2–15.

Nicolò, D., & Ricca, B. (2019). Under-capitalisation and other factors that influence the survival of young Italian companies. *International Journal of Advances in Management and Economics, 8*(2), 37–51.

Nosella, A., Petroni, G., & Verbano, C. (2006). Innovation development in biopharmaceutical startup firms: An Italian case study. *Journal of Engineering and Technology Management – JETM, 23*(3), 202–220. https://doi.org/10.1016/j.jengtecman.2006.06.005

Onesti, G., Monaco, E., & Palumbo, R. (2022). Assessing the Italian innovative startups performance with a composite index. *Administrative Sciences, 12*(4), 189. https://doi.org/10.3390/admsci12040189

Pais, I., Peretti, P., & Spinelli, C. (2018). *Crowdfunding. La via collaborativa all'imprenditorialità.* Egea, Milano.

Peruffo, E., Franco, S., Cappa, F., & Pinelli, M. (2018). Competenze dei fondatori e performance delle start-up: Un'analisi empirica. *Piccola impresa, 1*, 59–80.

Piccarozzi, M. (2017). Does social innovation contribute to sustainability? The case of Italian innovative startups. *Sustainability (Switzerland), 9*(12), 2376. https://doi.org/10.3390/su9122376

Powell, W. W., Koput, K. W., & Smith-Doerr, L. (1996). Interorganizational collaboration and the locus of innovation: Networks of learning in biotechnology. *Administrative Science Quarterly, 41*(1), 116–145. https://doi.org/10.2307/2393988

Presenza, A., Abbate, T., Meleddu, M., & Sheehan, L. (2019). Startup entrepreneurs' personality traits. An exploratory analysis of the Italian tourism industry. *Current Issues in Tourism, 23*(17), 2146–2164. https://doi.org/10.1080/13683500.2019.1677572

Ricci, S. (2015). *Social startup.* Maggioli, Sant'Arcangelo di Romagna.

Ries, E. (2011). *The lean startup: How today's entrepreneurs use continuous innovation to create radically successful businesses.* Crown Business.

Rippa, P., Ponsiglione, C., Bocanet, A., Capaldo, G., & Zollo, G. (2019). Do new ventures explore, exploit or both? A case-based analysis of six innovative Italian startups. *International Journal of Entrepreneurial Behavior & Research, 25*(7), 1515–1536. https://doi.org/10.1108/ijebr-12-2018-0817

Rosapepe, F. P. (2023). *Prodotti e start up innovative. Calcolo del loro valore commerciale.* Youcanprint, Tricase.

Ross, A., & Willson, V. L. (2017). One-way ANOVA. In A. Ross & V. L. Willson (Eds.), *Basic and advanced statistical tests* (pp. 21–24). Sense Publishers.

Santarelli, E. (1998). Startup size and post-entry performance: The case of tourism services in Italy. *Applied Economics, 30*(2), 157–163. https://doi.org/10.1080/000368498325967

Santarelli, E., & Piergiovanni, R. (1995). The determinants of firm startup and entry in Italian producer services. *Conference: 20th Annual E A R I E Conference Location: Tel Aviv, Israel,* SEP. 04-07, 1993. Small Business Economics, 7(3), 221–230. https://doi.org/10.1007/bf01135367

Scagnelli, S., Vasile, L., & Apostolov, M. (2019). Survival drivers of post-incubated startUPS: The effect of academic governance. *International Journal of Innovation Management, 23*(7), 1950062. https://doi.org/10.1142/s1363919619500622

Schaltegger, S., Lüdeke-Freund, F., & Hansen, E. G. (2016). Business models for sustainability: A co-evolutionary analysis of sustainable entrepreneurship, innovation, and transformation. *Organization & Environment, 29*(3), 264–289. https://doi.org/10.1177/1086026616633272

Shahriar, A. Z. M., Schwarz, S., & Newman, A. (2015). Profit orientation of microfinance institutions and provision of financial capital to business startups. *International Small Business Journal, 34*(4), 532–552. https://doi.org/10.1177/0266242615570401

Shinnar, R. S., Hsu, D. K., Powell, B. C., & Zhou, H. (2017). Entrepreneurial intentions and start-ups: Are women or men more likely to enact their intentions? *International Small Business Journal, 36*(1), 60–80. https://doi.org/10.1177/0266242617704277

Smeriglio, M. (2019). *L'impresa sociale, l'anima e le forme. Cooperazione, empowerment, territorio.* Anicia.

Taylor, D., King, R., & Smith, D. (2019). Management controls, heterarchy and innovation: A case study of a startup company. *Accounting, Auditing and Accountability Journal, 32*(6), 1636–1661. https://doi.org/10.1108/aaaj-11-2017-3208

Teece, D. J., Pisano, G., & Shuen, A. (1997). Dynamic capabilities and strategic management. *Strategic Management Journal, 18*(7), 509–533. https://doi.org/10.1002/(SICI)1097-0266(199708)18:7<509::AID-SMJ882>3.0.CO;2-Z

Tognazzo, A., & Mazzurana, P. A. M. (2017). Friends doing business. An explorative longitudinal case study of creativity and innovation in an Italian technology-based startup. *Journal of Entrepreneurship Management and Innovation, 13*(2), 77–103. https://doi.org/10.7341/20171324

Tukey, J. W. (1949). Comparing individual means in the analysis of variance. *Biometrics, 5*(2), 99–114. https://doi.org/10.2307/3001913

Tukey, J. W. (1953). The problem of multiple comparisons. Unpublished manuscript, in The Collected Works of John W Tukey VIII. *Multiple Comparisons: 1948–1983*. Chapman and Hall, New York.

Tukey, J. W. (1993). Where should multiple comparisons go next? In F. M. Hoppe (Ed.), *Multiple comparisons, selection, and applications in biometry* (pp. 187–207). Dekker.

Ulijn, J., Aaltio, I., Guerra, G., & Uhlaner, L. (2011). Cooperation and teamwork in technology startups: Reflected in some Italian, British, Dutch and German findings. *International Journal of Entrepreneurship and Small Business, 14*(1), 100–126. https://doi.org/10.1504/ijesb.2011.042165

Urso, A. (2023). *Relazione Annuale al Parlamento sullo stato di attuazione delle policy in favore delle startup e PMI innovative*. Ministero delle Imprese e del Made in Italy.

Venturi, P., & Zandonai, F. (2016). *Imprese ibride. Modelli d'innovazione sociale per rigenerare valore*. Egea, Milano.

Visconti, F. (Ed.). (2016). *Start up! 25 anni di università e impresa*. Guerini Next.

Zhou, Z., & Verburg, R. (2020). Open for business: The impact of creative team environment and innovative behaviour in technology-based startups. *International Small Business Journal: Researching Entrepreneurship, 38*(4), 318–336. https://doi.org/10.1177/0266242619892793

Chapter 6
Human Capital Qualification and Resilience of High-growth Start-ups (Gazelles). COVID-19 as a Natural Experiment

Domenico Nicolò and Bruno Ricca

6.1 Introduction

In the early stage, companies are very vulnerable. High-growth start-ups, also known as gazelle enterprises, are also very fragile, despite having gained a competitive advantage early in their lives that enabled them to grow rapidly into gazelles. Like mature high-growth firms, which are in the latter stages of their lives, these gazelles can suffer setbacks in their growth and even go into crisis and cease to exist (Garnsey & Heffernan, 2005). This is because rapid growth strains managerial, financial, and knowledge resources (Penrose, 1959). High-growth start-ups face a double challenge: the difficulties typical of the early stage of any enterprise and those of rapid growth.

The literature on business growth crisis is extensive and has attracted scholarly interest since the second half of the last century (Greiner, 1989; Lewis & Churchill, 1983; Chandler Jr, 1969). Only recently has the literature begun to study various aspects of fast-growing start-ups (Jansen et al., 2023). However, few studies have focused on the growth crisis of new ventures (Garnsey, 1998; Garnsey & Heffernan, 2005), while studies that focus on the resources that favour their survival are lacking.

To help fill this gap in the literature, we hypothesize a positive relationship between the endowment of human capital and intangible assets and the survival of gazelles. To test this hypothesis, we observed gazelles born in Italy in 2014 and

D. Nicolò (✉)
Department of Law, Economics and Human Sciences, University Mediterranea of Reggio Calabria, Reggio Calabria, Italy
e-mail: domenico.nicolo@unirc.it

B. Ricca
Department of Economics, University of Messina, Messina, Italy
e-mail: bricca@unime.it

S. Loprevite et al. (eds.), *Startups and Gazelle Enterprises*, SIDREA Series in Accounting and Business Administration,
https://doi.org/10.1007/978-3-031-90881-1_6

belonging to the 2014–2019 5-year cohort in the 2020–2022 3-year period following the attainment of gazelle status. The gazelle observation period coincides with an extraordinary event: the COVID-19 pandemic spread, which challenged the survival of all companies, not only that of high-growth start-ups. Thus, the pandemic was used as a natural experiment.

Focusing on some factors that contribute to the resilience of high-growth start-ups in the face of ordinary challenges, as well as external pressures from extraordinary critical events such as pandemics, has relevant practical implications. On the one hand, it helps founders create more resilient start-ups; on the other hand, it provides useful insights for policymakers to develop effective policies to support the survival of start-ups and high-growth companies, even in times of crisis.

6.2 Theoretical Background

Start-ups are highly vulnerable and many fail in the early stages after start-up (Nicolò, 2019; Knaup & Piazza, 2007; Audretsch & Mahmood, 1995). According to OECD data (OECD, 2003), about 20–40% of firms fail within the first 2 years, while only 40–50% survive beyond the seventh year (Bartelsman et al., 2005). This trend occurs in different countries at different periods, highlighting that a high probability of failure is a common feature of young firms, regardless of the context in which they operate and the trend of the business cycle (Nicolò, 2019).

Lack of reputation is a common vulnerability trait among start-ups. Start-ups lack a history and financial statements demonstrating their ability to meet their commitments to stakeholders, such as lenders, suppliers, customers, and employees. As a result, they struggle to establish strong bonds of trust with these stakeholders. Fragile trust relationships can easily break down when the company faces difficulties, leading stakeholders to not provide the company with the necessary resources. This can lead to a crisis due to the lack of essential human, technical, and financial resources (Bruna & Nicolò, 2020).

Most start-ups are small and often have the weaknesses common to small businesses, such as higher costs and lower efficiency than larger companies. The characteristics of the founders or co-founders, including risk tolerance, perseverance, education, competence, skill, and experience, can also influence the ability to cope with early stage challenges. In the early years, companies may face challenges such as conflicts among co-founders, planning errors related to demand or capacity estimation, financing, and other problems (Nicolò, 2017, 2019).

Many new businesses that survive the early stage remain small, while few experience high growth rates (Jansen et al., 2023; Gilbert et al., 2006; Garnsey & Heffernan, 2005; Audretsch, 1994). In the US, only 3.5% of new businesses become large companies (Acs & Armington, 2006; Mata, 1994). In Italy, only 1.2% of enterprises become high-growth enterprises in the initial stage (ISTAT, 2022).

Even successful gazelles can experience growth setbacks and fail. Scholars have not thoroughly explored the reasons for growth setbacks and subsequent crises experienced by early stage firms (Garnsey & Heffernan, 2005). However, some studies have highlighted the problems that young firms often face during growth phases. The first challenge they face is to attract investment because their future is uncertain (Penrose, 1955). Although their business model is promising, they use advanced technologies and sell innovative products, a high percentage of start-ups fail because they do not have the capital needed to sustain growth (Barkham et al., 2012; Garnsey & Heffernan, 2005). Young companies lack adequate market knowledge and are unable to adapt to changing customer needs (Garnsey & Heffernan, 2005). This can lead to under-utilization of production capacity (Garnsey, 1998) or setbacks in growth (Okrah & Nepp, 2018; Garnsey & Heffernan, 2005).

High growth can trigger a crisis because it saturates the resources available to the company. Especially in the start-up phase, in which they are small and have a modest endowment of resources. All other conditions being equal, we expect that the greater the endowment of distinctive, precious, and inimitable resources is, the longer the start-ups can sustain their competitive advantage and growth (Birley, 1987; Barney, 1991; Cooper et al., 1994). We refer to physical, human (Burvill et al., 2018), and organizational capital (Barney, 1991).

To demonstrate this hypothesis, we assume that the qualification of human capital, in terms of the ability to create value-added, positively affects the survival of these high-growth start-ups. This hypothesis is also based on the evidence of two of our previous research demonstrating the positive impact of human capital on the growth of gazelles in Italy. The first study found that human capital fosters the growth of gazelles operating in the third sector (Cattafi et al., 2023), while the second article demonstrated that investments in intangible assets and human capital positively contribute to gazelles' Enterprise Value (EV) (Cattafi et al., 2024).

Based on this research, we hypothesize that human capital (Eklund & Van Criekingen, 2022; Eklund, 2020) plays a positive role in the survival of gazelles. In line with this hypothesis, we pose the following research question: does human capital qualification positively influence the survival of gazelles?

Since young businesses often must wait a long time to acquire customers and achieve market goals, they risk going into crisis due to a lack of cash. This is especially true for fast-growing companies, which quickly burn money. Therefore, we also control liquidity (measured through the current ratio). We also control for other variables affecting the survival of businesses in general and gazelles in particular: intangible assets, financial risk (leveraged), operational risk, geographical area, and industry.

We observed gazelle firms in the 3 years following their achievement of gazelle status to test whether human capital plays a positive role in their survival. We have already said that these high-growth start-ups are under a lot of stress on their resources due to their high growth.

In the 3 years we studied, these gazelles were exposed to an extraordinary external shock of considerable magnitude: the COVID-19 pandemic, which put the resources of all firms under serious stress. The pandemic, therefore, plays the role of a natural experiment in this study as it put the resources of high-growth firms under significant additional stress and, indirectly, subjected our hypothesis about the positive role played by human capital to a severe robustness test. In other words, if a higher endowment of human capital helped these firms survive in such a challenging period, such as the pandemic, then the case for the validity of our hypothesis is strengthened.

In the international management and accounting literature, numerous contributions examine the pandemic from different aspects (Leoni et al., 2021, 2022). Some studies investigated the role of accounting (Ahmad et al., 2021; Antonelli et al., 2022) and budgeting (Heald & Hodges, 2020) in the choices made to deal with the pandemic (Ahmad et al., 2021; Ahrens & Ferry, 2020, 2021a, b; De Villiers et al., 2020). Other research has explored the accounting (Sargiacomo et al., 2021) and external reporting (Leoni et al., 2022) practices adopted by private and public organizations during the pandemic. Some scholars have emphasized the importance of accountability and governance during the pandemic crisis (Andreaus et al., 2021; Hopper, 2020; Koutoupis et al., 2021). This study adds to the existing management and accounting literature on extraordinary events (Sargiacomo, 2015; Sargiacomo & Walker, 2022; Sargiacomo et al., 2014). It specifically contributes to the literature on the impact of a particular extraordinary event, such as the COVID-19 pandemic, on businesses (Sargiacomo et al., 2021) and high-growth enterprises (Otola et al., 2023).

6.3 Sampling Techniques and Data Collection

We used the Eurostat-OECD (2007) definition of the gazelle enterprise as it is the most used in the literature (Daunfeldt et al., 2015; Coad et al., 2014; Audretsch, 2012). This makes it possible to compare the results of this study with other research and statistical reports published by leading international statistical institutes.

According to this definition, gazelles are enterprises up to 5 years old with an average annualized growth of more than 20% per year over 3 years and with ten or more employees at the beginning of the observation period, that is, the year in which they start to grow. Gazelles are not marginal entities since they have at least ten employees. Furthermore, the "gazelle status" is temporary, as companies can become gazelles in the fourth or fifth year of life and lose this status after the fifth year. Eurostat-OECD (2007) defines high-growth enterprises (HGEs) as all enterprises that reach these thresholds of growth in turnover and/or number of employees but are more than 5 years old.

This research examines the cohort of Italian start-ups born in 2014 and becoming gazelles by 2019 (in their fourth or fifth year of life) to verify whether those with a greater endowment of human capital had higher survival rates in the 3 years following the achievement of gazelle status (in our case from 2020 to 2022), in which they were severely hit by the negative effects of the COVID-19 pandemic on all businesses.

We relied on the Aida-Bureau Van Dijk database, which contains financial statements of Italian companies, to collect the data. Our dataset was created using the steps below. First, we determined the cohort of companies spanning 2014–2019, which included all Italian companies incorporated in 2014 and no older than 5 years by 2019. This time frame ensured that the pandemic did not affect the financial statements of these companies. Second, according to the OECD's definition of gazelle firms, we excluded companies with fewer than ten employees at the start of the 3-year growth period. Our sample comprised only those businesses with a 3-year average annualized growth rate of at least 20% in turnover (6.1) or employees (6.2).

$$\text{Average annualized growth rate of turnover} = \sqrt[3]{\frac{\text{Turnover}(t)}{\text{Turnover}(t-3)}} - 1 > 0.2 \qquad (6.1)$$

$$\begin{aligned}&\text{Average annualized growth}\\&\text{rate of employees} = \sqrt[3]{\frac{N.\text{Employees}(t)}{N - \text{Employees}(t-3)}} - 1 > 0.2\end{aligned} \qquad (6.2)$$

Using these criteria, we identified 2044 gazelles born in Italy in 2014, belonging to the 2014–2019 cohort. We excluded from the sample financial and insurance companies to avoid homogeneity problems arising from their balance sheet schemes, different from those of other companies. We also excluded companies with missing balance sheet data in the 3 years of the survey. Therefore, after these cleaning operations, our sample is 1665 companies active in 2019, of which 1508 are still active in 2023 while 158 have ceased due to the start of an extinction procedure in the 3 years 2020–2022 (Table 6.1).

For descriptive statistics and correlation matrix, see Tables 6.6 and 6.7 in the Appendix.

We used the following independent variables (Table 6.2).

We utilized various variables to assess the role of human capital in the survival of gazelle firms. The theoretical background of this study is the RBV which considers human capital a fundamental resource for sustained competitive advantage.

First, we considered the three variables constituting the intellectual capital according to the Value-Added Intellectual Coefficient (VAIC) developed by Pulic (2000: HCE (Human Capital Efficiency) (6.3), SCE (Structural Capital Efficiency) (6.4), and CEE (Capital Employed Efficiency) (6.5).

Table 6.1 Sample selection

Gazelles of the cohort 2014–2019	2044
Excluded because operating in financial and insurance industries	11
Excluded because of missing data	368
Sample	1665
Ceased in the years 2020, 2021, or 2022	158
Active in 2023	1508

Table 6.2 Independent variables

Abbreviation	Variables
HCE	Human Capital Efficiency
SCE	Structural Capital Efficiency
CEE	Capital Employed Efficiency
LCe	Labor cost per employee
VAe	Value added per employee
IR1	Intangible ratio (1)
IR2	Intangible ratio (2) Intangible fixed assets/Total fixed assets
CR	Current Ratio
FLev	Financial leverage
OLev	Operating leverage
SIZE	Company size
SECTOR	NACE2 aggregate sector: 1 = Manufacturing, mining and quarrying, and other industry 2 = Construction and Real estate activities 3 = Wholesale and retail trade, transportation and storage, accommodation, food 4 = Information and communication 5 = Professional, scientific, technical, administration, and support service activities 6 = Other services
[ZG] Geographical area	North, Central, and South Italy

$$\text{HCE}(\text{Human Capital Efficiency}) = \frac{\text{Value added}}{\text{Total employee costs}} \tag{6.3}$$

$$\text{SCE}(\text{Structural Capital Efficiency}) = \frac{\text{Structural capital}}{\text{Value added}} \tag{6.4}$$

$$\text{CEE}(\text{Capital Employed Efficiency}) = \frac{\text{Value added}}{\text{Capital employed}} \tag{6.5}$$

where:

$$\text{Capital employed} = \text{Total assets} - \text{Intangible fixed assets} \tag{6.6}$$

We also used the following two variables to assess the impact of the human capital on the resilience of gazelles: LCe (Labor Cost per employee) (6.7) as a proxy of the qualification of employees (García-Ayuso et al., 2000) and VAe (Value-Added per employee) (6.8) to assess the employee's productivity in terms of ability to create value-added.

$$\text{LCe}\left(\text{Labor Cost per employee}\right) = \frac{\text{Labor Cost}}{\text{Number of employees}} \tag{6.7}$$

$$\text{VAe}\left(\text{Value Added per employee}\right) = \frac{\text{Value Added}}{\text{Number of Employees}} \tag{6.8}$$

We assess the relative weight of intangible fixed assets over both the overall asset (6.9) and the fixed asset (6.10):

$$\text{IR1}\left(\text{Intangible ratio1}\right) = \frac{\text{Intangible fixed assets}}{\text{Total assets}} \tag{6.9}$$

$$\text{IR2}\left(\text{Intangible ratio2}\right) = \frac{\text{Intangible fixed assets}}{\text{Total fixed assets}} \tag{6.10}$$

Intangible fixed assets are a proxy of the investment in knowledge, innovation, and development of the companies. We have already discussed the importance of these resources in the achievement of a sustained competitive advantage, according to the RBV.

The balance sheets of start-ups and young companies may not fully highlight their intangible assets. For example, expenses for research and development, branding and human capital development are not fully considered by these two intangible assets ratios. Furthermore, various challenges emerge in determining the fair value of intangible assets, such as the lack of historical accounting data and start-ups' high levels of uncertainty. Therefore, they tend to represent these costs in the profit and loss statement rather than intangible assets in the balance sheet (Cattafi et al., 2024). Although there are some limitations, our model reflects the impact of intangible assets on both total assets (overall capital structure of companies) and total fixed assets (tangible and intangible).

We controlled gazelles' resilience also for the other following variables:

- [CR] Current ratio (6.11) (Bradley et al., 2011; George, 2005; Gill & Mathur, 2011), as a proxy for the available financial resource slack, that is, the pool of resources that exceed the minimum necessary to the routine operations of firms and readily available (Bourgeois III & Singh, 1983).
- [FLev] Financial leverage (6.12) was used to assess the potential slack in financial resources (George, 2005; Waddock & Graves, 1997), considering its positive impact on firms' growth (Baù et al., 2019).
- [OLev] Operating leverage (6.13) (Nicolò & Ricca, 2019). This ratio is used to estimate operational risk, that is, the risk that a negative change in sales produces a more than proportional negative change in operating profit. This operating leverage effect may also be positive since the increase in sales determines a more than proportional positive change in the operating result. The higher the fixed costs, the greater this effect, both when it is positive and negative. Given that fixed costs do not undergo variations when the quantities produced and sold vary (at least if this variation does not exceed the maximum production capacity), an

increase or reduction in sales produces a more than proportional variation in the operating result, positive or negative, respectively.

- Company size: to capture the size of gazelles we used the logarithmic transformation of total assets. We included this variable because it has been demonstrated that the survival probabilities of companies are positively correlated with their size (Evans, 1987a, b; Hall, 1986).
- Industry: we also control the industry, according to the two-digit NACE Rev2 classification. In the second step, we aggregate sectors in the following six classes:
  - 1 = Manufacturing, mining and quarrying, and other industry
  - 2 = Construction and real estate activities
  - 3 = Wholesale and retail trade, transportation and storage, accommodation, and food
  - 4 = Information and communication
  - 5 = Professional, scientific, technical, administration, and support service activities
  - 6 = Other services
- Geographical area: North, Central, and South Italy: to control for the influence on their contest for survival of the gazelles.

The continuous variables were all normalized in the range 0–100

$$\text{CR}\left(\text{Current ratio}\right) = \frac{\text{Current Assets}}{\text{Number of employees}} \tag{6.11}$$

$$\text{FLev}\left(\text{Financial Leverage}\right) = \frac{\text{Debt}}{\text{Equity}} \tag{6.12}$$

$$\text{OLev}\left(\text{Operating Leverage}\right) = \frac{\dfrac{\text{EBIT}_{t+1} - \text{EBIT}_t}{\text{EBIT}_t}}{\dfrac{\text{SALES}_{t+1} - \text{SALES}_t}{\text{SALES}_t}} \tag{6.13}$$

6.4 The Survey and Statistic Methodology

In this chapter, we estimate how human capital, intangibles, financial resources, and other variables affect the resilience of Italian firms born in 2014 that became "gazelles" in 2019, years in which COVID-19 has put the continuity of firms at serious risk. Therefore, we will study the bankruptcy risk function over 2020–2022 on human capital and financial resources magnitudes. Over the period considered, survival time is measured in months and is always positive. The data are right censored, and their distribution is not symmetric. For this reason, a linear regression model based on OLS estimation cannot be used to process the data. Therefore, the hazard ratio was estimated using Cox's (1972) semi-parametric proportional hazards model (1), which assumes no time distribution and that the effects of the variables on survival are constant over time and additive. Thus, the risk function represents the probability of a firm entering bankruptcy at a given time *t*.

Based on the Cox proportional hazards regression model, the hazard rate for the *j*th firm is:

$$h(t,X) = h_0(t)\exp(\beta X) \tag{6.14}$$

The β coefficients and robust standard errors are estimated by maximizing the partial log-likelihood function using the data (6.15):

$$\log L = \sum_{j=1}^{D}[\sum_{i\in D_j} x_i\beta - d_j \log\{\sum_{k\in R_j} \exp(x_k\beta) \tag{6.15}$$

where:

J is the index of ordered failure times *t*(*j*), with *j* = 1,2, …, *D*; *Dj* is the set of *dj* firms that fail at time *t*(*j*); *dj* is the number of failures at the time *t*(*j*); *Rj* is the set of *k* observations that are at risk at time *t*(*j*).

6.5 Data Analysis and Findings

The graph (Fig. 6.1) of the Nelson-Aalen estimate for the cumulative (integrated) hazard function shows that the risk rate indicating the onset of bankruptcy proceedings was very flat in 2020. It increases gradually in 2021 but rises significantly in 2022.

About the different geographical areas of Italy, Fig. 6.2 shows that the first bankruptcies in 2020 occurred in Southern Italy and the Islands. From mid-2021 until the end of the observation period, the Central Italy bankruptcy risk rate observed is the highest. In contrast, the risk rate for enterprises based in Northern Italy remained relatively stable, placing itself between the rates in Central and Southern Italy, which had the lowest rate at the end of 2022.

In examining the risk rates by sector (Fig. 6.3), we observe that the first bankruptcy procedures were initiated in 2020 by firms in the "Other Service" category (Sector 6). By 2022, the Industrial sector (Sector 1) exhibited a lower risk rate than all sectors, except for the "Information and Communication" sector (Sector 4). The sectors with the highest risk rates in 2022 continue to be "Professional, Scientific, Technical, Administration, and Support Service Activities" (Sector 5), "Wholesale and Retail Trade, Transportation and Storage, Accommodation, and Food" (Sector 3), and "Other Services" (Sector 6).

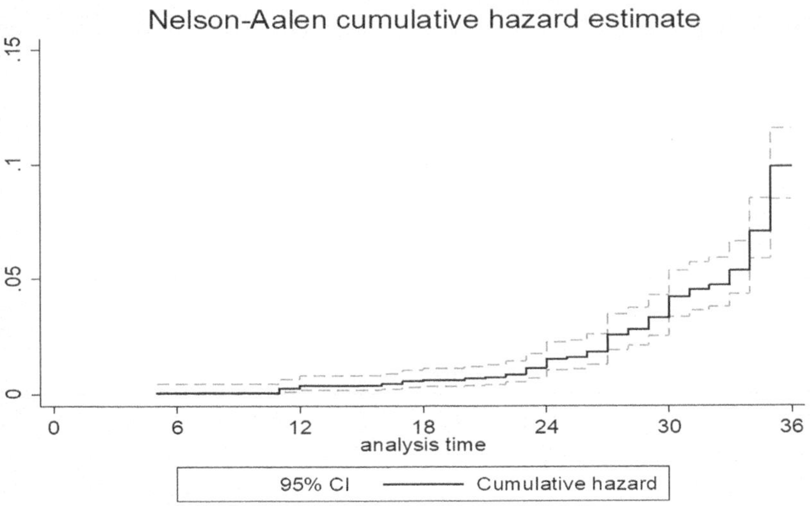

Fig. 6.1 Nelson-Aalen cumulative hazard estimate

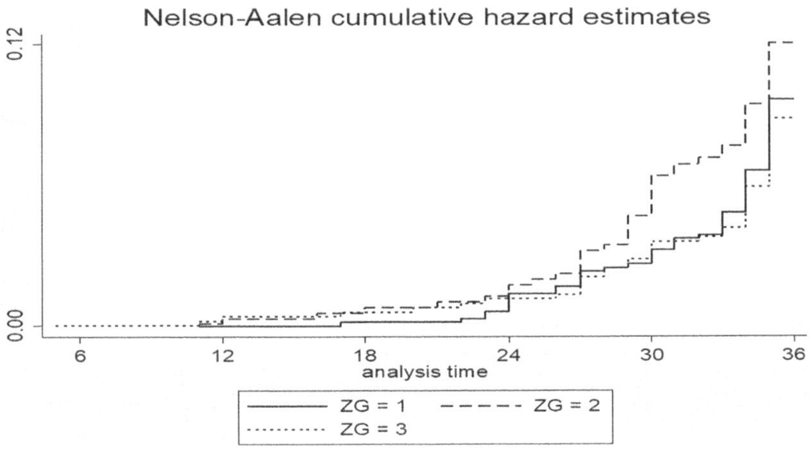

Fig. 6.2 Nelson-Aalen cumulative hazard estimates by ZG (Geographical area)

However, we must highlight that the plots of the categorical predictors ZG and SECTOR (Figs. 6.2 and 6.3) show overlapping and/or intersecting clusters in both cases. Therefore, at least graphically, they may violate the hypothesis of proportionality of predictors of the Cox model, so it will be necessary to perform the non-parametric log-rank test of equality between strata.

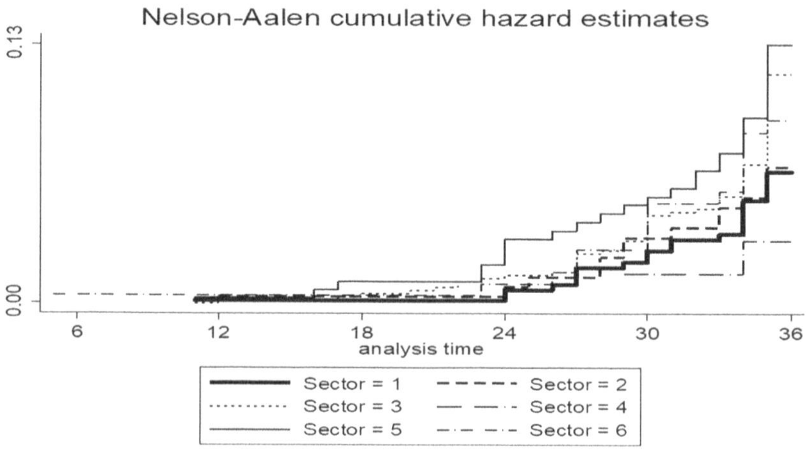

Fig. 6.3 Nelson-Aalen cumulative hazard estimates by sector

Table 6.3 Univariate regression model of semi-parametric Cox proportional hazard

Univariate regression model of semi-parametric Cox proportional hazards		
Continuous predictor	LR chi2(1)	Prob > chi2
CR	17.48	0.000
VAe	113.81	0.000
FLev	4.44	0.035
OLev	0.27	0.604
SIZE	123.56	0.000
LCe	53.98	0.000
HCE	15.73	0.000
SCE	2.06	0.152
CEE	50.46	0.000
IR1	6.71	0.010
IR2	4.55	0.033

To include the predictor in the final model, we first tested the proportionality of the survival functions by univariate analysis, which can be performed for categorical variables using the non-parametric log-rank test for equality of survival functions between strata and the continuous variables using a univariate semi-parametric Cox proportional hazards regression model. We included the predictor in the final model if the p-value of the Chi2 test was less than 0.25 (Tables 6.3 and 6.4).

In the following models, we include all predictors with a p-value below 0.25 in the univariate analyses, thus excluding the variables OLev and SCE and the categorical variable ZG (geographical area).

Therefore, we propose a model (1) (Table 6.5) with only continuous predictors. The variables are all significant, and the Hazard ratios of the predictors suggest that

Table 6.4 Log-rank test for equality of survivor functions

Log-rank test for equality of survivor functions			
Categorical predictor	df	chi2(df)	Pr > chi2
ZG	2	2.55	0.280
SECTOR	5	12.50	0.029

Table 6.5 Cox proportional hazards regression model (1)

Model (1)					
_t	Coef.	Haz. Ratio	Robust Std. Err.	z	P
CR	−0.015	0.986	0.002	−5.928	0.000
VAe	−0.146	0.864	0.019	−7.639	0.000
FLev	0.013	1.013	0.006	2.239	0.033
SIZE	−0.049	0.952	0.012	−4.016	0.000
LCe	0.011	1.011	0.002	4.965	0.000
HCE	0.008	1.008	0.004	2.360	0.025
CEE	0.009	1.009	0.004	2.292	0.029
IR1	0.004	1.004	0.002	2.273	0.030
IR2	−0.004	0.996	0.001	−3.345	0.001
Test Wald chi2(2) = 49.34 – Prob > chi2 = 0.00					

the Current Ratio (CR), Value Added per employee (VAe), Firm Size (SIZE), and the ratio of Intangible Fixed Assets to Total Fixed Assets (IR2) positively affect the probability of survival by reducing the risk of bankruptcy. The predictors with the higher impact on the bankruptcy risk rate are VAe and SIZE. A 1% increase in these variables, holding all other variables constant, reduces the risk of bankruptcy by 13.6% for VAe and 4.8% for SIZE. Instead, the variables FLev and LCe increase the risk of failure by 1.3% and 1.1%. For all other variables, the risk rate is flat, as the increase or decrease in the risk of default is less than 1% (Table 6.5).

Subsequently, we added the categorical variable SECTOR to model (2) to analyse how the economic and financial variables from model (1) impact bankruptcy probability in different product sectors. We have also included interactions between this variable and the continuous variables. It is important to note that we do not consider predictors or interactions that are not statistically significant when assessing the probability of bankruptcy (Table 6.8 in the Appendix).

The results of model (2) indicate that, unlike in model (1), the variables LCe and HCE are not significant at the 5% level. The remaining predictors are significant and show the same influence on the probability of failure compared to model (1), except for CEE, which indicates a 2.9% decrease in the risk of bankruptcy for each 1% increase, assuming all other predictors remain constant (Table 6.8).

For the estimation (Table 6.8) of the influence of the continuous predictors within the market sectors, we chose SECTOR = 1 (manufacturing, mining, quarrying, and other industries) as a benchmark. Thus, each 1% increase in one of the continuous variables, holding all other predictors constant, allows us to determine, compared to

Sector 1, the percentage increase or decrease in the probability of bankruptcy relative to the variables considered in the models.

The analysis of the results from model (2) compared to model (1) provides valuable insights into the various impacts of continuous predictors on the probability of failure in different sectors.

Interesting evidence concerns sectors 2 (Construction and Real Estate) and 3 (Wholesale and Retail Trade, Transport and Storage, Accommodation, and Food Service). We can see that the CEE and IR1 ratios have an opposing influence on the probability of bankruptcy. In fact, for Sector 2 versus Sector 1, CEE decreases the probability of bankruptcy by 28.8% and IR1 by 16.6%. The same ratios in Sector 3 increase the probability of bankruptcy by 11.5% and 3.2%, respectively. Furthermore, the IR1 ratio also has a different impact than model (1) in sectors 5 (professional, scientific, technical, administration, and support service activities) and 6 (Other services), decreasing the probability of bankruptcy by 3.9% and 22.2% versus Sector 1. Instead, the FLev ratio increases the probability of bankruptcy in all sectors except Sector 3 (9.7% decrease). The CR ratio has a similar impact to Model (1) for Sectors 3 and 6, but in Sectors 2 and 5 the probability of bankruptcy increases, compared to Sector 1, by 2.1% and 0.6%. The IR2 ratio, which has a negative but low impact on the risk of bankruptcy in Model 1, has a positive but still low impact in Sectors 2, 5, and 6. For Sector 4 (Information and communication), the only significant interaction concerns firm size SIZE, which highlights a high impact on the survival probability (53.2%). The variables VAe, HCE, and SIZE confirm the influence on the probability of failure found in the Model (1).

The hypothesis that model (2), which includes interactions, fits the data better than model (1), which does not include interactions, is supported by the results of the likelihood ratio test on the null hypothesis (see Table 6.9 in the Appendix). The *p*-value from this test indicates that we can reject the null hypothesis. In addition, the coefficient test of the variable sector (Table 6.10 in the Appendix), taken as a whole (2. Sector, 3. Sector, 4. Sector, 5. Sector, 6. Sector) reports a significant chi2 statistic (390.97) with a *p*-value equal to 0.00. Finally, although the proportionality test has been reported (Tables 6.3 and 6.4), we performed additional tests due to doubts raised by the graphical analysis:

1. To verify that the model with interactions satisfies the proportionality assumption, we use the scaled Schoenfeld and Schoenfeld residuals and the related nonzero slope test developed by Therneau and Grambsch (6.3) that allows us to test proportionality for each predictor. The results presented in Table 6.11 in the Appendix show that the *p*-value is greater than $\alpha = 0.05$ for all variables and interactions. Furthermore, using the plot option, we also obtained a graph of the scaled Schoenfeld assumption (Fig. 6.5 in the Appendix). The findings indicate that we cannot reject the principle of proportionality, and consequently, we conclude there is no violation of the proportionality hypothesis.
2. The goodness of fit of the final model: To graphically assess the goodness of fit of the regression model, we used the Nelson-Aalen cumulative risk function and Cox-Snell residuals. If the model goodness of fit is optimal, the residuals would have a standard censored exponential distribution with a hazard ratio equal to 1.

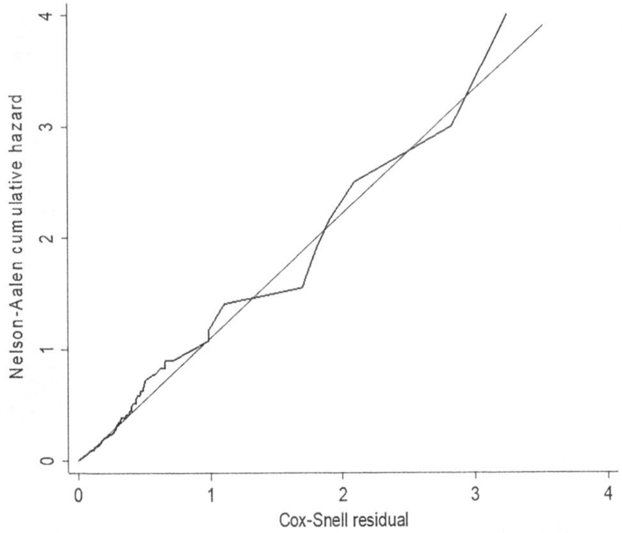

Fig. 6.4 Nelson-Aalen cumulative risk function and Cox-Snell residuals

The graph (Fig. 6.4) shows that the Cox model fits these data reasonably well; in fact, the risk function follows the trend of the 45-degree line quite closely, although with increasing fluctuations for larger time values.

6.6 Conclusion

This chapter focused on gazelles born in Italy in 2014 and belonging to the 2014–2019 cohort to identify the factors that influenced their resilience in the 3 years after achieving gazelle status (2020–2022). These start-ups were observed during a very challenging period characterized by high growth and an external shock of extraordinary intensity: the COVID-19 pandemic. The pandemic provided a natural experiment, making the research results robust.

The analysis revealed that the resilience of high-growth start-ups is positively influenced by the higher endowment of highly skilled human capital, financial resources, total assets, and lower debt. Interestingly, investment in intangibles, which is a proxy for investment in knowledge, did not influence the resilience of these firms. Human capital efficiency (HCE) was found to be detrimental to the resilience of these young and high-growth firms: gazelles with higher staff efficiency are less likely to survive major external shocks. This finding seems contradictory, but the contradiction is only apparent: firms with more qualified staff pay their employees more than the others and, therefore, have lower human capital efficiency; however, due to the high qualification of their staff, they are more resilient. This suggests that the qualification of staff boosts the resilience of gazelles more than the higher cost of more qualified staff negatively affects their survival.

Our analysis showed that the risk of termination of "gazelle" firms in Italy was very low in 2020. However, this risk increased in 2021 and grew even faster in 2022. Some of these firms were unable to withstand this challenge, which over time weakened their resilience. In the years we studied (2014–2019), these fast-growing companies faced a double source of pressure. In addition to the stress triggered by strong growth, they faced the crisis caused by the COVID-19 pandemic. Since 2020, the negative effects of the pandemic have affected all companies, not just high-growth start-ups, putting their survival at serious risk.

During the period examined, the risk of termination of "gazelle" enterprises in Italy differed across sectors and geographic areas. As depicted in Fig. 6.3, the "Manufacturing, mining and quarrying, and other industries" macro-sector (Sector = 1) had a lower failure risk rate in 2022 compared to all other sectors, except for the "Information and Communication" macro-sector (Sector = 4). Model 2 shows that continuous predictors have different effects on the probability of gazelles' failure across different sectors. We found interesting evidence related to the macro-sectors, which we identified by aggregating the two-digit breakdown of the NACE Rev. 2 industries. The results of this analysis can be found in Table 6.12 in the Appendix. Although we couldn't include the variable of geographical area [ZG] in the models, the univariate analysis, as shown in Fig. 6.1, indicates that gazelle companies in different geographical areas displayed varying levels of resilience. In 2020, the first gazelle companies to cease operations were in southern Italy and the islands. Subsequently, from mid-2021 until the end of the observation period (2023), the highest bankruptcy risk rate was observed in Central Italy. The risk rate for companies located in northern Italy falls between those of Central and southern Italy.

Our hypothesis is confirmed: qualification of employees, measured by the value added per employee, a proxy of human capital qualification, increases the probability of gazelles' survival in all industries.

In the macro-sectors "Construction and real estate" (Sector = 2) and "Wholesale and retail trade, transportation and storage, accommodation, and food" (Sector = 3), we observed that the intangible ratio IR1, calculated as the ratio of intangible assets to total assets, has an opposite impact on the probability of bankruptcy. These opposing effects of intangible assets on the survival rates of the observed gazelles explain why, in model 1, the coefficient of this indicator of investments in intangible assets approaches zero. Therefore, we can conclude that the overall impact of these investments on the probability of survival is not significant.

Financial leverage negatively affects the survival chances of the court gazelles we studied. The only exception is in macro-sector 3 "Wholesale and retail trade, transportation and storage, accommodation, food" where this index shows a different effect. Companies with higher debt and financial leverage are less resilient to unexpected external shocks due to their lower liquidity to handle crisis-related constraints.

The study also confirmed that liquidity positively impacts the survival of companies during crises, as indicated by the positive relationship between the current ratio (a measure of short-term resource availability) and the probability of survival of the gazelles. When comparing different sectors to the benchmark macro-sector 1, the positive effect of liquidity varies.

There are also contrasting effects regarding the current ratio. It positively impacts sectors "Wholesale and retail trade, transport and warehousing, accommodation and food" (Sector = 3) and "Other services" (Sector = 6), but increases the probability of failure in "Construction and real estate activities" (Sector = 2) and "Professional, scientific, technical, administrative, and support service activities" (Sector = 5) compared to Sector 1.

The size of the gazelles in terms of total assets has a high impact on their probability of survival (53.2%) as larger companies are more resilient.

The limitations of this study are that the results are valid only with regard to the geographic setting, Italy, and the cohort of gazelles examined, those born in 2014 and becoming gazelles by 2019. Similar studies conducted in different contexts and cohorts of gazelles might yield different results.

Start-uppers can gain useful insights from this study. It highlights the importance of human resource skills for the survival of high-growth start-ups. Policymakers can gain valuable insights from this study to develop more effective entrepreneurial policies and support businesses during major challenges, such as pandemics or other relevant external shocks.

Appendix

Table 6.6 Descriptive statistics

Var.	No. obs.	No. missing values	First quartile	Median	Third quartile	Mean	Standard deviation (*n*)
CR	4967	0	1.0	1.3	1.9	1.6	1.2
VAe	4967	0	17940.0	30700.0	48365.0	39835.5	41559.0
FLev	4967	0	2.1	4.6	10.5	9.7	418.2
OLev	4967	0	−0.1	0.1	0.3	3.2	199.6
SIZE	4967	0	6.4	7.2	8.2	7.4	1.5
LCe	4967	0	16835.0	26670.0	37210.0	28532.1	15916.3
HCE	4967	0	1.0	1.2	1.5	4.6	220.0
SC	4967	0	12465.0	84630.0	290270.0	690392.5	7955028.1
SCE	4967	0	0.0	0.2	0.4	0.1	13.6
CEE	4967	0	245.3	460.4	836.7	532.4	14292.6
IR1	4967	0	0.0	0.0	0.1	0.2	1.6
IR2	4967	0	0.0	0.1	0.5	0.3	0.3

Table 6.7 Correlation matrix (Pearson)

Variables	CR	VAe	FLev	RO	DIM	LCe	HCE	SC	SCE	CEE	IR1	IR2
CR	1.00	0.14	0.00	−0.01	0.00	0.08	0.00	0.00	0.01	0.01	0.00	−0.02
VAe	0.14	1.00	0.00	−0.01	0.50	0.64	0.05	0.23	0.01	0.00	−0.04	0.02
FLev	0.00	0.00	1.00	0.00	0.01	0.00	0.00	0.00	0.00	0.00	0.00	−0.01
OLev	−0.01	−0.01	0.00	1.00	0.00	0.00	0.00	0.00	0.00	0.00	0.00	0.03
DIM	0.00	0.50	0.01	0.00	1.00	0.56	−0.01	0.26	−0.01	−0.01	−0.12	0.14
LCe	0.08	0.64	0.00	0.00	0.56	1.00	−0.03	0.14	0.01	0.01	−0.05	0.07
HCE	0.00	0.05	0.00	0.00	−0.01	−0.03	1.00	0.00	0.00	0.00	0.00	−0.01
SC	0.00	0.23	0.00	0.00	0.26	0.14	0.00	1.00	0.00	0.00	0.00	0.07
SCE	0.01	0.01	0.00	0.00	−0.01	0.01	0.00	0.00	1.00	0.00	0.00	0.00
CEE	0.01	0.00	0.00	0.00	−0.01	0.01	0.00	0.00	0.00	1.00	−0.01	0.00
IR1	0.00	−0.04	0.00	0.00	−0.12	−0.05	0.00	0.00	0.00	−0.01	1.00	0.15
IR2	−0.02	0.02	−0.01	0.03	0.14	0.07	−0.01	0.07	0.00	0.00	0.15	1.00

Table 6.8 Cox proportional hazards regression model (2)

_t	Coef.	Haz. Ratio	Std. Err.	z	$P > z$
CR	−0.0813	0.9219	0.0208	−3.9185	0.0002
VAe	−0.1948	0.8230	0.0292	−6.6793	0.0000
FLev	0.2317	1.2607	0.1041	2.2246	0.0336
SIZE	−0.0463	0.9548	0.0152	−3.0360	0.0040
LCe	0.0140	1.0140	0.0050	0.2800	0.7800
HCE	0.5127	1.6698	7.5181	0.0682	0.3980
CEE	−0.0299	0.9706	0.0097	−3.0830	0.0034
IR1	−0.0123	0.9878	0.0035	−3.5298	0.0008
IR2	0.1305	1.1394	0.0191	6.8430	0.0000
Sector					
2	0.5186	1.6796	0.1533	3.3819	0.0013
3	−1.3507	0.2591	0.3281	−4.1169	0.0001
4	0.6586	1.9320	2.4800	0.2655	0.3851
5	−0.9911	0.3712	0.2591	−3.8249	0.0003
6	−0.4040	0.6676	0.1352	−2.9888	0.0046
Sector#c.CR					
2	0.1023	1.1077	0.0130	7.8456	0.0000
3	0.0775	1.0806	0.0156	4.9641	0.0000
4	−0.5787	0.5606	0.6769	−0.8550	0.2768
5	0.0874	1.0913	0.0305	2.8653	0.0066
6	−0.0027	0.9973	0.0012	−2.1706	0.0378
Sector#c.VAe					
2	0.1866	1.2052	0.0678	2.7541	0.0090
3	0.0343	1.0349	0.0133	2.5782	0.0144
4	−0.1647	0.8481	0.1305	−1.2623	0.1798
5	0.1805	1.1978	0.0442	4.0827	0.0001
6	−0.0116	0.9884	0.0050	−2.3479	0.0253
Sector#c.FLev					
2	−0.0017	0.9983	0.0008	−2.0654	0.0473
3	−0.3335	0.7164	0.1472	−2.2651	0.0307
4	0.1248	1.1329	0.1968	0.6340	0.3263
5	0.0842	1.0879	0.0343	2.4536	0.0197
6	0.1739	1.1900	0.0585	2.9745	0.0048
Sector#c.SIZE					
2	−0.0523	0.9490	0.0142	−3.6913	0.0004
3	0.0276	1.0280	0.0096	2.8840	0.0062
4	−0.7127	0.4903	0.1653	−4.3125	0.0000
5	−0.0262	0.9741	0.0061	−4.2832	0.0000
6	−0.0436	0.9573	0.0195	−2.2354	0.0328
Sector#c.LCe					
2	−0.0592	0.9425	0.0152	−3.8961	0.0002
3	−0.0113	0.9887	0.0539	−0.2097	0.3903

(continued)

Table 6.8 (continued)

_t	Coef.	Haz. Ratio	Std. Err.	z	$P > z$
4	0.1876	1.2064	0.1164	1.6120	0.1088
5	−0.0222	0.9781	0.0072	−3.0707	0.0036
6	0.0149	1.0151	0.0841	0.1777	0.3927
Sector#c.HCE					
2	−1.1830	0.3064	0.9343	−1.2662	0.1790
3	−0.5223	0.5932	0.8283	−0.6305	0.3270
4	0.0141	1.0142	0.7289	0.0193	0.3989
5	−0.9076	0.4035	0.3247	−2.7956	0.0080
6	−1.0086	0.3647	0.3572	−2.8237	0.0074
Sector#c.CEE					
2	−0.3101	0.7334	0.1214	−2.5546	0.0153
3	0.1388	1.1489	0.0521	2.6626	0.0115
4	−1.5414	0.2141	0.9524	−1.6185	0.1077
5	−1.5096	0.2210	0.9836	−1.5348	0.1228
6	0.1945	1.2147	0.0828	2.3498	0.0252
Sector#c.IR1					
2	0.0144	1.0145	0.0048	2.9782	0.0047
3	0.0038	1.0038	0.0031	1.2497	0.1827
4	−0.3353	0.7151	0.5789	−0.5791	0.3373
5	0.0186	1.0188	0.0012	15.9599	0.0000
6	0.0171	1.0173	0.0058	2.9450	0.0052
Sector#c.IR2					
2	−0.3125	0.7316	0.0284	−11.0067	0.0000
3	−0.0990	0.9058	0.0289	−3.4200	0.0012
4	−0.5433	0.5808	1.0249	−0.5301	0.3467
5	−0.1710	0.8428	0.0254	−6.7247	0.0000
6	−0.3815	0.6829	0.1301	−2.9314	0.0054
Test Wald chi2(2) = 145.11 – Prob > chi2 = 0.00					

Table 6.9 Likelihood ratio test

Likelihood-ratio test	LR chi2(43) = 77.95
	Prob > chi2 = 0.0009

Table 6.10 Likelihood ratio test on the null hypothesis

2.Sector = 0
3.Sector = 0
4.Sector = 0
5.Sector = 0
6.Sector = 0
Constraint 2 dropped
Constraint 3 dropped
chi2(3) = 390.97
Prob > chi2 = 0.0000

Table 6.11 Test of proportional hazards assumption

	rho	chi2	df	Prob>chi2
2.Sector	0.116	1.660	1.000	0.197
3.Sector	0.039	0.260	1.000	0.611
4.Sector	0.093	2.780	1.000	0.096
5.Sector	−0.003	0.000	1.000	0.960
6.Sector	−0.046	0.380	1.000	0.539
CR	0.060	2.230	1.000	0.136
VAe	−0.098	1.300	1.000	0.255
FLev	−0.006	0.000	1.000	0.982
SIZE	0.040	0.310	1.000	0.576
LCe	0.015	0.090	1.000	0.767
HCE	0.043	0.330	1.000	0.565
CEE	0.094	1.480	1.000	0.224
IR1	−0.057	0.520	1.000	0.470
IR2	0.050	0.450	1.000	0.502
2.Sector#c.CR	−0.042	0.990	1.000	0.320
3.Sector#c.CR	−0.051	1.510	1.000	0.219
4.Sector#c.CR	−0.113	0.020	1.000	0.891
5.Sector#c.CR	−0.062	2.230	1.000	0.135
6.Sector#c.CR	−0.020	0.130	1.000	0.720
2.Sector#c.VAe	0.099	2.240	1.000	0.134
3.Sector#c.VAe	0.098	1.400	1.000	0.237
4.Sector#c.VAe	0.006	0.000	1.000	0.992
5.Sector#c.VAe	0.089	1.120	1.000	0.290
6.Sector#c.VAe	−0.046	0.450	1.000	0.502
2.Sector#c.FLev	0.020	0.020	1.000	0.898
3.Sector#c.FLev	0.005	0.000	1.000	0.986
4.Sector#c.FLev	0.020	0.000	1.000	0.997
5.Sector#c.FLev	0.078	0.100	1.000	0.750
6.Sector#c.FLev	0.061	0.170	1.000	0.683
2.Sector#c.SIZEl	0.001	0.000	1.000	0.986
3.Sector#c.SIZEl	−0.035	0.250	1.000	0.620
4.Sector#c.SIZEl	−0.023	0.000	1.000	0.964
5.Sector#c.SIZEl	−0.047	0.440	1.000	0.508
6.Sector#c.SIZEl	−0.041	0.300	1.000	0.584
2.Sector#c.LCe	−0.053	0.740	1.000	0.388
3.Sector#c.LCe	0.011	0.040	1.000	0.841
4.Sector#c.LCe	0.008	0.000	1.000	0.985
5.Sector#c.LCe	−0.017	0.090	1.000	0.769
6.Sector#c.LCe	0.084	3.010	1.000	0.083
2.Sector#c.HCE	−0.120	1.720	1.000	0.190
3.Sector#c.HCE	−0.045	0.370	1.000	0.544

(continued)

Table 6.11 (continued)

	rho	chi2	df	Prob>chi2
4.Sector#c.HCE	0.035	0.020	1.000	0.895
5.Sector#c.HCE	−0.043	0.340	1.000	0.560
6.Sector#c.HCE	0.043	0.330	1.000	0.564
2.Sector#c.CEE	−0.030	0.050	1.000	0.820
3.Sector#c.CEE	0.049	0.330	1.000	0.565
4.Sector#c.CEE	−0.014	0.000	1.000	0.998
5.Sector#c.CEE	0.056	5.250	1.000	0.062
6.Sector#c.CEE	−0.025	0.080	1.000	0.784
2.Sector#c.IR1	0.087	1.530	1.000	0.216
3.Sector#c.IR1	0.054	0.500	1.000	0.477
4.Sector#c.IR1	0.009	0.000	1.000	0.977
5.Sector#c.IR1	−0.014	0.030	1.000	0.858
6.Sector#c.IR1	0.042	0.290	1.000	0.593
2.Sector#c.IR2	−0.023	0.050	1.000	0.823
3.Sector#c.IR2	−0.046	0.390	1.000	0.532
4.Sector#c.IR2	−0.009	0.000	1.000	0.977
5.Sector#c.IR2	−0.042	0.190	1.000	0.665
6.Sector#c.IR2	−0.034	0.160	1.000	0.689
global test	38.48	57	0.9716	

Table 6.12 Probability of bankruptcy risk, expressed as a percentage, for the significant variables in the model (2)

Sector	Interaction	Coef.	Haz. Ratio	P > z	Probability
2 = Construction and Real estate activities	Sector#c. CEE	−0.31	0.73	0.02	−28.82%
	Sector#c. IR1	−0.31	0.73	0.00	−16.64%
	Sector#c. SIZE	−0.05	0.95	0.00	−9.39%
	Sector#c. LCe	−0.06	0.94	0.00	−4.43%
	Sector#c. VAe	0.19	1.21	0.01	−0.81%
	Sector#c. IR2	0.01	1.01	0.00	0.21%
	Sector#c.CR	0.10	1.11	0.00	2.12%
	Sector#c. FLev	0.00	1.00	0.05	25.86%

(continued)

Table 6.12 (continued)

Sector	Interaction	Coef.	Haz. Ratio	P > z	Probability
3 = Wholesale and retail trade, transportation and storage, accommodation and food	Sector#c. VAe	0.03	1.03	0.01	−14.82%
	Sector#c. FLev	−0.33	0.72	0.03	−9.68%
	Sector#c. SIZE	0.03	1.03	0.01	−1.86%
	Sector#c.CR	0.08	1.08	0.00	−0.38%
	Sector#c. IR1	−0.10	0.91	0.00	3.20%
	Sector#c. CEE	0.14	1.15	0.01	11.50%
4 = Information and communication	Sector#c. SIZE	−0.71	0.49	0.00	−53.19%
5 = Professional, scientific, technical, administration and support service activities	Sector#c. HCE	−0.91	0.40	0.01	−32.63%
	Sector#c. SIZE	−0.03	0.97	0.00	−7.00%
	Sector#c. IR1	−0.17	0.84	0.00	−3.97%
	Sector#c. VAe	0.18	1.20	0.00	−1.42%
	Sector#c. LCe	−0.02	0.98	0.00	−0.82%
	Sector#c.CR	0.09	1.09	0.01	0.60%
	Sector#c. IR2	0.02	1.02	0.00	0.63%
	Sector#c. FLev	0.08	1.09	0.02	37.15%
6 = Other services	Sector#c. HCE	−1.01	0.36	0.01	−39.10%
	Sector#c. IR1	−0.38	0.68	0.01	−22.19%
	Sector#c. VAe	−0.01	0.99	0.03	−18.65%
	Sector#c. SIZE	−0.04	0.96	0.03	−8.60%
	Sector#c.CR	0.00	1.00	0.04	−8.06%
	Sector#c. IR2	0.02	1.02	0.01	0.49%
	Sector#c. CEE	0.19	1.21	0.03	17.89%
	Sector#c. FLev	0.17	1.19	0.00	50.02%

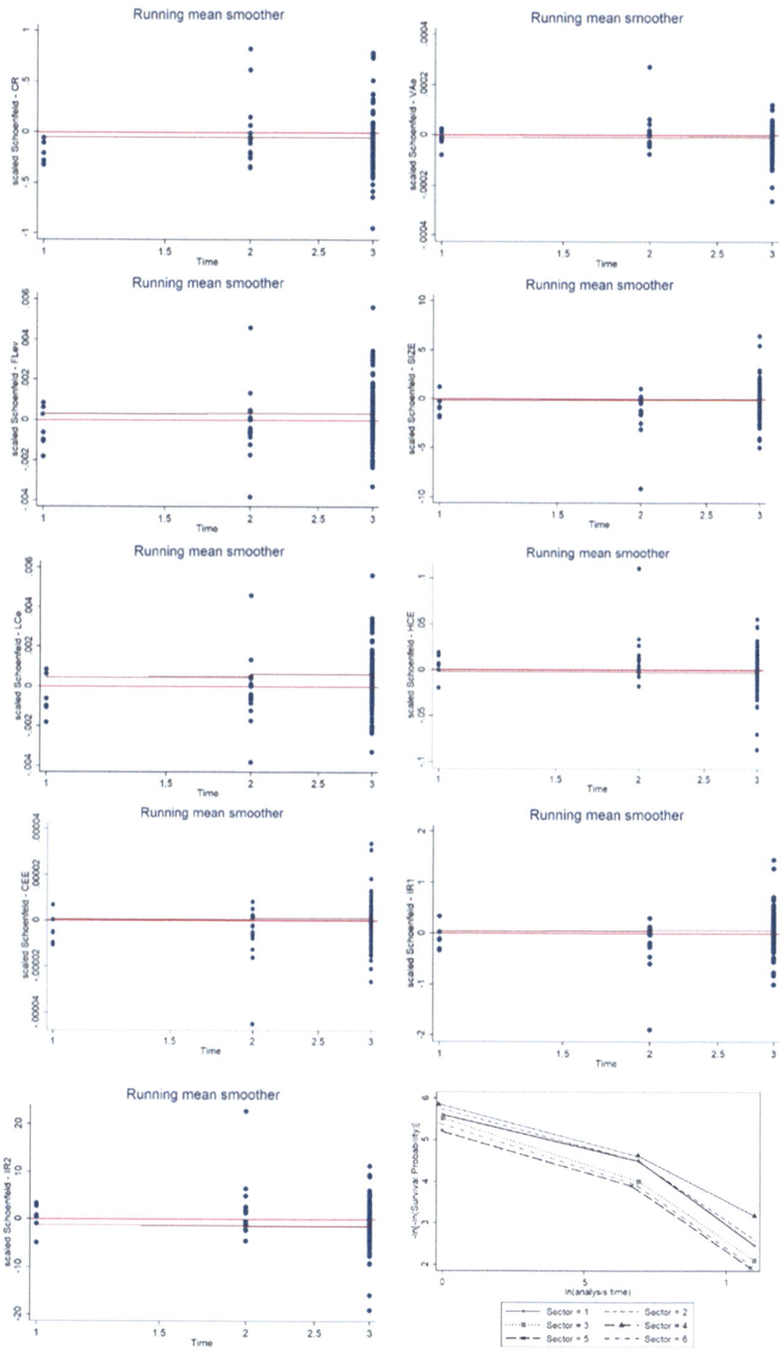

Fig. 6.5 Scaled Schoenfeld assumption

References

Acs, Z. J., & Armington, C. (2006). *Entrepreneurship, geography, and American economic growth*. Cambridge University Press.

Ahmad, S., Connolly, C., & Demirag, I. (2021). Testing times: governing a pandemic with numbers. *Accounting, Auditing and Accountability Journal, 34*(6), 1362–1375.

Ahrens, T., & Ferry, L. (2020). Financial resilience of English local government in the aftermath of COVID-19. *Journal of Public Budgeting, Accounting and Financial Management, 32*(5), 813–823.

Ahrens, T., & Ferry, L. (2021a). Accounting and accountability practices in times of crisis: A Foucauldian perspective on the UK government's response to COVID-19 for England. *Accounting, Auditing and Accountability Journal, 34*(6), 1305–1319.

Ahrens, T., & Ferry, L. (2021b). Debate: What support should local government expect from accounting during a sudden crisis such as Covid-19? *Public Money and Management, 41*(1), 12–14.

Andreaus, M., Rinaldi, L., Pesci, C., & Girardi, A. (2021). Accountability in times of exception: An exploratory study of account-giving practices during the early stages of the COVID-19 pandemic in Italy. *Journal of Public Budgeting, Accounting and Financial Management, 33*(4), 447–467.

Antonelli, V., Bigoni, M., Funnell, W., & Cafaro, E. M. (2022). Accounting for biosecurity in Italy under COVID-19 lockdown. *Accounting, Auditing and Accountability Journal, 35*(1), 120–130.

Audretsch, D. B. (1994). *Innovation and industry evolution*. MIT Press.

Audretsch, D. B. (2012). Determinants of high-growth entrepreneurship. In *Report prepared for the OECD/DBA International Workshop on "High-Growth Firms: Local policies and local determinants"*.

Audretsch, D. B., & Mahmood, T. (1995). New firm survival: New results using a hazard function. *The Review of Economics and Statistics*, 97–103.

Barkham, R., Gudgin, G., & Hart, M. (2012). *The determinants of small firm growth: An inter-regional study in the United Kingdom 1986–90*. Routledge.

Barney, J. (1991). Firm resources and sustained competitive advantage. *Journal of Management, 17*(1), 99–120.

Bartelsman, E., Scarpetta, S., & Schivardi, F. (2005). Comparative analysis of firm demographics and survival: Evidence from micro-level sources in OECD countries. *Industrial and Corporate Change, 14*(3), 365–391.

Baù, M., Chirico, F., Pittino, D., Backman, M., & Klaesson, J. (2019). Roots to grow: Family firms and local embeddedness in rural and urban contexts. *Entrepreneurship Theory and Practice, 43*(2), 360–385.

Birley, S. (1987). New ventures and employment growth. *Journal of Business Venturing, 2*, 155–165.

Bourgeois III, L. J., and Singh, J. V. (1983). Organizational slack and political behavior among top management teams. In Academy of management proceedings 1983, 1, pp. 43–47). : Academy of Management.

Bradley, S. W., Shepherd, D. A., & Wiklund, J. (2011). The importance of slack for new organizations facing 'tough'environments. *Journal of Management Studies, 48*(5), 1071–1097.

Bruna, M. G., & Nicolò, D. (2020). Corporate reputation and social sustainability in the early stages of start-ups: A theoretical model to match stakeholders' expectations through corporate social commitment. *Finance Research Letters, 35*, 101508.

Burvill, S. M., Jones-Evans, D., & Rowlands, H. (2018). Reconceptualising the principles of Penrose's (1959) theory and the resource based view of the firm: The generation of a new conceptual framework. *Journal of Small Business and Enterprise Development, 25*(6), 930–959.

Cattafi, G., Del Pozzo, A., & Nicolò, D. (2023). People first! Intellectual capital and growth of high-growth social cooperatives (social gazelles) in the startup stage. Evidence from Italy. *Piccola Impresa/Small Business, 1.*

Cattafi, G., Mariani, G., Pistolesi, F., and Nicolò, D. (2024). *Cheating in the evaluation. An expedient to estimate the impact of intangibles on the enterprise value of the high-growth start-ups.* MANAGEMENT CONTROL, (2023/3).

Chandler, A. D., Jr. (1969). *Strategy and structure: Chapters in the history of the American industrial enterprise* (Vol. 120). MIT Press.

Coad, A., Daunfeldt, S. O., Hölzl, W., Johansson, D., & Nightingale, P. (2014). High-growth firms: Introduction to the special section. *Industrial and Corporate Change, 23*(1), 91–112.

Cooper, A. C., Gimeno-Gascon, F. J., & Woo, C. Y. (1994). Initial human and financial capital as predictors of new venture performance. *Journal of Business Venturing, 9*, 371–395.

Daunfeldt, S. O., Johansson, D., & Halvarsson, D. (2015). Using the Eurostat-OECD definition of high-growth firms: a cautionary note. *Journal of Entrepreneurship and Public Policy, 4*(1), 50–56.

De Villiers, C., Cerbone, D., & Van Zijl, W. (2020). The South African government's response to COVID-19. *Journal of Public Budgeting, Accounting and Financial Management, 32*(5), 797–811.

Eklund, C. M. (2020). Why do some SME's become high-growth firms? The role of employee competences. *Journal of Intellectual Capital, 21*(5), 691–707.

Eklund, C., & Van Criekingen, K. (2022). Fast as a gazelle–young firms gaining from educational diversity. *Industry and Innovation, 29*(8), 927–947.

Eurostat-OECD. (2007). *Manual on business demography statistics.*

Evans, D. (1987a). Tests of alternative theories of firm growth. *Journal of Political Economy, 95*(4), 657–674.

Evans, D. (1987b). The relationship between firm growth, size, mad age – Estimates for 100 manufacturing industries. *Journal of Industrial Economics, 35*(4), 567–581.

García-ayuso, M. A., Moreno-campos, I., & Sierra-molina, G. (2000). Fundamental analysis and human capital: empirical evidence on the relationship between the quality of human resources and fundamental accounting variables. *Journal of Human Resource Costing & Accounting, 5*(1), 45–57.

Garnsey, E. (1998). A theory of the early growth of the firm. *Industrial and Corporate Change, 7*(3), 523–556.

Garnsey, E., & Heffernan, P. (2005). Growth setbacks in new firms. *Futures, 37*(7).

George, G. (2005). Slack resources and the performance of privately held firms. *Academy of Management Journal, 48*(4), 661–676.

Gilbert, B. A., McDougall, P. P., & Audretsch, D. B. (2006). New venture growth: A review and extension. *Journal of Management, 32*(6), 926–950.

Gill, A., & Mathur, N. (2011). Factors that affect potential growth of Canadian firms. *Journal of Applied Finance and Banking, 1*(4), 107.

Greiner, L. E. (1989). *Evolution and revolution as organizations grow* (pp. 373–387). Macmillan Education.

Hall, B. H. (1986). *The relationship between firm size and firm growth in the US manufacturing sector.*

Heald, D., & Hodges, R. (2020). The accounting, budgeting and fiscal impact of COVID-19 on the United Kingdom. *Journal of Public Budgeting, Accounting and Financial Management, 32*(5), 785–795.

Hopper, T. (2020). Swimming in a sea of uncertainty–business, governance and the coronavirus (COVID-19) pandemic. *Journal of Accounting and Organizational Change, 16*(4), 533–539.

ISTAT. (2022). *Annuario Statistico Italiano.*

Jansen, J. J., Heavey, C., Mom, T. J., Simsek, Z., & Zahra, S. A. (2023). Scaling-up: Building, leading and sustaining rapid growth over time. *Journal of Management Studies, 60*(3), 581–604.

Knaup, A. E., & Piazza, M. C. (2007). Business employment dynamics data: survival and longevity, II. *Monthly Labour Review, 130*, 3.
Koutoupis, A., Kyriakogkonas, P., Pazarskis, M., & Davidopoulos, L. (2021). Corporate governance and COVID-19: a literature review. *Corporate Governance: The International Journal of Business in Society, 21*(6), 969–982.
Leoni, G., Lai, A., Stacchezzini, R., Steccolini, I., Brammer, S., Linnenluecke, M., & Demirag, I. (2021). Accounting, management and accountability in times of crisis: Lessons from the COVID-19 pandemic. *Accounting, Auditing and Accountability Journal, 34*(6), 1305–1319.
Leoni, G., Lai, A., Stacchezzini, R., Steccolini, I., Brammer, S., Linnenluecke, M., & Demirag, I. (2022). The pervasive role of accounting and accountability during the COVID-19 emergency. *Accounting, Auditing and Accountability Journal, 35*(1), 1–19.
Lewis, V. L., and Churchill, N. C. (1983). *The five stages of small business growth*. University of Illinois at Urbana-Champaign's Academy for Entrepreneurial Leadership Historical Research Reference in Entrepreneurship.
Mata, J. (1994). Firm growth during infancy. *Small Business Economics, 6*, 27–39.
Nicolò, D. (2017). Young firms sustainability and corporate reputation: A comparison of the survival rates in the US and EU. In *Sustainable entrepreneurship and investments in the green economy* (pp. 1–27). IGI Global.
Nicolò, D. (2019). *La vulnerabilità delle imprese nella fase di start-up. interpretazione delle cause*. Giappichelli.
Nicolò, D., & Ricca, B. (2019). Under-capitalization and other factors that influence the survival of young Italian companies. *International Journal of Advances in Management and Economics, 8*(2), 37–51.
OECD. (2003). *The sources of economic growth in OECD countries, Paris.*
Okrah, J., & Nepp, A. (2018). Factors affecting startup innovation and growth. *Journal of Advanced Management Science, 6*(1), 34–38.
Otola, I., Grabowska, M., & Krupka, Z. (2023). Response of high-growth enterprises to the crisis caused by the Covid-19 pandemic. *Management: Journal of Contemporary Management Issues, 28*(2), 13–26.
Penrose, E. (1955). Limits to the growth and size of firms. *The American Economic Review, 45*(2), 531–543.
Penrose, E. (1959). *The theory of the growth of the firm*. Oxford University Press.
Sargiacomo, M. (2015). Earthquakes, exceptional government and extraordinary accounting. *Accounting, Organizations and Society, 42*, 67–89.
Sargiacomo, M., & Walker, S. P. (2022). Disaster governance and hybrid organizations: accounting, performance challenges and evacuee housing. *Accounting, Auditing and Accountability Journal, 35*(3), 887–916.
Sargiacomo, M., Ianni, L., & Everett, J. (2014). Accounting for suffering: Calculative practices in the field of disaster relief. *Critical Perspectives on Accounting, 25*(7), 652–669.
Sargiacomo, M., Corazza, L., D'Andreamatteo, A., Dumay, J., & Guthrie, J. (2021). COVID-19 and the governmentality of emergency food in the City of Turin. *Accounting, Auditing and Accountability Journal, 34*(6), 1457–1470.
Waddock, S. A., & Graves, S. B. (1997). The corporate social performance–financial performance link. *Strategic Management Journal, 18*(4), 303–319.

Chapter 7
Bank Financing and Survival Risk in New Entrepreneurial Ventures: The Controversial Effect of Credit Guarantee Schemes

Giulia Cattafi and Antonio Del Pozzo

7.1 Introduction

Young entrepreneurial firms represent a cornerstone of contemporary government policies. These dynamic enterprises not only stimulate industrial dynamism but also play a critical role in fostering technological advancements and employment growth (Coad et al., 2014; Henrekson & Johansson, 2010).

However, young firms often struggle to survive due to the challenges of the "Liability of newness"—a concept introduced by Stinchcombe (2000, 1965) to describe the competitive disadvantage of nascent organizations due to the lack of established routines, unstable customer bases, limited managerial expertise, and underdeveloped corporate reputations (Bruna & Nicolò, 2020; Gimenez-Fernandez et al., 2020; Nicolò, 2015).

The start-up phase is one of the most critical stages in a company's life-cycle (Garnsey, 1998; Phillips & Kirchhoff, 1989), representing a crucial transition from an entrepreneurial idea to a scalable and innovative business (Blank & Euchner, 2018). This shift often occurs under financial constraints and with limited managerial experience (Garnsey, 1998; Nicolò, 2019). Additionally, the absence of an established track record, limited access to comprehensive financial data, and an underdeveloped corporate reputation (Bruna & Nicolò, 2020) weaken trust relationship with key stakeholders, such as investors and banks. As a result, obtaining the resources necessary for growth and survival becomes more increasingly challenging (Schneider & Veugelers, 2010).

G. Cattafi (✉)
Magna Graecia University of Catanzaro, Catanzaro, Italy
e-mail: giulia.cattafi@unime.it

A. Del Pozzo
Department of Economics, University of Messina, Messina, Italy
e-mail: adelpozzo@unime.it

S. Loprevite et al. (eds.), *Startups and Gazelle Enterprises*, SIDREA Series in Accounting and Business Administration,
https://doi.org/10.1007/978-3-031-90881-1_7

Securing bank financing, in particular, poses significant challenge for start-ups due to inadequate or low-value collateral and pervasive information asymmetries (Binks & Ennew, 1996; Colombo & Grilli, 2007). To mitigate these issues, the Italian government has introduced a set of policy measures aimed at improving access to bank credit for innovative micro-, small-, and medium-sized enterprises (SMEs) (MIMIT, 2019). These measured include incentives for private equity and venture capital investments, exemption from chamber fees and stamp duty, tax breaks, remuneration tools like stock options and work-for-equity and streamlined access to the Italian Central Guarantee Fund (CGF).

The Italian CGF, established under Law no. 662/1996, aims to facilitate access to bank credit for young businesses by offering public guarantees that can cover up to 80% of a loan's amount. While these guarantees aim to alleviate the financial constraints of new ventures, they may inadvertently lead companies to take on excessive levels of debt. Such over-leveraging could increase failure rates among government-backed enterprises, potentially jeopardizing the objectives of the Start-up Act.

This raises questions about the effectiveness of the Italian CGF in supporting new entrepreneurial ventures, particularly whether its impact depends on the amount of bank debt.

To address these questions, this study examines the relationship between bank debt, the Italian CGF, and new venture survival over a 10-year period. The analysis is based on a longitudinal sample of 20,905 small enterprises (with fewer than 10 employees) from the 2013 birth cohort.

While extensive research has explored the determinants of new venture survival, few studies have investigated the influence of bank debt on the survival risk of new businesses (Wamba et al., 2017), particularly within the Italian context. The Italian entrepreneurial ecosystem, which has undergone significant transformation since the introduction of the Start-up Act (Legislative Decree 18/2012), represents a relevant setting for this analysis.

To our knowledge, no prior studies have empirically investigated the interaction between guarantee funds and the degree of bank indebtedness on new firms' survival risk. Existing literature has primarily focused on the relationship between CGF and survival risk (Biancalani et al., 2022; Caselli et al., 2021; Fasano et al., 2022; Ferrucci et al., 2021; Finaldi Russo et al., 2016), overlooking the moderating effect of bank debt.

This chapter aims to fill this gap by examining the impact of bank debt on new venture survival and analyzing the potential moderating effect of the Italian CGF.

This chapter is structured as follows. Section 7.2 presents the theoretical framework, discussing the effect of bank borrowing on new venture survival. Section 7.3 outlines the research design, while Sect. 7.4 presents the empirical findings. Section 7.5 discusses the results, highlights limitations, and offers suggestions for future research.

7.2 Theoretical Framework and Hypotheses

7.2.1 *The Effect of Bank Debt on Start-up Survival*

Financial constraints are among the most significant obstacles to the survival of new small businesses (Aghion et al., 2007). New ventures often struggle to establish trust-based relationships with key stakeholders, secure bank loans, and face high interest rates on such loans (Paulet et al., 2014; Wamba et al., 2017).

The vulnerability of these ventures stems from their limited resource base, lack of reliable financial records, and underdeveloped corporate reputations (Nicolò, 2015). Additionally, many new businesses lack high-quality collateral to support loan applications, further exacerbating their financial difficulties (Biancalani et al., 2022; Hall et al., 2016).

Despite the extensive body of research, empirical findings on the relationship between indebtedness and start-up survival remain inconclusive (Wamba et al., 2017).

An earlier strand of literature suggests that debt can enhance both the growth and survival of small businesses (Åstebro & Bernhardt, 2003; Boyer & Blazy, 2014; Castaldo et al., 2023; Cole & Sokolyk, 2018; Cooper et al., 1994). In an empirical study based on a longitudinal sample of Italian start-ups from 2004 to 2006, Castaldo et al. (2023) found that access to bank loans positively influences firm survival. Castaldo et al. (2020) found similar findings in an empirical analysis based on a sample of 49,111 Italian start-ups from the 2003, 2004, and 2005 birth cohorts.

Using a longitudinal sample of 12,771 French manufacturing microenterprises, Boyer and Blazy (2014) also confirmed the importance of bank loans in reducing the survival risk for these firms. In the U.S., Åstebro and Bernhardt (2003), using firm-level data from the "Characteristics of Business Owners" (CBO) database, showed that bank loans were positively associated with start-up survival, ceteris paribus.

However, recent empirical evidence has drawn attention to the potential risks of debt financing for the survival of young businesses. In this regard, Wamba et al. (2017) found that the marginal benefits of debt on the survival of young firms diminish once financial debt exceeds certain thresholds.

Building on this recent line of research, we hypothesize a U-shaped relationship between the amount of bank debt and the survival risk of new entrepreneurial ventures. Specifically, we hypothesize that moderate levels of bank debt can improve the survival prospects of these firms (Cole & Sokolyk, 2018). In contrast, excessive debt significantly increases survival risk, as these ventures often struggle to generate sufficient cash flows to meet their financial obligations and repay interest (Berger & Udell, 1998).

Based on these arguments, we propose the following hypothesis:

- *H1: There is a U-shaped relationship between the level of bank debt and the survival risk of new entrepreneurial ventures.*

7.2.2 The Moderating Effect of Government-backed Loans on New Venture Survival

Credit Guarantee Schemes (CGS) are policy tools aimed at improving access to bank credit for start-ups and SMEs while mitigating credit risk for lenders.

In Italy, the Italian CGF was established under Law n. 662/1996 and has been operational since 2000. This scheme provides government-backed guarantees on bank loans, reducing lenders' credit risk and enabling small businesses to access financing. The Italian CGF guarantees up to 80% of the loan amount, with a maximum guarantee of €2.5 million per beneficiary. Public guarantees are offered in two forms: a Direct Guarantee, which directly backs the loan transaction, or a Counter-Guarantee/Reinsurance, which secures intermediaries such as "confidi" or other financial entities that initially provide the loan guarantee.

The reform introduced in 2012 (known as "Decreto Crescita 2.0") expanded the accessibility and scope of the Italian CGFs by streamlining the application process and broadening eligibility criteria. This reform sought to address the financial barriers faced by small businesses, which often struggle to secure bank loans due to insufficient collateral and limited credit histories (Biancalani et al., 2022; Hall et al., 2016).

However, the widespread use of government guarantees can raise concerns about the potential for excessive indebtedness among young ventures. In other words, public guarantees could encourage businesses to adopt aggressive financing strategies that may not be sustainable in the long term. This could potentially increase default rates among guaranteed firms and jeopardize the primary objective of the Italian CGFs.

In recent years, there has been growing scholarly interest in examining the effects of CGSs on the survival rates of new ventures.

A recent study by Ferrucci et al. (2021) demonstrated that government guarantees have a positive effect on both business growth and survival rates of innovative Italian start-ups. Similarly, Caselli et al. (2021) investigated the impact of CGFs on default rates of government-backed loans, confirming their effectiveness in reducing financial risks for lenders and banks.

Beyond the Italian context, the empirical literature has highlighted the critical role of CGSs for SMEs. Hallberg (2000) emphasized the role of CGSs in reducing information asymmetries and fostering trust relationship between borrowers and banks, thereby enhancing survival prospects of SMEs. Similarly, Beck et al. (2011) underscored the role of CGSs as key instruments for improving SMEs' access to bank credit, thus enhancing their survival prospects. Finally, Hossain et al. (2023) examined the effect of government guarantees on SMEs' access to bank loans, highlighting the positive effect of CGSs on the survival rates of small businesses.

In summary, empirical evidence consistently suggests that CGSs can effectively alleviate financial constraints and improve firms' resilience, especially in times of crisis (Fasano et al., 2022).

Against this background, it is reasonable to hypothesize that the Italian CGF positively influences the survival rates of new entrepreneurial ventures.

Therefore, we propose the following hypothesis:

- *H2: The Italian CGF positively influences the survival rates of new ventures, with government-backed start-ups expected to exhibit lower failure rates compared to their non-government-backed counterparts.*

The empirical literature has extensively highlighted the pivotal role of government-backed loans in enhancing the survival prospects of new ventures. However, some studies suggests that further investigation is needed to better understand the potential drawbacks of CGSs (Saito, 2014).

The Interministerial Decree of April 26, 2013, marked a significant turning point for the Italian entrepreneurial ecosystem. This reform established a more streamlined process for accessing the Italian CGF, enabling start-ups to undergo a simplified creditworthiness assessment. Importantly, when an authorized guarantor entity (also known as "confidi") requests reinsurance or a counter-guarantee, start-ups can access the CGF without undergoing additional credit risk assessment by the Medio Credito Centrale (MCC).

While this streamlined process can offer significant benefits to emerging businesses, it can also introduce some significant risks. One primary concern is that guarantor entities may struggle to accurately differentiate between low- and high-risk borrowers (Kim et al., 2021; Saito & Tsuruta, 2018). Furthermore, the reliance on government-backed guarantees could encourage start-ups to adopt more aggressive financial strategies, potentially without fully assessing their ability to manage high levels of debt. This may exacerbate their financial risk, ultimately increasing the likelihood of failure among government-backed start-ups.

Therefore, we propose the following hypothesis:

- *H3: The Italian CGFs strengthen the U-shaped relationship between the level of bank debt and the survival risk of new firms. Specifically, the positive effect of the Italian CGF on firm survival diminishes as the level of bank debt increases.*

7.3 Research Design

This section describes the research design, including the data collection process and the sample used for the empirical analysis.

To examine the impact of bank financing on the survival risk new firms, we performed a panel survival analysis. The firms in our sample were tracked from their inception until the year they exited the dataset (i.e., the year of exit), with data collected at discrete annual intervals from 2013 to 2021. Therefore, a discrete time survival analysis was employed, consistent with prior research (Audretsch & Mahmood, 1995; Cheng et al., 2023; Choi et al., 2017; Ejermo & Xiao, 2014; Ferrucci et al., 2021; Zhou & Van Der Zwan, 2019).

The survival analysis was conducted in two stages. First, the Kaplan-Meier non-parametric analysis was used to compare the survival rates between firms supported by government guarantees and those without such support. Second, we performed a complementary log-log regression (cloglog) to analyze the impact of bank financing on the survival risk of new firms and assess the moderating effect of the Italian CGF.

The survival analysis was conducted on a longitudinal sample of 20,906 Italian new entrepreneurial ventures over the period 2013–2022.

7.3.1 Sample

This study uses secondary data from two main sources: (1) firm-level accounting data from AIDA-Bureau van Dijk and (2) the database on operations with CGFs provided by the Ministry of Enterprise and Made in Italy (MIMIT). The focus is on entrepreneurial small businesses from the 2013 birth cohort, tracked over a 10-year period (until 2023) to evaluate their post-entry survival performance.

A key challenge in empirical research on start-up survival is defining what constitutes a "new venture" (Johnson & Thomas, 1982). Consistent with Johnson and Cathcart (1979) and Ejermo and Xiao (2014), we define a new firm as a small, young, and independent organization (i.e., not part of any business group). This definition allows us to account for heterogeneity among the sampled firms (Davidsson, 2010; Rannikko et al., 2019).

The identification of "new firms" was based on the following criteria. First, we identified the population of new established, non-financial firms with fewer than ten employees founded in Italy in 2013 from the AIDA-BvD database ($n = 31{,}807$). To ensure the inclusion of only truly de novo ventures, we selected only independent firms (Ejermo & Xiao, 2014; Rannikko et al., 2019). Furthermore, consistent with Luger and Koo (2005), firms that changed their registration name in their founding year were excluded.

Finally, companies operating in the education and social assistance sectors (Divisions J-U of the NACE-Rev.2 classification), as well as public authorities and non-profit organizations, were excluded due to specific sectorial regulations (La Rocca et al., 2019, 2024).

7.3.2 Econometric Modeling

To analyze the impact of the Italian CGF on the survival rates of new ventures, we first estimated the non-parametric Kaplan-Meier (KM) function. The KM function calculates the probability that a business remains operational at a given time (t) (Kaplan & Meier, 1958).

Given a sample of n start-ups with observed failure event (i.e., exit) occurring at periods $t1 < t2 < (\ldots) < t_n$, where t_n represents the last observed cessation year (December 31, 2022).

The KM function, denoted as $S(t)$, is defined as:

$$\hat{S}(t) = \prod_{i:t_i \leq t} \left(1 - \frac{d_i}{n_i}\right) \tag{7.1}$$

In Eq. (7.1), t_i represents the year in which the exit event occurred (i.e., the year the business failed). d_i is the number of firms that failed at time t_i, while n_i is the number of enterprises at risk just before time t_i.

This function estimates the probability that a business will survive beyond time t_i, given its survival history up to that point.

To further analyze the effect of indebtedness on the survival rates of new businesses and the potential moderating effect of the Italian CGF, we performed a complementary log-log regression analysis.

Equation (7.2) represents the baseline hazard rate $h_{i,\,t}$:

$$h_{i,t} = \mathrm{P}\left(S_i < s_{t+1} \middle| S_i \geq s_t \geq X_{i,t}\right) = F\left(x'_{i,t}\beta + \gamma_t\right) \tag{7.2}$$

The hazard rate in Eq. (7.2) depends on time-dependent covariates $X_{i,\,t}$. F(.) represents a distribution function ensuring $0 \leq h_{i,\,t} \leq 1$ for all i at time t. x' is a vector of time-varying covariates, and γ_t is a time-dependent function. Due to the unknown nature of the underlying risk, γ_t is typically included in the model as set of dummy variables (Hess & Persson, 2010). Since a firm's survival risk is negatively associated with its age, incorporating the linear and quadratic terms of firm age can help control for γ_t (Eq. 7.2), as suggested by Cheng et al. (2023).

Various specifications can be used to estimate discrete-time survival models. For this study, the complementary log-log (cloglog) specification was used. Unlike the Cox model, the cloglog regression is better suited for survival data organized in discrete time intervals (Dai et al., 2020). Moreover, the cloglog specification is widely used in empirical research on start-up survival (e.g., Basile et al., 2017; Castaldo et al., 2023; Cheng et al., 2023).

Thus, we estimated the following baseline cloglog regression (Eq. 7.3):

$$\begin{aligned} \log\left(-\log\left(1 - h_{i,t}\right)\right) = a + \beta_1 \mathrm{BDR}_{i,t-1} + \beta_2 \mathrm{BDR}^2_{i,t-1} \\ + \sum_{j=1}^{N} \delta C_{i,t-1} + \mathrm{REG} + \mathrm{IND} + \varepsilon_{i,t-1} \end{aligned} \tag{7.3}$$

In Eq. (7.3), β_1 and β_2 are the 1-year lagged coefficients of the linear and quadratic terms for the independent variable of interest (i.e., Bank Debt Ratio, BDR). The quadratic term captures the nonlinear effect of bank financing on the survival risk of new ventures. $\delta C_{i,\,t-1}$ represents the vector of control variables lagged by 1 year. REG and IND are dummy variables accounting for industry type (at the two-digit level of the NACE Rev.2 classification) and regional effects (at level 2 of the NUTS classification).

All explanatory variables were lagged by 1 year to mitigate potential endogeneity issues (Cenciarelli et al., 2018). This approach enhances the robustness of the findings by reducing the risk of reverse causality and providing a clearer causal interpretation of the relationships under study.

To analyze the potential moderating effect of the Italian CGF on the survival risk of new firms, we extended Eq. (7.3) by introducing the moderating variable (Z). Both linear and quadratic interaction terms were included to assess the moderating effect of the Italian CGF on the relationship between bank debt and survival risk.

Therefore, we estimated the following Eq. (7.4):

$$\begin{aligned}\log\left(-\log\left(1-h_{i,t}\right)\right) = a + \beta_1 \mathrm{BDR}_{i,t-1} + \beta_2 \mathrm{BDR}^2_{i,t-1} + Z_i PG \\ + \left(\beta_1 \mathrm{DBDR}_{i,t-1} * Z_i \mathrm{PG}\right) + \left(\beta_2 \mathrm{BDR}^2_{i,t-1} * Z_i PG\right) \\ + \sum_{j=1}^{N} \delta C_{i,t-1} + \mathrm{REG} + \mathrm{IND} + \varepsilon_{i,t-1}\end{aligned} \tag{7.4}$$

7.3.3 Variables

In survival analysis, the primary focus is on survival duration, which represents the time between a firm's entry (i.e., birth) and the failure event (typically defined as failure or bankruptcy).

To distinguish between ceased and surviving firms (i.e., censored observations), companies were categorized based on their legal status as recorded in the AIDA database. Consistent with Cheng et al. (2023), bankruptcy was treated as the equivalent of a firm's exit. Survival duration was, therefore, measured by the length of time a firm remained in the AIDA database. If a firm disappeared from the database in a given year (t), it was considered a failure (Delmar et al., 2013). Firms that were still tracked in the database at the end of the observation period (i.e., December 31, 2022) were classified as "active" (i.e., censored).

The key independent variable is the weight of bank debt (BDR), which is defined as the ratio of total bank debt (including both short- and long-term debt) to total assets (Arcuri et al., 2024; D'Apolito et al., 2024).

The moderating variable is the Italian Central Guarantee Fund (CGF), measured as the natural logarithm of the guaranteed loan amount (Ferrucci et al., 2021).

Before conducting the moderation analysis, the independent variables were mean-centered to mitigate multicollinearity concerns (Aiken & West, 1991; Chirico et al., 2011).

Several control variables were included in the regression analysis to account for firm-level characteristics that may influence new venture survival.

First, we controlled for liquidity (CASH), measured as the natural logarithmic of cash flow (Oliveira & Fortunato, 2006). Firms with positive cash flows are generally more resilient to financial difficulties and exhibit higher survival rates (Wilcox, 1973).

Second, we controlled for firm profitability, using Return on Asset (ROA). Higher ROA implies higher profitability and greater chances of survival (Baumöhl et al., 2020; Carretero-Gómez et al., 2023).

Patents (INN) were also included in the analysis as a measure of innovation. Patent filings not only offer legal protection against competitors, but also foster long-term growth and improve survival prospects of new businesses.

Investment rate (INV_R) also plays a key role in survival dynamics, reflecting the company's commitment to investing in fixed capital. Higher investment rates often indicate proactive growth strategies, positively influencing new venture survival.

The variable "CRAFT" is a dummy indicating whether the firm is registered in the special section of the business register for artisan firms. The distinctive characteristics of this sector can have a significant effect on start-up survival (Solomon & Mathias, 2020).

Additionally, we controlled for firm size and age. Firm size was measured as the natural logarithm of total assets, which helps account for the structural characteristics of the firm. Larger firms generally have more resources at their disposal to overcome financial challenges, increasing their likelihood of survival (Audretsch & Mahmood, 1995; Castaldo et al., 2023).

Regarding firm age, older businesses benefit from accumulated experience, stronger corporate reputation, and greater stability compared to younger firms (Ericson & Pakes, 1995; Jovanovic, 1982). To account for potential nonlinear effects, we included the quadratic specification of firm age (Bruderl & Schussler, 1990; Esteve-Pérez & Mañez-Castillejo, 2008).

7.4 Results

This section presents the results of the analysis examining the relationship between bank debt and the survival risk of new entrepreneurial ventures. It also discusses the findings related to the potential moderating effect of the Italian CGF.

7.4.1 Descriptive Statistics and Non-parametric Survival Analysis

This section provides the descriptive statistics for the variables used in the empirical analyses. It also presents the results from the non-parametric survival analysis, which estimates the survival rates of the Italian new ventures included in our sample.

Table 7.1 summarizes the financial and operational characteristics of the companies included in the analysis.

Table 7.1 Descriptive statistics

Variables	*N*	Mean	SD	Min	Max
Total bank debt (/000€)	45,715	0.202	6.04	0	1278
Banking debt ratio (%)	45,715	0.141	0.221	0	0.965
CGFs (nlog)	12,985	1.267	2.693	0	16.001
CGFs (/000€)	12,985	14,425	105,458	3	3300
Cash flow (/000€)	60,073	12.988	1485	−31.64	175,282
Cash Flow (nlog)	54,754	3.480	1.477	−6.908	12.074
Patents	62,726	0.021	0.144	0	1
Investment rate (%)	60,073	0.288	0.742	−0.442	7.684
Total assets (/000€)	60,073	1733	19,805	0.893	19,184
Total Assets (nlog)	60,073	6.202	1.253	−0.113	14.467
Firm Age	62,726	8.365	1.054	1	10

"Total bank debt" represents the total amount of bank debt (in thousands of euros) for the companies included in our sample. On average, the total bank debt of the sample is approximately 201,542 euros, while the average bank debt ratio (BDR) is equal to 0.141.

The average value of government-guaranteed loans, expressed both in logarithmic and nominal terms, is, respectively, equal to 1267 and 14,425 thousand euros.

The operating cash flow has an average value of approximately 120,988 thousand euros, indicating that the companies in the sample generate positive cash flows from their operating activities.

The average number of patents held by companies is 0.021, suggesting a low propensity for innovation in the companies included in the sample.

The average investment rate is 0.288%, reflecting a cautious approach to investment management. The sampled companies have an average total asset of approximately 1733 thousand euros, which represents the capital base necessary to support operations and grow. Lastly, the companies in the sample have an average age of 8 years.

Figure 7.1 illustrates the distribution of new Italian ventures across different industry sectors, according to the European Classification of Economic Activities (NACE Rev. 2).

To address potential multicollinearity issues, we conducted a correlation analysis before running the regression analyses.

Table 7.2 presents the correlation matrix along with the Variance Inflation Factor (VIF) for each variable. Both the mean VIF and the VIF for each individual variable are well below the critical threshold of 5.00 (Becker et al., 2015), confirming that multicollinearity does not represent a significant concern.

Table 7.3 presents the survival and failure rates of firms during their first 10 years of operation.

In the first year, the failure rate is approximately 3%. However, failure rates increase steadily over time. By the fifth year, the survival rate drops to 76%, with the failure rate rising to 24%. This pattern is consistent with previous research, which

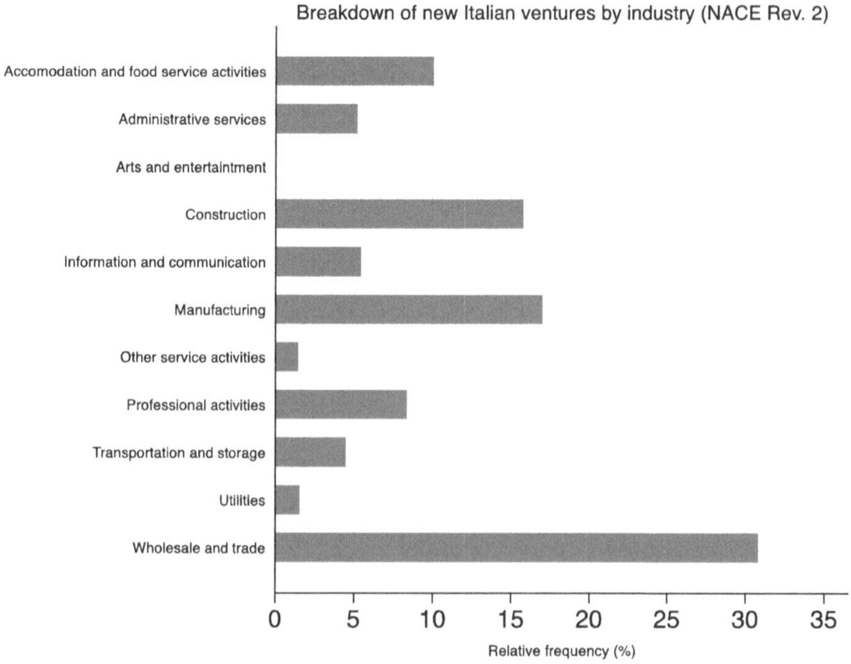

Fig. 7.1 Distribution of Firms by Industry Type

emphasizes that the early years are particularly critical for the survival of new ventures (Audretsch & Mahmood, 1995; Boyer & Blazy, 2014; Bruderl et al., 1992; Nicolò, 2019; Nicolò & Ricca, 2019; Phillips & Kirchhoff, 1989).

By the tenth year, the survival rate further decreases to 62%, while the failure rate climbs to 38%.

Figure 7.2 illustrates the survival and failure rates of businesses 10 years after birth. The graph clearly shows a steady upward trend in failure rates over time, consistent with the data shown in Table 7.3.

Figure 7.3 displays the Nelson-Aalen cumulative hazard function for the sampled firms over the study period. This graph shows how the cumulative risk of failure evolves over time. Sharp increases in the curve correspond to periods of heightened risk, while flatter sections indicate lower risk periods. The most significant increases in failure risk occur from the fifth year of operation, corroborating the findings of previous studies (Nicolò, 2019; Nicolò & Ricca, 2019).

Figure 7.4 presents the KM survival curves for firms backed by government guarantees (CGFs) and those without. The KM analysis was conducted to assess the impact of CGFs on the survival risk of start-ups during their first 10 years of operation.

The findings indicate that, on average, government-backed firms exhibit higher survival rates compared to those without government guarantees. This underscores the critical role of public guarantees in enhancing new venture survival (Caselli et al., 2021).

Table 7.2 Pairwise correlation matrix and VIF

Variables	BDR	GF	CASH_FLOW	ROA	PATENTS	INV_R	SIZE	AGE	VIF	1/VIF
BDR	1								1.02	0.98
GF	0.033*	1							1.01	0.99
CASH_FLOW	−0.036*	0.049*	1						3.66	0.27
ROA	−0.082*	−0.023*	0.330*	1					1.99	0.50
PATENTS	0.031*	0.012*	0.096*	−0.017*	1				1.02	0.98
INV_R	0.026*	−0.021	−0.050*	0.080*	0–007*	1			1.03	0.97
SIZE	−0.022*	0.061*	0.693*	0.034*	0.107*	−0.026*	1		3.41	0.29
AGE	0.076*	0.004	0.178*	0.064*	0.039*	−0.132*	0.183*	1	1.04	0.96
Mean VIF										

Table 7.3 Yearly survival and failure rates. Source: Authors' elaboration

		Survival rates		Failure rates	
Firm Age	Year	*n*	Frequency (%)	*n*	Frequency (%)
1	2013	20,247	0.97	659	0.032
2	2014	18,998	0.91	1908	0.091
3	2015	17,791	0.85	3115	0.149
4	2016	16,722	0.80	4184	0.200
5	2017	15,799	0.76	5107	0.244
6	2018	15,015	0.72	5891	0.282
7	2019	14,276	0.68	6630	0.317
8	2020	13,328	0.64	7578	0.362
9	2021	12,985	0.62	7921	0.379
10	2022	12,888	0.62	8018	0.384

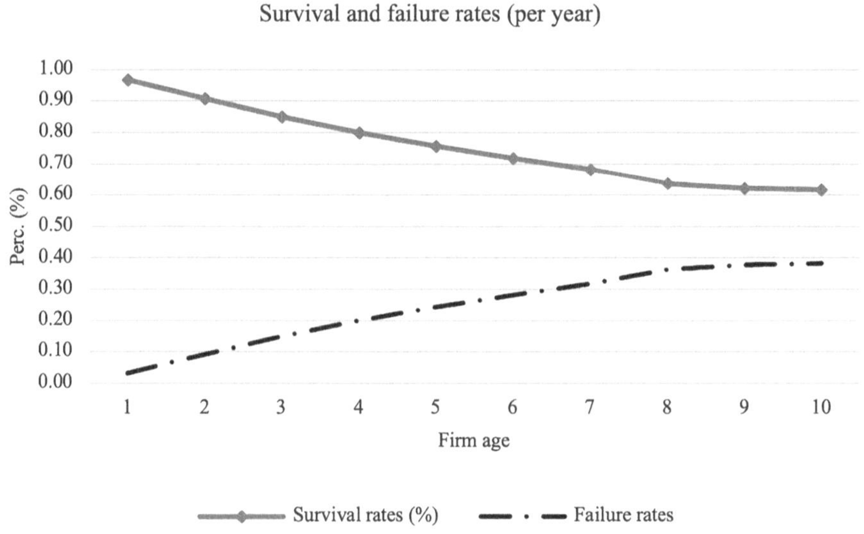

Fig. 7.2 Survival and failure rates (per year). Source: Own elaboration

7.4.2 *Discrete-Time Survival Analysis: Complementary Log-log Regression*

Table 7.4 presents the results from the complementary log-log regression.

In Model 1 (Col. 1), the coefficient for the BDR variable is negative and statistically significant at the 1% level ($p < 0.01$), suggesting that bank financing reduces the risk of failure for young firms. This finding supports previous research highlighting the beneficial effect of bank loans on the survival prospects of new ventures (Åstebro & Bernhardt, 2003; Boyer & Blazy, 2014; Castaldo et al., 2023).

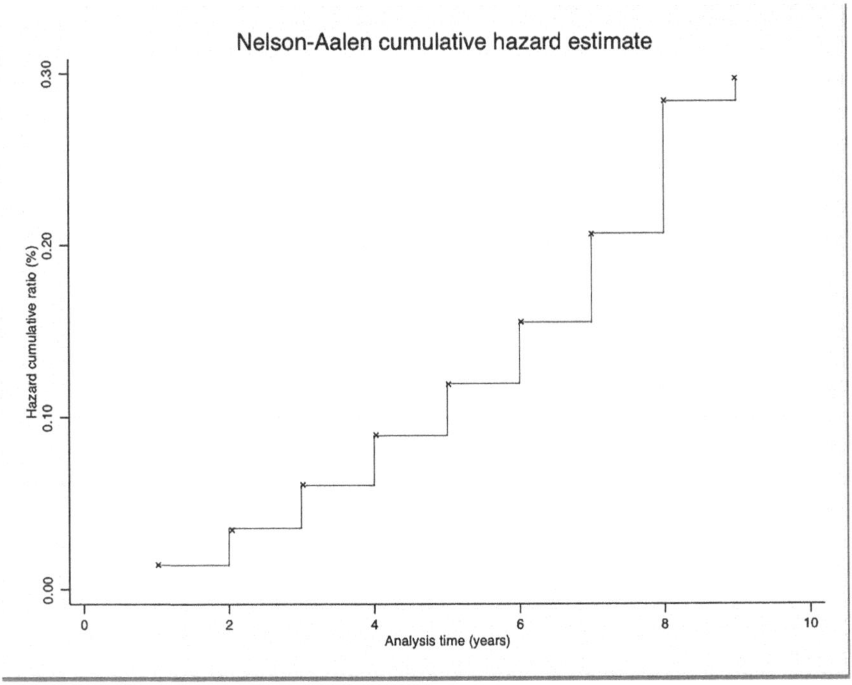

Fig. 7.3 Nelson-Aalen cumulative hazard estimates. Source: Own elaboration

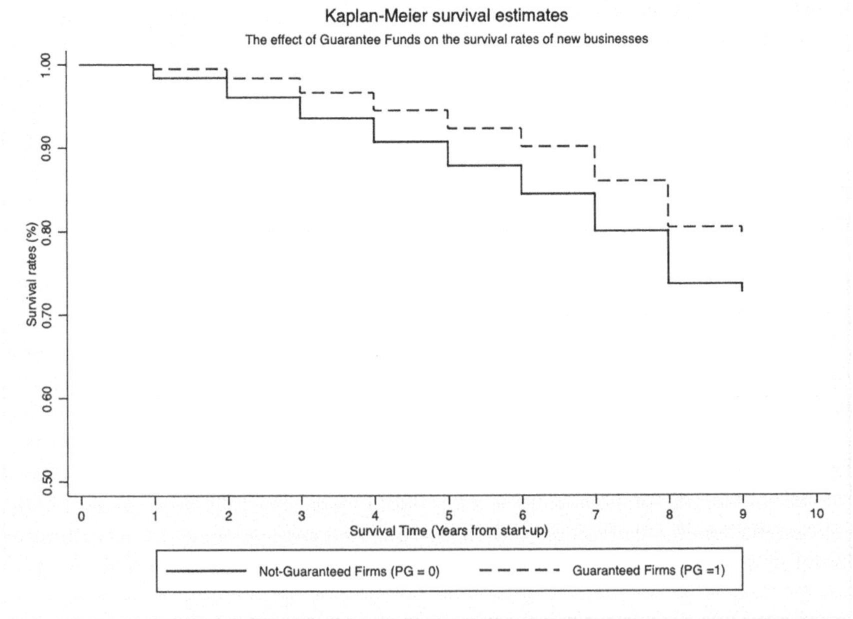

Fig. 7.4 Kaplan-Meier survival analysis. The effect of the Italian CGF on the survival rates of new businesses. Source: Own elaboration

Table 7.4 Estimation results from log-log complementary regression

	(1)	(2)	(3)	(4)
Variables	Coef./ (SE)	Coef./ (SE)	Coef./ (SE)	Coef./ (SE)
BDR(*t*–1)	−0.346**	−0.946***	−0.944***	−0.929***
	(0.140)	(0.336)	(0.336)	(0.336)
BDR2 (*t*–1)		0.888*	0.885*	0.860*
		(0.458)	(0.458)	(0.460)
GFs (*t*–1)			−0.004	0.045
			(0.021)	(0.032)
BDR (*t*–1) × CGFs(*t*–1)				−0.544**
				(0.242)
BDR2 (*t*–1) × CGFs(*t*–1)				0.639**
				(0.266)
CASH(*t*–1)	−0.061**	−0.061**	−0.061**	−0.061**
	(0.026)	(0.026)	(0.026)	(0.026)
ROA (*t*–1)	−0.002	−0.002	−0.002	−0.002
	(0.003)	(0.003)	(0.003)	(0.003)
PATENTS (*t*–1)	−0.022	−0.017	−0.017	−0.013
	(0.180)	(0.179)	(0.179)	(0.179)
INV_R (*t*–1)	−0.226***	−0.227***	−0.227***	−0.227***
	(0.022)	(0.022)	(0.022)	(0.022)
SIZE (*t*–1)	0.271***	0.273***	0.273***	0.273***
	(0.030)	(0.030)	(0.030)	(0.030)
AGE (*t*–1)	0.486***	0.485***	0.484***	0.484***
	0.073)	(0.073)	(0.073)	(0.073)
AGE2 (*t*–1)	−0.115***	−0.115***	−0.115***	−0.115***
	(0.006)	(0.006)	(0.006)	(0.006)
INTERCEPT	−1.394***	−1.372***	−1.372***	−1.369***
	(0.278)	(0.278)	(0.278)	(0.278)
Observations	60,253	60,253	60,253	60,253
Region Fixed-Effects	Yes	Yes	Yes	Yes
Industry Fixed-Effects	Yes	Yes	Yes	Yes
IC	4	4	4	4
N. Clusters	15,311	15,311	15,311	15,311
Log-Likelihood	−5714	−5712	−5712	−5710
Null Log-Likelihood	−8733	−8733	−8733	−8733
Wald Chi2	94.27***	94.41***	94.48***	94.43***

Notes: Clustered standard errors are reported in parentheses. *** $p < 0.01$, ** $p < 0.05$, * $p < 0.1$. Region and industry effects were omitted due to space constraints. Model (1) represents the baseline cloglog model including the linear coefficient of the BDR variable along with a set of control variables. Model (2) includes the quadratic term of the BDR variable. Model (3) adds the moderating variable "CGF". Model (4) introduces the interaction term "DEBT × CGFs" and its quadratic term. IC = Akaike Information Criterion. ll = Log-Likelihood

Model 2 (Col. 2) introduces the quadratic term for the BDR variable. The estimated coefficient for the BDR variable is positive and statistically significant ($p < 0.001$), revealing a U-shaped relationship between bank debt and survival risk, as shown in Fig. 7.5. This suggests that, initially, bank debt leverage reduces survival risk. However, once a certain threshold is exceeded, bank debt increases the failure risk of new business ventures, thus reducing their survival prospects. These findings align with the research of Wamba et al. (2017) and Huynh et al. (2012).

Model 3 (Col. 3) introduces the moderating variable, that is, the natural logarithm of the government-guaranteed loan (CGF) amount. The coefficient for the CGF variable is negative but not statistically significant ($p > 0.10$). Although this result does not support hypothesis 2, it aligns with previous research that highlights the positive impact of public guarantees on the survival prospects of small businesses (Ferrucci et al., 2021). According to Kang and Heshmati (2008), this positive effect stems from the critical role of public guarantees in alleviating the financial constraints of young businesses.

Model 4 (Col. 4) examines the interaction effect between BDR and CGFs. The linear coefficient of the interaction term (BDR × CGF) is negative and statistically significant ($p < 0.05$). In contrast, the quadratic coefficient of the interaction term (BDR2 × CGF) is positive and statistically significant ($p < 0.001$). This suggests that the effectiveness of public guarantees may diminish as debt financing increases, which is consistent with previous research (Kang & Heshmati, 2008; Saito, 2014; Saito & Tsuruta, 2018). Fig. 7.6. provides a visual representation of this relationship.

Regarding the control variables, the results highlight the importance of cash flow for the survival prospects of new businesses. The coefficient of the CASH FLOW

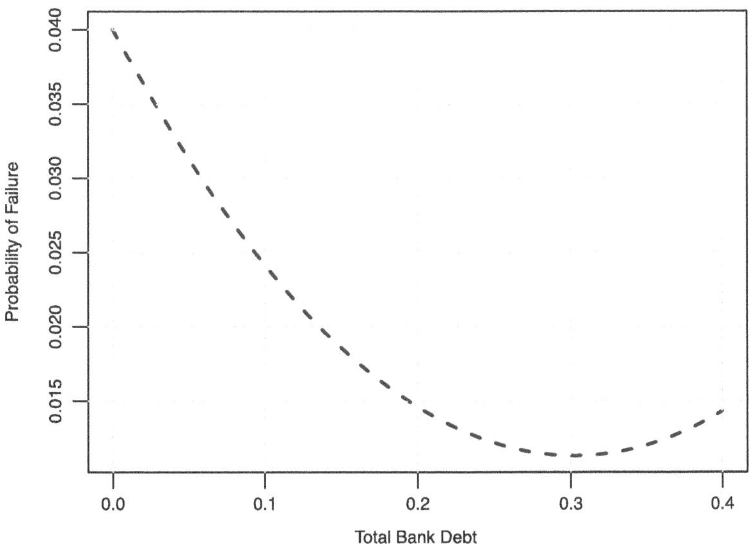

Fig. 7.5 The U-shaped relationship between bank debt and new venture survival

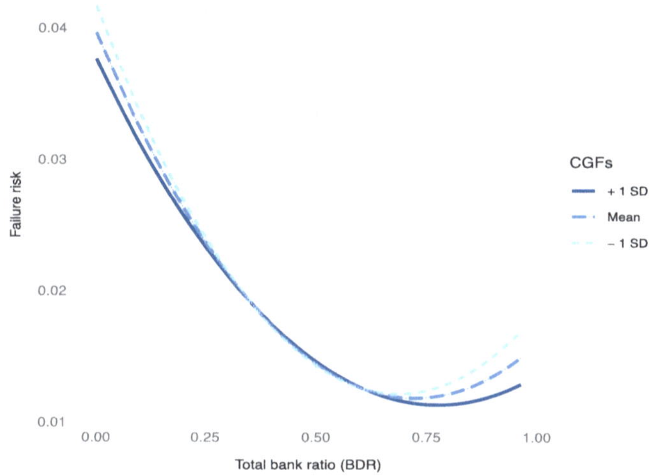

Fig. 7.6 The moderating effect of CGFs on the relationship between bank financing and new venture survival

variable is negative and statistically significant at the 5% level ($p < 0.05$) across all estimated models (Cols. 1–4). As stated by Liu et al. (2006), liquidity reserves are critical assets for new ventures, acting as a buffer to cover economic losses and manage adverse conditions, thus reducing the risk of exit.

Contrary to expectations, larger firms are less likely to fail compared to smaller ones. This may be because larger companies often require more complex organizational structures and routines, which can lead to inefficiencies and difficulties, particularly in the early stages of development (Garnsey, 1998; Greiner, 1998).

Consistently with Wennberg et al. (2016), the investment rate (INV_R) is critical for new venture survival ($p < 0.001$).

Lastly, the results indicate an inverted U-shaped relationship between firm age and survival risk. This can be explained by the so-called "liability of newness" (Stinchcombe, 1965, 2000), which postulates a negative relationship between firm age and new venture survival (Bruderl & Schussler, 1990).

7.4.3 Robustness Checks

To assess the robustness of the empirical findings, we conducted additional analyses.

First, to account for potential unobserved heterogeneity (Farnworth, 2012), we estimated the regression models using a complementary log-logistic regression with Random-Effects (RE). Second, recognizing that the hazard function often includes both logistic and normal distributions (Cheng et al., 2023), we estimated Eqs. (7.2–7.4) using logistic regression.

Table 7.5 presents the cloglog-RE regression estimates (Cols. 5–8), while Table 7.6 presents the results from the logistic regression (Cols. 9–12).

Table 7.5 Estimation results from the complementary log-log regression with Random Effects (RE) (controlling for unobserved heterogeneity)

	(5)	(6)	(7)	(8)
Variables	Coef./ (SE)	Coef./ (SE)	Coef./ (SE)	Coef./ (SE)
BDR(*t*–1)	−0.346**	−0.946***	−0.944***	−0.929***
	(0.140)	(0.336)	(0.336)	(0.336)
BDR 2 (*t*–1)		0.888*	0.885*	0.860*
		(0.458)	(0.458)	(0.460)
CGFs (*t*–1)			−0.004	0.045
			(0.021)	(0.032)
BDR (*t*–1) × CGFs(*t*–1)				−0.544**
				(0.242)
BDR2 (*t*–1) × CGFs(*t*–1)				0.639**
				(0.266)
CASH(*t*–1)	−0.061**	−0.061**	−0.061**	−0.061**
	(0.026)	(0.026)	(0.026)	(0.026)
ROA (*t*–1)	−0.002	−0.002	−0.002	−0.002
	(0.003)	(0.003)	(0.003)	(0.003)
PATENTS (*t*–1)	−0.022	−0.017	−0.017	−0.013
	(0.180)	(0.179)	(0.179)	(0.179)
INV_R (*t*–1)	−0.226***	−0.227***	−0.227***	−0.227***
	(0.022)	(0.022)	(0.022)	(0.022)
SIZE (*t*–1)	0.0271***	0.273***	0.273***	0.273***
	(0.030)	(0.030)	(0.030)	(0.030)
AGE(*t*–1)	0.486***	0.485***	0.484***	0.484***
	(0.073)	(0.073)	(0.073)	(0.073)
AGE2 (*t*–1)	−0.115***	−0.115***	−0.115***	−0.115***
	(0.006)	(0.006)	(0.006)	(0.006)
INTERCEPT	−1.394***	−1.372***	−1.372***	−1.369***
	(0.278)	(0.278)	(0.278)	(0.278)
Observations	60,253	60,253	60,253	60,253
N. of clusters	15,311	15,311	15,311	15,311
Region Fixed-Effects	Yes	Yes	Yes	Yes
Industry Fixed-Effects	Yes	Yes	Yes	Yes
IC	7	7	7	7
Log-Likelihood	−5714	−5712	−5712	−5710
Chi2	60,85***	60,93***	60,93***	60,93***
Rho	3.17e-06	3.17e-06	3.17e-06	3.17e-06

Notes: $p < 0.01$, $^{**}p < 0.05$, $^{*}p < 0.1$. Clustered standard errors are reported in parentheses. Region and Industry effects were omitted due to space constraints. Model (5) represents the baseline cloglog model including the linear coefficient of the BDR variable and a set of control variables. Model (6) includes the quadratic term of the BDR variable of the debt variable based on Model (5). Model (7) introduces the moderating variable "CGFs". Model (8) incorporates the interaction term "DEBT × CGFs" and its quadratic term

Table 7.6 Estimation results from the Logistic Regression analysis

Variables	(9) Coef./ (SE)	(10) Coef./ (SE)	(11) Coef./ (SE)	(12) Coef./ (SE)
BDR(*t*–1)	−0.386**	−1.090***	−1.088***	−1.072***
	(0.154)	(0.377)	(0.377)	(0.377)
BDR2 (*t*–1)		1.013**	1.011**	0.982**
		(0.499)	(0.499)	(0.501)
CGFs (*t*–1)			−0.004	0.052
			(0.024)	(0.038)
BDR (*t*–1) × CGFs(*t*–1)				−0.612**
				(0.268)
BDR2 (*t*–1) × CGFs(*t*–1)				0.708**
				(0.282)
CASH (*t*–1)	−0.080***	−0.080***	−0.080***	−0.080***
	(0.031)	(0.031)	(0.031)	(0.031)
ROA (*t*–1)	−0.002	−0.002	−0.002	−0.002
	(0.004)	(0.004)	(0.004)	(0.004)
PATENTS (*t*–1)	−0.055	−0.055	−0.054	−0.052
	(0.196)	(0.195)	(0.195)	(0.194)
INV_R (*t*–1)	−0.274***	−0.275***	−0.275***	−0.275***
	(0.024)	(0.024)	(0.024)	(0.024)
SIZE (*t*–1)	0.322***	0.324***	0.325***	0.325***
	(0.035)	(0.035)	(0.035)	(0.035)
AGE (*t*–1)	0.467***	0.465***	0.465***	0.464***
	(0.081)	(0.081)	(0.081)	(0.081)
AGE2 (*t*–1)	−0.123***	−0.122***	−0.122***	−0.122***
	(0.007)	(0.007)	(0.007)	(0.007)
INTERCEPT	−0.991***	−0.964***	−0.965***	−0.959***
	(0.322)	(0.323)	(0.323)	(0.322)
Observations	60,253	60,253	60,253	60,253
Region Fixed-Effects	Yes	Yes	Yes	Yes
Industry Fixed-Effects	Yes	Yes	Yes	Yes
IC	7	7	7	7
N. of clusters	15,311	15,311	15,311	15,311
Log-Likelihood	−5676	−5674	−5674	−5672
Null Log-Likelihood	−8733	−8733	−8733	−8733
Wald Chi2	7552***	7559***	7563***	7557***
Pseudo R2	0.350	0.350	0.350	0.351

Notes: $p < 0.01$, **$p < 0.05$, *$p < 0.1$. Clustered standard errors are reported in parentheses. ***$p < 0.01$, **$p < 0.05$, *$p < 0.1$. Region and industry effects were omitted due to space constraints. Model (9) presents the baseline cloglog model, including the linear coefficient of the independent variable of interest (BDR) and a set of control variables. Model (10) extends the baseline model by adding the quadratic term of the BDR variable. Model (11) incorporates the moderating variable "CGFs". introduces the interaction term "DEBT × CGFs" along with its quadratic term

Table 7.7 Empirical Fluctuation Process (EFP) test

Test	Statistic	Value
M-fluctuation Test	f(efp)	4.3268
	p-value	4.00E-15

Notes: f(efp) indicates the empirical fluctuation process

Both econometric specifications confirm the U-shaped relationship between bank debt and survival risk. Furthermore, the findings underscore the potential risks underlying the government guarantees, raising concerns about the controversial effect of CGFs on the survival prospects of new businesses.

To identify potential structural breaks within our data resulting from the COVID-19 pandemic, we first conducted the Chow Test for Structural Breaks using the R routine for the Empirical Fluctuation Process (EFP) (Zeileis et al., 2002). This test was designed to detect significant changes in the regression coefficients associated with the onset of the pandemic.

The EFP test (Table 7.7) clearly indicates the presence of a structural break in 2020. Consequently, we repeated the regression analysis, limiting the study period to 2013–2019 (the final year of observation). This adjustment effectively mitigates potential biases in the results caused by the impact of the COVID-19 pandemic.

Table 7.8 reports the regression estimates obtained after excluding the years impacted by the COVID-19 pandemic. The findings confirm the U-shaped relationship between bank debt and survival risk, supporting Hypothesis 1. They also provide support for Hypothesis 2, showing that public guarantees have a positive effect on the survival prospects of new entrepreneurial ventures. However, as bank indebtedness increases, the positive impact of guarantees diminishes, further strengthen the U-shaped relationship between bank debt and survival risk (Hypothesis 3).

7.5 Discussion, Implications, and Limitations

This study contributes to the literature on new venture survival by examining the role of bank debt and government-backed loans, with a particular focus on the Italian Central Guarantee Fund ("Fondo di Garanzia"). While access to debt capital is essential for entrepreneurial growth, new ventures often face significant financial constraints due to limited collateral and information asymmetries (Bertoni et al., 2023; Ferrucci et al., 2021; Hall et al., 2016).

In response to these challenges, the Italian government has introduced several reforms designed to support new venture creation and improve access to bank financing (Law 221/2012). A key element of these reforms is the Credit Guarantee

Table 7.8 Regression Estimates using complementary log-log models (Period 2013–2019)

	(13)	(14)	(15)	(16)
Variables	Coef./ (SE)	Coef./ (SE)	Coef./ (SE)	Coef./ (SE)
BDR(*t*–1)	–0.094	–1.571***	–1.412***	–1.519***
	(0.235)	(0.521)	(0.535)	(0.521)
BDR2 (*t*–1)		2.212***	2.063***	2.144***
		(0.712)	(0.725)	(0.712)
GFs (*t*–1)			–0.022*	–0.010
			(0.014)	(0.049)
BDR (*t*–1) × GFs(*t*–1)				–0.576
				(0.390)
BDR2 (*t*–1) × GFs(*t*–1)				0.885**
				(0.429)
CASH (*t*–1)	–0.001	–0.007	–0.004	–0.008
	(0.038)	(0.038)	(0.038)	(0.037)
ROA (*t*–1)	–0.006	–0.006	–0.006	–0.006
	(0.004)	(0.004)	(0.004)	(0.004)
PATENTS (*t*–1)	0.578*	0.604**	0.611**	0.610**
	(0.310)	(0.296)	(0.295)	(0.291)
INV_R (*t*–1)	–0.185***	–0.186***	–0.186***	–0.187***
	(0.022)	(0.022)	(0.022)	(0.022)
SIZE (*t*–1)	0.241***	0.251***	0.254***	0.254***
	(0.045)	(0.045)	(0.045)	(0.045)
AGE(*t*–1)	0.457***	0.457***	0.458***	0.450***
	(0.092)	(0.092)	(0.092)	(0.092)
AGE2(*t*–1)	–0.159***	–0.159***	–0.159***	–0.159***
	(0.008)	(0.008)	(0.008)	(0.008)
INTERCEPT	–0.770**	–0.722**	–0.742**	–0.728**
	(0.353)	(0.352)	(0.353)	(0.350)
Observations	41,217	41,217	41,217	41,217
Region Fixed-Effects	Yes	Yes	Yes	Yes
Industry Fixed-Effects	Yes	Yes	Yes	Yes
IC	4	4	4	4
N. of clusters	14,381	14,381	14,381	14,381
Log-Likelihood	–1866	–1861	–1860	–1859
Null Log-Likelihood	–4802	–4802	–4802	–4802
Wald Chi2	90,57***	89,99***	90,00***	89,84***

Notes: $p < 0.01$, $^{**}p < 0.05$, $^{*}p < 0.1$. Clustered standard errors in parentheses. Region and industry effects were omitted due to space constraints. Model (13) represents the baseline complementary log-log (cloglog) model, including the linear coefficient of the independent variable of interest (BDR) and a set of control variables. Model (14) incorporates the quadratic term of the BDR variable. Model (15) includes the moderating variable "CGFs". Model (16) introduces the interaction term "DEBT × CGFs" and its quadratic term

Systems (CGS), established by Law no. 662/96[1] with the aim of promoting access to credit for SMEs.

Given the importance of these policy instruments, in recent years a large body of literature has examined the impact of CGS on the survival rates of SMEs. However, the existing literature has predominantly highlighted the "bright sides" of government-backed loans, while neglecting the potential risks of these measures (Saito, 2014; Saito & Tsuruta, 2018).

This study seeks to fill this gap by examining not only the direct impact of bank loans on the survival of new businesses, but also whether the effectiveness of CGFs varies depending on the amount of debt.

This study contributes to the literature in several ways. First, while recognizing the importance of bank debt for the survival of new businesses, the results of this research call for caution in defining corporate debt policies. The empirical analysis has indeed revealed a U-shaped relationship between the level of bank debt and survival risk, indicating that excessive dependence on debt can significantly reduce the survival prospects of young businesses (Wamba et al., 2017).

Second, the empirical analysis was based on a large and representative sample of early stage microenterprises from the 2013 birth cohort. The cohort approach allowed for a more consistent and homogeneous analysis, as it tracks firms born in the same year until their exit (Rannikko et al., 2019).

Third, unlike previous studies, this research focused on the moderating effect of CGFs to assess how their impact on firm survival varies based on the level of debt. As discussed previously, as the amount of bank debt increases, and consequently the value of the public guarantee, the risk of adverse effects on the survival of new businesses also increases. High leverage can weaken a firm's financial stability, leading to increased debt servicing costs that may be unsustainable for start-ups. Furthermore, while government-backed guarantees are intended to ease financing challenges, they can also create moral hazard and adverse selection risks, which could ultimately undermine the goals of the Start-up Act.

The empirical findings have relevant practical and policy implications. Specifically, managers of new firms should exercise caution when adopting debt policies, even in the presence of public subsidies such as CGFs. The results underline the importance of carefully evaluating financial leverage to avoid excessive debt, which could jeopardize a firm's financial stability and increase the likelihood of failure.

Although this study provides valuable insights on the relationship between bank debt, government guarantees and new venture survival, some limitations should be highlighted.

First, the analysis is based on a single group of companies. While representative, analysis of a single cohort of businesses may not fully capture the effects of

[1] Decree-Law No. 23 of 8 April 2020 ("Liquidity Decree"), for example, introduced transitional provisions aimed at increasing the guarantees percentage and the maximum guaranteed amount to facilitate access to credit for companies in the crisis phase caused by the Covid-19 emergency.

economic fluctuations or policy changes over time. Future research could expand this analysis by comparing multiple cohorts of firms across different periods.

Second, the study is limited to Italian firms, potentially limiting the generalizability of these findings to other countries with different regulatory frameworks, entrepreneurial ecosystems, or government support policies. Therefore, future studies could explore the impact of similar policies in different geographic contexts.

Third, this study primarily investigates the impact of bank debt on new venture survival but does not consider alternative financing sources, such as equity financing, venture capital, or crowdfunding. Future research could broaden the scope to examine how these alternative financing mechanisms influence the survival prospects of new ventures, providing a more comprehensive understanding of the various factors that affect new venture survival.

Authors' contributions: Both authors conceived the study. A.D.P. wrote sections 1 and 5. G.C. wrote sections 2, 3 and 4. G.C. revised the article in accordance with the reviewers' comments.

References

Aghion, P., Fally, T., & Scarpetta, S. (2007). Credit constraints as a barrier to the entry and post-entry growth of firms. *Economic Policy, 22*, 732–779. https://doi.org/10.1111/j.1468-0327.2007.00190.x

Aiken, L. S., & West, S. G. (1991). *Multiple regression: Testing and interpreting interactions*. Sage.

Arcuri, M. C., Di Tommaso, C., & Pisani, R. (2024). Does gender matter in financing SMEs in green industry? *Research in International Business and Finance, 69*, 102222. https://doi.org/10.1016/j.ribaf.2024.102222

Åstebro, T., & Bernhardt, I. (2003). Start-up financing, owner characteristics, and survival. *Journal of Economics and Business, 55*, 303–319. https://doi.org/10.1016/S0148-6195(03)00029-8

Audretsch, D. B., & Mahmood, T. (1995). New firm survival: New results using a hazard function. *The Review of Economics and Statistics, 77*, 97. https://doi.org/10.2307/2109995

Basile, R., Pittiglio, R., & Reganati, F. (2017). Do agglomeration externalities affect firm survival? *Regional Studies, 51*, 548–562. https://doi.org/10.1080/00343404.2015.1114175

Baumöhl, E., Iwasaki, I., & Kočenda, E. (2020). Firm survival in new EU member states. *Economic Systems, 44*, 100743. https://doi.org/10.1016/j.ecosys.2020.100743

Beck, T., Demirgüç-Kunt, A., & Pería, M. S. M. (2011). Bank financing for SMEs: Evidence across countries and bank ownership types. *Journal of Financial Services Research, 39*, 35–54. https://doi.org/10.1007/s10693-010-0085-4

Becker, J.-M., Ringle, C. M., Sarstedt, M., & Völckner, F. (2015). How collinearity affects mixture regression results. *Marketing Letters, 26*, 643–659. https://doi.org/10.1007/s11002-014-9299-9

Berger, A. N., & Udell, G. F. (1998). The economics of small business finance: The roles of private equity and debt markets in the financial growth cycle. *Journal of Banking & Finance, 22*, 613–673. https://doi.org/10.1016/S0378-4266(98)00038-7

Bertoni, F., Colombo, M. G., & Quas, A. (2023). The long-term effects of loan guarantees on SME performance. *Journal of Corporate Finance, 80*, 102408. https://doi.org/10.1016/j.jcorpfin.2023.102408

Biancalani, F., Czarnitzki, D., & Riccaboni, M. (2022). The Italian Start Up Act: A microeconometric program evaluation. *Small Business Economics, 58*, 1699–1720. https://doi.org/10.1007/s11187-021-00468-7

Binks, M. R., & Ennew, C. T. (1996). Growing firms and the credit constraint. *Small Business Economics, 8*, 17–25. https://doi.org/10.1007/BF00391972

Blank, S., & Euchner, J. (2018). The genesis and future of lean startup: An interview with Steve Blank. *Research-Technology Management, 61*, 15–21. https://doi.org/10.1080/08956308.2018.1495963

Boyer, T., & Blazy, R. (2014). Born to be alive? The survival of innovative and non-innovative French micro-start-ups. *Small Business Economics, 42*, 669–683. https://doi.org/10.1007/s11187-013-9522-8

Bruderl, J., & Schussler, R. (1990). Organizational mortality: The liabilities of newness and adolescence. *Administrative Science Quarterly, 35*, 530. https://doi.org/10.2307/2393316

Bruderl, J., Preisendorfer, P., & Ziegler, R. (1992). Survival chances of newly founded business organizations. *American Sociological Review, 57*, 227. https://doi.org/10.2307/2096207

Bruna, M. G., & Nicolò, D. (2020). Corporate reputation and social sustainability in the early stages of start-ups: A theoretical model to match stakeholders' expectations through corporate social commitment. *Finance Research Letters, 35*, 101508. https://doi.org/10.1016/j.frl.2020.101508

Carretero-Gómez, J. M., Forteza, F. J., & Estudillo, B. (2023). Linking occupational accidents and construction firm survival. *Journal of Safety Research, 85*, 485–491. https://doi.org/10.1016/j.jsr.2023.05.002

Caselli, S., Corbetta, G., Cucinelli, D., & Rossolini, M. (2021). A survival analysis of public guaranteed loans: Does financial intermediary matter? *Journal of Financial Stability, 54*, 100880. https://doi.org/10.1016/j.jfs.2021.100880

Castaldo, A., De Luca, G., & Barile, B. (2020). Does Initial Access To Bank Loans Predict Startups'future Default Probability? Evidence From Italy. *Contemporary Economic Policy, 39*(1), 83–106.

Castaldo, A., Pittiglio, R., Reganati, F., & Sarno, D. (2023). Access to bank financing and start-up resilience: A survival analysis across business sectors in a time of crisis. *The Manchester School, 91*, 141–170. https://doi.org/10.1111/manc.12433

Cenciarelli, V. G., Greco, G., & Allegrini, M. (2018). Does intellectual capital help predict bankruptcy? *JIC, 19*, 321–337. https://doi.org/10.1108/JIC-03-2017-0047

Cheng, R., Yuan, P., & Jiang, G. (2023). Growth, agglomeration externalities, and survival: Evidence from Chinese manufacturing start-ups. *Journal of Business Research, 154*, 113319. https://doi.org/10.1016/j.jbusres.2022.113319

Chirico, F., Sirmon, D. G., Sciascia, S., & Mazzola, P. (2011). Resource orchestration in family firms: Investigating how entrepreneurial orientation, generational involvement, and participative strategy affect performance. *Strategic Entrepreneurship, 5*, 307–326. https://doi.org/10.1002/sej.121

Choi, T., Rupasingha, A., Robertson, J. C., & Leigh, N. G. (2017). The effects of high growth on new business survival. *Review of Regional Studies, 47*. https://doi.org/10.52324/001c.8025

Coad, A., Daunfeldt, S.-O., Holzl, W., Johansson, D., & Nightingale, P. (2014). High-growth firms: Introduction to the special section. *Industrial and Corporate Change, 23*, 91–112. https://doi.org/10.1093/icc/dtt052

Cole, R. A., & Sokolyk, T. (2018). Debt financing, survival, and growth of start-up firms. *Journal of Corporate Finance, 50*, 609–625. https://doi.org/10.1016/j.jcorpfin.2017.10.013

Colombo, M. G., & Grilli, L. (2007). Funding gaps? Access to bank loans by high-tech start-ups. *Small Business Economics, 29*, 25–46. https://doi.org/10.1007/s11187-005-4067-0

Cooper, A. C., Gimeno-Gascon, F. J., & Woo, C. Y. (1994). Initial human and financial capital as predictors of new venture performance. *Journal of Business Venturing, 9*, 371–395. https://doi.org/10.1016/0883-9026(94)90013-2

D'Apolito, E., Galletta, S., Iannuzzi, A. P., & Labini, S. S. (2024). Sustainability and bank credit access: New evidence from Italian SMEs. *Research in International Business and Finance, 69*, 102242. https://doi.org/10.1016/j.ribaf.2024.102242

Dai, M., Liu, H., & Lin, L. (2020). How innovation impacts firms' export survival: Does export mode matter? *The World Economy, 43*, 81–113. https://doi.org/10.1111/twec.12847

Davidsson, P. (2010). Small firm growth. *FNT in Entrepreneurship, 6*, 69–166. https://doi.org/10.1561/0300000029

Delmar, F., McKelvie, A., & Wennberg, K. (2013). Untangling the relationships among growth, profitability and survival in new firms. *Technovation, 33*, 276–291. https://doi.org/10.1016/j.technovation.2013.02.003

Ejermo, O., & Xiao, J. (2014). Entrepreneurship and survival over the business cycle: How do new technology-based firms differ? *Small Business Economics, 43*, 411–426. https://doi.org/10.1007/s11187-014-9543-y

Ericson, R., & Pakes, A. (1995). Markov-perfect industry dynamics: A framework for empirical work. *The Review of Economic Studies, 62*, 53. https://doi.org/10.2307/2297841

Esteve-Pérez, S., & Mañez-Castillejo, J. A. (2008). The resource-based theory of the firm and firm survival. *Small Business Economics, 30*, 231–249. https://doi.org/10.1007/s11187-006-9011-4

Farnworth, M. G. (2012). Faster estimation of a discrete-time proportional hazards model with gamma frailty. *Stata Journal, Stata Corp LP, 12*, 242–256.

Fasano, F., Javier Sánchez-Vidal, F., & La Rocca, M. (2022). The role of government policies for Italian firms during the COVID-19 crisis. *Finance Research Letters, 50*, 103273. https://doi.org/10.1016/j.frl.2022.103273

Ferrucci, E., Guida, R., & Meliciani, V. (2021). Financial constraints and the growth and survival of innovative start-ups: An analysis of Italian firms. *Eur Financial Management, 27*, 364–386. https://doi.org/10.1111/eufm.12277

Finaldi Russo, P., Magri, S., & Rampazzi, C. (2016). Innovative start-ups in Italy: Their special features and the effects of the 2102 law. *Politica Economica*, 297–330. https://doi.org/10.1429/83967

Garnsey, E. (1998). A theory of the early growth of the firm. *Industrial and Corporate Change, 7*, 523–556. https://doi.org/10.1093/icc/7.3.523

Gimenez-Fernandez, E. M., Sandulli, F. D., & Bogers, M. (2020). Unpacking liabilities of newness and smallness in innovative start-ups: Investigating the differences in innovation performance between new and older small firms. *Research Policy, 49*, 104049. https://doi.org/10.1016/j.respol.2020.104049

Greiner, L. E. (1998). Evolution and revolution as organizations grow. *Harvard Business Review Home, 76*, 55–67.

Hall, B. H., Moncada-Paternò-Castello, P., Montresor, S., & Vezzani, A. (2016). Financing constraints, R & D investments and innovative performances: New empirical evidence at the firm level for Europe. *Economics of Innovation and New Technology, 25*, 183–196. https://doi.org/10.1080/10438599.2015.1076194

Hallberg, K. (2000). *A market-oriented strategy for small and medium scale enterprises*. The World Bank. https://doi.org/10.1596/0-8213-4727-6

Henrekson, M., & Johansson, D. (2010). Gazelles as job creators: A survey and interpretation of the evidence. *Small Business Economics, 35*, 227–244. https://doi.org/10.1007/s11187-009-9172-z

Hess, W., Persson, M., 2010. The duration of trade revisited: Continuous-time vs. discrete-time hazards. *SSRN Journal*. doi:https://doi.org/10.2139/ssrn.1684615.

Hossain, M., Yoshino, N., & Tsubota, K. (2023). Sustainable financing strategies for the SMES: Two alternative models. *Sustainability, 15*, 8488. https://doi.org/10.3390/su15118488

Huynh, K. P., Petrunia, R. J., & Voia, M. (2012). Duration of new firms: The role of startup financial conditions, industry and aggregate factors. *Structural Change and Economic Dynamics, 23*, 354–362. https://doi.org/10.1016/j.strueco.2012.03.008

Johnson, P. S., & Cathcart, D. G. (1979). New manufacturing firms and regional development: Some evidence from the Northern Region. *Regional Studies, 13*, 269–280. https://doi.org/10.1080/09595237900185241

Johnson, P. S., & Thomas, R. B. (1982). New firms and employment creation. *Managerial and Decision Economics, 3*(4), 218–224. https://doi.org/10.1002/mde.4090030408

Jovanovic, B. (1982). Selection and the evolution of industry. *Econometrica, 50*, 649. https://doi.org/10.2307/1912606

Kang, J. W., & Heshmati, A. (2008). Effect of credit guarantee policy on survival and performance of SMEs in Republic of Korea. *Small Business Economics, 31*, 445–462. https://doi.org/10.1007/s11187-007-9049-y

Kaplan, E. L., & Meier, P. (1958). Nonparametric estimation from incomplete observations. *Journal of the American Statistical Association, 53*, 457–481. https://doi.org/10.1080/01621459.1958.10501452

Kim, S. S., Kesller, T., Lee, H., & Khan, M. S. (2021). *Policies to optimize the performance of credit guarantee schemes during financial crises (ADB Briefs), ADB Briefs*. Asian Development Bank. https://doi.org/10.22617/BRF210074-2

La Rocca, M., Staglianò, R., La Rocca, T., Cariola, A., & Skatova, E. (2019). Cash holdings and SME performance in Europe: The role of firm-specific and macroeconomic moderators. *Small Business Economics, 53*, 1051–1078. https://doi.org/10.1007/s11187-018-0100-y

La Rocca, M., Fasano, F., La Rocca, T., & Neha, N. (2024). Women in CEO duality and firm performance in Europe. *Journal of Management and Governance, 28*, 177–214. https://doi.org/10.1007/s10997-023-09669-6

Liu, S., Woodlock, P., Qi, H., & Xie, Y. A. (2006). Cash reserve and venture business survival probability. *The Journal of Entrepreneurial Finance, 11*, 123–136. https://doi.org/10.57229/2373-1761.1042

Luger, M. I., & Koo, J. (2005). Defining and tracking business start-ups. *Small Business Economics, 24*, 17–28. https://doi.org/10.1007/s11187-005-8598-1

MIMIT. (2019). *The Italian Startup Act. Italy's national strategy to support innovative startups and innovative SMES*. Ministry of Economic Development. Directorate-General for Industrial Policy, Competitiveness, and SMEs.

Nicolò, D. (2015). Towards a theory on corporate reputation and survival of young firms. *Procedia Economics and Finance, 22*, 296–303. https://doi.org/10.1016/S2212-5671(15)00289-0

Nicolò, D. (2019). *La vulnerabilità delle imprese nella fase di start-up: Analisi ed interpretazione delle cause*. G. Giappichelli.

Nicolò, D., & Ricca, B. (2019). Under-capitalization and other factors that influence the survival of young Italian companies. *International Journal of Advances in Management and Economics, 8*, 37–51.

Oliveira, B., & Fortunato, A. (2006). Firm growth and liquidity constraints: A dynamic analysis. *Small Business Economics, 27*, 139–156. https://doi.org/10.1007/s11187-006-0006-y

Paulet, E., Parnaudeau, M., & Abdessemed, T. (2014). The SME struggle for financing: A clampdown in European banks post-crisis. *Journal of Business Strategy, 35*, 36–45. https://doi.org/10.1108/JBS-09-2013-0089

Phillips, B. D., & Kirchhoff, B. A. (1989). Formation, growth and survival; Small firm dynamics in the U.S. Economy. *Small Business Economics, 1*, 65–74. https://doi.org/10.1007/BF00389917

Rannikko, H., Tornikoski, E. T., Isaksson, A., & Löfsten, H. (2019). Survival and growth patterns among new technology-based firms: Empirical study of cohort 2006 in Sweden. *Journal of Small Business Management, 57*, 640–657. https://doi.org/10.1111/jsbm.12428

Saito, K. (2014). *Do credit guarantees encourage moral hazard?* World Economic Forum.

Saito, K., & Tsuruta, D. (2018). Information asymmetry in small and medium enterprise credit guarantee schemes: Evidence from Japan. *Applied Economics, 50*, 2469–2485. https://doi.org/10.1080/00036846.2017.1400651

Schneider, C., & Veugelers, R. (2010). On young highly innovative companies: Why they matter and how (not) to policy support them. *Industrial and Corporate Change, 19*, 969–1007. https://doi.org/10.1093/icc/dtp052

Solomon, S. J., & Mathias, B. D. (2020). The artisans' dilemma: Artisan entrepreneurship and the challenge of firm growth. *Journal of Business Venturing, 35*, 106044. https://doi.org/10.1016/j.jbusvent.2020.106044

Stinchcombe, A. L. (1965). Social structure and organizations. In *Handbook of organizations* (pp. 142–193). Rand McNally.

Stinchcombe, A. L. (2000). Social structure and organizations. In *Advances in strategic management* (pp. 229–259). Emerald (MCB UP). https://doi.org/10.1016/S0742-3322(00)17019-6

Wamba, L. D., Hikkerova, L., Sahut, J.-M., & Braune, E. (2017). Indebtedness for young companies: Effects on survival. *Entrepreneurship and Regional Development, 29*, 174–196. https://doi.org/10.1080/08985626.2016.1255435

Wennberg, K., Delmar, F., & McKelvie, A. (2016). Variable risk preferences in new firm growth and survival. *Journal of Business Venturing, 31*, 408–427. https://doi.org/10.1016/j.jbusvent.2016.05.001

Wilcox, J. W. (1973). A prediction of business failure using accounting data. *Journal of Accounting Research, 11*, 163. https://doi.org/10.2307/2490035

Zeileis, A., Leisch, F., Hornik, K., & Kleiber, C. (2002). strucchange: An R package for testing for structural change in linear regression models. *The Journal of Statistical Software, 7*, 1–38. https://doi.org/10.18637/jss.v007.i02

Zhou, H., & Van Der Zwan, P. (2019). *Is there a risk of growing fast? The relationship between organic employment growth and firm exit*. Industrial and Corporate Change. https://doi.org/10.1093/icc/dtz006

Part III
Growth and Success Factors

Chapter 8
The Development of Gazelles at the Turn of the Pandemic Crisis: Greater Attention to the Generation of Social and Environmental Well-being?

Rodolfo Damiano and Marcantonio Ruisi

8.1 Introduction

Systemic crises, such as COVID-19, have challenged our economic and social system. In such disruptive situations, entrepreneurs must provide ingenious solutions not to fail and contribute to generating a more sustainable and resilient economy. In this respect, start-ups and gazelles could be key to our socio-economic system's well-being. However, many start-ups fail in the early stages of their entrepreneurial journey (Aminova & Marchi, 2021; Beresford & Saunders, 2005), while others are not capable of achieving high levels of growth (Jansen et al., 2023; Radácsi & Filep, 2021). In this study, we assume this may be due to a misunderstanding of their role in our economic and social system.

In this regard, following the economia aziendale theory (Costa & Ramus, 2012; Zappa, 1927), we hypothesize that mainly firms that have understood their role as agents of sustainability and common-good generation can survive and achieve gazelle status in times of crisis. To demonstrate this, we also employ upper echelons theory (Hambrick & Mason, 1984), according to which the characteristics of managers and entrepreneurs leading the firm are transmitted to such an entity and will determine its results in both financial and non-financial terms.

Therefore, our research question is: are firms that survived and rose to gazelle status characterized by a higher consciousness of their role as sustainable agents than the others?

We focus on the Italian context to perform such an investigation for two reasons. First of all, this country was the first and one of the most affected by the COVID-19 crisis in Europe (Bruni et al., 2023; Fezzi & Fanghella, 2020; Lazzerini & Putoto,

R. Damiano (✉) · M. Ruisi
Department of Economics, Business and Statistics, University of Palermo, Palermo, Italy
e-mail: rodolfo.damiano@unipa.it; marcantonio.ruisi@unipa.it

S. Loprevite et al. (eds.), *Startups and Gazelle Enterprises*, SIDREA Series in Accounting and Business Administration,
https://doi.org/10.1007/978-3-031-90881-1_8

2020; Possenti et al., 2021). Second, this country is the homeland of the economia aziendale theory and of other economic theories—such as the economia civile (Becchetti et al., 2019)—emphasizing the social role that the entrepreneurs should have in the social system to make this and the firm prosper (Costa & Ramus, 2012; Zappa, 1927, 1962). Specifically, we will use a matched sample of gazelles and non-gazelles and, using a quasi-Poisson regression model, we will try to understand whether being a gazelle implies a significantly greater orientation toward sustainability. We expect that the gazelles formed during the crisis period are characterized by a greater intention to contribute to social and environmental well-being than non-gazelles.

Overall, the work advances the readers' knowledge by linking the literature on start-ups and gazelles with firms' sustainability and resilience literature under the theoretical framework of economia aziendale, potentially nudging new research on the role of firms in our society. Further, the findings of this research also have implications for managers and policymakers by providing suggestions to orient, or re-orient, and support new entrepreneurial initiatives.

The remainder of the work is as follows: the next section will present the research context. The third section will discuss the research design, providing information on the theoretical framework, the sample selection and the analysis. The fourth section will provide the results of the analysis. Lastly, the fifth section will be used to discuss the work results and draw conclusions.

8.2 Research Context: Start-up, Sustainability, and Entrepreneurs

According to Paul Graham, start-ups are firms that are designed for rapid growth (Cattafi et al., 2023; Graham, 2012). Such firms present relevant innovative traits that can lead them to excel in terms of financial and non-financial performance (Carle & Rayna, 2024; Lamperti et al., 2023; Sreenivasan & Suresh, 2024). On this line, several entrepreneurship researchers (Carle & Rayna, 2024; Gionfriddo & Piccaluga, 2024; Lamperti et al., 2023; Zhu et al., 2023) posit that start-ups can play a pivotal role in addressing sustainable growth and development due to their capacity of bringing technologies, innovation, and new business models.

For instance, Malpani et al. (2024) investigate the nexus between corporate social responsibility, innovations, and financial performances in start-ups, noting that due to the rapid growth in the number of start-ups, their corporate social responsibility can strongly contribute to national socio-economic development. Further, the authors noticed that start-ups' corporate social responsibility and financial performance have a significant relationship. Specifically, they show that start-ups' corporate social responsibility can enhance innovation culture, generating long-term financial and non-financial value. In another study, Lamperti et al. (2023) highlight that start-ups can introduce business models that are valuable in addressing environmental and social issues and that the benefits they create can be spread to society overall. Pornparnomchai and Rajchamaha (2021) emphasize the importance of start-ups transitioning to more sustainable business models because of the growing consumption of the population and the limited resources of our planet. Nunes et al. (2022) analyze the implementation of business models for sustainability in start-ups. However, they found that such firms face relevant challenges in this respect and suggest that public policies should support them in doing so. Similarly, Cacciolatti et al. (2020) highlight that start-ups pursuing social missions can raise skepticism from investors due to the fact that they often operate in novel markets.

Therefore, while innovation with a social purpose is strictly related to entrepreneurship for sustainable growth, it needs to attract investments that could be lacking. In another study, Malpani and Ghosh (2023) report that experts state that corporate social responsibility practices are relevant for start-ups' success and long-term survival. However, the researchers also posited that performing such practices is challenging for start-ups (Salamzadeh, 2015). In this respect, they demonstrate that policymaker interventions can be useful in helping start-ups succeed in achieving societal well-being.

The insights from these studies highlight the importance of start-ups in allowing our society to achieve sustainable development. However, these studies also emphasize that letting start-ups follow the sustainability path is not trivial. It risks to be really challenging. Therefore, entrepreneurs guiding such firms must cope with difficult tasks and demonstrate relevant skills and perseverance. In this respect, while several studies have addressed different nuances and determinants of the relationship between start-ups and sustainability, a part of these studies has focused on the human factor behind sustainable start-ups. For instance, Carle and Rayna (2024) reveal that integrating the triple bottom line (Elkington, 1997) in the entrepreneurial process highly influences start-ups' sustainability. They demonstrate that start-ups born to be sustainable since the idea generation have greater sustainability consciousness and better control tools than start-ups that transitioned toward sustainability. In another study, Verma et al. (2023) demonstrate that greener intellectual capital influences societal sustainability and the co-creation of customer values. Further, Koe Hwee Nga and Shamuganathan (2010) examine demographic and personality traits that influence social entrepreneurship start-up intentions. They posit that to adopt an integrative view of financial with social and environmental objectives, entrepreneurs should be deeply committed to a social vision, sustainable practices, innovativeness, and relationality. In this respect, their findings suggest that such a commitment is related to certain personality characteristics and values defining entrepreneurial behaviors. Thus, according to the researchers, traits such as innate nurturing, socialization, education, agreeableness, and openness play an important role in generating effective and socially impactful entrepreneurship.

Lastly, studies have also investigated start-ups' resilience in relation to the COVID-19 crisis. In particular, Sreenivasan and Suresh (2023) identified the lean-sustainability enablers for start-ups during the COVID-19 epidemic, demonstrating that these are mainly related to the firms' human factor, and in particular, among these, there are leadership and managerial commitment and employees' skills and abilities, and engagement.

Following this brief literature review, it is possible to notice that addressing the role of start-ups in supporting sustainable development is a relevant topic that deserves more attention from researchers. In this regard, relying on the economia aziendale theory, suggesting that successful firms should play a pivotal social role in our social system oriented to the creation of the common good (Costa & Ramus, 2012), we investigate whether highly successful start-ups (i.e., gazelles) are characterized by a strong sustainability orientation, in particular in times of crisis, when a resilient response is needed.

8.3 Methodology

8.3.1 Theoretical Framework

To perform our investigation, we rely on a theoretical framework combining the economia aziendale[1] and upper echelons theory. Under the premise that the primary goal of economic units, whether for profit or not, public or private, is satisfying human needs and generating the common good rather than maximizing profit, economia aziendale is a person-centered business economics theory that connects organization, managerial, and accounting studies (Costa & Ramus, 2012; Zan, 1994; Zappa, 1962). According to the economia aziendale theory, human nature should be characterized by cooperation, solidarity, and benevolence rather than being only driven by utilitarian objectives (Costa & Ramus, 2012; Masini, 1960; Zappa, 1962). This perspective mitigates the distinction between ethics and business (Costa & Ramus, 2012; Masini, 1960; Zappa, 1962). According to this notion, a well-managed firm can benefit society as a whole in addition to creating financial value for its owners (Onida, 1968). Further, according to economia aziendale theory, a firm capable of merging this propensity to satisfying human needs, the primary aim of the firm, with the one of making profits, the physiological need of the firm, will prosper (Costa & Ramus, 2012; Zappa, 1927, 1962).

Regarding upper echelons theory (Hambrick & Mason, 1984), this theory posits that managers' and entrepreneurs' backgrounds and characteristics can significantly affect firms' strategies, operations and results. Researchers have largely applied such a theory to justify firms' behavior, focusing on factors such as demographic and cognitive ones and the values of the firms' decision-makers (D'Allura & Bannò, 2022).

---

[1] The definition of economia aziendale used in this work is that provided by Costa and Ramus (2012). Regarding economia aziendale see, among others, Pietro Onida's methodological and precursor study (1951). Furthermore, see Carlo Masini's ideas for a discussion of the common good as it relates to economia aziendale studies (Ruisi, 2016).

In this work, we combine these two theories, testing whether firms demonstrating a greater understanding of their role in society, according to the economia aziendale perspective, and thus guided by managers or entrepreneurs demonstrating such consciousness, according to upper echelons theory, are also more capable of prospering and becoming gazelles.

8.3.2 Sample Selection

We retrieved the sample for our analysis from the Bureau van Dijk AIDA database. This database contains Italian firms' financial and non-financial information. Following the definition provided by the Italian Institute of Statistics (ISTAT) in their 2018 annual report (ISTAT, 2018), we retrieved from the AIDA database the gazelles born in 2018. We decided to focus on this year because it allows us to deal with firms that became gazelles while coping with the COVID-19 crisis. Indeed, according to the ISTAT definition, gazelles have to be not older than 4 or 5 years and must have experienced high rates of growth in terms of sales or number of employees for three consecutive periods in such a time span.

Following the criteria provided by the ISTAT (2018), AIDA allowed us to retrieve 210 gazelles. Further, we gained a total population of 2098 non-gazelles from the AIDA database born in the same period. We retrieved the main financial pieces of information for all these firms, such as the total assets and sales. We also retrieved information regarding the board, such as the ages and genders of the directors. However, the AIDA database does not provide data that can be interpreted as proxies of sustainability or innovation orientation, nor does it provide data on entrepreneurial culture and values. In this regard, we performed an extra step to obtain our final sample. Indeed, while AIDA does not offer such measures, the database provides the firms' purpose statements and the link to their websites. Therefore, we gained extra information on sustainability orientation and entrepreneurial culture and values on which the firms rely by retrieving and analyzing texts from the firms' declared purposes and websites.

Particularly, while AIDA already provides the firms' purposes, we checked the websites to find the section in which a description of the firm, its mission, vision, and values are described. Such a section is usually titled "Who are we?" or also "The company." We retrieved all the texts in this section to gain insights into entrepreneurial orientation toward sustainability issues. In particular, we did so by performing an automated content analysis (Beattie, 2014; Krippendorff, 2012; Loughran & McDonald, 2011, 2015; Pencle & Mălăescu, 2016) on the statements of purpose and website texts using the Pencle and Mălăescu (2016) corporate social responsibility dictionary allowing to quantify the references to four different dimensions of sustainability, that is, "human rights," "employees," "environment," and "community." After this step, we performed a propensity score analysis (Austin, 2011) to match every gazelle in our sample (and the related information) with the most similar non-gazelle on the basis of total assets, region, and industry in which the firm operates. We decided to perform such a match on these measures because these represent measures related to the context in which the firm operates and to the stock of resources the firm has. We decided not to use measures of performance because gazelle differs from non-gazelle due to performance, so such variables in a matching procedure could lead to unreliable results. In other words, the match was performed on the stock of resources the firms have to operate instead of their results.

8.3.3 Variables and Inferential Analysis

To test whether gazelles show a higher orientation toward sustainability, we perform a quasi-poisson regression analysis using the R software (R Core Team, 2024). We use this extension of the Poisson regression because it guarantees more robust estimates when the model presents high levels of dispersion. Poisson is a generalized linear model that can be used instead of the traditional linear regression model when the response variable is not normally distributed. In particular, Poisson regression should be preferred to the traditional linear regression model when the response variable is a discrete variable such as a count. In our study, it is not possible to gain relevant traditional proxies of firms' sustainability orientation for our sample. This is because while most literature uses the texts within the sustainability reports as a proxy for this orientation (Beattie, 2014), such reporting practice is mainly diffuse among large companies and not in smaller ones. Therefore, we used the count of the terms of the Pencle and Mălăescu dictionary (2016) within the corporate purpose statement and the section dedicated to the description of the firm within the firms' websites as a proxy of the sustainability orientation for the firms in our sample.

However, considering that not all the firms in our sample provided a perfectly functioning website, our study's first source of sustainability orientation is the number of terms related to sustainability within the firm's purpose statement. So, this count is the primary response variable of our quasi-poisson regression model.

Then, we performed a second model using as a response variable the count of terms related to sustainability within the firm's purpose statement plus the count of the same terms in the description of the firm provided on the website.

We regress such measures of sustainability orientation using the following independent variables. We use a binary variable as the main independent variable, denoting whether the firm is or is not a gazelle. Then, we use board-related variables such as the average age of the board and the proportion of males and females in it. Lastly, we use the firm's size expressed in terms of total assets and the industrial sector as control variables.

8.4 Results

Table 8.1 shows the results of the analysis for the first regression model. As can be seen from the table, the model presents a high level of dispersion; therefore, performing a quasi-binomial model is a better fit than relying on the traditional Poisson regression. The results show that several variables significantly influence the sustainability-related terms in the firms' purpose statement. However, our main interest regards the significance of being a gazelle in influencing such a count. Overall, it is possible to notice that this variable significantly and positively affects the count of terms related to sustainability in the firm purpose statement.[2]

Now, we perform model 2 to test whether such a significant result also persists for the terms in the website's description of the firm. Also, in this case (see Table 8.2), it is possible to see that using a quasi-binomial model represents a better fit than running a Poisson regression model. Then, we can see that several variables affect the number of sustainability-related terms in the firms' purpose statement and website description of the firm. Notably, this regression model also confirms that being a gazelle positively affects such a measure.

Table 8.1 Quasi-Poisson regression model (response variable: number of sustainability-related terms within the firm's purpose statement)

	Estimate	Std. Error	t value	Pr(>|t|)	
Intercept	3.07E+00	4.73E-01	6.504962058	3.23E-10	***
Total assets	−4.10E-07	8.98E-07	−0.456484147	6.48E-01	
ATECO 2007 = 581300	1.18E+00	5.26E-01	2.241081381	2.57E-02	*
ATECO 2007 = 812202	8.50E-01	5.09E-01	1.668239497	9.63E-02	.
ATECO 2007 = 812999	9.40E-01	4.79E-01	1.961008626	5.08E-02	.
ATECO 2007 = 821909	1.12E+00	4.99E-01	2.236722739	2.60E-02	*
ATECO 2007 = 829999	7.48E-01	4.69E-01	1.594108745	1.12E-01	
ATECO 2007 = 853120	1.06E+00	5.35E-01	1.974855746	4.92E-02	*
ATECO 2007 = 855930	9.42E-01	4.92E-01	1.912391342	5.68E-02	.
ATECO 2007 = 873000	1.08E+00	4.88E-01	2.209282264	2.79E-02	*
ATECO 2007 = 960300	8.27E-01	4.88E-01	1.694622273	9.12E-02	.
Board female proportion	−8.42E-03	6.08E-02	−0.138420461	8.90E-01	
Board average age	5.35E-04	1.85E-03	0.289733673	7.72E-01	
Gazella = Yes	7.94E-02	3.91E-02	2.032412988	4.30E-02	*

Signif. codes: 0 '***' 0.001 '**' 0.01 '*' 0.05 '.' 0.1" 1 (Dispersion parameter for quasi-poisson family taken to be 5.083314)

Null deviance: 3132.6 on 417 degrees of freedom, Residual deviance: 1624.4 on 301 degrees of freedom

Number of Fisher Scoring iterations: 5

[2] For reasons of space, the tables with the results of the regression models present only a part of the industrial sectors analysed.

Table 8.2 Quasi-Poisson regression model (response variable: number of sustainability-related terms within the firm's purpose statement and firm description provided on the firm website)

	Estimate	Std. Error	t value	Pr(>|t|)	
Intercept	3.88E+00	4.51E-01	8.597186386	4.54E-16	***
Total assets	6.32E-07	1.20E-06	0.524586588	6.00E-01	
ATECO 2007 = 152010	−8.40E-01	4.91E-01	−1.709098152	8.85E-02	.
ATECO 2007 = 231100	1.55E+00	4.89E-01	3.174254908	1.66E-03	**
ATECO 2007 = 463210	−1.21E+00	7.20E-01	−1.679150484	9.42E-02	.
ATECO 2007 = 471990	−8.81E-01	4.86E-01	−1.813554208	7.07E-02	.
ATECO 2007 = 475910	−1.19E+00	7.09E-01	−1.677579702	9.45E-02	.
Board female proportion	4.62E-02	8.58E-02	0.538311326	5.91E-01	
Board average age	2.51E-03	2.62E-03	0.957620435	3.39E-01	
Gazella = Yes	2.37E-01	5.44E-02	4.361751989	1.77E-05	***

Signif. codes: 0 '***' 0.001 '**' 0.01 '*' 0.05 '.' 0.1″ 1 (Dispersion parameter for quasi-poisson family taken to be 12.8047)
Null deviance: 7609.9 on 417 degrees of freedom, Residual deviance: 3711.7 on 301 degrees of freedom
Number of Fisher Scoring iterations: 5

8.5 Discussion and Conclusions

The results of the analysis allow us to answer our research question on whether entrepreneurial orientation toward innovation and sustainability significantly distinguishes gazelles from non-gazelles. In particular, our study answers affirmatively to this research question, demonstrating that gazelles show more sustainability-related terms in their firm purpose statement and their descriptions of themselves on their websites.

Overall, in line with previous studies positing a great orientation of start-ups toward sustainability (Carle & Rayna, 2024; Gionfriddo & Piccaluga, 2024; Lamperti et al., 2023; Zhu et al., 2023), the results of the analysis found a great orientation of Italian gazelles toward sustainability in times of crisis and suggest that gazelles can play a pivotal role for sustainable development.

In this regard, while previous studies have already demonstrated that several factors can contribute to making firms more sustainable (Carle & Rayna, 2024; Verma et al., 2023), our study is the first to provide evidence of an underlying tension toward sustainability of gazelle firms. In particular, we do so in alignment with the economia aziendale theory, according to which the role of successful firms is to create sustainable value for the entire society and not only maximize profits. In line with these results, our study adds to these previous findings that firms becoming gazelles during a crisis are guided by an intrinsic orientation to creating the common good (see, Costa & Ramus, 2012).

Such new understanding can be useful in comprehending that economia aziendale principles can stimulate the birth of gazelles, reminding entrepreneurs that whether they want their firms to achieve high success, they should bet on satisfying human needs by solving societal problems orienting their purposes and their vision of the firms toward sustainable development principles (Costa & Ramus, 2012; Zappa, 1927).

Overall, this work advances the literature on the relationship between start-ups and sustainability that has demonstrated that start-ups can be pivotal in achieving sustainable development (Carle & Rayna, 2024; Gionfriddo & Piccaluga, 2024; Lamperti et al., 2023; Malpani et al., 2024; Zhu et al., 2023) and stating that implementing sustainability-related processes and practices is relevant for start-ups long-term survival (Malpani & Ghosh, 2023), by adding that start-ups explicitly showing their willingness to contribute to sustainable development are more likely to evolve into gazelles (highly successful start-ups). Therefore, the originality of the work consists in demonstrating that an underlying tension to solve sustainable development challenges can characterize highly successful start-ups. We have done this in light of the framework economia aziendale and upper echelons theory showing that the communication in the firm's purpose declaration and the firm's website description—as representations of the vision and mission of the management (upper echelons) that could be animated by higher values regarding the firm purpose (economia aziendale)—can lead to the birth of a gazelle.

To sum up, the present chapter demonstrated that the gazelles born in Italy at the turn of the pandemic crisis show a significantly higher sustainability orientation through their statements of purpose and websites with respect to their non-gazelle counterparts. In particular, in light of previous literature showing that an orientation of start-ups toward sustainable development and the strong role these entrepreneurial entities can achieve in such a global mission, we add that highly successful start-ups (gazelles) in the Italian context at the turn of the pandemic crisis show an intrinsic orientation toward sustainability.

Our work has several implications. Particularly, our study does not only provide empirical evidence on the phenomenon of gazelles at the turn of a global crisis, but it also contributes theoretically to the literature demonstrating that such firms align their purposes with the economia aziendale theory principles.

Then, as regards managerial and policymaker implications, according to our results, betting on sustainability is the way to go to develop gazelles in times of crisis. In this regard, entrepreneurs searching for the generation of successful gazelles in such disruptive periods should address societal challenges and contribute to sustainable development and common good creation to gain more chances of achieving such a result. Similarly, policymakers should provide support for the generation of such realities. This could be done by investing in training entrepreneurs on sustainability and economia aziendale principles to allow them to cope better with the social role the society needs them to comply with. In this respect, for example, the Italian legal environment already offers incentives for supporting innovative start-ups. However, such incentives do not consider the purpose of the start-up other than developing technological products and services. Such incentives are provided on the basis of the means (e.g., the level of education of members and patents) instead of the purpose of the start-up. In this regard, policymakers could consider developing new incentivizing strategies, taking into account both the level of innovativeness and the declared purposes of the firm in order to further incentivize those realities intended to leverage innovativeness to solve environmental and social problems. Such an incentivizing scheme could combine policies planned to support innovative start-ups with those proposed to support other forms of firms that are more socially and environmentally committed (see "imprese sociali" and "società benefit"). Obviously, such incentives should be subordinated to reporting information on the progress of the start-up in coping with the environmental and social challenges it decided to address. Although there are already incentives for realities of this type in Italy (the so-called start-ups with a social vocation or SIAVS), these realities present some heavy constraints in terms of non-distribution of profits and constraints on the sectors in which they can operate (Damiano, 2022). This risks limiting their competitiveness by making these forms of organizations closer to the non-profit world than to the for-profit or hybrid organizations (potentially inhibiting the generation of gazelles) (Battilana et al., 2012).

Lastly, this study is not without limitations. First of all, we investigated a very specific sample: the gazelles born at the turn of the COVID-19 crisis in the Italian context. Our study demonstrates that gazelles born in this period have a greater orientation toward sustainability than non-gazelles. However, while choosing such a specific sample allows us to answer our research question, it is not possible for us to discern whether such a characteristic is only proper for gazelles developed at the turn of the COVID-19 crisis or gazelles overall. In this regard, we strongly recommend future studies rely on the insights provided in this study by repeating the present analysis in a larger context in terms of territories and time span to corroborate and provide more generalizable results on the relationship between sustainability orientation and gazelles' generation. Then, as regards other future lines of research, other studies can rely on the content of this chapter to conduct case studies on gazelles (or potential ones) to unveil whether and how these firms align their purposes, objectives, and strategies with the economia aziendale theory.

References

Aminova, M., & Marchi, E. (2021). The role of innovation on start-up failure vs. its success. *International Journal of Business Ethics and Governance*, 41–72. https://doi.org/10.51325/ijbeg.v4i1.60

Austin, P. C. (2011). An introduction to propensity score methods for reducing the effects of confounding in observational studies. *Multivariate Behavioral Research, 46*(3), 399–424. https://doi.org/10.1080/00273171.2011.568786

Battilana, J., Lee, M., Walker, J., & Dorsey, C. (2012). In search of hybrid ideal. *Stanford Social Innovation Review, 10*(3), 51–55.

Beattie, V. (2014). Accounting narratives and the narrative turn in accounting research: Issues, theory, methodology, methods and a research framework. *The British Accounting Review, 46*(2), 111–134. https://doi.org/10.1016/j.bar.2014.05.001

Becchetti, L., Bruni, L., & Zamagni, S. (2019). *Economia civile e sviluppo sostenibile. Progettare e Misurare Un Nuovo Modello Di Benessere*. Ecra, Rome.

Beresford, R., & Saunders, M. N. K. (2005). Professionalization of the business start-up process. *Strategic Change, 14*(6), 337–347. https://doi.org/10.1002/jsc.734

Bruni, M. E., Masali, G., & Perboli, G. (2023). The effect of COVID-19 on the economic systems: Evidence from the Italian case. *2023 IEEE 47th annual computers, software, and applications conference (COMPSAC)* (pp. 1745–1749). doi:https://doi.org/10.1109/COMPSAC57700.2023.00269.

Cacciolatti, L., Rosli, A., Ruiz-Alba, J. L., & Chang, J. (2020). Strategic alliances and firm performance in startups with a social mission. *Journal of Business Research, 106*, 106–117. https://doi.org/10.1016/j.jbusres.2019.08.047

Carle, A., & Rayna, T. (2024). Where to start? Exploring how sustainable startups integrate sustainability impact assessment within their entrepreneurial process. *Journal of Management and Organization, 30*(1), 148–164. https://doi.org/10.1017/jmo.2023.46

Cattafi, G., Del Pozzo, A., & Nicolò, D. (2023). People first! Intellectual capital and growth of high-growth social cooperatives (social gazelles) in the startup stage. Evidence from Italy. *Piccola Impresa/Small Business, 1*. https://doi.org/10.14596/pisb.3500

Costa, E., & Ramus, T. (2012). The Italian economia aziendale and catholic social teaching: How to apply the common good principle at the managerial level. *Journal of Business Ethics, 106*(1), 103–116. https://doi.org/10.1007/s10551-011-1056-x

D'Allura, G., & Bannò, M. (2022). *Mariasole Bannò DONNE E GOVERNO D'IMPRESA Prospettive teoriche ed evidenze empiriche*. FrancoAngeli, Milan.

Damiano, R. (2022). *Multidimensionalità del valore aziendale e valutazione dell'impatto sociale: nuove prospettive di indagine*. Aracne, Rome.

Elkington, J. (1997). *Cannibals with Forks: The triple bottom line of 21st century business*. Capstone, Oxford.

Fezzi, C., & Fanghella, V. (2020). Real-time estimation of the short-run impact of COVID-19 on economic activity using electricity market data. *Environmental and Resource Economics, 76*(4), 885–900. https://doi.org/10.1007/s10640-020-00467-4

Gionfriddo, G., & Piccaluga, A. (2024). Startups' contribution to SDGs: A tailored framework for assessing social impact. *Journal of Management and Organization, 30*, 1–29. https://doi.org/10.1017/jmo.2024.3

Graham, P. (2012). *Startup = growth*. Internet access: http://www.paulgraham.com/growth.html, 1.

Hambrick, D. C., & Mason, P. A. (1984). Upper echelons: The organization as a reflection of its top managers. *The Academy of Management Review, 9*(2), 193. https://doi.org/10.2307/258434

ISTAT. (2018). *Annuario Statistico Italiano*. Istituto Nazionale di Statistica, Rome.

Jansen, J. J. P., Heavey, C., Mom, T. J. M., Simsek, Z., & Zahra, S. A. (2023). Scaling-up: Building, leading and sustaining rapid growth over time. *Journal of Management Studies, 60*(3), 581–604. https://doi.org/10.1111/joms.12910

Koe Hwee Nga, J., & Shamuganathan, G. (2010). The influence of personality traits and demographic factors on social entrepreneurship start up intentions. *Journal of Business Ethics, 95*(2), 259–282. https://doi.org/10.1007/s10551-009-0358-8

Krippendorff, K. (2012). *Content analysis: An introduction to its methodology*. Sage, Los Angeles London New Delhi Singapore.

Lamperti, S., Sammut, S., & Courrent, J.-M. (2023). From incubator's knowledge transfer to sustainability start-ups' impact: A case study in a French support program. *Journal of Knowledge Management, 27*(9), 2393–2413. https://doi.org/10.1108/JKM-09-2022-0690

Lazzerini, M., & Putoto, G. (2020). COVID-19 in Italy: Momentous decisions and many uncertainties. *The Lancet Global Health, 8*(5), e641–e642. https://doi.org/10.1016/S2214-109X(20)30110-8

Loughran, T., & McDonald, B. (2011). When is a liability not a liability? Textual analysis, dictionaries, and 10-Ks. *The Journal of Finance, 66*(1), 35–65. https://doi.org/10.1111/j.1540-6261.2010.01625.x

Loughran, T., & McDonald, B. (2015). The use of word lists in textual analysis. *Journal of Behavioral Finance, 16*(1), 1–11. https://doi.org/10.1080/15427560.2015.1000335

Malpani, R., & Ghosh, A. (2023). Corporate social responsibility practices: A strategy for indian startups to sustain. *Business Perspectives and Research, 11*(2), 246–268. https://doi.org/10.1177/22785337211070357

Malpani, R., Baral, M. M., Panigrahi, R. R., & Chittipaka, V. (2024). Unveiling the dynamic nexus between corporate social responsibility, innovations and financial performances in 21st-century Indian start-ups. *International Journal of Organizational Analysis*. https://doi.org/10.1108/IJOA-01-2024-4239

Masini, C. (1960). *L'organizzazione del lavoro nell'impresa* (Vol. 1). Giuffrè, Milan.

Nunes, A. K. d. S., Morioka, S. N., & Bolis, I. (2022). Challenges of business models for sustainability in startups. *RAUSP Management Journal, 57*(4), 382–400. https://doi.org/10.1108/RAUSP-10-2021-0216

Onida, P. (1951). *Le discipline economico-aziendali: Oggetto E metodo* (2nd ed.). A. Giuffre, Milan.

Onida, P. (1968). *Economia d'azienda*. Unione Tipografica—Editrice Torinese, Turin.

Pencle, N., & Mălăescu, I. (2016). What's in the words? Development and validation of a multidimensional dictionary for CSR and application using prospectuses. *Journal of Emerging Technologies in Accounting, 13*(2), 109–127. https://doi.org/10.2308/jeta-51615

Pornparnomchai, M., & Rajchamaha, K. (2021). Sharing knowledge on the sustainable business model: An aquaculture start-up case in Thailand. *Cogent Business and Management, 8*(1), 1924932. https://doi.org/10.1080/23311975.2021.1924932

Possenti, V., Minardi, V., Contoli, B., Lana, S., Scardetta, P., & Masocco, M. (2021). Impact of COVID-19 on economic and working conditions in Italy. Data from PASSI and PASSI d'Argento. *European Journal of Public Health, 31*(Supplement_3), ckab165.083. https://doi.org/10.1093/eurpub/ckab165.083

R Core Team. (2024). *R: A language and environment for statistical computing*. R Foundation for Statistical Computing. https://www.R-project.org/

Radácsi, L., & Filep, J. C. (2021). Survival and growth of Hungarian start-ups. *Entrepreneurship and Sustainability Issues, 8*(4), 262–279. https://doi.org/10.9770/jesi.2021.8.4(15)

Ruisi, M. (2016). Bene comune e Dottrina Sociale della Chiesa in Carlo Masini. In E. Borgonovi & G. Invernizzi (Eds.), *Scienza, umanità e visione nel pensiero e nell'azione di Carlo Masini* (pp. 254–261). Egea, Milan.

Salamzadeh, A. (2015). New venture creation: Controversial perspectives and theories. *Economic Analysis, 48*(3–4), 101–109.

Sreenivasan, A., & Suresh, M. (2023). Readiness for lean-sustainability in start-ups during the COVID-19 era. *International Journal of Organizational Analysis, 31*(1), 124–148. https://doi.org/10.1108/IJOA-09-2021-2963

Sreenivasan, A., & Suresh, M. (2024). Start-up sustainability: Does blockchain adoption drives sustainability in start-ups? A systematic literature reviews. *Management Research Review, 47*(3), 390–405. https://doi.org/10.1108/MRR-07-2022-0519

Verma, R., Arya, V., Thomas, A., Bolognesi, E., & Mueller, J. (2023). Does startup culture in the emerging country grow around societal sustainability? An empirical study through the lens of co-creational capital and green intellect. *Journal of Intellectual Capital, 24*(4), 1047–1074. https://doi.org/10.1108/JIC-07-2022-0162

Zan, L. (1994). Toward a history of accounting histories: Perspectives from the Italian tradition. *European Accounting Review, 3*(2), 255–310.

Zappa, G. (1927). *Tendenze nuove negli studi di ragioneria: Discorso inaugurale dell'anno accademico 1926–27 nel R.* Istituto Superiore di Scienze Economiche e Commerciali di Venezia.

Zappa, G. (1962). *L'economia delle aziende di consumo*. Giuffrè, Milan.

Zhu, B., Liang, C., Mirza, N., & Umar, M. (2023). What drives gearing in early-stage firms? Evidence from blue economy startups. *Journal of Business Research, 161*, 113840. https://doi.org/10.1016/j.jbusres.2023.113840

Chapter 9
Sustainability in Innovative Start-Ups: Exploring Drivers, Barriers, and Tools for Performance Accountability

Monica Veneziani, Laura Rocca, Andrea Caccialanza, and Dina Lucia Todaro

9.1 Introduction

It is widely recognized that entrepreneurs, and the diffusion of entrepreneurship as attitude, can significantly drive sustainable development by linking entrepreneurial processes, market transformations, and large-scale societal changes (e.g., Horne et al., 2020; Johnson & Schaltegger, 2020; Volkmann et al., 2021). In the field of entrepreneurship studies, sustainable entrepreneurship is a trending and yet established concept aimed at "equally" prioritizing economic, social, and environmental objectives (e.g., Hörisch et al., 2015; Loprevite, 2020). Consequently, the diffusion of the term "sustainability impact" denotes the meaningful contribution of sustainable entrepreneurship to development across these three dimensions of value creation (e.g., Di Vaio et al., 2022; Figge & Hahn, 2004). Within this debate, sustainable entrepreneurship studies are also playing an active role in the achievement of sustainable development goals (e.g., Johnson & Schaltegger, 2020). These studies vary and has an impact on these goals through different mechanisms and a differentiated efforts depending also on the dimensional level of ventures (e.g., Carle & Rayna, 2023).

M. Veneziani (✉) · D. L. Todaro
Department of Business and Social Sciences, Catholic University of the Sacred Heart, Piacenza, Italy
e-mail: monica.veneziani1@unicatt.it; dinalucia.todaro@unicatt.it

L. Rocca
Department of Economics and Management, University of Brescia, Brescia, Italy
e-mail: laura.rocca@unibs.it

A. Caccialanza
Department of Management, University of Bologna, Bologna, Italy
e-mail: andrea.caccialanza@unibo.it

S. Loprevite et al. (eds.), *Startups and Gazelle Enterprises*, SIDREA Series in Accounting and Business Administration,
https://doi.org/10.1007/978-3-031-90881-1_9

According to Cohen and Winn (2007), start-ups are crucial in this context due to their potential for radical innovation in order exploit significant opportunities and to improve social and environmental conditions. Consequently, these emerging young ventures with innovative products and services represent and unicum in terms of peculiar characteristics that distinguish them in the comparison to established firms, thus driving societal and environmental shifts toward sustainability thanks to their transition-oriented business models and innovation practices (e.g., Schaltegger & Wagner, 2011; Sreenivasan & Suresh, 2024). Furthermore, Hockerts and Wüstenhagen (2010) emphasize that start-ups play a key role in the initial and early growth stages of market development, whereas larger, established companies become more influential during the growth and mature stages of an industry.

However, it remains of primary importance to understand from the outset the impacts an organization generates, not only to appreciate the achieved internal efficiency graph but also with a view toward transparency and accreditation for the various categories of stakeholders (e.g., Davidsson et al., 2020). In fact, according to several scholars, such as Di Vaio et al. (2022, 2023) and Venturelli et al. (2017), the development of innovative and sustainable business model has been proven to be a key for the minimization of impacts thanks to the integration of sustainability assessment processes. Moreover, the diffusion of sustainable-oriented start-ups may facilitate the transition process to optimal and more sustainable managerial practices according to Horne and Fichter (2022, p. 2), while on the other side "Little is known about the factors that influence their growth and the link between entrepreneurial ventures and the social or environmental outcomes and impacts they generate". In line, as noted by Boar-Boar and Oliveras-Villanueva (2019, p. 2), there are at least two elements that complicate the analysis of the results of this literature: the rapidity of the changes in the operating environment of start-ups on the managerial side and the limited number of unstructured studies on this topic on the theoretical one. Furthermore, we acknowledge the lack of an established and cross-sectoral tool to evaluate the impacts (e.g., Carle & Rayna, 2023; Fichter et al., 2023; Trautwein, 2021), since every tool might be evaluated with reference to the appropriateness referred to the stage of start-ups' specific needs and contexts. In this perspective and conscious of the importance of this topic, the chapter aims to trace the evolution of the literature by presenting a systematic and bibliometric review on the topic. More specifically, it intends to understand sustainability-orientation of start-ups evolved over the time (RQ1), identify and systematize the recognized drivers and discussed barriers to its implementation (RQ2), and analyze the assessment tools that have been employed for this purpose (RQ3).

The reminder of the chapter is the following. Next section introduces the background of the debate, then methodological aspects of the review are presented. In addition, results and discussion are addressed; finally, contributions to the debate and conclusion are exposed.

9.2 Background

9.2.1 Start-Ups and Sustainability

Broadly speaking, the debate in the literature on entrepreneurship for sustainable development has sparked growing interest in the ability of individuals (i.e., entrepreneurs) and (new) ventures to act as agents of change and transformation, including on social and environmental levels (e.g., Cohen & Winn, 2007). According to Johnson and Schaltegger (2020, p. 1242), the entrepreneurship for sustainable development literature has "two common traits: (i) the depiction of processes and (ii) the description of challenges and opportunities on multiple levels". Consequently, on one hand they focus on the process of value co-creation contributing to the achievement of macro-level targets; on the other Scholars analyze how entrepreneurial activities act within markets and try to fix failures and promote the co-evolution of players for value co-creation. Within this debate, as anticipated in the introduction, start-ups play a significant role in the promotion of sustainability transition and the evolution of business models to a sustainability-oriented perspective. In line, scholars such as Bidmon and Knab (2018) or Broccardo et al. (2023) in their studies analyze the connections between business models and transition (theory) research, but they also focus on the role of start-ups as agent that succeed if they demonstrate the ability to adapt their technological solution to a viable and sustainable business model. As a consequence, it can be noted as their innovation propensity must be not only anchored to a feasibility study but should also include an assessment of their capability to find an equilibrium in this socio-technical system (e.g., Elzen & Wieczorek, 2005). For start-ups this equilibrium might be more difficult to reach, even if temporarily. For this purpose, several strategies aimed at improving its performance in the start-up phase of the business have been developed both in the literature and in practice. For example, Deyanova et al. (2022) have recently systematically analyzed the role of business incubators as a potential solution to the problem in terms of both resources and strategy formulation. Moreover, on the investors side, several contributes supported as sustainability orientation of business models are increasingly part of the evaluation of the positioning and strategy of start-ups, with specific tools that help to estimate this effort such as the "triple-layered business model canvas" (e.g., Joyce & Paquin, 2016). Furthermore, some (institutional) investors are specifically selecting investments with a specific focus on sustainability issues (e.g., Auzepy et al., 2024), such as in the case of "sustainable venture capital" investors (e.g., Bocken, 2015). In addition, Boar-Boar and Oliveras-Villanueva (2019), on the behavioral-individual side, mapped in their review the characteristics of entrepreneurs and investors in relation to their propensity to invest in sustainability-oriented start-ups, especially on social side. They propose an analysis of existing start-ups and, finally, the evaluation of impact of institutional support. If financial and institutional support is proved to be relevant, also the market and demand side remains critical for sustainable start-ups' resilience and survival. In line, Hockerts and Wüstenhagen (2010) analyzed the strategies of sustainable new entrants in the market compared to existing incumbent firms, while Parrish (2010) pointed out drivers of sustainability-driven entrepreneurship depending on contextual values and motives. Although the urgency of action to orient businesses toward sustainability criteria is relevant according to both perspectives adopted (investor and market-demand), the debate on the identification, quantification, and disclosure of impact remains an open issue.

9.2.2 *Assessment of Sustainability Performance*

In the attempt to contribute both to the theoretical and practical debate, several studies have been published in the attempt to better understand the definitions, processes, and dynamics of sustainability assessment in the context of start-ups. Accordingly, with Trautwein (2021, p. 4), there are at least five characteristics that challenges the establishment of an effective assessment tool: (1) informal and fast-moving working and management structures, which affect the replicability of that assessment; (2) the resource restrictions, that limit the competition of the assessment and the effective communication of results; (3) volatility in business model and value chain, since they deal with unpredictable change in the context; (4) they are new to the market, so no past performance data available; and (5) the lack of specific knowledge, that incentive them to pick the simplest assessment tool.

In fact, these newly introduced realities in the market live in a condition that presents a strong contradiction. On the one hand, they are typically small, informal structures with a flat and smooth organizational structure precisely for being particularly responsive or proactive to changes in context. On the other they are urged to formalize procedures, models (including business models) and having to report performance without often having a comparative history or a competitor or benchmark as reference point (e.g., Comin et al., 2020).

As a result, it becomes clear that a start-up will only effectively promote sustainability if it is genuinely aware of and motivated by a comprehensive sustainability management approach (e.g., Boar-Boar & Oliveras-Villanueva, 2019). This approach should also include the consideration and assessment of both positive and negative externalities for all categories of stakeholders (e.g., Hörisch et al., 2014). Moreover, this effort is not only linked or focused to the reporting activity (or period) but includes all the activities and function involved in the creation of value in order to effectively disclose its distribution (e.g., Lüdeke-Freund et al., 2024). All these processes and procedures are linked to the issue of sustainability impact assessment (SIA) in literature, which is strictly connected to the evaluation of (past) present and expected future performances (e.g., Carle & Rayna, 2023).

9.2.3 Hypothesis Development and Research Questions

Albeit the review proposed by Trautwein (2021, p. 6) mapped and discussed 23 original assessments approaches in literature for the SIA of start-ups performances, the variety of activities, sectors, dimensions, and impacts still requires a reduction in the fragmentation of approaches and a deeper understanding of specific contexts (e.g., Di Vaio et al., 2022). Furthermore, in line with this reasoning, Fichter et al. (2023) stressed that the sustainability assessment of start-ups impacts is still a neglected area of intervention and study, albeit the performance evaluation, value distribution, and impact of incumbent firms has been a key topic of sustainability accounting research for a long time. This led to our research gap and the development our of research questions. In fact, as mentioned above, our hypothesis is that sustainability orientation is one of the emerging factors in the evaluation of start-ups, both from a perspective of their performance and the quality of corporate disclosure and communication, and for an assessment of current and prospective competitiveness in the market (e.g., Carle & Rayna, 2023). Furthermore, this is also reflected in their current (or potential) ability to exploit resources, nor promote circular initiatives, proving differentiated resilience to the impacts of climate change. Therefore, we formulated the following research questions (RQs):

- *RQ1: How has the sustainability-orientation of start-ups evolved over time?*
- *RQ2: What have been the driving factors or barriers to their implementation?*
- *RQ3: Specifically, what tools have been used to improve sustainability performance accountability?*

9.3 Methodology

With references to methodological aspects, we decided to adopt a bibliometric approach and to operationalize this we employed the bibliometric software Scival[1] in which we imported the results from Scopus database. We used the Scival research performance analysis tool provided by Elsevier, since it is designed to offer insights into the research performance of individuals, institutions, and countries. It leverages data from Scopus and provided different data analysis and interpretation such as descriptive statistics and/or visualizations. We adopted this strategy for the analysis of results since it allows to group the selected articles in a less subjective perspective and cluster them in a way that allow us to comment on the evolution of topics in the last few years (e.g., Tranfield et al., 2003). In fact, as Donthu et al. (2021) pointed out, the bibliometric analysis "Summarizes large quantities of bibliometric data to present the state of the intellectual structure and emerging trends of a research topic

[1] For further information on the tool adopted visit the official website: https://www.scival.com/home

or field" and can be used with a broad scope of the research and with a dataset that is too large for being reviewed manually. Previous studies, both bibliometric (e.g., Sreenivasan & Suresh, 2024) and systematic (e.g., Horne & Fichter, 2022), have already covered the prior decades as periods of analysis (from 2000).

The adopted research criteria includes several combination and synonyms of the following areas "start-up" AND "sustainability" AND "assessment". More specifically, the research adopted the following "title-abstract-keyword" research strategy in Scopus database,[2] adapting the strategy from the one proposed by Trautwein (2021, see his "Appendix A") to ensure consistency of results:

> TITLE-ABS-KEY (startup OR start-up OR "start up" OR "new venture*" OR "new enterprise*" OR "new business*" OR "new compan*") AND TITLE-ABS-KEY (sustain* OR "triple bottom line" OR "triple-bottom-line") AND TITLE-ABS-KEY (analys* OR assess* OR controll* OR ac-count* OR apprais* OR evaluat* OR measure* OR benchmark* OR report*) AND PUBYEAR > 2017 AND PUBYEAR < 2025 AND (LIMIT-TO (SUBJAREA, "BUSI")) AND (LIMIT-TO (SRCTYPE, "j")) AND (LIMIT-TO (LANGUAGE, "English")) AND (LIMIT-TO (PUBSTAGE, "final")).

In addition, the process of filtering, exclusion, and inclusion of studies is presented according to the PRISMA checklist to reduce arbitrariness in content selection and ensure replicability of the study (e.g., Page et al., 2021). This element of disclosure also has the advantage of ensuring full replicability of the data, transparently showing the steps and reasons behind the exclusion of filtered papers, as highlighted in other similar reviews on entrepreneurship and the accountability of developed sustainability assessments (e.g., Tranfield et al., 2003).

More in detail, Fig. 9.1 proposes the selection and filtering approach adopted. In particular, it can be noted as the filtering approach limited the analysis to peer-reviewed articles published in journals, pertaining to the "Business, management and accounting" area in Scopus, published in "English" at "Final stage" in the timespan 2018–2024.

The rationale behind the following selection is the need to choose reviewed contributions that generated more impact within the academic debate, in order to monitor the trend of the most recurring and growing themes in studies from the past 7 years (e.g., Donthu et al., 2021). In regard to the choice of the database for our study, we acknowledge that relying on a single source, such as Scopus, could be seen as a potential limitation compared to using a combination of sources, such as integrating EBSCO. However, given the number of studies retrieved from Scopus, the variety of topics covered in these studies within the specific literature niche considered, and the additional search for relevant papers on Google Scholar, we believe that this study successfully captures the complexity of the phenomenon analyzed and contributes to the debate with an updated overview of the topic. Specifically, the next section provides a detailed description of the historical distribution of filtered paper, the share of publications by journal and journal quartile, the list of most productive authors, countries and universities in this scope of research.

[2] Extraction occurred on April 30, 2024; while the analysis of results in Scival the May 9, 2024.

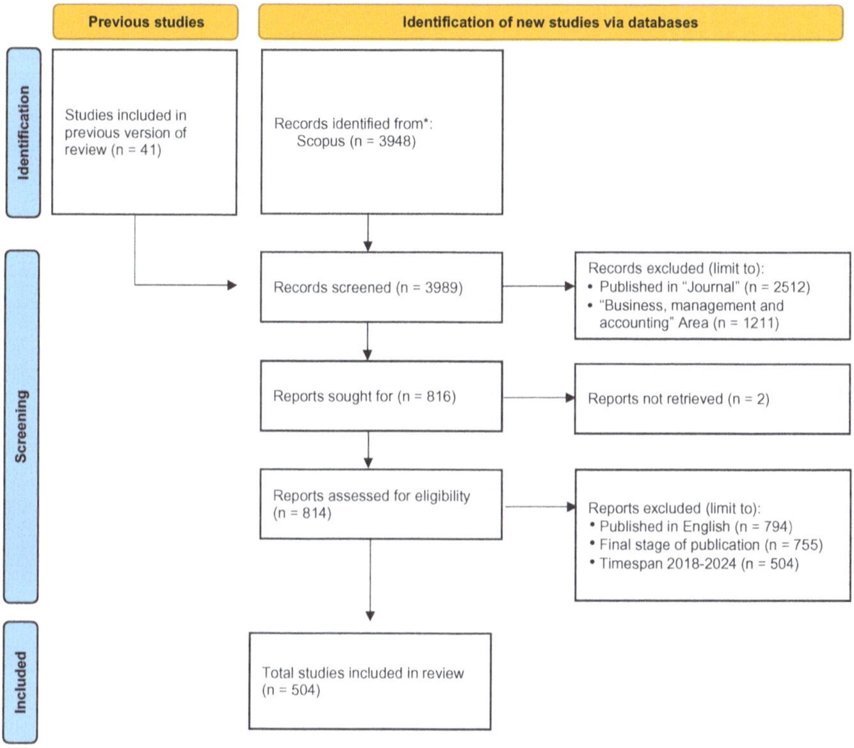

Fig. 9.1 PRISMA selection and filtering approach adopted [*Source*: PRISMA scheme adapted from Page et al. (2021)]

Finally, the list of eight most productive topics by scholarly output will be presented and discussed.

9.4 Results

The distribution of publications shows a significant number of studies among the most cited worldwide. Italy is clearly emerging as a leader in academic research on start-up sustainability, with a significant number of publications, high citation impact, and high number of views. In fact, as showed in Table 9.1, Italy is the second largest country in terms of number of publications, demonstrating considerable academic commitment and interest in this field.

Between 2018 and 2024, 20.8% of the publications are in the top 10% of the most cited publications. This data is significant as it indicates that the topic of innovative start-ups and their focus on sustainability is of great interest and relevance to

Table 9.1 Distribution of contributions by geographical area (*Source*: Scival analysis on Scopus data)

Country and territories	Scholarly output	Views count	Field-weighted citation impact	Citation count
India	75	5081	1.07	365
Italy	55	9817	3.45	1578
United States	46	5762	1.92	936
Germany	45	8166	2.62	1332
United Kingdom	45	7927	2.70	943
Brazil	29	4106	1.48	639
Netherlands	25	7350	3.21	1296
China	23	2878	1.53	675
Spain	22	2488	1.71	292
Australia	19	2370	1.95	377

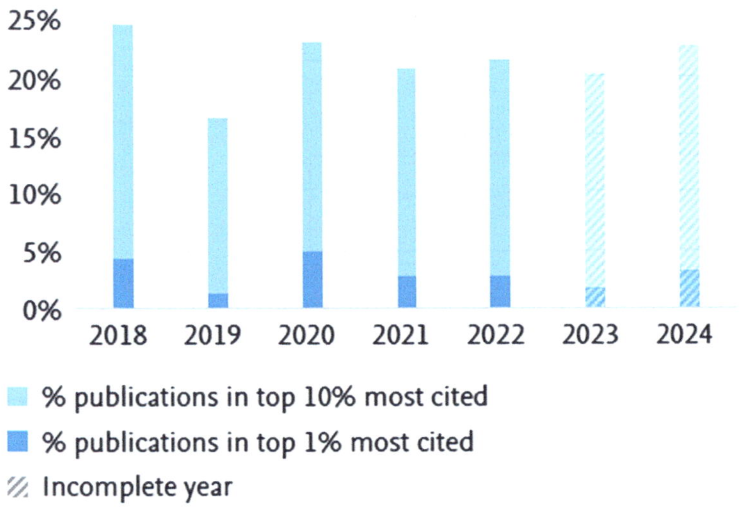

Fig. 9.2 Share of publications that are among the most cited publications worldwide (n = 105) (*Source*: Scival analysis on Scopus data)

the scientific community. The temporal distribution of the top 10% publications is shown in Fig. 9.2.

Almost 40.9% of the publications are found in top journals by CiteScore, an indicator that measures the impact of scientific journals. This high ranking of publications suggests that research is not only prolific but also recognized as high-quality contributions published on prestigious academic platforms. The temporal distribution of the publications with the highest CiteScore is shown in Fig. 9.3.

This positive trend could be attributed to various factors, including improved research methodologies, increased investment in innovation and greater awareness of the importance of start-ups in the global economic landscape. From an

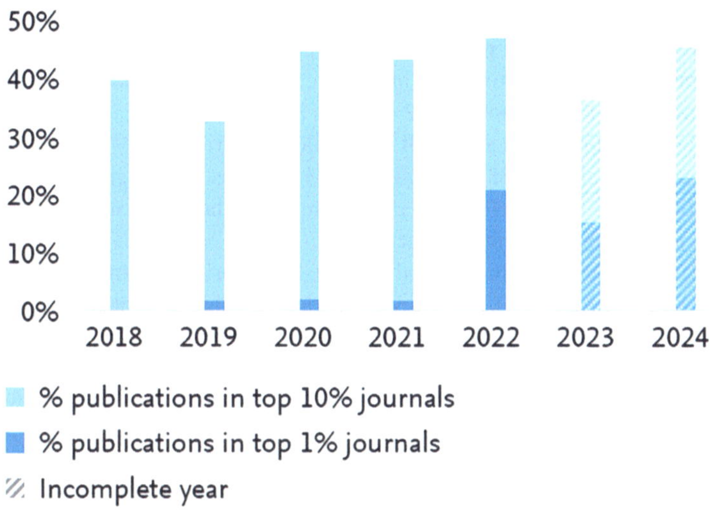

Fig. 9.3 Share of publications that are among the most cited publications worldwide (n = 196) (*Source*: Scival analysis on Scopus data)

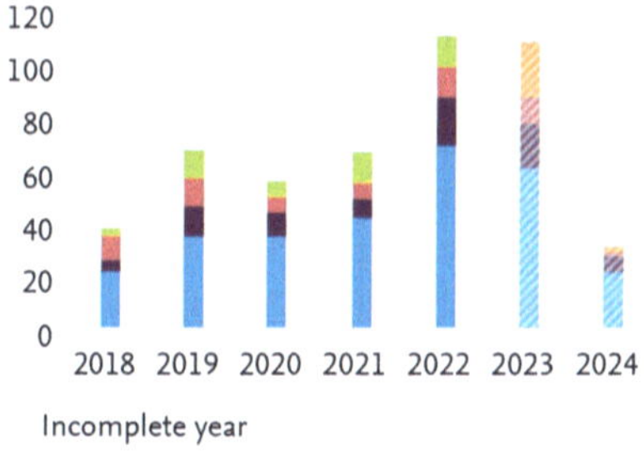

Quartiles	Publications	Publication share (%)
Q1 (top 25%)	285	59.5
Q2 (26% - 50%)	71	14.8
Q3 (51% - 75%)	56	11.7
Q4 (76% - 100%	67	14.0

Fig. 9.4 Share of publications per journal quartile (*Source*: Scival analysis on Scopus data)

examination of the evolution of academic publications relating to innovative start-ups we explore the impact of published research, their distribution in high-impact journals and emerging trends in the field. The volume of publications shows a steady increase over the years, peaking in 2022. The temporal distribution of the publications per journal quartile is shown in Fig. 9.4.

The distribution of publications across journal quartiles highlights the high quality of research, with nearly 60% of publications appearing in journals in the first quartile (Q1). This high rate suggests a strategic focus on publication in top-ranked journals, likely contributing to the high-citation impact. From 2018 to 2024, research on innovative start-ups produced a total of 479 published articles.

Confirming the above, 2022 was a record year with 111 publications, including 69 in Q1, reflecting a peak in productivity and quality. In particular, this year represents a turning point, indicating that innovative start-ups have reached significant academic maturity. Furthermore, 2022 emerges as a watershed year with the maximum number of publications across all percentile categories. 20.7% of publications are in top 1% journals, and 38.7% are in top 5% journals. This significant increase suggests not only an increase in the quantity of research, but also a notable improvement in its quality and academic impact.

In 2022, the studies by Schiuma et al. (2022), Mansouri and Momtax (2022), and Padilla-Lozano and Colazzo (2022) have provided valuable insights into how start-ups can leverage digitization and sustainability to remain competitive and attract investment. The COVID-19 pandemic has had a devastating impact on global economies, prompting many nations to seek new sources of growth and innovation. Start-ups have been identified as a key driver of economic recovery, being agile and able to adapt quickly to market changes (Akpan et al., 2022). According to Padilla-Lozano and Colazzo (2022), the adoption of technologies such as blockchain-based crowdfunding has facilitated transparency and analysis of start-ups' sustainability practices, increasing investor confidence. Indeed, sustainability has become a global priority, with a growing awareness of the need to address environmental and social challenges. Mansouri and Momtax (2022) highlighted how corporate social responsibility (CSR) practices and green innovation have become crucial for the competitiveness of start-ups, especially in emerging markets. Their research showed that start-ups that adopt sustainable practices can attract talent and investment by improving their credibility and transparency through green certifications and blockchain technologies. Interest in sustainability has also been reflected in investment criteria, with an increasing focus on ESG (Environment, Society, and Governance) aspects (Padilla-Lozano and Colazzo, 2022).

The most prominent research themes include Business Model Innovation, Digital Transformation, Entrepreneurial Intention, Circular Economy, and Social Entrepreneurship. These themes reflect the growing interest in how innovative start-ups are influencing and transforming various sectors. Specifically, Industry 4.0 and Sustainable Development Goals (SDGs) are frequently mentioned, indicating significant attention toward sustainability and technological integration.

From the analysis of the top ten cited topic (Table 9.2), it clearly emerges the crucial role of start-ups in terms of innovation in emerging and developing economic contexts (EMDE). As highlighted by Akpan et al. (2022), SMEs in EMDEs face significant challenges in adopting advanced digital technologies, with start-ups emerging as catalysts for digital innovation and economic resilience during the COVID-19 pandemic. Furthermore, start-ups facilitate open innovation to address sustainability challenges in the food and beverage sector, as illustrated by Bogers et al. (2020). Hahn (2020) highlight how start-ups adopt advanced operating models in Industry 4.0, promoting flexibility and scalability in supply chain management. Henry et al. (2020) and Leising et al. (2018) explore how start-ups accelerate the adoption of circular and sustainable business models, overcoming organizational barriers and promoting innovative practices. Moreover, Henry et al. (2020)

Table 9.2 Top ten topics by scholarly output (*Source*: Scival analysis on Scopus data)

Topic	Scholarly output	Publication share (%)	Field-weighted citation impact	Prominence
Business Model Innovation; Innovation; Digital Transformation	46	0.77	3.03	99.828
Entrepreneurial Intention; Effectuation; Entrepreneurship	42	0.35	0.94	99.904
Alliance Portfolios; Firm; Open Innovation	25	0.19	3.15	99.946
Industrial Symbiosis; Sustainable Development; Circular Economy	20	0.36	3.53	99.906
Social Entrepreneurship; Innovation; Impact Investing	19	0.41	0.77	99.447
Business Development; Science Parks; Incubators	19	2	1.26	95.761
Cause-Related Marketing; Corporate Social Responsibility; Corporate Philanthropy	13	0.08	2.13	99.964
Crowdfunding; Lending; Fintech	11	0.25	1.55	99.64
Entrepreneurial Activity; New Firm Formation; Economic Growth	10	0.75	4.04	98.322
Sustainable Entrepreneurship; Entrepreneurial Activity; Sustainability	9	2.57	1.95	94.017

demonstrate a significant growth in the number of circular start-ups, highlighting their progressive adoption of business models that incorporate circularity principles, which in turn contributes to environmental sustainability of production systems. In addition, Hahn (2020) shows that the introduction of digital technologies, as part of the Fourth Industrial Revolution, has driven start-ups to innovate in a more agile and sustainability-focused manner.

Franceschelli et al. (2018) and Leising et al. (2018) indicate that start-ups integrate environmental and social considerations into their business models, thus contributing to sustainable value creation. Criticizing the lack of shared understanding and effective tools for sustainability-oriented business models, Cosenz and Noto (2018) propose a theoretical approach that aims to overcome these limitations by emphasizing accountability in enhancing collaboration and the development of sustainable business models.

We report in Table 9.3 the most mentioned articles on innovative and sustainable start-ups.

The analysis of the various studies reveals a common theme: digital transformation and the adoption of sustainable business models are key to addressing contemporary challenges. These studies underline the importance of integrating digital innovation and sustainability into business models to effectively respond to global challenges and promote inclusive and sustainable growth. Innovation in KMSs shows how digitization can optimize the use of knowledge and improve corporate

Table 9.3 Top five most cited publications (*Source*: Scival analysis on Scopus data)

Title	Authors	Year	Scopus source title	Citations	Field-weighted citation impact
Artificial intelligence in sustainable energy industry: Status Quo, challenges, and opportunities	Ahmad, T.; Zhang, D.; Huang, C.; Zhang, H.; Dai, N.; Song, Y.; Chen, H.	2021	Journal of Cleaner Production	298	8.72
Circular Economy in the building sector: Three cases and a collaboration tool	Leising, E.; Quist, J.; Bocken, N.	2018	Journal of Cleaner Production	286	9.38
Industry 4.0: a supply chain innovation perspective	Hahn, G.J.	2020	International Journal of Production Research	223	11.83
The role of digital innovation in knowledge management systems: A systematic literature review	Di Vaio, A.; Palladino, R.; Pezzi, A.; Kalisz, D.E.	2021	Journal of Business Research	211	10.24
A typology of circular start-ups: Analysis of 128 circular business models	Henry, M.; Bauwens, T.; Hekkert, M.; Kirchherr, J.	2020	Journal of Cleaner Production	210	9.39

governance (Di Vaio et al., 2021). In parallel, AI in the energy sector is a powerful lever to improve efficiency and competitiveness. Industry 4.0 and supply chain innovation highlight the importance of adaptability and scalability, especially for start-ups (Ahmad et al., 2021).

The circular economy, both in the context of start-ups and in the construction sector, shows how new approaches and collaborations can lead to a more sustainable use of resources. Circular start-ups emerge as pioneers in adopting business models that promote sustainability (Henry et al., 2020), while innovations in the construction sector demonstrate the need for shared visions and extended collaborations to achieve circularity goals (Leising et al., 2018).

Each tool and approach, as discussed by the respective authors, provides different methodologies and frameworks for improving sustainability performance accountability, focusing on both internal processes and external collaborations to achieve long-term sustainable business practices. The adoption of digital technologies such as FinTech, analytical algorithms, cloud computing, "Big Data", predictive analytics, disruptive technologies, data analytics, and the Internet of Things (IoT) is crucial to improve business models and digitize business operations, especially for SMEs in developing and emerging markets (Akpan et al., 2022).

9.5 Discussion

In recent years, the interest in innovative start-ups has grown significantly, driven by the increasing recognition of their role in fostering economic growth and addressing contemporary global challenges. In this section, we explore the evolution of sustainability focus in start-ups, the factors driving or hindering their implementation, and the tools utilized to enhance sustainability performance accountability. In particular, we answer the research questions through the analysis of the most cited papers, and which find allocation in high-ranking scientific journals.

9.5.1 Start-Ups' Sustainability-Orientation over the Time

The focus on sustainability for start-ups has evolved significantly over the past decades. This section of the work analyses its evolution to answer RQ1. In the early stages of start-up development, the emphasis was primarily on rapid growth and immediate profitability. This approach was reflected in business models that prioritized short-term economic return rather than environmental and social impacts.

However, as global awareness of environmental problems such as climate change, biodiversity loss, and pollution increased, along with social issues such as economic inequality and working conditions, start-ups began to recognize the importance of sustainability. From analysis of the review carried out by Boar-Boar and Oliveras-Villanueva (2019), it is stated that Schick et al. (2002) argue that the distinctive element between conventional start-ups and those oriented toward sustainability is the attitude of the entrepreneur. Sustainable entrepreneurs show a very strong initial commitment to sustainability. In more recent times authors such as Smith (2021) have documented this shift, indicating that new generations of entrepreneurs are more inclined to integrate sustainability values into their business models from the start.

Market studies show that consumers are willing to pay more for products that respect the environment and workers' rights, which has prompted many startups to review their business practices. According to Brown et al. (2019a, 2019b), this demand has incentivized many emerging companies to differentiate themselves through the adoption of sustainable practices, not only to satisfy customers but also to build a positive and lasting reputation.

The emphasis on sustainability within start-ups has evolved markedly from 2018 to 2024, reflecting a broader trend in the global business and academic communities. The analysis of publication data reveals that innovative start-ups are increasingly viewed as crucial players in promoting sustainable business practices and contributing to the United Nations' SDGs. This period saw 479 articles published on the topic, with a significant portion appearing in high-impact journals, underscoring the importance and relevance of sustainability in this sector.

Our analysis revealed that sustainability was an emerging theme, with initial research focusing on the underlying concepts and potential benefits of sustainable practices. Early publications, such as those by Franceschelli et al. (2018) and Leising et al. (2018), highlighted the integration of environmental and social considerations into start-up business models. Their work emphasized the need for start-ups to align their strategies with broader sustainability goals, setting the stage for future research and application. By 2020 and 2021, sustainability had become a central theme, with research emphasizing the practical application of sustainable business models. Notable works by Henry et al. (2020) and Hahn (2020) discussed the adoption of circular economy principles and Industry 4.0 technologies, respectively, highlighting how start-ups are driving innovation in these areas. Henry et al. (2020) explored how start-ups integrate circularity principles into their operations, promoting resource efficiency and waste reduction. Hahn (2020) research on Industry 4.0 illustrated the role of digital technologies in enhancing operational efficiency and sustainability. The year 2022 marked a significant peak, with 111 publications, 69 of which were in Q1 journals. This indicates a heightened focus on both the quantity and quality of research in sustainable start-ups. Studies during this period, such as those by Bogers et al. (2020), explored the role of start-ups in addressing sustainability challenges in specific sectors, such as the food and beverage industry. Bogers et al. (2020) highlighted how start-ups facilitate open innovation to tackle sustainability issues, demonstrating the importance of collaborative efforts in achieving sustainable outcomes. By 2024, partial data suggest a continued strong focus on sustainability, reflecting its entrenched importance in start-up research and practice. The ongoing interest in this area is likely driven by the increasing recognition of the critical role start-ups play in addressing environmental and social challenges. The evolution of sustainability focus in start-ups underscores the sector's adaptability and commitment to aligning with global sustainability trends.

9.5.2 Driving Factors and Barriers to Sustainability Implementation

Several driving factors and barriers influence the implementation of sustainability practices in start-ups (RQ2). According to the literature review applied for this chapter, the key drivers include the increasing awareness of environmental issues, regulatory pressures, market demand for sustainable products, and the potential for cost savings through efficient resource use.

Governments and international bodies have introduced regulations and incentives to promote sustainable practices. This has motivated start-ups to adopt environmentally friendly practices to comply with regulations and benefit from financial incentives. As highlighted by Cosenz and Noto (2018), regulatory frameworks can foster a culture of accountability and collaboration in developing sustainable business models. The introduction of sustainability-related policies has created a favorable environment for start-ups to innovate and implement sustainable solutions. Munaro et al. (2020) highlight the importance of subsidies, laws, and tax incentives in promoting circular economy practices in the built environment.

Looking at the market perspective, there is a growing consumer preference for sustainable products and services. Start-ups that align their business models with sustainability principles can tap into this market demand, enhancing their competitiveness and brand reputation. Studies such as those by Mansouri and Momtaz (2022) illustrate how start-ups leverage sustainability to attract investment and customers. This market-driven approach has led to the development of products and services that meet the evolving preferences of environmentally conscious consumers. Increasing consumer awareness about environmental issues and demand for sustainable products is a significant driver. As Baipai et al. (2022) note, consumers are more interested in healthy and high-quality products, pushing, for example, the agricultural sector toward sustainable practices.

The advent of digital technologies, such as blockchain, AI, and IoT, has enabled start-ups to implement and track sustainable practices more effectively. These technologies provide tools for better resource management, supply chain transparency, and performance measurement, as discussed by Di Vaio et al. (2021). The integration of digital technologies has facilitated real-time monitoring and optimization of sustainable practices, allowing start-ups to enhance their operational efficiency (and resource use) and sustainability outcomes.

On the other hand, the barriers to implementing sustainability issues into start-ups business models are seen as mainly: financial constraints, lack of expertise, and resistance to change.

Many start-ups operate with limited financial resources, making it challenging to invest in sustainable technologies and practices. This is particularly pronounced in emerging and developing economic contexts (EMDEs), where access to funding is more restricted (Akpan et al., 2022). The high initial costs associated with sustainable technologies and practices can deter start-ups from pursuing sustainability initiatives. Long et al. (2018) identify low financial rewards and lack of legislative support as significant barriers. Start-ups often struggle with limited financial resources, making it challenging to invest in sustainable practices.

Implementing sustainability requires specific knowledge and skills, which start-ups may lack. The need for expertise in areas such as sustainable supply chain management and circular economy practices can be a significant barrier (Leising et al., 2018). The absence of trained personnel and technical knowledge can hinder the effective implementation of sustainability strategies (Henry et al., 2020; Awana et al., 2024).

Finally, as emphasized by Schiuma et al. (2022), he reluctance to change established practices and the perceived risks associated with new approaches can slow down the adoption of sustainability measures. Guldmann and Huulgaard (2020) mention that most barriers to circular business model innovation are encountered at the organizational level. Resistance to change within companies can hinder the adoption of sustainable practices. Moreover, Akpan et al. (2022) discuss the slow adoption of state-of-the-art technologies in SMEs in emerging markets. Despite the potential benefits, technological challenges and the lack of infrastructure can be significant obstacles.

9.5.3 Tools for Improving Sustainability Performance Accountability

Various tools and methodologies have been developed to enhance sustainability performance accountability in start-ups. These tools help measure, report, and improve sustainable practices, ensuring that start-ups can demonstrate their commitment to sustainability to stakeholders. In response to RQ3, we outline the main tools and methodologies that the literature review we performed has provided. That tools have enabled start-ups to measure, analyze, and improve their sustainability practices, ensuring greater accountability and alignment with broader sustainability goals. We summarize that in the following Table 9.4.

These findings collectively provide a comprehensive overview of various assessment approaches tailored for start-ups. By detailing the advantages and disadvantages of each method, they guide stakeholders in selecting appropriate tools based on specific needs and contexts. The insights are essential for start-ups aiming to effectively measure and enhance their social and environmental impacts, ensuring they adopt the most suitable and impactful assessment methodologies.

However, the main result from that final RQ is that the accountability for measuring the sustainability of start-ups is still an emerging field and there is a lot of work to do in research to really conceptualize an assessment tool for that; the work of Fichter et al. (2023) on sustainability impact assessment of new ventures concludes on the same line evaluating that *"First, existing assessment approaches do not apply a multi-level view, ..., and work with rather fuzzy conceptualizations of sustainability effects. Thus, an elaborated concept of system-level effects is missing. Second, while most approaches consider environmental impacts, other system-level impacts such as market changes or wider social impacts beyond single stakeholders of focal organizations are not systematically considered. Third, most existing assessment approaches focus on methodologies that help to evaluate environmental impacts (mostly LCA approaches), but do not provide a holistic multi-level assessment methodology. Thus, while sustainable business model research has emphasized the importance of considering sustainability impacts, no elaborated conceptualization of system level impacts has yet been provided, nor have there been any empirical investigations into the system level effects of business models beyond environmental impact assessments"* (Fichter et al., 2023, p. 10).

Table 9.4 Tools and methodologies for sustainability performance of start-ups [*Source*: Authors' elaboration adapted from Trautwein (2021). The references for the tools are respectively: Lingane and Olsen (2004), Puttick and Ludlow (2012), Halberstadt and Johnson (2014), Judl et al. (2015), Obst (2015), Varga (2018) and Horne (2019)]

Assessment approaches	PROS	CONS
Standard for Social Return on Investment Analysis (SSROI) This is a framework for measuring and accounting for the value created by social, environmental, and economic outcomes. It goes beyond traditional financial ROI by incorporating social value into the analysis.	The SSROI is appreciated for its simplicity and ease of calculation, making it highly accessible and consultancy oriented.	This approach can be subjective, influenced by personal and political factors. The focus on quantification may overlook qualitative impacts, and it often lacks data from large companies. Moreover, SSROI is just one of many measures of success, which can limit its standalone utility.
Standards of Evidence for Impact Investing That refer to the criteria and methodologies used to rigorously evaluate the social and environmental impact of investments. These standards help ensure that impact investments are effectively generating the intended positive outcomes.	This approach is inclusive, considering multiple stakeholders in the investment process and aiming to increase the scale of impact.	Its matrix-based and conceptual nature can be complex and is more suited to decision-making and communication rather than quantitative reporting.
Sustainability Quick-Check (SQC) model This is a rapid assessment tool used to evaluate the sustainability performance of projects, products, or organizations. It provides a concise yet comprehensive analysis of environmental, social, and economic impacts, helping stakeholders make informed decisions quickly.	The SQC model is useful for identifying and mapping key social and environmental issues, involving activities, partners, and resources	The reliance on self-assessment can lead to biased results, and it lacks a double materiality perspective, crucial for comprehensive sustainability evaluation.
LCA clinic This is a specialized service or framework designed to provide expertise and support in conducting Life Cycle Assessments (LCA). LCA is a methodology for assessing the environmental impacts associated with all stages of a product's life, from raw material extraction through production, use, and disposal.	This approach lowers barriers and enables fast implementation ("Life cycle assessment and ecodesign in a day"), aiding in identifying bottlenecks in a short time frame.	There are doubts about its reliability, and it emphasizes quick access to certification over a sustainable transition path.

(continued)

Table 9.4 (continued)

Assessment approaches	PROS	CONS
SPI-Framework (Sustainability oriented version of Business model Canvas) This is a strategic tool designed to integrate sustainability into business model planning and innovation. It adapts the traditional Business Model Canvas to emphasize sustainability considerations, helping organizations develop business models that are economically viable while also being socially and environmentally responsible.	This framework helps startups combine business model formulation with performance measurement.	Its implementation is context-specific, primarily applicable in Germany, which can limit its generalizability.
Triple-Bottom-Line Impact Analysis Framework of Fintech Companies This is a comprehensive evaluation tool designed to measure the sustainability performance of financial technology firms. It focuses on assessing the impact across three dimensions: economic, social, and environmental. This framework helps fintech companies align their operations and strategies with sustainable development goals.	This framework supports a progressive orientation toward sustainability, as outlined by Baumgartner and Ebner (2010).	It is limited to specific areas of intervention and follows a predefined context, initially focusing on economic reporting, followed by voluntary disclosure and audit.
Lean Impact Measurement This is an approach designed to evaluate the effectiveness and impact of social and environmental initiatives using principles from the Lean methodology. It focuses on maximizing value and minimizing waste by rapidly testing and iterating on impact measurement processes.	It emphasizes the prioritization of issues and a clear structure, with public data collection enhancing transparency.	It is mainly adopted for conceptualization, focusing on the structure and influencing factors of ideal solutions, which may limit practical application.

9.6 Implications

The results of this bibliometric analysis have several implications for future research directions and policies. High citation impact and publication quality indicate that current research strategies are effective, but there is always room for improvement. For example, enhancing international collaborations can further increase the impact and relevance of research. Institutions can also focus on emerging research areas identified in this analysis, such as digital transformation and sustainability, to stay abreast of global research trends.

From a policy perspective, supporting research initiatives that align with global sustainability goals and technological advancements can have far-reaching impacts. Policymakers can leverage these insights to fund and promote research areas that address critical global challenges, such as climate change, sustainable development, and digital innovation. Supportive policies for the start-up ecosystem, such as tax incentives and access to funding, can further stimulate innovation and create a virtuous cycle of collaboration between academia and industry. This not only improves the quality of research, but also contributes to economic growth and solving pressing social and environmental problems by aligning academic research with SDGs.

9.7 Conclusions and Research Agenda

According to the aim of the current literature review of understanding how the sustainability of the start-ups has been studied, measured, and disclosed, we conclude that the assessment of start-ups' social and environmental impacts requires a nuanced approach that balances various dimensions and trade-offs. The analysis presented in the tables underscores several key dimensions that must be considered when selecting appropriate assessment tools. In our avenues for future research, we highlight them, suggesting the promotion of an awareness in tool selection that is informed about the impacts this choice has on various dimensions.

First, there is the trade-off between consultancy-oriented solutions and conceptually groundbreaking approaches. Lingane and Olsen (2004) highlight the simplicity and accessibility of consultancy-oriented methods such as the Standard for Social Return on Investment Analysis (SSROI), which are easy to apply and calculate. However, these may lack the depth and innovation of more conceptually robust frameworks. In our study, we presented tools that were discussed both in the scientific literature and in the gray literature commonly used by practitioners. This certainly raises concerns about the methodological consistency of the tools discussed, which was not addressed here for reasons of brevity. Acknowledging this as a limitation of the chapter, we consider a more in-depth analysis of these aspects as one of the future directions for the development of this study.

Another critical dimension is the orientation toward disclosure, specifically whether the emphasis should be on communicating with investors or clients. Puttick and Ludlow (2012) illustrate that different stakeholders may require different types of information, and thus, the chosen methodology must be capable of addressing these diverse needs. Aware that each communication and disclosure tool may have different informational purposes, depending on the category of stakeholders considered as the primary recipients of the performance disclosure, we consider a systematization and discussion of these aspects as a further direction for the development of this study.

The context-specific nature of some solutions versus the applicability across sectors or countries also presents a significant consideration. For example, Hall et al. (2010), and Varga (2018) for Fintech, point out that while tailored, context-specific solutions can be highly effective in particular settings, there is a risk that these solutions may not be transferable or comparable across different contexts.

Speed versus reliability is another essential trade-off in the evolving context of start-ups. As discussed, Halberstadt and Johnson (2014) and Judl et al. (2015) emphasize the importance of quick assessments in dynamic environments. However, this speed must not compromise the reliability and thoroughness of the evaluations performed. In line with this suggestion, we propose that future studies could empirically analyze differences in the quantity and quality of disclosure, potentially identifying specific and effective drivers and barriers for fostering a culture more oriented toward measuring sustainability performance. This constrain could also take into account the dynamic nature of the context, as well as the responsiveness of entities to significant changes in the environment, which may affect the nature and quality of the disclosure provided.

Moreover, the trade-off between tailored solutions that fit specific business models and the need for comparability of measures is crucial. Hansen et al. (2009), Obst (2015), and Maas et al. (2016) suggest that while bespoke assessments can provide valuable insights tailored to individual business models, there is also a need for standardized metrics that allow for comparison across different entities. A fourth direction identified by this study is the further classification of contexts, sectors, and operational dimensions that could enhance the likelihood of a more reliable (voluntary) disclosure scheme. Specifically, we propose positioning this expected behavior in a matrix format to enable effective visualization based on specific contextual factors and the propensity for tool adoption.

Finally, the prioritization of themes and issues versus the growing trend toward voluntary, partial disclosure needs to be balanced. Horne (2019) and Varga (2018) indicate that while focusing on specific themes can drive targeted improvements, there is increasing pressure for broader, more comprehensive disclosure practices. In line with this reasoning a further direction for future studies might be suggested. A further avenue for developing this study could involve identifying the key characteristics that differentiate one sustainability assessment tool from another. Specifically, a practitioner could benefit from a classification and comparison system for these tools, allowing them to select the one that is most effective and insightful for their particular context.

In conclusion, the choice of assessment methodology for start-ups should be guided by a careful consideration of these dimensions and trade-offs (see Fichter et al., 2023). A balanced approach that integrates the strengths of various methodologies while mitigating their weaknesses will be essential for effectively measuring and enhancing the social and environmental impacts of start-ups. This will ensure that the chosen solutions are both practical and robust, providing meaningful insights that can drive sustainable growth and development for born sustainable start-ups. As Fichter et al. (2023) underlined, "*there is a clear gap in sustainable business model research with regard to the conceptualization of system level impacts and related empirical evidence* [for new ventures and start-ups]" (p. 10).

References

Ahmad, T., Zhang, D., Huang, C., Zhang, H., Dai, N., Song, Y., & Chen, H. (2021). Artificial intelligence in sustainable energy industry: Status Quo, challenges and opportunities. *Journal of Cleaner Production, 289*, 125834.

Akpan, I. J., Udoh, E. A. P., & Adebisi, B. (2022). Small business awareness and adoption of state-of-the-art technologies in emerging and developing markets, and lessons from the COVID-19 pandemic. *Journal of Small Business & Entrepreneurship, 34*(2), 123–140.

Auzepy, A., Bannier, C. E., & Gärtner, F. (2024). *Looking beyond ESG preferences: The role of sustainable finance literacy in sustainable investing*. Center for Financial Studies Working Paper, 719. https://doi.org/10.2139/ssrn.4773211.

Awana, S., Chavan, M., Sedera, D., Cheng, Z., & Ganzin, M. (2024). Unlocking circular start-ups: A model of barriers. *Business Strategy and the Environment, 33*(3), 2546–2577.

Baipai, R., Chikuta, O., Gandiwa, E., & Mutanga, C. N. (2022). *Critical success factors for sustainable agritourism development in Zimbabwe: A multi-stakeholder perspective.*

Baumgartner, R. J., & Ebner, D. (2010). Corporate sustainability strategies: Sustainability profiles and maturity levels. *Sustainable Development, 18*(2), 76–89.

Bidmon, C. M., & Knab, S. F. (2018). The three roles of business models in societal transitions: New linkages between business model and transition research. *Journal of Cleaner Production, 178*, 903–916. https://doi.org/10.1016/j.jclepro.2017.12.198

Boar-Boar, A., & Oliveras-Villanueva, M. (2019). Systematic literature review: Sustainability practices in start-ups. *European Accounting and Management Review, 6*(1), 53–80. https://ssrn.com/abstract=3486127

Bocken, N. M. (2015). Sustainable venture capital–catalyst for sustainable start-up success? *Journal of Cleaner Production, 108*, 647–658. https://doi.org/10.1016/j.jclepro.2015.05.079

Bogers, M., Chesbrough, H., & Strand, R. (2020). Sustainable open innovation to address a grand challenge: Lessons from Carlsberg and the Green Fiber Bottle. *British Food Journal, 122*(5), 1505–1517.

Broccardo, L., Vola, P., Zicari, A., & Alshibani, S. M. (2023). Contingency-based analysis of the drivers and obstacles to a successful sustainable business model: Seeking the uncaptured value. *Technological Forecasting and Social Change, 191*, 122513. https://doi.org/10.1016/j.techfore.2023.122513

Brown, R., Mawson, S., & Rowe, A. (2019a). Start-ups, entrepreneurial networks and equity crowdfunding: A processual perspective. *Industrial Marketing Management, 80*, 115–125.

Brown, R., Mawson, S., Lee, N., & Peterson, L. (2019b). Start-up factories, transnational entrepreneurs and entrepreneurial ecosystems: Unpacking the lure of start-up accelerator programmes. *European Planning Studies, 27*(5), 885–904.

Carle, A., & Rayna, T. (2023). Where to start? Exploring how sustainable startups integrate sustainability impact assessment within their entrepreneurial process. *Journal of Management & Organization*, 1–17. https://doi.org/10.1017/jmo.2023.46

Cohen, B., & Winn, M. I. (2007). Market imperfections, opportunity and sustainable entrepreneurship. *Journal of Business Venturing, 22*(1), 29–49. https://doi.org/10.1016/j.jbusvent.2004.12.001

Comin, L. C., Aguiar, C. C., Sehnem, S., Yusliza, M. Y., Cazella, C. F., & Julkovski, D. J. (2020). Sustainable business models: a literature review. *Benchmarking: An International Journal, 27*(7), 2028–2047. https://doi.org/10.1108/BIJ-12-2018-0384

Cosenz, F., & Noto, G. (2018). A dynamic business modelling approach to design and experiment new business venture strategies. *Long Range Planning, 51*(1), 127–140.

Davidsson, P., Recker, J., & Von Briel, F. (2020). External enablement of new venture creation: A framework. *Academy of Management Perspectives, 34*(3), 311–332. https://doi.org/10.5465/amp.2017.0163

Deyanova, K., Brehmer, N., Lapidus, A., Tiberius, V., & Walsh, S. (2022). Hatching start-ups for sustainable growth: A bibliometric review on business incubators. *Review of Managerial Science, 16*(7), 2083–2109. https://doi.org/10.1007/s11846-022-00525-9

Di Vaio, A., Hasan, S., Palladino, R., & Hassan, R. (2023). The transition towards circular economy and waste within accounting and accountability models: A systematic literature review and conceptual framework. *Environment, Development and Sustainability, 25*(1), 734–810.

Di Vaio, A., Hassan, R., Chhabra, M., Arrigo, E., & Palladino, R. (2022). Sustainable entrepreneurship impact and entrepreneurial venture life cycle: A systematic literature review. *Journal of Cleaner Production, 134469.*

Di Vaio, A., Palladino, R., Pezzi, A., & Kalisz, D. E. (2021). The role of digital innovation in knowledge management systems: A systematic literature review. *Journal of Business Research, 123*, 220–231.

Donthu, N., Kumar, S., Mukherjee, D., Pandey, N., & Lim, W. (2021). How to conduct a bibliometric analysis: An overview and guidelines. *Journal of Business Research, 133*, 285–296. https://doi.org/10.1016/j.jbusr.es.2021.04.070

Elzen, B., & Wieczorek, A. (2005). Introduction: Transitions towards sustainability through system innovation. *Technological Forecasting and Social Change, 72*, 651–661. https://doi.org/10.1016/j.techfore.2005.04.002

Fichter, K., Lüdeke-Freund, F., Schaltegger, S., & Schillebeeckx, S. J. (2023). Sustainability impact assessment of new ventures: An emerging field of research. *Journal of Cleaner Production, 384*, 135452. https://doi.org/10.1016/j.jclepro.2022.135452

Figge, F., & Hahn, T. (2004). Sustainable value added—measuring corporate contributions to sustainability beyond eco-efficiency. *Ecological Economics, 48*(2), 173–187. https://doi.org/10.1016/j.ecolecon.2003.08.005

Franceschelli, M. V., Santoro, G., & Candelo, E. (2018). Business model innovation for sustainability: A food start-up case study. *British Food Journal, 120*(10), 2483–2494.

Guldmann, E., & Huulgaard, R. D. (2020). Barriers to circular business model innovation: A multiple-case study. *Journal of Cleaner Production, 243*, 118160.

Hahn, G. J. (2020). Industry 4.0: A supply chain innovation perspective. *International Journal of Production Research, 58*(5), 1425–1441.

Halberstadt, J., & Johnson, M. (2014). Sustainability management for startups and micro-enterprises: Development of a sustainability-quick-check and reporting scheme. In *EnviroInfo* (pp. 17–24).

Hall, J. K., Daneke, G. A., & Lenox, M. J. (2010). Sustainable development and entrepreneurship: Past contributions and future directions. *Journal of Business Venturing, 25*(5), 439–448.

Hansen, E. G., Große-Dunker, F., & Reichwald, R. (2009). Sustainability innovation cube. A framework to evaluate sustainability-oriented innovations. *International Journal of Innovation Management, 13*, 683–713.

Henry, M., Bauwens, T., Hekkert, M., & Kirchherr, J. (2020). A typology of circular start-ups: An Analysis of 128 circular business models. *Journal of Cleaner Production, 245*, 118528.

Hockerts, K., & Wüstenhagen, R. (2010). Greening Goliaths versus emerging Davids—Theorizing about the role of incumbents and new entrants in sustainable entrepreneurship. *Journal of Business Venturing, 25*(5), 481–492. https://doi.org/10.1016/j.jbusvent.2009.07.005

Hörisch, J., Freeman, R. E., & Schaltegger, S. (2014). Applying stakeholder theory in sustainability management: Links, similarities, dissimilarities, and a conceptual framework. *Organization & Environment, 27*(4), 328–346. https://doi.org/10.1177/1086026614535786

Hörisch, J., Johnson, M. P., & Schaltegger, S. (2015). Implementation of sustainability management and company size: A knowledge-based view. *Business Strategy and the Environment, 24*(8), 765–779. https://doi.org/10.1002/bse.1844

Horne, J. (2019). *The sustainability impact of new ventures: Measuring and managing entrepreneurial contributions to sustainable development* (Doctoral dissertation, Technische Universität Berlin).

Horne, J., Recker, M., Michelfelder, I., Jay, J., & Kratzer, J. (2020). Exploring entrepreneurship related to the sustainable development goals-mapping new venture activities with semi-automated content analysis. *Journal of Cleaner Production, 242*, 118052.

Horne, J., & Fichter, K. (2022). Growing for sustainability: Enablers for the growth of impact start-ups–A conceptual framework, taxonomy, and systematic literature review. *Journal of Cleaner Production, 349*, 131163. https://doi.org/10.1016/j.jclepro.2022.131163

Johnson, M. P., & Schaltegger, S. (2020). Entrepreneurship for sustainable development: A review and multilevel causal mechanism framework. *Entrepreneurship Theory and Practice, 44*(6), 1141–1173. https://doi.org/10.1177/1042258719885368

Joyce, A., & Paquin, R. L. (2016). The triple layered business model canvas: A tool to design more sustainable business models. *Journal of Cleaner Production, 135*, 1474–1486. https://doi.org/10.1016/j.jclepro.2016.06.067

Judl, J., Mattila, T., Manninen, K., & Antikainen, R. (2015). Life cycle assessment and ecodesign in a day. Lessons learned from a series of LCA clinics for start-ups and small and medium enterprises (SMEs). *Suomen ympäristö, 18*.

Leising, E., Quist, J., & Bocken, N. (2018). Circular economy in the building sector: Three cases and a collaboration tool. *Journal of Cleaner Production, 176*, 976–989.

Lingane, A., & Olsen, S. (2004). Guidelines for social return on investment. *California Management Review, 46*(3), 116–135. https://doi.org/10.2307/41166224

Loprevite, S. (2020). Vocazione sociale, profitto e nuovi modelli ibridi d'impresa: paradigmi e realtà in prospettiva economico-aziendale. *Vocazione sociale, profitto e nuovi modelli ibridi d'impresa*, 1–148.

Long, T. B., Looijen, A., & Blok, V. (2018). Critical success factors for the transition to business models for sustainability in the food and beverage industry in the Netherlands. *Journal of Cleaner Production, 175*, 82–95.

Lüdeke-Freund, F., Froese, T., Dembek, K., Rosati, F., & Massa, L. (2024). What makes a business model sustainable? Activities, design themes, and value functions. *Organization & Environment*, (head-of-print). https://doi.org/10.1177/10860266241235212.

Maas, K., Schaltegger, S., & Crutzen, N. (2016). Advancing the integration of corporate sustainability measurement, management and reporting. *Journal of Cleaner Production, 133*, 859–862.

Mansouri, S., & Momtaz, P. P. (2022). Financing sustainable entrepreneurship: ESG measurement, valuation, and performance. *Journal of Business Venturing, 37*(6), 106258.

Munaro, M. R., Tavares, S. F., & Bragança, L. (2020). Towards circular and more sustainable buildings: A systematic literature review on the circular economy in the built environment. *Journal of Cleaner Production, 260*, 121134.

Obst, L. (2015). *Utilizing the business model canvas to enable sustainability measurement on the business model level: An indicator framework supplementing the business model canvas* (Master's thesis, University of Twente).

Padilla-Lozano, C. P., & Collazzo, P. (2022). Corporate social responsibility, green innovation and competitiveness–causality in manufacturing. *Competitiveness Review: An International Business Journal, 32*(7), 21–39.

Page, M. J., McKenzie, J. E., Bossuyt, P. M., Boutron, I., Hoffmann, T. C., Mulrow, C. D., et al. (2021). The PRISMA 2020 statement: An updated guideline for reporting systematic re-views. *BMJ, 372*. https://doi.org/10.1136/bmj.n71

Parrish, B. D. (2010). Sustainability-driven entrepreneurship: Principles of organization design. *Journal of Business Venturing, 25*(5), 510–523. https://doi.org/10.1016/j.jbusvent.2009.05.005

Puttick, R., & Ludlow, J. (2012). *Standards of evidence for impact investing*. Nesta.

Schaltegger, S., & Wagner, M. (2011). Sustainable entrepreneurship and sustainability innovation: Categories and interactions. *Business Strategy and the Environment, 20*(4), 222–237. https://doi.org/10.1002/bse.682

Schick, H., Marxen, S., & Freimann, J. (2002). Sustainability issues for start-up entrepreneurs. *Greener Management International, 38*, 59–70.

Schiuma, G., Schettini, E., Santarsiero, F., & Carlucci, D. (2022). The transformative leadership compass: Six competencies for digital transformation entrepreneurship. *International Journal of Entrepreneurial Behavior & Research, 28*(5), 1273–1291.

Smith, A. D. (2021). *Strategies for small business owners to succeed beyond five years* (Doctoral dissertation, Walden University).

Sreenivasan, A., & Suresh, M. (2024). Start-up sustainability: Does blockchain adoption drives sustainability in start-ups? A systematic literature reviews. *Management Research Review, 47*(3), 390–405. https://doi.org/10.1108/MRR-07-2022-0519

Tranfield, D., Denyer, D., & Smart, P. (2003). Towards a methodology for developing evidence-informed management knowledge by means of systematic review. *British Journal of Management, 14*(3), 207–222. https://doi.org/10.1111/1467-8551.00375

Trautwein, C. (2021). Sustainability impact assessment of start-ups–Key insights on relevant assessment challenges and approaches based on an inclusive, systematic literature review. *Journal of Cleaner Production, 281*, 125330. https://doi.org/10.1016/j.jclepro.2020.125330

Varga, D. (2018). Triple-bottom-line impact analysis framework of FinTech companies. *Vezetéstudomány-Budapest Management Review, 49*(11), 24–34.

Venturelli, A., Caputo, F., Leopizzi, R., Mastroleo, G., & Mio, C. (2017). How can CSR identity be evaluated? A pilot study using a Fuzzy Expert System. *Journal of Cleaner Production, 141*, 1000–1010. https://doi.org/10.1016/j.jclepro.2016.09.172

Volkmann, C., Fichter, K., Klofsten, M., & Audretsch, D. B. (2021). Sustainable entrepreneurial ecosystems: An emerging field of research. *Small Business Economics, 56*(3), 1047–1055. https://doi.org/10.1007/s11187-019-00253-7

Chapter 10
Critical Success Factors for Healthcare Services Gazelles: An Empirical Analysis of Italian Companies

Marianna Mauro, Giulia Cattafi, Elisa Rita Ferrari, and Monica Giancotti

10.1 Introduction

In recent years, research on high-growth firms (HGFs), also known as gazelles (Birch, 1981), has increased (Rocha & Ferreira, 2021; Coad & Guenther, 2014; Goswami et al., 2019; Henrekson & Johansson, 2010; Monteiro, 2019; Coad & Srhoj, 2020; Fotopoulos, 2023).

The studies on this topic offer a comprehensive overview of their peculiarities, which in turn justify the growing interest from the literature.

Monteiro (2019), for example, provides an extensive review of HGFs, highlighting their fundamental characteristics: gazelles are distinguished by their rapid growth rates and their substantial contributions to economic development (Stangler, 2010; Bos & Stam, 2014; Heimonen & Virtanen, 2012; Bleda et al., 2013), job creation (Birch, 1981; Coad & Guenther, 2014; Henrekson & Johansson, 2010; OECD, 2010; Heimonen & Virtanen, 2012), and knowledge generation (Henrekson & Johansson, 2010; Bleda et al., 2013).

More recent studies (such as Pereira et al., 2020 & Cristofaro et al., 2024) have highlighted their innovative capabilities and agility in adapting to market changes and exploit new opportunities, fostering a dynamic business environment.

In summary, given their significant role in job creation and productivity growth, HGFs have become a focal point for research.

M. Mauro · G. Cattafi · M. Giancotti (✉)
Magna Graecia University of Catanzaro, Catanzaro, Italy
e-mail: mauro@unicz.it; giulia.cattafi@unicz.it; mgiancotti@unicz.it

E. R. Ferrari
Kore University of Enna, Enna, Italy
e-mail: elisarita.ferrari@unikore.it

S. Loprevite et al. (eds.), *Startups and Gazelle Enterprises*, SIDREA Series in Accounting and Business Administration,
https://doi.org/10.1007/978-3-031-90881-1_10

Although research is expanding, the empirical evidence regarding the financial performance drivers which contribute to their rapid growth (Delmar et al., 2013) remains fragmented (Gaikwad, 2022).

Prior studies showed that the growth trajectory of gazelles is rarely linear (Delmar et al., 2003). These companies often undergo phases of rapid expansion followed by phases of stabilization or even decline (St-Jean et al., 2008; Chae, 2024). A deeper understanding of the factors influencing their financial performance and success, which underlie these fluctuations, would be useful (St-Jean et al., 2008; Acs & Mueller, 2015). However, to the best of our knowledge, empirical literature addressing these dynamics is scarce.

This chapter fills this gap, offering evidence from the private healthcare sector. The focus on this specific sector is justified by the following considerations.

First, the healthcare sector represents a fundamental component of the Italian economy, significantly contributing to the country's GDP. According to the European Commission,[1] in 2021 the healthcare sector accounted for 9.4% of the national GDP, surpassing key sectors such as construction (6.2%) and non-food manufacturing (8.9%) (ISTAT[2]). Moreover, the healthcare sector has experienced a steady growth of 3.1% due to investments in technology and the rising demand for healthcare services from the aging population.

Compared to other strategic sectors of the Italian economy, the healthcare sector exhibits unique growth dynamics, making it particularly relevant for the analysis of gazelle firms. The complexity of regulations, technological challenges, and the need to adapt quickly to demographic and healthcare changes create a fertile environment for the emergence of high-growth potential firms. Second, the healthcare industry stands out because of its rapid technological advancements and increasing demand for innovative solutions, making it a highly conducive environment for HGFs (Achilladelis & Antonakis, 2001; Mazzucato & Parris, 2015; Srinivasan & Chandwani, 2014). In this context, gazelles play a pivotal role by fostering innovation and introducing new models of care that improve accessibility, efficiency, and patient satisfaction (Mazzucato & Parris, 2015). These companies often focus on creating advanced medical technologies, medicines, and healthcare models, which improve patient results and make the overall system more efficient (Achilladelis & Antonakis, 2001; Mazzucato & Parris, 2015; Srinivasan & Chandwani, 2014). The private healthcare sector's unique characteristics make it a relevant and interesting case for examining the critical success factors (CSFs) of gazelle enterprises.

The chapter is structured as follows: the following paragraph (background) provides a framework of the role of gazelles in the Italian healthcare sector. Section 10.2 (literature review) provides a synthesis of the previous literature on the CSFs in HGFs. Section 10.3 describes the research design, while Sect. 10.4 illustrates the research findings. Finally, Sect. 10.5 reports the discussion and concluding remarks.

---

[1] https://health.ec.europa.eu/document/download/1f348745-341f-425a-8dd6-28ff2fbd8ea3_en?filename=2023_chp_it_italian.pdf

[2] https://www.istat.it/storage/settori-produttivi/2022/Capitolo-2.pdf

10.1.1 Background: The Role of Gazelles in Italian Healthcare Sector

Gazelles exist in all sectors, primarily in services (Henrekson & Johansson, 2010). They focus mainly on knowledge production, science, and research (OECD, 2010), which is characteristic for sub-sector of business services. This chapter is focused on gazelles operating in the healthcare sector. This choice is justified by the importance of the private healthcare sector in the Italian context.

The Italian National Health Service (NHS) operates under a universal coverage model, offering free access to an array of healthcare services for all citizens (Fattore, 2019; Ricciardi & Tarricone, 2021). It is funded through a taxation system. The NHS is currently managed and organized at the regional level, with two main types of agencies: Public Hospitals (also referred to as "Aziende Ospedaliere"), which deliver specialized medical care, surgeries, emergency services, or take part in medical research and education ("Aziende Ospedaliere Universitarie"—Teaching hospitals), and Local Health Authorities, which provide primary care and community health services.

When public structures experience a deficiency in internal resources, governments establish partnerships with private healthcare providers to enhance care quality, maximize efficiency, and increase productivity (Vecchi et al., 2022). By providing services to patients for free or a minimal fee, private providers become integral to a sustainable solution for improving access to high-quality care, later seeking reimbursement from the NHS.

Historically, this system has provided high-quality care at affordable costs. Recently, however, it has encountered significant challenges because of factors, including (a) budget cuts stemming from financial crises and inefficiencies in expenditure management, (b) increasing demands driven by demographic shifts and changing population behaviors, such as an aging population requiring more comprehensive care and a general desire for higher quality and expedited treatment, (c) insufficient coverage of highly demanded services, including dental, rehabilitative, home-care, and childcare services, which are under-funded and often offered at high costs by private providers (Pinto & Baracsi, 2012; Gorli et al., 2014).

As a result, the Italian NHS has seen a reduction in its capacity. Budget constraints have led to longer waiting lists and fewer agreements with private providers, limiting healthcare services. The current system is insufficient to meet the comprehensive healthcare and welfare needs of all families. In response to the reduction in public services, there has been a rise in demand for private healthcare, which has spurred an increase in healthcare-related start-ups (Gorli et al., 2014; Morande et al., 2020).

To date, few studies have dealt with factors affecting the financial performance of private healthcare providers (Forgione & Noto, 2023). However, the specific factors that affect the financial performance of healthcare start-ups, contributing to the achievement of the "gazelle" status, remain unknown.

The topic is relevant considering that healthcare start-ups play a crucial role in shaping the landscape of healthcare in Italy, offering models of scalability and innovation that contribute significantly to the sector's evolution. Understanding the CSFs in private healthcare gazelles provides useful insights applicable to the public healthcare sector. CSFs identified in the private sector can serve as useful benchmarks for public healthcare organizations (Eeckloo et al., 2007).

10.2 Critical Success Factors in Gazelles: Literature Review

CSFs refer to the essential elements or critical areas that require efficient management for the attainment of success by an individual or organization (Rockart, 1979; Chung, 1987). Identifying and understanding the CSFs that enable start-ups to achieve sustained performance is crucial for reducing failures and enhancing the likelihood of continued success for HGFs (Chung, 1987).

The literature on CSFs for gazelle enterprises is fragmented and ambiguous. On one hand, additional research is needed as there is currently no comprehensive theoretical framework that adequately encompasses all the factors influencing their growth (Hechavarria et al., 2019). Conversely, certain studies show that the triumph of gazelles can be attributed to the interplay of diverse endogenous (i.e., firm-level) and external factors (Gaikwad, 2022). Endogenous factors encompass internal dynamics like innovation, human capital, and effective management practices, whereas external factors mainly refer to market conditions and policy environment. The interplay of these factors contributes to the multifaceted nature of rapid business growth (Steffens et al., 2009; Davidsson, 1989). Other studies suggest specific CSFs may vary across different sectors where gazelles operate (Delmar et al., 2003).

This research aims to address this knowledge gap, offering evidence from the healthcare sector; we investigate—on the one hand—the existence of common factors, on the other, the existence of specific CSFs for gazelles operating in the healthcare sector.

Building on previous studies, we begin by discussing the major factors that contribute to the success of gazelles. The following subsections provide a detailed description of these factors.

10.2.1 Owner-Manager Orientation and Background

Several studies have investigated the personality traits and characteristics of entrepreneurs that impact business growth (Gupta et al., 2019; Bendell et al., 2019; Cassar, 2007; Stanworth & Curran, 1976; Baum et al., 2000; Eisenhardt & Schoonhoven, 1990; Perren, 2000; Feindt et al., 2002). Educational background, including training, industry experience, or prior entrepreneurial experience, significantly influences business growth (Baum et al., 2000; Eisenhardt & Schoonhoven,

1990; Lee, 2014; Monteiro, 2019). In effect, studies show that a lack of managerial skills is a major obstacle for firms during high growth periods (Lee, 2014; Monteiro, 2019; Greiner, 1997).

More recently, Rocha and Ferreira (2021) summarize academic literature on HGFs from 2000 to 2021 by analyzing 84 peer-reviewed articles. Regarding the role of entrepreneurial characteristics and personality, the study confirms that factors such as risk-taking, motivation, and learning orientation play a significant role in a gazelle's growth (Slevin & Covin, 1997; Brännback et al., 2009; Ingolfsdotter & Viklund, 2017), enhancing process improvement (OECD, 2010; Ireland et al., 2003), and fostering a positive business environment (OECD, 2010).

10.2.2 Human Capital

The skills and experience of the human resources is another significant factor that impact growth (Rocha & Ferreira, 2021; Demir et al., 2017; Parker et al., 2010; Cooper et al., 1994; Hechavarria et al., 2019). Studies show that human capital plays a relevant role in explaining the non-uniform distribution of the growth rate of firms in the economy (Klette & Kortum, 2004; Rossi-Hansberg & Wright, 2007; Feindt et al., 2002). The recruitment and training of employees are critical issues, especially when considering that HGFs are most prevalent in knowledge-intensive industries (Delmar et al., 2003; Daunfeldt et al., 2016; Coad et al. 2014a, 2014b, 2016; Coad & Guenther, 2014).

10.2.3 Innovation Strategies

Innovation is frequently cited in previous studies as a key driver for the growth of gazelle companies (Henrekson & Johansson, 2010; Megaravalli & Sampagnaro, 2018; Rocha & Ferreira, 2021; Feindt et al., 2002; Goedhuys & Sleuwaegen, 2016; Gundry & Welsch, 2001). For example, Parker et al. (2010) analyzed over 100 HGFs from a novel British dataset, tracking their growth over two periods: 1992–1996 and 1996–2001. They conclude that companies that innovate and adopt new technologies experience faster, sustainable growth, especially in dynamic markets. The impact of innovation, however, varies depending on enterprise diversity and the specific innovation types pursued (Hölzl, 2014; Rocha & Ferreira, 2021).

Two main types of innovation—product and process innovation—play pivotal roles. Product innovation involves developing new or significantly improved goods/services to meet growing customer requirements and capitalize on market opportunities (Schilling, 2017). This type can influence a company's market position and revenue streams. For example, in healthcare, introducing advanced medical devices enhances the experiences of users (Feindt et al., 2002; Christensen, 1997).

Process innovation, on the other hand, focuses on implementing new or significantly improved production or delivery methods (Laforet, 2012). It enhances efficiency, reduces costs, improves quality, and increases flexibility. Examples include adopting automation technologies or lean manufacturing principles (Davenport, 1993). While less visible to consumers, process innovation is crucial for competitiveness and operational excellence. Both innovation types are essential for long-term business growth. Product innovation drives market expansion and consumer satisfaction, while process innovation ensures efficient delivery. Companies excelling in both areas can adapt to market changes, optimize operations, and maintain a competitive edge (Tidd & Bessant, 2020; Danneels, 2002; Christensen, 1997; Dobbs & Hamilton, 2007; Verhees & Meulenberg, 2004; Capelleras & Greene, 2008). Additionally, innovation fosters a culture of continuous improvement, encouraging employees to enhance their work, contributing to a dynamic business environment (Dyer, 2023). Research and Development (R&D) also plays a vital role in innovation (Feindt et al., 2002; Hölzl, 2009). Continuous R&D investment is characteristic of gazelles, enabling them to meet growing market demands and outperform competitors. However, the impact of R&D on firm performance is inconsistent: some studies suggest R&D allows gazelles to lead in technological advancements (Coad et al., 2014a, 2014b), while others report a negative or negligible effect on HGFs (Daunfeldt et al., 2016). Finally, evolutionary innovation, involving incremental improvements to products, services, or processes, is essential for maintaining competitiveness and responding to market changes (Tidd & Bessant, 2020; Danneels, 2002; Christensen, 1997). This approach fosters resilience and agility in a rapidly changing marketplace.

10.2.4 Market Orientation: Strategy Management and Organizational Systems

Operating in dynamic environments, HGFs must adapt to internal and external changes to maintain growth (Chandler & Hanks, 1994; Eisenhardt & Schoonhoven, 1990; Hofer & Sandberg, 1987). Adapting to environmental changes allows firms to leverage opportunities and mitigate negative impacts (Kazanjian & Drazin, 1990; Garnsey et al., 2006; Chandler & Baucus, 1996; St-Jean et al., 2008). Static strategies are inadequate; a flexible management approach is needed (Parker et al., 2010; Davila et al., 2010). In this framework, market orientation is crucial. For example, the study of Mason et al. (2015) investigates the role and characteristics of HGFs, using Scotland as a case study. Authors find successful HGFs emphasize understanding market needs and maintaining close relationships with customers, suggesting that market orientation is a significant factor in driving the growth of gazelle firms.

10.2.5 The Role of Information Technology (IT)

Several studies have examined IT's impact on gazelle enterprises' productivity and growth. While some research found no link between IT and firm performance (Brynjolfsson, 1993; Wilson, 1993, 1995; Solow, 1987), others confirmed IT's significant role in fostering service innovation across sectors (Barras, 1986; Hilkevics & Hilkevica, 2017; Luhn et al., 2017) and enhancing resilience. For example, Coad et al. (2023) found that digitized gazelles handled the COVID-19 shock better. Effective knowledge management, supported by IT, is crucial for HGFs, enabling swift information access (Davenport, 2007). Yet, adopting rigid systems can hinder growth, demanding more adaptation from employees (Chae, 2024). For optimal growth, gazelles should adopt dynamic, flexible systems to address coordination issues (Brnjas et al., 2015; Edberg & Ryss, 2019; Schlichter et al., 2021).

10.2.6 The Role of Internationalization

The geographic location is a notable factor in the HGF literature (Kelley et al., 2017; McDougall et al., 1994; Baum et al., 2000), though evidence remains ambiguous. Some studies link internationalization strategies to the success of gazelles (Nightingale & Coad, 2014; Zhao & Aram, 1995). Keen and Etemad (2012) emphasize that gazelles engaged in alliances within global networks perform better than domestic-oriented ones, benefiting from strengthened stakeholder relations, positive externalities, and reduced transaction costs (Chetty & Campbell-Hunt, 2003). International operations offer access to more financial resources (St-Jean et al., 2008). However, geographic expansion also exposes firms to diverse regulatory, cultural, economic, and social challenges that can affect growth. For example, the study by Barringer et al. (2005), which aimed to identify characteristics distinguishing rapid-growth from slow-growth firms, shows that geographic location can influence knowledge absorption. Firms in areas rich with external knowledge sources, such as clusters of high-tech companies, gain access to specialized suppliers, scientific knowledge, and technological expertise, which support growth.

10.2.7 Relational Capital: Relationships and Relationships with Customers and Key Stakeholders

Building strong relationships with customers, suppliers, and stakeholders offers gazelles valuable resources, market insights, and collaboration opportunities (Spitsin et al., 2023; Laur & Mignon, 2021). Understanding and meeting market demands, particularly through close customer relationships, enables firms to gather critical information and respond effectively, which is essential for launching new products and sustaining growth (Rocha & Ferreira, 2021; Siegel et al., 1993; Chandler & Baucus, 1996; Manev et al., 2005). Engaging with customers not only enhances responsiveness but also builds trust and loyalty, fostering both new and repeat business. In effect, the study of Feindt et al. (2002), which aims to identify CSFs for rapid growth in SME E-commerce ventures, concludes that baby gazelles should address key success factors, such as commitment, interaction, and control, from the start of their business. These factors give gazelles a competitive advantage by building customer trust and delivering effective customer support.

10.2.8 Financing Methods and Access to Financial Capital for Gazelle Companies

A crucial factor for gazelle enterprises is securing the financial resources necessary for growth (Feindt et al., 2002). The capital structure, comprising personal funds, bank loans, owner's equity, and business angel investments, is vital for their success (Ingolfsdotter & Viklund, 2017; Colombo & Grilli, 2010; Cooper et al., 1994; Hechavarria et al., 2019). As HGFs expand, access to venture capital, private equity, and other funding sources becomes essential for scaling operations and pursuing growth opportunities, thus driving innovation (Brown et al., 2014).

10.3 Method

10.3.1 Data and Sample

The study examines the population of Italian HGFs within the private healthcare sector (Division 86–88 NACE Rev.2 Classification[3]), also referred to as "HealthCare gazelles". The analysis covers the period from 2015 to 2022.

Data for the empirical analysis were gathered through a two-step process.

First, the healthcare gazelles were identified using the AIDA-Bureau van Dijk database. Subsequently, an online electronic questionnaire was sent to chairmen/chief executives of the selected enterprises.

10.3.1.1 Identifying Gazelle Enterprises

This research employs the definition of gazelle firm as introduced by Eurostat-OECD (2008) in the Manual on Business Demography Statistics. While there are concerns that this size threshold may exclude many small entrepreneurial firms with

[3]The selected two-digit NACE Rev.2 codes correspond to the following sectors: (1) Healthcare services activities, (2) Residential Care Services, (3) Non-residential Social Services.

high-growth potential, Daunfeldt et al. (2015) support its use in empirical research on HGFs.[4]

The OECD-Eurostat definition defines gazelles as new ventures less than 5 years old, with at least ten employees at the beginning of the growth period and an annualized growth rate in either sales revenues or employees exceeding 20% over a 3-years period.

In this research, two growth periods were identified:[5] 2015–2018 and 2016–2019. Business growth was measured using the 3-years annualized growth rate of sales revenues (10.1) and employment (10.2).

$$Sales\ growth = \sqrt[3]{\frac{Revenues_T}{Revenues_{T-3}}} - 1 > 20\% \tag{10.1}$$

$$Employment\ growth = \sqrt[3]{\frac{N.of\ employees_T}{N.of\ employees_{T-3}}} - 1 > 20\% \tag{10.2}$$

Figure 10.1 illustrates the growth periods and the two cohorts of gazelles identified in this study.

Based on the above-mentioned criteria, 82 healthcare gazelles were identified using the AIDA-BvD database. To ensure the quality of the data for the empirical analysis, the dataset was carefully screened to remove firms with unreliable accounting values, such as negative assets or turnover.

As a result, 13 firms were removed from the sample, leaving a balanced panel of 483 firm-year observation, corresponding to 69 healthcare Italian gazelles.

Figure 10.2 shows the geographical distribution of healthcare gazelles across the different Italian regions.

Lombardy has the highest concentration of healthcare gazelles, accounting for approximately 18.84% of the sample. This reflects the region's well-developed infrastructure and strong support for entrepreneurship. Campania follows with 12 healthcare gazelles (17.40%), while Sicily also shows a notable presence with 7 health gazelles (10.15%). Piedmont and Sardinia count six and five healthcare gazelles, respectively. Tuscany, Emilia-Romagna, Lazio, and Abruzzo each have between four and five healthcare gazelles, indicating moderate entrepreneurial activity. Apulia, Marche, Friuli-Venezia Giulia, Molise, Trentino-Alto Adige, and Umbria show the lowest share of healthcare gazelles (ranging from one to three).

[4] Furthermore, using the Eurostat-OECD definition ensures comparability between empirical studies. This definition has been applied in several empirical studies with similar purposes, including Coad et al. (2014b), Coad and Srhoj (2020), Colombelli et al. (2014), Lee (2014).

[5] Since the Eurostat-OECD (2008) definition allows for the high-growth period to begin in the first or at most the second year of a firm's existence, this study identifies two growth periods: (1) 2015–2018 for firms that had at least 10 employees in their second year (2015), and (2) 2016–2019 for firms that reached the 10-employee threshold in their second year of their life (2016).

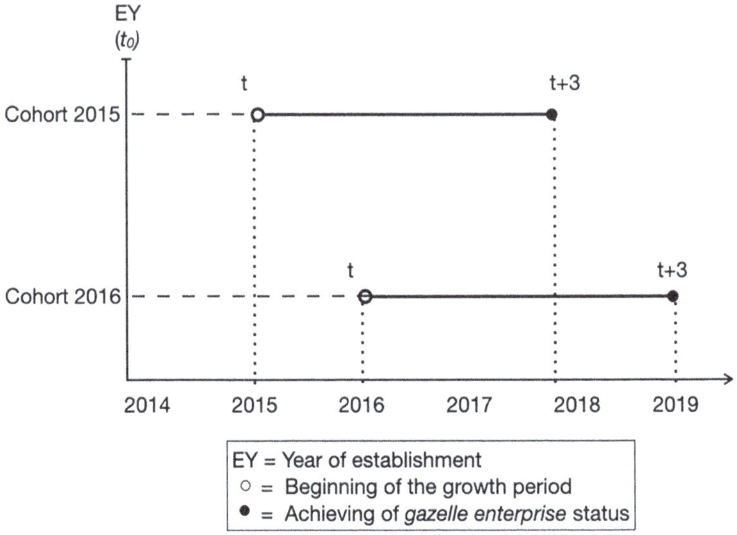

Fig. 10.1 Growth periods and sample structure. *Source*: Author's own elaboration

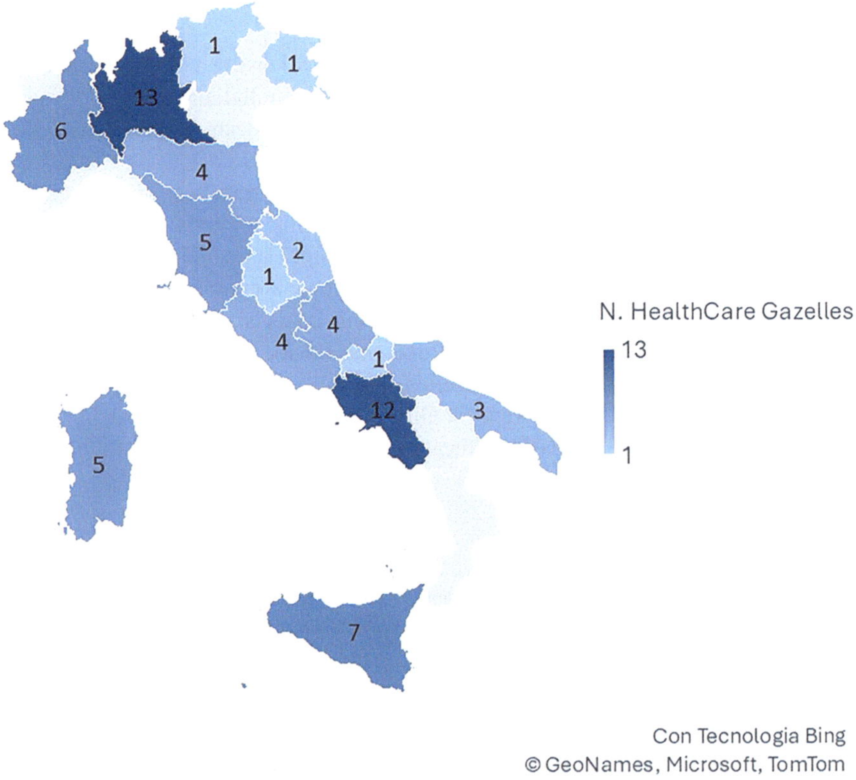

Fig. 10.2 Distribution of healthcare gazelles across Italy. *Source*: Author's elaboration

10.3.1.2 Questionnaire Design, Survey Data, and Respondents' Characteristics

This study identifies the most relevant CSFs driving the financial performance and success of healthcare gazelles.

To identify the major CSFs for rapidly expanding healthcare start-ups, a questionnaire was formulated based on a synthesis of the existing literature (refer to the Appendix). We focused on the following areas: (a) staff education; (b) innovation strategies; (c) structural and relational capital; (d) systems of planning and control; (e) type of start-up financing.

To investigate the role of these factors, the electronic questionnaire was sent via email to the founders/CEOs of gazelles.

A total of 69 questionnaires were sent to the CEOs and/or managers of Italian healthcare gazelles in January 2024. These individuals were selected for their ability to provide accurate information about their firms, given their positions and direct access to internal information (Muda et al., 2020).

Participants were asked to complete questionnaires provided through an online platform. They were given four weeks to complete the questionnaire. After the 1-month period, participants who did not respond were sent reminder emails with a link to the electronic questionnaire attached.

Fifty-eight responses were received, resulting in a response rate of approximately 85%.

Table 10.1 summarizes the demographic characteristics of the respondents. Of the respondents, 57% were male and 43% were female. Regarding age, most interviewees were in the 45–54 (34%) and 35–44 (24%) year age groups. Only a small portion was in the early stage of their career, with the smallest group (5%) in the 25–34 age group. Most of the respondents hold the position of president of the Board of Directors (41%) or CEO (55%). Only 3% of the responses came from founders. In terms of education, most respondents have a master's degree (17%) or a postgraduate master's degree (21%). Only 5% of respondents have a PhD.

Respondents exhibit many years of prior experience, with 38% reporting having 10 or more years of experience in the industry. Smaller portions of respondents have between 1 and 9 years of experience, with the largest group after the 10 or more years category consisting of respondents with 5 years of experience (16%). The size of the founding team also varies, with 36% of respondents reporting a single founder, 34% having three to five founders, and 29% having two founders.

10.3.2 Empirical Analysis

According to the studies conducted by Sebora et al. (2009) and Kumar et al. (2015), bivariate correlation analysis and multivariate regression analysis were employed to analyze the relationship between CSFs and the financial performance of healthcare gazelles.

Table 10.1 Demographic characteristics of the respondents

	n = 58	
Description	Frequency	Percent (%)
Gender		
Male	33	0.57
Female	25	0.43
	Age	
25–34 years	3	0.05
35–44 years	14	0.24
45–54 years	20	0.34
55–64 years	10	0.17
64 years or more	11	0.19
	Position	
CEO	32	0.55
Founder	2	0.03
President	24	0.41
	Education of the founders	
Bachelor's Degree (Old system)	8	0.14
Bachelor's Degree	9	0.16
Master's Degree	17	0.29
PhD	3	0.05
Postgraduate Masters	21	0.36
	Years of experience	
1 year	2	0.03
2 years	7	0.12
3 years	3	0.05
4 years	4	0.07
5 years	9	0.16
6 years	1	0.02
7 years	1	0.02
8 years	7	0.12
8 years	1	0.02
9 years	1	0.02
10 or more years	22	0.38
	Size of the founding team	
1 founder	21	0.36
2 founders	17	0.29
3–5 founders	20	0.34

Bivariate correlation analysis was used to measure the strength and direction of the relationship between each CSF and the financial performance of healthcare gazelles. According to Cohen's (1988) classification, the correlation coefficients (r) were categorized as follows:

Very weak correlation: $|r|<0.1$
Weak correlation: $0.1\leq|r|<0.3$
Moderate correlation: $0.3\leq|r|<0.5$
Strong correlation: $|r|\geq0.5$

This classification allowed for a clear interpretation of the strength of the relationship between each individual CSF and financial performance. For instance, a strong correlation ($|r|\geq0.5$) would indicate a significant linear positive relationship, while a weak or very weak correlation would suggest a low or negligible association.

Multivariate regression analysis was employed to examine the joint impact of multiple independent variables (CSFs and control variables) on the dependent variables (financial performance ratios). This approach helps determine the individual contribution of each CSF to financial performance, while controlling for the influence of other variables.

The regression model was estimated using the following Eq. (10.3):

$$Fin\_perf_{i,t} = \alpha + \partial_{CSF_s} + \varphi_{Control_{i,t}} + \varepsilon_{i,t} \tag{10.3}$$

where $Fin\_perf_{i,t}$ indicates the financial performance of gazelle i in year t, ∂_{CSF_s} is a vector of explanatory variables related to CSFs, $\varphi_{i,t}$ denotes the vector of firm-level control variables, and ε is the error term.

10.3.2.1 Variables

Dependent Variable

The financial performance represents the outcome variable in this research. Consistent with prior studies (Bornhäll et al., 2015; Onesti et al., 2022; Senderovitz et al., 2016), the following metrics were employed as dependent variables: (1) Return on Asset (ROA), defined as the ratio of Earnings Before Interests and Taxes (EBIT) to total assets; (2) Return on Equity (ROE), obtained by dividing net income by the book value of equity; (3) Return on Sales (ROS), measured as the ratio of EBIT to total sales; (4) EBITDA-to-sales ratio, operationalized as Earnings Before Interest, Taxes, Depreciation, and Amortization (EBITDA) divided by revenues.

Independent Variable

The independent variables were collected from the questionnaire and organized into six categories: (1) Staff Education, (2) Innovation, (3) Structural Capital, (4) Relational Capital, (5) Systems of Planning and Control, and (6) Firm Financing.

In the Education category (1), two items were used to measure the educational attainment among employees within Italian healthcare gazelles. These items measure the presence of employees with bachelor's or master's degrees, and those with a PhD. Responses to questions in categories (2–5) were coded using a binary scale (Yes/No). For category (6), related to start-up financing, responses were encoded as a categorical variable with eight response items. Table 10.2 provides details of the variables used in the empirical analysis, along with their average scores.

Control Variables

In the regression analyses, a set of firm-level control variables was included to account for factors that may affect the financial performance of healthcare gazelles. First, the analysis control for firm size measured by the natural logarithm of sales. This variable helps to understand how the scale or revenue size of these organizations influences their performance. Larger firms, for instance, might benefit from economies of scale or have different operational dynamics compared to smaller ones. Second, indebtedness is controlled using the Debt-to-Equity ratio, which provides insights into the extent to which firms rely on debt financing versus equity, thus potentially affecting their financial stability and risk management strategies.

Table 10.2 Critical Success Factors (CSF) variables used in the empirical analysis

Category	Description	Variable
1. Staff Education	Measures the number of employees with a bachelor's or master's degree.	Employees with Bachelor's/Master's Degree/Total number of employees
	Measures the number of employees with a Ph.D.	Employees PhD/Total number of employees
2. Innovation	Measures whether the firm is oriented toward the continuous improvement of its products/services and production processes.	Efficiency Innovation
	Assesses if the firm is constantly working to increase its market competitiveness.	Evolution Innovation
	Looks at whether the firm explores, identifies, and selects new opportunities and ideas.	New Opportunities and Ideas
	Checks if the firm promotes internationalization and develops policies and strategies to ensure its presence in international markets.	Internationalization Strategies
	Examines if the firm has a plan for innovation that is integrated with its policies and strategies.	Integrated Innovation Plan
	Assesses if the firm adopts approaches and initiatives to train and develop human resources to support innovation.	Human Resource Development
3. Structural Capital	Measures if the firm has a high level of codified knowledge within digital documents and databases.	Codified Knowledge
	Checks if these documents and databases are updated promptly.	Timely Updates
4. Relational Capital	Evaluates if there is a designated contact point for customers that addresses user needs and dedicates the necessary time to them.	Customer Contact Point
	Assesses if there is a well-established trust relationship between the customer and the firm.	Customer Trust Relationship
	Looks at if communication between the firm and its stakeholders (suppliers, banks, public institutions, etc.) is constant and effective.	Stakeholder Communication

(continued)

Table 10.2 (continued)

Category	Description	Variable
5. Systems of Planning and Control	Evaluates if the phases of entrepreneurial idea development and business start-up are supported by a business plan.	Business Plan Utilization
	Assesses if there are systems in place for controlling costs and payments, including sufficient cash flow/ reserves, to avoid payment delays.	Cost and Payment Control Systems
6. Firm Financing	Determines which financing instruments were used during the startup phase of the firm. The options include: (1) Founder self-financing, (2) debt and equity from founders' family, friends, and employees; (3) Public subsidies and grants; (4) Financing from parent companies; (5) Equity provided by linked companies; (6) Financing from private financial institutions (such as commercial banks, credit unions, and credit institutes, associations); (7) Financing from other financiers; (8) Equity from Venture Capitalists and Private Equity funds; (9) Equity from business angels	Start-up financing

In addition to these firm-level controls, several governance-related variables potentially affecting the financial performance of healthcare gazelles were included in the regression analyses. First, the CEO's age was considered a control variable, as the CEO's experience and tenure can significantly influence the strategic direction and firm performance (Tarus & Aime, 2014). Older CEOs might bring more experience and stability, while younger CEOs might introduce more innovative and risky approaches (Sitthipongpanich & Polsiri, 2015). Second, gender diversity in the Board of Directors (BoD) was considered, measured as the proportion of women in the BoD. Gender diversity has been increasingly recognized as a factor that can influence decision-making processes, business behaviors, and, ultimately, financial outcomes (Mauro et al., 2023; Reguera-Alvarado et al., 2017; Campbell and Mínguez-Vera, 2008).

The size of the BoD (measured by the number of directors) was also controlled for, as the number of directors can affect the firm's governance efficiency and performance (Topal & Dogan, 2014). Larger boards may benefit from a wider range of expertise, but they might suffer from slower decision-making processes, whereas smaller boards might be more agile but lacking of different skills and perspectives.

Finally, CEO duality was included as a governance-related control variable. CEO duality refers to the situation where the CEO also holds the position of the chairman of the BoD. CEO duality can lead to stronger, more centralized leadership, but it can also reduce the checks and balances within the governance structures, thus potentially affecting firm performance (La Rocca et al., 2024; Elsayed, 2007).

Additionally, the Industry Fixed Effects based on the four-digit NACE Rev.2 classification are included to control for industry-specific factors. Finally, a set of temporal dummies was introduced to capture time-related effects or trends that may affect financial performance across different periods. Economic cycles, policy changes, or industry trends over time can all influence the financial health of these firms.

10.4 Results

This section provides the results of the empirical analysis, including the descriptive statistics and the correlation analyses regarding the relationship between the financial performance and the CSFs of the healthcare gazelles.

10.4.1 Descriptive Statistics and Results from Questionnaire-Based Survey

Table 10.3 presents descriptive statistics for the variables used in the empirical analysis and summarizes the main findings from the questionnaire-based survey.

Performance ratios provide direct proxies for business success. Modest profitability is evident as the average ROA reaches 3.67. With a mean ROE of 24.56%, shareholders are enjoying strong returns. The overall profitability in relation to sales is displayed by an average ROS of 3.13. The EBITDA to sales ratio of 0.06 suggests that earnings before interest, taxes, depreciation, and amortization represent 6% of sales, highlighting strong operational efficiency.

Employee education levels play a critical role in a firm success. On average, about 62% of employees in healthcare gazelles hold a bachelor's or master's degree. Nonetheless, the survey data highlights a significantly low percentage of employees holding a PhD.

Regarding innovation, approximately 81% of companies focus on continuous improvement of their products, services, and processes. Similarly, 88% of companies engage in activities to increase market competitiveness. The average scores for "New Opportunities and Ideas" and "Internationalization Strategy" are 0.88 and 0.76, respectively, showing a strong orientation toward exploring and implementing new opportunities and promoting internationalization strategies among surveyed companies.

As for structural capital, about 83% of companies declare a high level of knowledge codified within digital documents and databases. The variable "Timely Updates", with a mean score of 0.47, suggests that nearly half of the companies ensure prompt updates of their documents and databases.

Regarding the relational capital, the variable "Customer Contact Point" has an average value of 0.41, showing that 41% of companies have a specific contact point to meet customer needs. Conversely, "Customer Trust Relationship" and "Stakeholder Communication" achieve above average scores of 0.98 and 0.97,

Table 10.3 Descriptive statistics and results from questionnaire-based survey

Variable	Obs.	Mean	Std.	Min	Max
Dependent variables					
ROA[a]	502	3.67	14.48	−34.47	29.21
ROE[a]	430	24.56	28.47	−13.27	76.56
ROS[a]	446	3.13	7.30	−15.41	15.60
EBITDA/Sales[a]	471	0.06	0.19	−0.29	3.08
Critical Success Factors (CSFs)					
Employee Education					
Proportion of graduate employees	316	0.62	0.23	0.04	0.98
Proportion of Ph.D.	469	0.00	0.02	0.00	0.22
Innovation					
Efficiency Innovation	580	0.81	0.39	0.00	1.00
Evolution Innovation	580	0.88	0.33	0.00	1.00
New Opportunities and Ideas	580	0.88	0.33	0.00	1.00
Internationalization Strategies	580	0.76	0.43	0.00	1.00
Integrated Innovation Plan	580	0.40	0.49	0.00	1.00
Human Resource Development	580	0.45	0.50	0.00	1.00
Structural capital					
Codified Knowledge	580	0.83	0.38	0.00	1.00
Timely Updates	580	0.47	0.50	0.00	1.00
Relational capital					
Customer Contact Point	580	0.41	0.49	0.00	1.00
Customer Trust Relationship	580	0.98	0.13	0.00	1.00
Stakeholder Communication	580	0.97	0.18	0.00	1.00
Planning and control systems					
Business Plan Utilization	580	0.16	0.36	0.00	1.00
Cost and Payment Control Systems	580	0.93	0.25	0.00	1.00
Start-up financing					
1) Self-Financing	580	0.09	0.28	0.00	1.00
2) Public subsidies and grants	580	0.91	0.28	0.00	1.00
Firm-level control variables					
Firm size (Turnover sales_nlog)	471	6.49	1.46	−3.41	10.79
Debt-to-equity ratio[a]	361	1.21	2.31	−0.12	8.65
Board size	580	3.03	1.44	1	8
CEO Duality	580	.517	.501	0	1
CEO age	580	47	11	23	66
Gender diversity	580	.477	.349	0	1

[a]Variables winsorized at the 5th and 95th percentiles to mitigate the impact of outliers

respectively. This shows strong customer trust and effective communication with key stakeholders for most of the companies.

Planning and control systems exhibit variability: "Business Plan" averages 0.16, showing that only 16% of firms consistently used a business plan in the start-up phase. Conversely, "Cost and Payment Control Systems" score an average of 0.93, suggesting widespread implementation of systems for controlling costs and payments. In terms of start-up funding, most companies used public subsidies and grants, while the remaining 9% relied on founder personal funds.

10.4.2 Correlation Analysis and Regression Estimates

The correlation analysis of CSFs for healthcare gazelles provides an overview of the key factors driving business success. Among the examined metrics of financial performance—ROA, ROE, ROS, and EBITDA/Sales—several CSFs stand out significantly. According to Cohen's (1988) classification, correlation coefficients were categorized as very weak ($|r| < 0.1$), weak ($0.1 \leq |r| < 0.3$), moderate ($0.3 \leq |r| < 0.5$), and strong ($|r| \geq 0.5$). This approach facilitates the examination of the strength of correlation coefficients, going beyond mere evaluation of the significance levels (Garousi et al., 2019). The correlation analysis shown in Table 10.4 indicates that the presence of employees with bachelor's or master's degrees shows moderate positive correlations with ROA ($r = 0.1670$, $p < 0.05$), ROE ($r = 0.1217$, $p < 0.05$), and ROS ($r = 0.2661$, $p < 0.05$). Similarly, healthcare gazelles with a higher proportion of employees with the PhD qualification exhibit moderate positive correlations with ROA ($r = 0.0592$, $p < 0.05$) and ROS ($r = 0.1453$, $p < 0.05$).

In terms of innovation, CSFs such as Efficiency Innovation and an Integrated Innovation Plan show strong positive correlations across all financial metrics. Conversely, factors related to the Structural Capital, such as Timely Updates, exhibit moderate correlations with ($r = 0.1013$, $p < 0.05$) and ROS ($r = 0.1677$, $p < 0.05$).

The relationships observed in Relational Capital highlight the significance of customer trust and effective stakeholder communication, particularly in terms of ROE and ROS. Meanwhile, robust Systems of Planning and Control, particularly effective Cost and Payment Control Systems, demonstrate moderate positive correlations with ROA ($r = 0.1420$, $p < 0.05$), ROE ($r = 0.1181$, $p < 0.05$) and ROS ($r = 0.0861$, $p < 0.05$).

Table 10.5 presents the results of regression estimates regarding the relationship between CSFs and the financial performance of healthcare gazelles. Financial performance was measured through multiple indicators: ROA, ROE, ROS, and EBITDA-to-Sales ratio.

The findings strongly support the critical role of qualified human capital plays a vital role in driving the financial performance of healthcare gazelles. Specifically, the percentage of employees holding a degree shows a significant positive effect on most performance measures: ROA ($\beta = 10.20$, $p < .05$), ROE ($\beta = 14.41$, $p < .05$), ROS ($\beta = 12.23$, $p < .01$). However, its effect on the EBITDA-to-sales ratio was not statistically significant ($\beta = .08$, $p > 0.10$). In addition, the percentage of PhD employees also demonstrates a positive effect across most financial metrics, except for ROE, which do not show a significant relationship.

Table 10.4 Correlation analysis between CSFs and financial performance metrics in healthcare gazelles

Categories	CSFs	r ROA	r ROE	r ROS	r Ebitda/ Sales
(1) Staff Education	% of employees with Bachelor's/ Master's Degree	.1670[a]	.1217[a]	.2661[a]	.0827
		W	W	W	N/W
	% Employees with Ph.D.	.0592	−.0309	.1453[a]	.043
		N/W	N/W	W	N/W
(2) Innovation	Efficiency Innovation	.237[a]	.187[a]	.217[a]	.105[a]
		W	W	W	W
	Evolution Innovation	−.013	−.010	.091	.048
		N/W	N/W	N/W	N/W
	New Opportunities and Ideas	−.016	.007	.073	.022
		N/W	N/W	N/W	N/W
	Internationalization Strategies	−.002	−.031	.086	.083
		N/W	N/W	N/W	N/W
	Integrated Innovation Plan	.175[a]	.091	.233[a]	.112[a]
		W	N/W	N/W	W
	Human Resource Development	.137[a]	.103[a]	.223[a]	.090
		W	N/W	N/W	N/W
(3) Structural Capital	Codified Knowledge	.098[a]	.042	.043	−.049
		N/W	N/W	N/W	N/W
	Timely Updates	.101[a]	.056	.168[a]	.067
		W	N/W	W	N/W
(4) Relational Capital	Customer Contact Point	.009	.053	−.025	.030
		N/W	N/W	N/W	N/W
	Customer Trust Relationship	.084	.170[a]	.072	.065
		N/W	W	N/W	N/W
	Stakeholder Communication Efficiency	.149[a]	−.037	.125[a]	.082
		W	N/W	W	N/W
(5) Planning and control systems	Business Plan	.082	.083	.146[a]	.029
		N/W	N/W	W	N/W
	Cost and Payment Control Systems	.151[a]	.142[a]	.118[a]	.086
		W	W	W	N/W
(6) Start-up financing	Founder self-financing	−.064	.059	−.088	−.059
		N/W	N/W	N/W	N/W
Cohen's classification	N/W	9	12	9	14
	W	7	4	7	2
	Moderate correlation [M]	0	0	0	0
	Strong correlation [S]	0	0	0	0

Notes: CSFs = Critical success factors; r = correlation coefficient. N/W = none or very weak correlation ($|r|<.01$); W = weak correlation ($.1\leq|r|<.3$); M = moderate correlation ($.3\leq|r|<.5$); S = strong correlation ($|r|\geq.5$)

[a]Correlation is significant at the .05 level (two-tailed)

Table 10.5 The relationship between CSFs and financial performance in healthcare gazelles

	(1) ROA	(2) ROE	(3) ROS	(4) EBITDA/ sales
Staff education (bachelor's or master's degree)	10.20**	14.41**	12.23***	.08
	(4.67)	(11.80)	(4.07)	(.10)
Employees with PhD	96.67***	143.44	94.46***	1.24**
	(27.45)	(94.11)	(23.77)	(.52)
Innovation				
Efficiency Innovation	10.90**	16.38	4.31	.06
	(5.13)	(11.97)	(3.67)	(.15)
Evolution Innovation	−11.05*	−8.89	−9.01*	−.18**
	(5.65)	(13.52)	(5.44)	(.08)
New Opportunities and Ideas	1.53	17.66**	2.55	.002
	(3.57)	(8.31)	(3.12)	(.06)
Internationalization Strategies	12.03***	1.69	9.95**	.25**
	(4.18)	(9.05)	(4.05)	(.01)
Integrated Innovation Plan	−12.51***	−13.27	−10.05**	−0.17**
	(4.57)	(10.05)	(4.30)	(.06)
Human Resource Development	11.53*	.87	8.01	.06
	(6.32)	(16.87)	(5.10)	(.07)
Structural Capital				
Codified Knowledge	−4.79	.72	−3.853	−.082
	(3.70)	(9.71)	(3.44)	(.054)
Timely Updates	−1.29	6.51	−.126	−.050
	(3.15)	(12.51)	(1.827)	(.048)
Relational Capital				
Customer Contact Point	18.20***	4.55	12.27***	.004
	(5.42)	(14.78)	(4.562)	(0.20)
Customer Trust Relationship	11.39*	27.16*	10.07*	0.01
	(6.37)	(14.89)	(5.88)	(0.13)
Stakeholder Communication Efficiency	15.44	−65.21	−13.07	−.044
	(11.06)	(25.83)	(10.29)	(.20)
Planning and control systems				
Business Plan	0.60	4.04	0.73	−.023
	(3.72)	(8.36)	(2.59)	(.042)
Cost and Payment Control Systems	−2.91	12.61	−.085	.233
	(5.05)	(13.96)	(2.97)	(.234)
Firm financing				
Founder self-financing (reference category: Public subsidies and grants)	0.37	−3.26	0.78	−.057
	(4.45)	(15.09)	(3.66)	(.06)
Control variables				

(continued)

Table 10.5 (continued)

	(1) ROA	(2) ROE	(3) ROS	(4) EBITDA/ sales
Firm size (ln_sales)	4.18**	6.23*	3.70***	.053
	(1.65)	(3.25)	(1.27)	(.035)
Debt-to-Equity Ratio	−.34	−.68	−.60	.001
	(.410)	(.996)	(.428)	(.007)
Size of the BoD	1.03	−8.41***	1.05	.008
	(1.14)	(3.09)	(1.02)	(.016)
CEO Duality	3.76	1.63	2.67	.039
	(3.24)	(7.56)	(2.59)	(.038)
CEO Age	.274*	−.426	.203	.004
	(.164)	(.356)	(.175)	(.003)
Gender diversity in the BoD	16.91**	−14.04	13.49*	−.055
	(8.26)	(22.06)	(7.81)	(0.213)
Intercept	−89.90***	13.81	−75.47***	−0.96*
	(23.65)	(49.42)	(20.04)	(0.53)
Industry FE (4-digit NACE Rev.2)	Yes	Yes	Yes	Yes
Time dummies	Yes	Yes	Yes	Yes
# Obs.	240	207	229	240
F-stat	10.69***	7.44***	7.88***	7.55***
R2	0.42	0.45	0.57	0.31
R2_adj.	0.29	0.31	0.47	0.17

Efficiency innovation exhibits a positive impact on ROA ($\beta = 10.90$, $p < .01$), emphasizing its importance in improving asset utilization and overall financial performance. Evolutionary innovation, in contrast, has a negative relationship with most financial indicators, including ROA ($\beta = -11.05$, $p < .05$) and ROS ($\beta = -9.01$, $p < .05$), suggesting that incremental innovation strategies may negatively affect profitability in healthcare gazelles. This could indicate that radical or transformative innovations are better suited for high-growth environments in this sector. Furthermore, evolutionary innovation negatively impacts EBITDA-to-sales ($\beta = -0.18$, $p < .05$), which underscores its negative impact on the operational efficiency.

Internationalization strategies also exert a significant positive impact on the financial performance of healthcare gazelles. Firms that engage in internationalization strategies see significant improvements in ROA ($\beta = 12.03$, $p < .01$) and ROS ($\beta = 9.95$, $p < .01$), implying that expanding into global markets enhances overall profitability and operational returns. The positive effect on the EBITDA-to-sales ratio ($\beta = 0.25$, $p < .05$) also suggests that internationalization contributes to better cost management and operational efficiency.

Contrary to expectations, integrated innovation plans show a significant negative effect on ROA ($\beta = -12.50$, $p < .01$), ROS ($\beta = -10.05$, $p < .01$), and EBITDA-to-sales ($\beta = -0.17$, $p < .05$). This could indicate that highly structured innovation processes might stifle flexibility and agility in high-growth healthcare firms, which rely on dynamic responses to emerging market opportunities.

Investment in human resource development shows a significant positive effect on ROA ($\beta = 11.52$, $p < .10$), highlighting the role of workforce training and development in enhancing asset returns. However, its effect on other performance metrics, such as ROE and ROS, was not significant.

Structural capital factors like codified knowledge and timely updates do not demonstrate significant effects on financial performance.

Relational capital, particularly customer contact points, shows a strong positive relationship with ROA ($\beta = 18.20$, $p < .01$) and ROS ($\beta = 12.27$, $p < .01$), indicating that maintaining strong customer relationships is essential for achieving business success. Furthermore, trust-based customer relationships positively impact ROA ($\beta = 11.39$, $p < .10$) and ROS ($\beta = 10.07$, $p < .10$), confirming the importance of trust and effective communication in driving firm performance.

Stakeholder communication efficiency and planning and control systems do not show any significant effect across all financial performance metrics.

The results indicate that founder self-financing does not significantly influence financial performance across the examined metrics. This suggests that relying solely on internal funding may not be a key driver of success for healthcare gazelles. Instead, these firms might benefit more from external funding sources, such as venture capital or grants, to improve their performance.

Control variables indicate that larger firms (as measured by the natural logarithm of sales) have significantly better financial performance across all measures, with significant positive effects on ROA ($\beta = 4.18$, $p < .05$), ROE ($\beta = 6.23$, $p < .10$), and ROS ($\beta = 3.70$, $p < .01$). The debt-to-equity ratio does not show significant effects on the financial performance of healthcare gazelles.

Regarding governance-related variables, gender diversity within the board of directors significantly improves ROA ($\beta = 16.91$, $p < .05$) and ROS ($\beta = 13.48$, $p < .10$), suggesting that a higher female representation on board contribute to better financial performance. However, this diversity negatively affects ROE ($\beta = -14.04$, $p > .10$), which may indicate trade-offs between profitability and shareholder returns in highly gender-diverse boards. Additionally, CEO age shows a modest positive and significant effect on ROA ($\beta = 0.27$, $p < .10$), implying that more experienced management can enhance the financial performance of healthcare gazelles (Sitthipongpanich & Polsiri, 2015).

Overall, the F-statistics and R-squared values suggest the models explain a reasonable portion of the variance in financial performance. Including industry and time dummies ensures these results account for sector-specific and temporal factors.

10.4.3 Critical Success Factors in Healthcare Gazelles: Additional Comments

Interesting results also emerged in the last section of the questionnaire, named "additional comments" (open section).

The section allowed to provide evidence that—while some of the general CSFs for gazelles apply to HGFs operating in the healthcare sector—there are additional specific variables that influence their success: the highly regulated nature of healthcare, the complexity of medical research, and the critical importance of patient outcomes all necessitate a unique set of success factors for healthcare gazelles.

According to the additional comments provided by respondents, it is possible to classify these factors as follows:

- *Regulatory Compliance and Navigational Expertise*: Healthcare gazelles must navigate a complex regulatory landscape to bring their products and services to the market. Success in this area requires a thorough understanding of regulatory requirements, as well as the ability to manage the approval process for new drugs, devices, and treatments efficiently. Regulatory compliance ensures that healthcare products and services meet safety and efficacy standards, which is crucial for patient trust and market acceptance.
- *Clinical Validation and Evidence-Based Practice*: Healthcare gazelles must demonstrate the clinical efficacy and safety of their innovations through rigorous testing and validation. Evidence-based practice is essential for gaining regulatory approval, securing funding, and achieving market adoption. Clinical trials and studies serve as indispensable sources of data, providing evidence to validate the effectiveness of emerging medical technologies and treatments.
- *Patient-Centered Approach*: A patient-centered approach is critical for healthcare gazelles, as it ensures that innovations address patient needs and improve health outcomes. Engaging patients in the development process and prioritizing their experiences and feedback can lead to more effective and user-friendly healthcare solutions. This approach also enhances patient satisfaction and loyalty.
- *Ethical Considerations and Social Responsibility*: Given the sensitive nature of healthcare, ethical considerations and social responsibility are paramount for healthcare gazelles. Ensuring ethical conduct in clinical trials, patient data handling, and marketing practices builds trust with stakeholders and enhances the firm's reputation. Social responsibility initiatives, such as improving access to care and addressing health disparities, further contribute to the firm's positive impact on society.
- *Leveraging Digital Health Technologies*: The integration of digital health technologies, such as telemedicine, electronic health records, and mobile health applications, can significantly enhance the reach and effectiveness of healthcare gazelles. These technologies enable more efficient healthcare delivery, improved patient engagement, and better health outcomes. Leveraging digital health innovations is essential for staying competitive in the modern healthcare landscape.

10.5 Discussion and Conclusion

This study is an empirical study designed to gather information that can help in the development of future theories (Helfat, 2007).

We contribute to the literature on the CSFs in gazelle enterprises, offering evidence from the Italian private healthcare sector. Research on CSFs in gazelle enterprises has been inconclusive because of contradictory findings in prior literature, requiring additional research and evidence. We provide additional findings offering new empirical evidence from the healthcare sector: to the best of our knowledge, no empirical studies exist testing the relationship between CSFs and financial performance in private healthcare gazelles.

The regression analyses confirm that the CSFs for healthcare gazelles encompass most variables identified in the previous studies. Consistent with prior literature (e.g., Eklund & Van Criekingen, 2022), our findings indicate staff training as a primary CSF factor of gazelles.

Regarding innovation, strategies aimed at efficiency (focusing on continuous improvement of products/services and production processes) and internationalization (developing policies to ensure presence in global markets) play a key role in enhancing the financial performance of gazelle enterprises.

Factors of structural capital, such as codified knowledge and timely updates, show no significant impact on financial performance. This finding partially supports literature suggesting that highly complex and rigid knowledge coding systems can impede growth by requiring considerable time and resources for new employees to adapt (Chae, 2024).

Regarding the Relational Capital, the importance of customer trust and effective stakeholder communication is confirmed, particularly in relation to ROA, ROE, and ROS.

Effective planning and control systems, notably efficient Cost and Payment Control Systems, do not exhibit statistically significant associations across all financial performance metrics.

Similarly, the impact of financing methods, in particular founder self-financing, on financial performance changes in relation to the performance indicator used but, in any case, is not statistically significant across all models.

Some interesting findings concern the impact of governance-related variables on the financial performance of healthcare gazelles. Our results indicate that female representation in the Board of Directors has a positive impact on the financial performance of healthcare providers, particularly in terms of ROA and ROS. Likewise, the age of the CEO positively affects the operational profitability (ROA) of healthcare gazelles, confirming the importance of managerial skills and experience in shaping the success of small businesses.

Finally, our results indicate a negative relationship between board size and financial performance, measured in terms of ROE. As stated previously, a smaller board can increase the efficiency of small business decision making, thus leading to higher business performance.

The combination of these factors enables a new venture to establish a strong vision, clear objectives, and strategies that foster patient trust and rapid growth.

In the additional comments section of the questionnaire, specific CSFs for healthcare gazelles emerge, including (a) regulatory compliance, (b) clinical validation and evidence-based practice, (c) patient-centered approach, (d) ethical considerations and social responsibility, and (e) leveraging digital health technologies. The highly regulated nature of healthcare, the complexity of medical research, and the critical importance of patient outcomes cause a distinct set of success factors for gazelles operating in this sector.

Results also provide several practical implications for stakeholders in the private healthcare sector. Identifying the CSFs for high-growth firms allows young firms to understand which variables enable the transition from start-up to gazelle firms. In effect, recent study shows that gazelles may address most or all the CSFs in their start-up phase (Feindt et al., 2002), and that potential CSFs relevant have to be considered at the very beginning of the venture.

According to our results, managers involved with gazelle enterprises, particularly in the first years of activity, should (a) emphasize continuous training and development programs for staff, (b) prioritize strategies that focus on continuous improvement of products/services and production processes, (c) develop policies that facilitate entry into global markets, as these strategies positively affect financial performance, (d) ensure that knowledge management systems are agile and adaptable to avoid hindering growth, (e) implement efficient cost and payment control systems to enhance firm's financial performance, (f) strengthen customer trust and ensure an effective stakeholder communication, as these factors notably influence financial metrics; considering the healthcare sector, this includes integrating patient-centric approaches and leveraging digital health technologies effectively.

The impact of financing methods on financial performance requires further investigation. Founder self-financing in the healthcare sector appears to have a negative impact on financial ratios like ROS and EBITDA-to-Sales ratio, when compared to obtaining public subsidies or grants. Understanding these implications can guide strategic decisions regarding financing sources.

Policymakers should recognize the unique challenges and opportunities within the healthcare sector, such as regulatory compliance, clinical validation, patient-centered care, ethical considerations, and leveraging digital health technologies. These specific factors are crucial for success in healthcare gazelles because of the sector's highly regulated and complex nature.

In summary, stakeholders in the private healthcare sector, especially those involved with gazelle enterprises, should leverage these practical implications to refine their strategies, enhance operational efficiencies, and ultimately drive superior financial performance and growth.

This research has some limitations.

First, the study's sample size might limit the generalizability of findings beyond the specific context studied, potentially limiting the broader applicability of the results. Moreover, due to the specific characteristics of healthcare gazelles and the specific context under study, the findings may not easily apply to other industries or countries. Future studies could benefit from comparing healthcare gazelles across different countries or industries. This approach would help to assess the impact of varying regulatory environments, market structures, and cultural factors on CSFs and financial performance.

Second, it is important to highlight that the results of this study are not directly tied to a pre-existing theoretical framework, given that research on healthcare gazelles is still in its nascent stages. As a result, there is a limited body of literature addressing the applicability of specific theories to this context. However, this exploratory approach is justified, as it aims to identify and understand key factors that influence the success of gazelles in this sector, providing a foundation for future theoretical development.

From a methodological perspective, the use of advanced econometric techniques, such as Structural Equation Models (SEM) could enhance the empirical findings presented in this chapter. SEM allows for the simultaneous examination of multiple relationships between variables, offering a more comprehensive understanding of how CSFs interact and influence financial outcomes. However, the decision not to apply SEM in this study was primarily influenced by concerns regarding the small sample size. SEM typically requires a large number of observations to produce reliable and robust results. A common guideline suggests a minimum sample size of 200 units (Kline, 2023). A smaller sample size ($n < 200$) increases the risk of biased estimates and decreases the power of the analysis, potentially leading to unstable and biased model results (Kelcey, 2019). In this study, the sample size ($n = 69$) did not reach these thresholds necessary for effective application of SEMs. Despite these limitations, by employing more traditional regression methods, we were still able to provide reliable information on the association between CSFs and the financial performance of healthcare gazelles.

10.5.1 Future Research Directions

The conclusions of this chapter open up several avenues for future research on gazelle firms in the healthcare sector. First, further investigation into the role of innovation strategies for the success of gazelle firms would be valuable. While this study highlighted the importance of innovation for financial growth, future studies could delve deeper into how different types of innovation (such as technological, process, or customer-oriented) influence long-term performance in various contexts.

Second, the implications of employee skills warrant further exploration. It would be relevant to investigate how continuous training, and the development of healthcare-specific competencies contribute to the sustainability and growth of gazelle firms, particularly in a sector where highly specialized knowledge is crucial.

Another direction for research could be to examine the specific challenges related to regulatory compliance and how gazelle firms navigate these complexities. Given that regulatory requirements are a critical factor in the healthcare sector, future studies could focus on analyzing effective strategies for obtaining necessary approvals and meeting required standards.

Additionally, considering the significance of a patient-centered approach and the integration of digital health technologies, further research could explore how these practices can be leveraged to achieve a competitive advantage. Investigating how the adoption of digital tools, such as telemedicine or mobile health applications, influences the growth and scalability of gazelle firms could provide valuable insights for both managers and policymakers.

In summary, research on healthcare gazelles is still in its early stages, and there are numerous opportunities to deepen our understanding of how these firms can continue to grow and thrive in such a challenging and vital sector.

Authors' contributions *M.M.* conceived the study and wrote Sect. 10.1. *E.R.F.* contributed to the administration of the questionnaires and wrote Sect. 10.5.1. *G.C.* wrote Sects. 10.3 and 10.4 (Sects. 10.4.1 and 10.4.2). *M.G.* wrote Sects. 10.2, 10.4.3, and 10.5. All authors contributed to the revision of the paper in accordance with the reviewers' suggestions.

Appendix

The Questionnaire

Presentation Letter

Welcome to the online survey for the research study "Critical Success Factors of Healthcare Gazelles". This survey is conducted to delve into the factors contributing to the success of companies during their early years. The information collected will remain anonymous and help new businesses consider factors that ensure long-term success.

If you have been invited to complete this questionnaire, it is because your company was selected from the AIDA-Bureau van Dijk database and is considered a high-growth company (i.e., gazelle firm), characterized by rapid revenue growth in its early years.

We invite you to answer the questions in the questionnaire thoroughly. It will take approximately 5 min to complete.

Thank you for your cooperation.

The Study Coordinator

Part One
Respondent Information

1. Position of the respondent:

   ○ CEO
   ○ Founder
   ○ President
   ○ Board Member
   ○ Other (please specify) ___________

2. Gender:

   ○ Male
   ○ Female

3. Age:

   ○ 18–24
   ○ 25–34
   ○ 35–44
   ○ 45–54
   ○ 55–64
   ○ Over 64

4. Education:

   ○ Middle school
   ○ High school (Classical, Scientific, etc.)
   ○ Bachelor's degree
   ○ Master's degree
   ○ Old system diploma
   ○ Postgraduate Master's
   ○ PhD
   ○ Other (please specify) _________

5. Experience:

How many years of experience have you accumulated in the industry? (express the number) _______________

Part Two
Basic Characteristics of the Company
Ownership Information

1. Number of owners:

   ○ 1
   ○ 2
   ○ 3 to 5
   ○ 6 or more

2. Educational background of owners:

How many owners have a Bachelor's, Master's, or equivalent degree? (express the number) _______________

Employee Information

1. Educational background of employees:

How many employees have a Bachelor's or Master's degree? (express the number) _______________

2. How many employees have a PhD? (express the number) ___________

Markets

Select the markets in which your company operates (you can select more than one option):

○ Italy
○ Europe
○ North America
○ Central and South America
○ Australia-Oceania
○ Asia
○ Africa

Part Three: Identifying Critical Success Factors
Innovation

1. The company is oriented toward continuous improvement of the products/services offered as well as the production/delivery processes (efficiency innovation—product and process innovation):

   ○ Yes
   ○ No

2. The company is constantly committed to increasing its competitiveness in the market (evolution innovation):

   ○ Yes
   ○ No

3. The company can make structural and drastic changes to its entire business if necessary (radical innovation):

   ○ Yes
   ○ No

4. Do you explore, identify, and select new opportunities and ideas?

   ○ Yes
   ○ No

5. Do you promote and support the culture of internationalization and develop policies and strategies to ensure the organization's presence in international markets?

   ○ Yes
   ○ No

6. Do you develop an innovation plan integrated with policies and strategies?

   ○ Yes
   ○ No

7. Do you adopt approaches and promote initiatives to train and develop human resources to support innovation?

   ○ Yes
   ○ No

Structural Capital

1. The company has a high level of codified knowledge within digital documents and databases:

   ○ Yes
   ○ No

2. Documents and/or databases are updated promptly:

   ○ Yes
   ○ No

Relational Capital

1. There is a dedicated customer contact point that addresses user needs and dedicates all the necessary time:

   ○ Yes
   ○ No

2. There is a well-established trust relationship between the customer and the company:

   ○ Yes
   ○ No

3. Communication between the company and its stakeholders (suppliers, banks, public institutions, etc.) is constant and effective:

   ○ Yes
   ○ No

Planning and Control Systems

1. The phases of the entrepreneurial idea development and subsequent start-up were supported by creating a business plan:

○ Yes
○ No

2. Cost control and payment systems are in place, as well as sufficient cash flows/ reserves to avoid payment delays:

   ○ Yes
   ○ No

Company Financing

Which of the following tools were used in the start-up phase of the company? (you can indicate more options):

○ Self-financing by founders (including savings and pension allowances) or financing through debt and equity from family and friends of the founders and employees
○ Public subsidies and grants
○ Financing from affiliated companies
○ Equity from affiliated companies
○ Financing from private financial institutions (e.g., commercial banks, credit cooperatives, and credit institutions)
○ Financing from other lenders
○ Equity from Venture Capitalists and Private Equity funds
○ Equity from individual business angels

Part Four: Additional Comments

Please add any other considerations you think are useful for the study (e.g., key factors not identified in the questionnaire or strategies useful for success):

____

____

References

Achilladelis, B., & Antonakis, N. (2001). The dynamics of technological innovation: The case of the pharmaceutical industry. *Research Policy, 30*(4), 535–588.

Acs, Z. J., & Mueller, P. (2015). Employment effects of business dynamics: Mice, gazelles and elephants. In *Global entrepreneurship, institutions and incentives* (pp. 304–319). Edward Elgar.

Barras, R. (1986). Towards a theory of innovation in services. *Research Policy, 15*(4), 161–173.

Barringer, B. R., Jones, F. F., & Neubaum, D. O. (2005). A quantitative content analysis of the characteristics of rapid-growth firms and their founders. *Journal of Business Venturing, 20*(5), 663–687.

Baum, J. A., Calabrese, T., & Silverman, B. S. (2000). Don't go it alone: Alliance network composition and startups' performance in Canadian biotechnology. *Strategic Management Journal, 21*(3), 267–294.

Bendell, B. L., Sullivan, D. M., & Marvel, M. R. (2019). A gender-aware study of self-leadership strategies among high-growth entrepreneurs. *Journal of Small Business Management, 57*(1), 110–130.

Birch, D. L. (1981). Who creates jobs? *The Public Interest, 65*, 3–14.

Bleda, M.., Morrison, K., & Rigby, J. (2013). The role and importance of gazelles and other growth firms for innovation and competitiveness: Mercedes Bleda, Kathryn Morrison and John Rigby. In *Innovation Policy Challenges for the 21st Century* (pp. 118–142). Routledge.

Bornhäll, A., Daunfeldt, S. O., & Rudholm, N. (2015). Employment protection legislation and firm growth: Evidence from a natural experiment. *Industrial and Corporate Change* dtw017.

Bos, J. W., & Stam, E. (2014). Gazelles and industry growth: A study of young high-growth firms in The Netherlands. *Industrial and Corporate Change, 23*(1), 145–169.

Brännback, M., Carsrud, A., Renko, M., Östermark, R., Aaltonen, J., & Kiviluoto, N. (2009). Growth and profitability in small privately held biotech firms: Preliminary findings. *New Biotechnology, 25*(5), 369–376.

Brnjas, Z., Vulićević, V., & Čanaićević, D. (2015). Importance and role of fast-growing companies–Gazelles in modern economies. *Economic Analysis, 48*(3–4), 44–61.

Brown, R., Mason, C., & Mawson, S. (2014). *Increasing 'the Vital 6 Percent': Designing effective public policy to support high growth firms*. Working paper series.

Brynjolfsson, E. (1993). The productivity paradox of information technology. *Communications of the ACM, 36*(12), 66–77. http://ccs.mit.edu/papers/CCSWP130/ccswp130.html. Accessed 28 June 2024

Campbell, K., & Mínguez-Vera, A. (2008). Gender diversity in the boardroom and firm financial performance. *Journal of Business Ethics, 83*, 435–451.

Capelleras, J. L., & Greene, F. J. (2008). The determinants and growth implications of venture creation speed. *Entrepreneurship and Regional Development, 20*(4), 317–343.

Cassar, G. (2007). Money, money, money? A longitudinal investigation of entrepreneur career reasons, growth preferences and achieved growth. *Entrepreneurship and Regional Development, 19*(1), 89–107.

Chandler, G. N., & Baucus, D. A. (1996). Gauging performance in emerging businesses: Longitudinal evidence and growth pattern analysis. *Frontiers in Entrepreneur Research, 1996*, 491–504.

Chandler, G. N., & Hanks, S. H. (1994). Market attractiveness, resource-based capabilities, venture strategies, and venture performance. *Journal of Business Venturing, 9*(4), 331–349.

Chae, H. C. (2024). In search of gazelles: Machine learning prediction for Korean high-growth firms. *Small Business Economics, 62*(1), 243–284.

Chetty, S., & Campbell-Hunt, C. (2003). Explosive international growth and problems of success amongst small to medium-sized firms. *International Small Business Journal, 21*(1), 5–27.

Christensen, C. M. (1997). *The innovator's dilemma: When new technologies cause great firms to fail*. Harvard Business Review Press.

Chung, K. H. (1987). *Management: Critical success factors*. Allyn and Bacon.

Coad, A., Bauer, P., Domnick, C., Harasztosi, P., Pál, R., & Teruel, M. (2023). From rapid decline to high growth: Where in the distribution did COVID hit hardest? *Journal of Small Business and Enterprise Development, 30*(6), 1178–1209. https://doi.org/10.1108/JSBED-02-2023-0061

Coad, A., Daunfeldt, S. O., Hölzl, W., Johansson, D., & Nightingale, P. (2014a). High-growth firms: Introduction to the special section. *Industrial and Corporate Change, 23*(1), 91–112.

Coad, A., Daunfeldt, S. O., Johansson, D., & Wennberg, K. (2014b). Whom do high-growth firms hire? *Industrial and Corporate Change, 23*(1), 293–327.

Coad, A., & Guenther, C. (2014). Processes of firm growth and diversification: Theory and evidence. *Small Business Economics, 43*(4), 857–871.

Coad, A., Segarra, A., & Teruel, M. (2016). Innovation and firm growth: Does firm age play a role? *Research Policy, 45*(2), 387–400.

Coad, A., & Srhoj, S. (2020). Catching Gazelles with a Lasso: Big data techniques for the prediction of high-growth firms. *Small Business Economics, 55*(3), 541–565.

Colombelli, A., Krafft, J., & Quatraro, F. (2014). High-growth firms and technological knowledge: Do gazelles follow exploration or exploitation strategies? *Industrial and Corporate Change, 23*(1), 261–291.

Colombo, M. G., & Grilli, L. (2010). On growth drivers of high-tech start-ups: Exploring the role of founders' human capital and venture capital. *Journal of Business Venturing, 25*(6), 610–626.

Cooper, A. C., Gimeno-Gascon, F. J., & Woo, C. Y. (1994). Initial human and financial capital as predictors of new venture performance. *Journal of Business Venturing, 9*(5), 371–395.

Cristofaro, M., Abatecola, G., Giannetti, F., & Zannoni, A. (2024). The survival of the fastest: Unveiling the determinants of Unicorns and Gazelles' early success. *Scandinavian Journal of Management, 40*(2), 101335.

Danneels, E. (2002). The dynamics of product innovation and firm competences. *Strategic Management Journal, 23*(12), 1095–1121.

Davenport, T. H. (1993). *Process innovation: Reengineering work through information technology*. Harvard Business Press.

Davenport, T. H. (2007). Information technologies for knowledge management. In *Knowledge creation and management: New challenges for managers* (pp. 97–117).

Davidsson, P. (1989). Entrepreneurship—and after? A study of growth willingness in small firms. *Journal of Business Venturing, 4*(3), 211–226.

Davila, A., Foster, G., & Jia, N. (2010). Building sustainable high-growth startup companies: Management systems as an accelerator. *California Management Review, 52*(3), 79–105.

Daunfeldt, S. O., Elert, N., & Johansson, D. (2016). Are high-growth firms overrepresented in high-tech industries? *Industrial and Corporate Change, 25*(1), 1–25.

Daunfeldt, S. O., Johansson, D., & Halvarsson, D. (2015). Using the Eurostat-OECD definition of high-growth firms: A cautionary note. *Journal of Entrepreneurship and Public Policy, 4*(1), 50–56.

Delmar, F., Davidsson, P., & Gartner, W. B. (2003). Arriving at the high-growth firm. *Journal of Business Venturing, 18*(2), 189–216.

Delmar, F., McKelvie, A., & Wennberg, K. (2013). Untangling the relationships among growth, profitability and survival in new firms. *Technovation, 33*(8–9), 276–291.

Demir, R., Wennberg, K., & McKelvie, A. (2017). The strategic management of high-growth firms: A review and theoretical conceptualization. *Long Range Planning, 50*(4), 431–456.

Dobbs, M., & Hamilton, R. T. (2007). Small business growth: Recent evidence and new directions. *International Journal of Entrepreneurial Behavior and Research, 13*(5), 296–322.

Dyer, C. (2023). *The power of company culture: How any business can build a culture that improves productivity, performance and profits*. Kogan Page.

Eeckloo, K., Delesie, L., & Vleugels, A. (2007). Where is the pilot? The changing shapes of governance in the European hospital sector. *The Journal of the Royal Society for the Promotion of Health, 127*(2), 78–86.

Edberg, E., & Ryss, J. (2019). *Managing the social-and financial dimensions in Swedish gazelle companies-A qualitative study from the founder's perspective* [Master's thesis, Uppsala University].

Eisenhardt, K. M., & Schoonhoven, C. B. (1990). Organizational growth: Linking founding team, strategy, environment, and growth among US semiconductor ventures, 1978-1988. *Administrative Science Quarterly*, 504–529.

Elsayed, K. (2007). Does CEO duality really affect corporate performance? *Corporate Governance: An International Review, 15*(6), 1203–1214.

Eklund, C., & Van Criekingen, K. (2022). Fast as a gazelle–young firms gaining from educational diversity. *Industry and Innovation, 29*(8), 927–947.

Eurostat-OECD. (2008). *Eurostat-OECD Manual on business demography statistics*. Office for Official Publications of the European Communities.

Fattore, G. (2019). Cost containment and reforms in the Italian National Health Service. In *Health care and cost containment in the European Union* (pp. 513–546). Routledge.

Feindt, S., Jeffcoate, J., & Chappell, C. (2002). Identifying success factors for rapid growth in SME e-commerce. *Small Business Economics, 19*, 51–62.

Fotopoulos, G. (2023). Knowledge spillovers, entrepreneurial ecosystems and the geography of high growth firms. *Entrepreneurship Theory and Practice, 47*(5), 1877–1914.

Forgione, A. F., & Noto, G. (2023). Exploring the determinants of private healthcare providers' market power: A performance-based perspective. *Health Services Management Research*, 09514848231194850.

Gaikwad, P. (2022). Catching up with Gazelles: A systematic literature review of high growth antecedents. In *The promises and properties of rapidly growing companies: Gazelles* (pp. 7–38).

Garnsey, E., Stam, E., & Heffernan, P. (2006). New firm growth: Exploring processes and paths. *Industry and Innovation, 13*(1), 1–20.

Garousi, V., Pfahl, D., Fernandes, J. M., Felderer, M., Mäntylä, M. V, Shepherd, D., et al. (2019). Characterizing industry-academia collaborations in software engineering: Evidence from 101 projects. *Empirical Software Engineering, 24*(4), 2540–2602. https://doi.org/10.1007/s10664-019-09711-y

Gorli, M., Galuppo, L., Pezzana, P., Scaratti, G., & Shani, A. B. (2014). Innovating health care through multi-stakeholder partnership: The Welfare Italia Servizi Case. In *Building networks and partnerships* (pp. 133–164). Emerald Group.

Goswami, A. G., Medvedev, D., & Olafsen, E. (2019). *High-growth firms: Facts, fiction, and policy options for emerging economies*. World Bank Publications.

Greiner, L. E. (1997). Evolution and Revolution as Organizations Grow: A company's past has clues for management that are critical to future success. *Family Business Review, 10*(4), 397–409.

Gundry, L. K., & Welsch, H. P. (2001). The ambitious entrepreneur: High growth strategies of women-owned enterprises. *Journal of Business Venturing, 16*(5), 453–470.

Gupta, V. K., Wieland, A. M., & Turban, D. B. (2019). Gender characterizations in entrepreneurship: A multi-level investigation of sex-role stereotypes about high-growth, commercial, and social entrepreneurs. *Journal of Small Business Management, 57*(1), 131–153.

Hechavarria, D., Bullough, A., Brush, C., & Edelman, L. (2019). High-growth women's entrepreneurship: Fueling social and economic development. *Journal of Small Business Management, 57*(1), 5–13.

Heimonen, T., & Virtanen, M. (2012). Characteristics of successful gazelles–problems in approaches and methods of analysing the data. *International Journal of Business and Globalisation, 9*(1), 12–41.

Helfat, C. E. (2007). Stylized facts, empirical research and theory development in management. *Strategic Organization, 5*(2), 185–192.

Henrekson, M., & Johansson, D. (2010). Gazelles as job creators: A survey and interpretation of the evidence. *Small Business Economics, 35*, 227–244.

Hilkevics, S., & Hilkevica, G. (2017). New information technologies use for Latvian stock companies financial health evaluation. *Entrep Sustain Issues, 5*(2), 178–189.

Hofer, C. W., & Sandberg, W. R. (1987). Improving new venture performance: Some guidelines for success. *American Journal of Small Business, 12*(1), 11–26.

Hölzl, W. (2009). Is the R&D behaviour of fast-growing SMEs different? Evidence from CIS III data for 16 countries. *Small Business Economics, 33*, 59–75.

Hölzl, W. (2014). Persistence, survival and growth: A closer look at 20 years of fast growing firms in Austria. *Industrial and Corporate Change, 23*(1), 199–231.

Ingolfsdotter, H., & Viklund, S. (2017). *Success factors of Swedish sequential Gazelle companies: A study on differentiating firm attributes and the significance of using external professional business services*.

Ireland, R. D., Hitt, M. A., & Sirmon, D. G. (2003). A model of strategic entrepreneurship: The construct and its dimensions. *Journal of Management, 29*(6), 963–989. https://doi.org/10.1016/S0149-2063(03)00086-2

Kazanjian, R. K., & Drazin, R. (1990). A stage-contingent model of design and growth for technology based new ventures. *Journal of Business Venturing, 5*(3), 137–150.

Keen, C., & Etemad, H. (2012). Rapid growth and rapid internationalization: The case of smaller enterprises from Canada. *Management Decision, 50*(4), 569–590.

Kelcey, B. (2019). A robust alternative estimator for small to moderate sample SEM: Bias-corrected factor score path analysis. *Addictive Behaviors, 94*, 83–98.

Kelley, D., et al. (2017). *Global Entrepreneurship Monitor 2016/2017 Report on Women's Entrepreneurship*. Babson College.

Klette, T. J., & Kortum, S. (2004). Innovating firms and aggregate innovation. *Journal of Political Economy, 112*(5), 986–1018.

Kline, R. B. (2023). Principles and practice of structural equation modeling. *Guilford*. publications.

Kumar, R., Singh, R. K., & Shankar, R. (2015). Critical success factors for implementation of supply chain management in Indian small and medium enterprises and their impact on performance. *IIMB Management Review, 27*(2), 92–104.

La Rocca, M., Fasano, F., La Rocca, T., & Neha, N. (2024). Women in CEO duality and firm performance in Europe. *Journal of Management and Governance, 28*(1), 177–214.

Laforet, S. (2012). *Innovation in small family businesses*. Edward Elgar.

Laur, I., & Mignon, I. (2021). Match or mismatch between gazelle companies' challenges and the support provided by intermediary actors–an empirical example of the construction industry. *European Planning Studies, 29*(10), 1845–1869.

Lee, N. (2014). What holds back high-growth firms? Evidence from UK SMEs. *Small Business Economics, 43*(1), 183–195. https://doi.org/10.1007/s11187-013-9525-5

Luhn, A., Aslanyan, S., Leopoldseder, C., & Priess, P. (2017). An evaluation of knowledge management system's components and its financial and non-financial implications. *Entrepreneurship and Sustainability Issues, 5*(2), 315–329.

Manev, I. M., Gyoshev, B. S., & Manolova, T. S. (2005). The role of human and social capital and entrepreneurial orientation for small business performance in a transitional economy. *International Journal of Entrepreneurship and Innovation Management, 5*(3–4), 298–318.

Mason, C., Brown, R., Hart, M., & Anyadike-Danes, M. (2015). High growth firms, jobs and peripheral regions: The case of Scotland. *Cambridge Journal of Regions, Economy and Society, 8*(2), 343–358.

Mauro, M., Giancotti, M., Ferrari, E. R., & Cattafi, G. (2023). Board gender diversity and performance in gazelles: Evidence from a sample of Italian private hospitals. *Piccola Impresa/Small Business, 2*. https://doi.org/10.14596/pisb.3698

Mazzucato, M., & Parris, S. (2015). High-growth firms in changing competitive environments: The US pharmaceutical industry (1963 to 2002). *Small Business Economics, 44*(1), 145–170.

McDougall, P. P., Covin, J. G., Robinson, R. B., & Herron, L. (1994). The effects of industry growth and strategic breadth on new venture performance and strategy content. *Strategic Management Journal, 15*(7), 537–554.

Megaravalli, A. V., & Sampagnaro, G. (2018). Predicting the growth of high-growth SMEs: Evidence from family business firms. *Journal of Family Business Management, 9*(1), 98–109.

Monteiro, G. F. A. (2019). High-growth firms and scale-ups: A review and research agenda. *RAUSP Manag J, 54*, 96–111.

Morande, S., Del Vacchio, E., & Ranieri, A. (2020). Digital innovations in healthcare startups: Transforming service ecosystem. *Journal of Business and Management Studies, 2*(1), 26–39.

Muda, S., Rahman, M. R. C., Hamzah, N., & Saleh, N. M. (2020). Intellectual capital and SMEs' business performance from an organisational lifecycle perspective. *The South East Asian Journal of Management, 14*(1), 5.

Nightingale, P., & Coad, A. (2014). Muppets and gazelles: Political and methodological biases in entrepreneurship research. *Industrial and Corporate Change, 23*(1), 113–143.

OECD. (2010). *High-growth enterprises: What governments can do to make a difference. OECD Studies on SMEs and Entrepreneurship*. OECD Publishing. https://doi.org/10.1787/9789264048782-en

Onesti, G., Monaco, E., & Palumbo, R. (2022). Assessing the Italian innovative start-ups performance with a composite index. *Administrative Sciences, 12*(4), 189.
Parker, S. C., Storey, D. J., & Van Witteloostuijn, A. (2010). What happens to gazelles? The importance of dynamic management strategy. *Small Business Economics, 35*, 203–226.
Pereira, D., Leitão, J., & Baptista, R. (2020). Who's winning the "survivor" race? Gazelle or non-gazelle startups. In *Intrapreneurship and sustainable human capital: Digital transformation through dynamic competences* (pp. 169–208).
Perren, L. (2000). Factors in the growth of micro-enterprises (Part 2): Exploring the implications. *Journal of Small Business and Enterprise Development, 7*(1).
Pinto, R., & Baracsi, M. (2012). Creating an environment for innovative start-ups in healthcare. *Health Policy and Technology, 1*(4), 187–192.
Reguera-Alvarado, N., De Fuentes, P., & Laffarga, J. (2017). Does board gender diversity influence financial performance? Evidence from Spain. *Journal of Business Ethics, 141*, 337–350.
Ricciardi, W., & Tarricone, R. (2021). The evolution of the Italian national health service. *Lancet, 398*(10317), 2193–2206.
Rocha, R. G., & Ferreira, J. J. (2021). Gazelles (high-growth) companies: A bibliometric science map of the field. *Journal of the Knowledge Economy*, 1–24.
Rockart, J. F. (1979). Chief executives define their own data needs. *Harvard Business Review, 57*(2), 81–93.
Rossi-Hansberg, E., & Wright, M. L. J. (2007). Establishment size dynamics in the aggregate economy. *The American Economic Review, 97*(5), 1639–1666.
Schilling, M. A. (2017). *Strategic management of technological innovation*. McGraw-Hill.
Schlichter, J., Klyver, K., & Haug, A. (2021). The moderating effect of ERP system complexity on the growth–profitability relationship in young SMEs. *Journal of Small Business Management, 59*(4), 601–626.
Sebora, T. C., Lee, S. M., & Sukasame, N. (2009). Critical success factors for e-commerce entrepreneurship: An empirical study of Thailand. *Small Business Economics, 32*, 303–316.
Senderovitz, M., Klyver, K., & Steffens, P. (2016). Four years on: Are the gazelles still running? A longitudinal study of firm performance after a period of rapid growth. *International Small Business Journal, 34*(4), 391–411.
Siegel, R., Siegel, E., & Macmillan, I. C. (1993). Characteristics distinguishing high-growth ventures. *Journal of Business Venturing, 8*(2), 169–180.
Sitthipongpanich, T., & Polsiri, P. (2015). Do CEO and board characteristics matter? A study of Thai family firms. *Journal of Family Business Strategy, 6*(2), 119–129.
Slevin, D. P., & Covin, J. G. (1997). Strategy formation patterns, performance, and the significance of context. *Journal of Management, 23*(2), 189–205.
Solow, R. M. (1987). *We'd better watch out.* Times Book Rev.
Spitsin, V., Vukovic, D., Mikhalchuk, A., Spitsina, L., & Novoseltseva, D. (2023). High-tech gazelle firms at various stages of evolution: Performance and distinctive features. *Journal of Economics Studies, 50*(4), 674–695.
Srinivasan, V., & Chandwani, R. (2014). HRM innovations in rapid growth contexts: The healthcare sector in India. *International Journal of Human Resource Management, 25*(10), 1505–1525.
Stangler, D. (2010). *High-growth firms and the future of the American economy*. Available at SSRN 1568246. Accessed June 28, 2024.
Stanworth, M. J. K., & Curran, J. (1976). Growth and the small firm--an alternative view. *Journal of Management Studies, 13*(2).
St-Jean, E., Julien, P. A., & Audet, J. (2008). Factors associated with growth changes in "gazelles". *Journal of Enterprising Culture, 16*(2), 161–188.
Steffens, P., Davidsson, P., & Fitzsimmons, J. (2009). Performance configurations over time: Implications for growth–and profit–oriented strategies. *Entrepreneurship Theory and Practice, 33*(1), 125–148.
Tarus, D. K., & Aime, F. (2014). Board demographic diversity, firm performance and strategic change: A test of moderation. *Management Research Review, 37*(12), 1110–1136.

Tidd, J., & Bessant, J. R. (2020). *Managing innovation: Integrating technological, market and organizational change*. Wiley.

Topal, Y., & Dogan, M. (2014). Impact of board size on financial performance: The case of BIST manufacturing industry. *International Journal of Business Management and Economic Research, 5*(4), 74–79.

Vecchi, V., Tanese, A., & Osborne, S. (2022). Do public-private partnerships still have a future? *Public Works Management and Policy, 27*(4), 337–341.

Verhees, F. J., & Meulenberg, M. T. (2004). Market orientation, innovativeness, product innovation, and performance in small firms. *Journal of Small Business Management, 42*(2), 134–154.

Wilson, D. (1993). Assessing the impact of information technology on organizational performance. In R. Banker, R. Kauffman, & M. A. Mahmood (Eds.), *Strategic information technology management*. Idea Group.

Wilson, D. (1995). IT investment and its productivity effects: An organizational sociologist's perspective on direction for future research. *Economics of Innovation and New Technology, 4*(3), 235–251. https://doi.org/10.1080/10438599500000005

Zhao, L., & Aram, J. D. (1995). Networking and growth of young technology-intensive ventures in China. *Journal of Business Venturing, 10*(5), 349–370.

Chapter 11
Does Culture Matter for a FinTech New Venture?

Paola Demartini and Mara Del Baldo

11.1 Introduction

"FinTech refers to the application of technology to finance" (Arner et al., 2017, p. 377).

This is one of the most frequently quoted definitions to explain the phenomenon of the emergence of Fintech. It includes not only the high-tech "new incumbents" in the financial sector but also the new digital banks. It is an economic sector composed of companies that aim to compete with traditional financial methods and shape the future of the banking sector. All of these companies are targeting customers through process or product innovation, or through new channels and distribution methods, to create a match between supply and demand for financial services (Schueffel, 2016). The growth of FinTech worldwide is rapid and exponential in terms of number and business volume, and it counts for a high number of unicorns (according to CB Insights).

Most of the literature that has studied the fintech phenomenon has focused on issues related to the application of new technologies (Milian et al., 2019) and the emergence of new business models (Lee & Shin, 2018). This chapter, on the other hand, seeks to take a different perspective in the analysis of such a complex and varied phenomenon, focusing on the cultural factors that can characterize a new fintech venture.

P. Demartini (✉)
Department of Business Studies, Roma Tre University, Rome, Italy
e-mail: paola.demartini@uniroma3.it

M. Del Baldo
Department of Economics, Society and Politics, University of Urbino Carlo Bo, Urbino, Italy
e-mail: mara.delbaldo@uniurb.it

S. Loprevite et al. (eds.), *Startups and Gazelle Enterprises*, SIDREA Series in Accounting and Business Administration,
https://doi.org/10.1007/978-3-031-90881-1_11

The etymology of the word "fintech" originates from the crasis of the words "Finance" (from old French finance: *settlement of a debt, payment*) and "Technology" (from ancient Greek *tékhnē*). Our interest lies in the reinterpretation of the ancient Greek word *tékhnē*, whose literal meaning is "*art, skill, craft*". Not surprisingly, this meaning recalls the synonym word "culture":

- as in *education*: art, practice, skill;
- as in *ideas, value of a people*: civilization, knowledge, society, way of life (synonyms can be inferred from thesaurus.com).

This is the intrinsic meaning, little explored to date, that we are most interested in exploring in the creation of a fintech.

Therefore, our Research Question (RQ) is the following:

– *Why and how does culture matter for a new fintech venture?*

We state that important factors influencing the foundation, launch and growth of a high-tech, in general, are not only due to the application of innovative information and digital technologies, Big Data, algorithms, analytics but more generally to cultural factors that represent the antecedents of that destructive and regenerative process at the basis of doing business that is fueled by the "art, skills, practices and values" proposed by the entrepreneur, shared by the start-up team and by the workmates, which creates a symbolic meaning system. The latter is the driving force that fuels corporate identity and legitimizes it in front of investors and customers.

The theoretical lens we intend to use is neo-institutional theory. This perspective conceptualizes institutions as generative of interests, identities, and appropriate models of practice that take shape in broader socio-cultural contexts. Under the umbrella of neo-institutional theory, Lounsbury and Glynn (2001, 2019) and Glynn and Lounsbury (2022) lay the groundwork for a broad research agenda called "cultural entrepreneurship". They highlight the central role of culture in entrepreneurial and innovative practice, facilitating the creation of a new venture identity that serves as a touchstone upon which investors and other stakeholders can confer legitimacy.

We can address the first RQ (i.e., why) by examining the development of arguments and thinking within this field of research.

Building on this theoretical lens, we aim to answer the second RQ (i.e., how) by focusing on one of the first and most important digital banks in Italy, Banca Widiba (that is the acronym of Wise Dialogue Bank), launched on the market in September 2014 as a start-up of one of the oldest Italian banks and a case of success, both in terms of the level of innovation achieved and awarded several times, including internationally, within the reference sector, and for its financial and sustainability performance, having achieved the breakeven within 5 years after its launch, and an income of 54 million and a Return on Equity of 31% in 2023, after 10 years.

According to our interpretative theory, our focus is not on the entrepreneurial judgmental decision-making, which translates into action and execution, but on "the process of storytelling that mediates between extant stocks of entrepreneurial resources and subsequent capital acquisition and wealth creation" (Lounsbury & Glynn, 2001, p. 545).

In particular, to understand how cultural processes take place and enable the consolidation of collective sense-making (Weick, 1995), we will analyze, through the methodology of content analysis, the story of the first few years of the company's life through thoughts, opinions, and emotions. Our timeline of analysis embeds the seed phase (2013), the launch (2014), and the early growth (2015) of the company.

This research was possible thanks to the realization of a book, titled *Cronaca Pop*—Pop Chronicle of Widiba (2018), in which, voluntarily, board members, start-up team, managers, employees and professionals have responded to the invitation to "telling what Widiba was for them, even describing a moment, an experience they consider particularly memorable". This book is an example of collective storytelling that, to our knowledge, is unparalleled and has proven to be an interesting field of study to contextualize the latest research in the field of cultural entrepreneurship theory (Lounsbury & Glynn, 2019; Glynn & Lounsbury, 2022). Therefore, our fieldwork aims to understand how collective storytelling is realized through the writing of the book Pop Chronicle of Widiba, which will be successful if it reinforces or extends the entrepreneurial story told by the founder into a coherent narrative.

The information gathered was obtained from multiple sources to gain a deeper understanding of the context. These included corporate sources, newspapers, social media, and communication events organized by the bank itself. Moreover, one of the chapters' authors was directly involved in the launch of the new venture as an independent board member until 2019. The involvement of one of the researchers in the field enabled the authors to develop a broad understanding of the major concerns and challenges "behind the scenes". This has facilitated comprehension of the narratives while also being a potential source of bias, as remarked by Unluer (2012) and Aguinis and Solarino (2019). Recognizing that there is no absolute truth and that qualitative research is not generalizable (Guba, 1981), the validity of qualitative research can be described as trustworthiness (Anney, 2014), which is supported by verification processes during the study (Morse et al., 2002).

Our research provides manifold contributions.

First, the results of our study offer a cultural-based interpretation of a phenomenon such as the launch of a FinTech venture, which cannot be read only from the partial perspective of how new technologies enable new business models.

Second, previous literature and the media often portray high-tech entrepreneurs as brilliant "individuals" who face challenges and difficulties alone and make "judgmental choices under uncertain market conditions" (i.e., think of the launch stories of Apple, Google, Spotify), neglecting the efforts of teams, communities, or collective processes at the field level. In light of Lounsbury and Glynn's appeal, our contribution intends to emphasize that, in contrast, in high-tech settings, innovative and creative processes are boosted through storytelling, first nurtured by the entrepreneur, and then consolidated at a broader, collective level.

Our findings contribute to advancing the theory of cultural entrepreneurship by adopting a processual approach, as advocated by Glaser and Lounsbury (2021) and focusing on the role of the company's human resources and demonstrating how workers, especially those involved in the creative process, can strengthen corporate storytelling by providing new content to the entrepreneurial story.

Finally, the analysis of the words and meanings emerging from the stories offers some insights for advancing research about the role of culture in two main directions. The first direction explores the relevance of cultural value (Throsby, 1999, 2003) for the people involved in the innovative and creative processes that characterize new ventures. The second direction explores how workers exhibiting passion, need for achievement, responsibility, and a willingness to take risks—key motivational factors of intrapreneurship (Antoncic & Hisrich, 2001)—can contribute to the success of new ventures and enrich research on cultural entrepreneurship.

This chapter continues as follows. Section 11.2 presents the theoretical background, and Sect. 11.3 describes the research methodology. Section 11.4 presents and discusses the findings, and, finally, Sect. 11.5 provides a summary of the research constituents and concludes with an analysis of the limitations of the study and suggestions for further research.

11.2 Why Culture Matters: The Theory of Cultural Entrepreneurship

Having superior technology and a strong business model is essential, but it alone does not guarantee entrepreneurial success. Culture plays a critical role.

Lounsbury and Glynn introduced the concept of cultural entrepreneurship nearly two decades ago in an article published in the *Strategic Management Journal* (2001). The Theory of Cultural Entrepreneurship was conceptualized as a way to bridge multiple theoretical strands, including the resource-based view of the firm (Penrose, 1959; Barney, 1991; Teece et al., 1997), institutional theory (DiMaggio & Powell, 1983; Aldrich & Fiol, 1994; Scott, 1995), and organizational identity (Elsbach & Kramer, 1996; Gioia et al., 2013; Glynn, 2000), among others.

This theory integrates strategic management considerations of effective resource use with an institutionalist perspective that emphasizes the constraining and enabling effects of culture on action. The term "culture" is used in this context to refer to processes of meaning-making, to account for different meanings, and to examine their effects on social life (Lounsbury & Glynn, 2001, p. 546).

The central argument is that entrepreneurs need to establish a distinctive identity in a social context through meaning-making devices, including stories, narratives, analogies, frames, and symbols. Positive social recognition from key resource-holding audiences—such as consumers, investors, employees, the media, or other stakeholders—enhances resource allocation, which is crucial for wealth creation.

In the contribution "Beyond Homo Entrepreneurs", Lounsbury et al. (2019) highlight the specifics of the foundations of their theory by comparing key aspects concerning differences in the definition and role of entrepreneurs, key mechanisms, and the role of context (see Table 11.1).

Table 11.1 Comparing key aspects of *Homo Entrepreneurus* approach and Cultural Entrepreneurship approach

Aspect	Homo Entrepreneurus	Cultural Entrepreneurship
Definition of entrepreneurship	"Judgmental decision-making which takes place in a market setting under uncertainty"	"Process of storytelling that mediates between extant stocks of entrepreneurial resources and subsequent capital acquisition and wealth creation" (Lounsbury & Glynn, 2001, p. 545).
Role of entrepreneur	"Entrepreneurs combine heterogeneous assets, and deploy these assets […] within a firm to the production of new offerings that may satisfy customer wants at a profit"	"Entrepreneurs must be skilled cultural operators who shape interpretations of the nature and potential of their new venture to those who may supply needed resources" (Lounsbury & Glynn, 2001, p. 549).
Core mechanism	Judgment: "The need for individuals to make decisions about the future without access to a formal model of decision rule"	Storytelling: "A primary mechanism employed in this process, we propose, is that of storytelling" (Lounsbury & Glynn, 2001, p. 549) that shapes the interpretations and valuations of key stakeholders.

Source: Our extraction of the most relevant categories (Lounsbury et al., 2019, p. 1218) and Lounsbury and Glynn (2001, pp. 545, 549)

In short, *Homo Entrepreneurus* focuses on making judgments and decisions in uncertain markets while combining diverse resources to build profitable ventures. *Cultural Entrepreneurship Theory* emphasizes the entrepreneur's role as a skilled cultural operator, adept at crafting narratives and leveraging storytelling to shape stakeholder perceptions, and secure essential resources for venture growth. While the former highlights decision-making and resource coordination, the latter prioritizes cultural and narrative expertise as key drivers of entrepreneurial success.

In the book *Cultural Entrepreneurship: A New Agenda for the Study of Entrepreneurial Processes and Possibilities*, Lounsbury and Glynn (2019) suggest new directions for future research. They highlight three biases in mainstream literature on entrepreneurship: the start-up bias, the opportunity discovery bias, and the individual bias alone.

The *start-up bias* is a focus on for-profit business model ventures that tend to neglect social entrepreneurs and intrapreneurs. Social entrepreneurs are driven by a desire to create societal impact, while intrapreneurs are individuals within established companies who are encouraged to identify new solutions, products or processes and other change agents, such as internal and external communities (i.e., communities of practice, communities of followers) motivated by a desire to contribute to change.

The *opportunity bias* refers to the prevailing focus in the entrepreneurship literature on economic, psychological, and cognitive aspects of opportunity discovery and exploitation. Such perspectives neglect the constitutive nature of opportunities and treat processes of resource assembly as a black box. It is in this domain where the authors make their significant contributions by pointing out, through a relational, contextualized perspective, how (collective) actors create and exploit entrepreneurial possibilities, which "*must be understood as part of a field of action where there is an ever-evolving ecology of entrepreneurial possibilities, as well as a wide variety of potential and actual entrepreneurs, and other actors, who are variously involved in the construction and exploitation of such possibilities*" (Lounsbury & Glynn, 2019, p. 57).

Finally, the *individual bias* is that the literature often portrays entrepreneurs as "heroic individuals", thereby neglecting the efforts of teams, communities, or collective processes at the field level. Understanding relational and institutional fields at the heart of entrepreneurial possibilities, Lounsbury and Glynn call for examining entrepreneurship processes at higher levels of analysis based on collective efforts and see the need for a multilevel approach.

These ideas paved the way for a cultural turn in studying entrepreneurial processes, which captivated scholars within organization studies, strategy, and entrepreneurship (e.g., Golant & Sillince, 2007; Überbacher, 2014; Van Werven et al., 2015).

To sum up, while scholars have long examined the economic drivers of innovation and entrepreneurship, still less is known about the cultural forces that shape these dynamics.

11.2.1 How Culture Matters: Entrepreneurial Stories and Collective Storytelling

Expanding their initial definition (Lounsbury & Glynn, 2001), the authors systematize their theoretical model (see Fig. 11.1) and define cultural entrepreneurship as the "processes by which actors draw upon cultural resources (e.g., discourse, language, categories, logics, and other symbolic elements) to advance entrepreneurship or to facilitate organization or institutional innovation" (Lounsbury & Glynn, 2019, p. 3).

Entrepreneurs must be skilled cultural operators (Lounsbury & Glynn, 2001, p. 549) who pursue legitimacy by shaping how different kinds of audiences understand, evaluate, and reward them (Fisher et al., 2017). To achieve this, entrepreneurs construct coherent narratives that rationalize the purpose and functioning of their new ventures. This enables them to establish their organizational identities and make their activities comprehensible, meaningful, and appealing to relevant audiences (Czarniawska, 1997; Grimes, 2018; Vaara et al., 2016) to attract resources and finally generate wealth creation.

Such entrepreneurial narratives may be regarded as framing devices, whereby information about nascent ventures is structured and organized by focusing attention on a limited set of key dimensions (Giorgi, 2017, p. 713).

The majority of research into cultural entrepreneurship has concentrated on the consequences of such narratives, particularly how they facilitate the *identity*

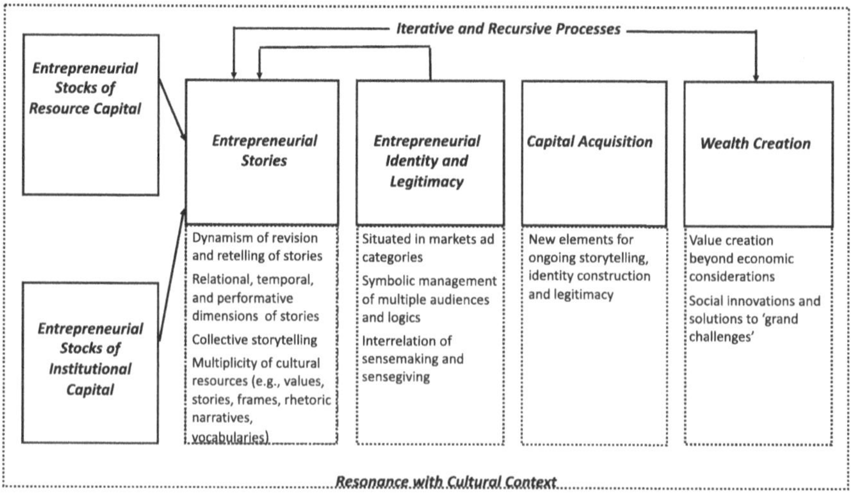

Fig. 11.1 Expanded theoretical model of cultural entrepreneurship [Source: Lounsbury & Glynn, 2019, figure 2, p. 3, adapted from Lounsbury et al., 2019]

formation and the legitimization of new enterprises. This is achieved by enabling the acquisition of resources and growth (Glynn & Lounsbury, 2005; Wry et al., 2011; Überbacher, 2014; Gehman & Soublière, 2017).

The process of *identity formation* entails the creation of identity claims that strike a balance between *conformity* and *uniqueness* within the context of an institutional field. *Conformity* serves to guarantee that the actions and narratives of the entrepreneur are acknowledged and validated within the institutional field. The aspect of *uniqueness* captures the audience's interest and enables the entrepreneur to differentiate themselves from their competitors. By achieving this balance, entrepreneurs can effectively navigate their institutional field, simultaneously gaining legitimacy and standing out.

In addition to previous studies that have emphasized the concept of legitimacy (cognitive, moral, and pragmatic) as the primary social evaluation by audiences, Lounsbury and Glynn (2019) have proposed the notion of *cultural resonance.*

The concept of *cultural resonance* has been introduced to explain the extent to which a narrative or identity claim resonates with audiences who possess the relevant resources. The emphasis is placed on the significance of both the cognitive and emotional aspects of storytelling. In more detail, cultural resonance can be defined as the degree to which a narrative or identity story effectively engages and aligns with the values, beliefs, and emotions of an audience, leading to greater acceptance, support, and legitimacy. In their contribution, Glaser and Lounsbury (2021) in deepening the concept of cultural resonance, underline that entrepreneurial narratives unfold and develop over time and, therefore, argue that is necessary to adopt a processual perspective (Wegener & Lorino, 2021) to more fully explain that there is a substantive difference between early stage stories and later stage thanks to "*collective adjusting and reconciling of the story*" (p. 8).

In light of Glaser and Lounsbury's (2021) call for a more detailed understanding of the construction and evolution of entrepreneurial narratives, and in consideration of the limited attention devoted to this process in the context of ongoing dialogue and collective storytelling, we propose to address this matter through a case study. In particular, we aim to examine the formation of a collective history of a start-up through the voices of not only the founder but also those who have participated in its creation and contributed to its early years, from the seed phase to the early growth phase. We believe that an analysis of the cultural resonance at an early stage, with its initial human capital (i.e., board members, professionals, managers, and employees), is fundamental to verify the existence of a collective identity that reinforces the sense of participation and commitment of qualified human resources, in a critical and delicate period for the survival of a company.

11.3 Research Design and Methodology

This section presents the research design and empirical approach used to contextualize the theory of cultural entrepreneurship within the empirical setting of the launch of a new venture in the fintech field.

The authors initially present the rationale behind the case study selection (Sect. 11.3.1), before outlining the data gathering methodology (Sect. 11.3.2). In Sect. 11.3.3, they define the constructs to address the second RQ: "How does culture matter?" Finally, in the last section (Sect. 11.3.4), they discuss their approach to content analysis.

11.3.1 Selection of the Case Study

The rationale behind the selection of this particular case study can be attributed to two key factors.

First, the emergence of a new bank online from one of the oldest banks in Italy, which was experiencing a period of financial and reputational crisis, entailed an enormous amount of hype—both positive and negative. The negative hype was especially dramatic and created enormous legitimacy challenges.

Second, Widiba (an acronym for Wise Dialogue Bank), one of the first digital banks in Italy, launched on the market in September 2014, can be considered a success story, based on the following aspects:

Table 11.2 Widiba KPIs

Fiscal year	No of clients (at 31.12)	Employees	Net income (Euros mln)	Common Equity Tier 1 (CET1) ratio (%)
2013	–	17	n.a.	n.a.
2014	95,000	87	(7.7)	112.98
2015	140,000	163	(11.0)	46.74
2016	161,200	177	(12.2)	27. 4
2017	200,000	199	(14.9)	35.2
2018	>300,000	229	1.5	24.4
……….				
2023	270,000	235	54	38.2

Source: Widiba's financial statements available on Widiba website

- the degree of innovation, which has been recognized with several awards (see Widiba's website at www.widiba.it),
- the financial performance and capital adequacy, as the bank reached breakeven five years after its launch, and as it is shown by the indicators in Table 11.2.

For our research, we are interested in focusing on the first 3 years of fintech's life (2013–2015), a period that formed the identity and DNA of the company. Although evolving over the years, the company has maintained and developed its distinctive and unique characteristics, even within a regulatory and institutional framework as tightly regulated as banking.

11.3.1.1 A Brief History of Widiba in the First Three Years

2013 The Seed Phase

In line with the objectives of its new industrial plan and the evolution of the market, the group launched the online bank project, a key pillar for the revitalization and repositioning of its business model. The project is aimed at customers who prefer digital banking but have complex service needs and relationship expectations.

In more detail, the online bank project is targeting people who are comfortable with and prefer to manage their banking primarily through digital channels, such as online banking or mobile apps, rather than through traditional, in-person branch services. These are customers who value the convenience and efficiency of handling financial transactions remotely but whose financial situations or goals require personalized or advanced solutions, not just simple, transactional banking. These customers also value a deeper, more personalized relationship with their bank, even though they prefer digital channels. They might want access to expert advice or feel valued through personalized services and communication, which goes beyond what a basic digital interface can offer.

Launched in 2013, the project included the creation of a digital community to build brand awareness and a waiting list of potential clients. For the first time in the banking sector, the name Widiba (hereafter W.), an acronym for WIse-DIalog-BAnking, was co-created through collective brainstorming.

2014 The Launch

The launch on the market was in September 2014. In about 3 months of activity, W. recorded over 15,000 new account opening requests (more than 200 per day). This innovative digital bank attracted over 150,000 users in the "Say&Play community management platform", contributing around 3500 suggestions for service improvement, supported by an effective social media strategy, and engaging digital influencers through nationwide events.

Widiba's business model focus on merging the *convenience of digital banking* with the *high-touch, tailored services* that more traditional banks offer to clients with complex financial needs. The goal is likely to create a sophisticated digital banking experience that still prioritizes client relationships and personalized service.

A major initiative was to create a trading platform from the ground up, rather than using pre-existing systems or third-party software. The platform gives users access to 18 major financial markets across the globe. This means W. customers can trade in a diverse range of international markets, allowing them to invest in a wide variety of stocks, bonds, and other financial instruments. The platform boasts 50 advanced functions, including tools for technical analysis, portfolio management, automated trading, alerts, and customizable interfaces. By providing a broad array of tools, W. is enhancing the user experience and empowering traders to make informed decisions.

2015 Early Growth

A few months after its launch, the digital bank completes its service model.

In January 2015, EFMA (the European Financial Management Association), an international organization that aims to identify and reward the most innovative best practices in finance praised W. as one of the most innovative banks in the world. W. won the award for the quality of its customer experience, thanks to the Widiba 2020 project. Specifically, the bank's new web interface provides a google-like intelligent search engine, developed entirely in W. labs with use of Big Data, that allows customers to conduct transactions and operations just by entering a keyword.

The technological evolution continues and in June 2015 the first banking app for Apple Watch was launched. The consecration of the high level of innovation comes in 2016 with the awarding of the National Prize for Innovation for the WidiExpress project, the first all-digital account portability, a national award for Innovation promoted by the presidency of the Council of Ministers and delivered by the president of the Italian Republic.

11.3.2 Data Gathering

The information gathered to understand the context was multiple coming from different sources: corporate sources, newspapers, social media, and communication events organized by the bank itself. Moreover, one of the chapter's authors was directly involved in the launch of the new venture as an independent board member of the new venture. Our involvement in the field enabled us to develop a broad understanding of the major concerns as well as challenges "behind the scenes". This facilitated comprehension of the individual narratives, yet it can also be a potential source of bias (Unluer, 2012; Aguinis & Solarino, 2019). Because there is no absolute truth and the purpose of qualitative inquiry is to develop idiographic knowledge (Guba, 1981), the validity of qualitative research can thus be described as trustworthiness (Anney, 2014), which is supported by processes of verification during the study (Morse et al., 2002). In particular, a detailed and systematic approach was employed in the analysis of the textual data. The information was then collected and compared by the authors on a case-by-case basis, with the aim of identifying any discrepancies or inconsistencies. The findings presented here have been the result of a comprehensive and ongoing discussion among the authors, which has been subject to further reflection and analysis over time.

According to our interpretative theory, our interest is not the entrepreneurial judgmental decision-making, which translates into action and execution, but "the process of storytelling that mediates between extant stocks of entrepreneurial resources and subsequent capital acquisition and wealth creation" (Lounsbury & Glynn, 2001, p. 545), with specific reference to the audience made up of the people who have contributed to the creation and growth of the company (i.e., board members, professionals, managers, and employees), who are crucial human resources for the creation of the company's wealth.

In particular, to understand how cultural processes take place and allow for the consolidation of collective sensemaking (Weick, 1995), we will analyze, through the methodology of text analysis, the story of the first few years of the fintech's life through the thoughts, opinions, and emotions of the people who contributed to its birth and growth. The timeline of analysis embeds the seed phase (2013), the launch (2014), and the early growth (2015) of the company.

This is possible thanks to the realization of a book, titled *Pop Chronicle of Widiba* (2018), in which, voluntarily, board members, start-up team, professionals, managers, and employees responded to the invitation to "tell their stories". This is an example of collective storytelling that, to our knowledge, is unparalleled and has proven to be an interesting field of study to contextualize the latest research in the field of the theory of cultural entrepreneurship.

We will analyze the content of these texts with the assumption that individuals' attitudes, cognitions, and values are reflected in the language they use (Gabriel, 2000).

11.3.3 Defining the Construct of Cultural Resonance

After positioning our research within a specific strand of studies, our following step is to outline the constructs of the framework of analysis.

According to the Theory of Cultural Entrepreneurship, the key components of cultural resonance are: (a) cognitive alignment and (b) emotional impact. The rationale we are going to illustrate is summarized in Fig. 11.2.

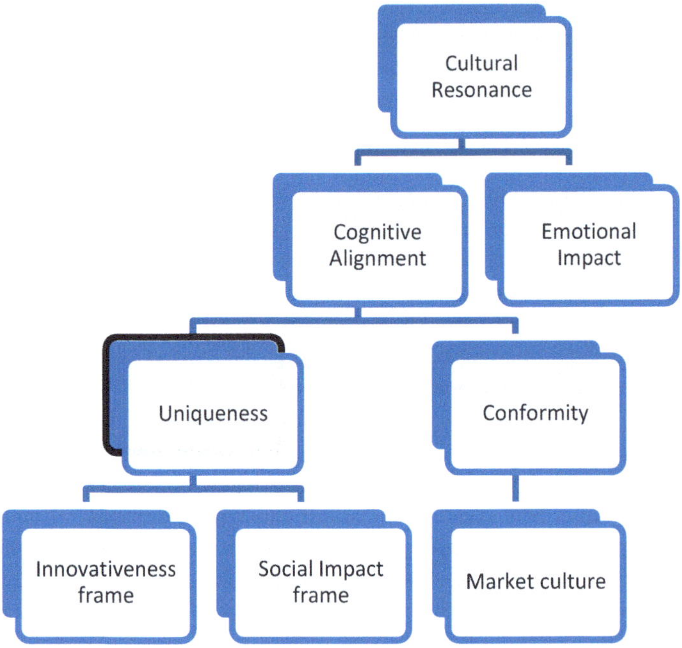

Fig. 11.2 Key components of the construct "Cultural Resonance". *Source*: Our elaboration

11.3.3.1 Cognitive Alignment

The cognitive alignment is the extent to which the story fits with the existing knowledge, beliefs, and expectations of the audience. This requires a balance between the uniqueness of a new venture and familiar concepts. A narrative that aligns well with familiar concepts and frames of reference in the field is more likely to be understood and accepted.

Uniqueness as a framing mechanism reflects a perception that the entrepreneurial venture and its offering meaningfully differ from existing organizations and their offerings. Such a perception matters because distinctiveness often represents an important element in the evaluation of entrepreneurial ventures (e.g., Navis & Glynn, 2011).

Entrepreneurial ventures commonly deploy an innovativeness frame—broadly defined as a frame that emphasizes the innovativeness or disruptiveness of the entrepreneurial venture and offering (e.g., Ansari et al., 2016; Snihur et al., 2018; Pan et al., 2020). Another line of entrepreneurship research particularly highlights innovative social impact frames—defined as frames that present an entrepreneurial venture in light of its desirable impact on society (Lee & Huang, 2018). As such, a social impact frame "*emphasizes the social–environmental welfare benefits of a venture and its activities*" (Lee & Huang, 2018, p. 1).

To analyze familiar concepts for the audience, we rely on the "market culture" construct as developed by Cameron et al. (2006), which is widely used in the literature on corporate culture evaluation. This cultural dimension focuses on a firm's external effectiveness by pursuing enhanced competitiveness and emphasizing organizational effectiveness, fast response, and customer focus. Firms with market culture attach the highest priority to customers and judge success based on indicators such as market value, revenues, and meeting budgetary targets.

11.3.3.2 Emotional Impact

Emotional impact refers to the capacity of entrepreneurial narratives and actions to evoke emotions that resonate with stakeholders, thereby influencing their perceptions, decisions, and behaviors. In the context of cultural entrepreneurship, emotional impact is achieved through the strategic use of storytelling, symbols, and cultural meanings that connect with the audience on an emotional level. This emotional engagement is essential for entrepreneurs to gain legitimacy, mobilize resources, and build support for their ventures.

The entrepreneurial story should tap into the audience's emotional landscape, resonating with their passions, desires, and aspirations. This emotional connection makes the narrative more compelling and memorable. By addressing the hopes and dreams of the audience, the story fosters a deeper connection and motivates the audience to support the narrative or identity claim.

To sum up, emotional impact in the theory of cultural entrepreneurship by Lounsbury and Glynn (2001, 2019) is about the ability of entrepreneurs to use narratives and symbolic actions to evoke emotions that resonate with their audience. This emotional connection is essential for gaining legitimacy, mobilizing resources, and building a supportive network for the entrepreneurial venture.

11.3.4 Our Approach to Text Analysis

The objective of our field research is to understand how, through the writing of the book *Pop Chronicle of Widiba*, a collective storytelling is realized, which will be successful if it reinforces or extends the entrepreneurial story told by the entrepreneur. We will focus on the seed phase (2013), the launch (2014), and the early growth phase (2015).

We use text analysis to capture, in a systematic and in as much as is achievable objective manner, the characteristics specific to a text (Stone et al., 1966). Our text analysis is motivated by the notion that words and expressions used by members of an organization (labeled "vocabulary") represent the outcome of an organizational culture that has developed over time (Levinson, 2003).

After delving into the concept of cultural resonance and defining its main key components (i.e., cognitive alignment and emotional resonance), we will proceed with a text analysis that first requires us to highlight our unit of analysis and how we will develop the coding of the text.

The target audience consists of board members of the holding company, who represent the investors, board members of the new venture appointed by the holding and for this reason considered as delegated by the investors, professionals, and experts in the field, who collaborated to the seed and launch phases, managers and employers with expertise in the creative and information technology sector, who consider themselves as founders of the new venture. The narratives were composed and collated in 2018; however, in the book, they have been structured according to a consistent chronological sequence and delineated according to key phases that characterize the life cycle of a start-up. Our object of analysis is to compare their stories to see whether or not certain themes occur—then a context unit—a chunk of text that reflects a theme—is likely to be the appropriate unit of analysis.

11.3.4.1 Wordlists, Coding, and Text Analysis

In this section, we focus on vocabularies/wordlists related to the above-identified themes (i.e., Innovativeness, Social Impact, Market Culture, and Emotional Impact). Vocabularies are essential elements in creating meaning (Meyer & Höllerer, 2010; Lockwood et al., 2019) and we used "words" to tag the most expressive sentences (i.e., a chunk of text that reflects a theme) and to code them. Instead of computer-aided text analysis (CATA) tools, we read all the stories and directly coded the text to provide deep insight into a particular phenomenon (i.e., cultural resonance), those multifaceted aspects, not yet well defined in the literature and yet to be explored, could be missed by a computer.

One could use a variety of sources for producing wordlists:

- We began with "start words" because these words are created based on our conceptual definitions for concepts, and they are chosen based on theoretical reasoning.
- Then, to augment term expansion, the researcher could look up each term in a dictionary or thesaurus and add these to the list. We did this in the current research using the online WordNet lexical database (Miller, 1995), extracting its synonyms for each word. Nouns, verbs, adjectives, and adverbs are grouped into sets of cognitive synonyms, each expressing a distinct concept. Those synonyms are interlinked by means of conceptual-semantic and lexical relations. WordNet's structure makes it a useful tool for computational linguistics and natural language processing. An additional dictionary was the Harvard-IV-4 Psycho-Social Dictionary.
- Another source the researcher could use is from prior text-mining research that may have produced special lexicons for a concept (see Table 11.3).

For *innovativeness*, we use the wordlist as formally developed and validated by McKenny et al. (2018). The wordlist, which was also developed specifically for the context of entrepreneurial ventures, consists of 147 words (e.g., creative, innovate,

Table 11.3 Framework for text analysis

Cultural resonance key components	Framing mechanisms as for the TOCE	Concepts	Sources for wordlists to tag our unit of analysis	Example of key words
Cognitive alignment	Entrepreneurial venture uniqueness	Innovativeness orientation (Ansari et al., 2016; Pan et al., 2020; Snihur et al., 2018)	Innovativeness wordlist (McKenny et al., 2018). Synonims of the word "innovativeness" as for WordNet lexical database	Originality, ability, cognition, knowledge, abstraction, novelty
		Social value orientation (Lee & Huang, 2018)	Social value orientation wordlist (Moss et al., 2018)	Equality, humankind, empowerment, benefits, society
	Conformity, situated in market and familiar categories	Market orientation (Cameron et al., 2006)	Words and synonyms suggested by Cameron et al. (2006)	Achievement, challenge, clients, competitiveness, fast, goal, growth, market, perform, position, profit, result, strong, value, win
Emotional impact	Audience's emotional response, resonating with their passions, desires, and aspirations	Lounsbury and Glynn (2001, 2019)	Harvard-IV-4 Psycho-Social Dictionary from the list of words indicating both emotion and affiliation or supportiveness	Attachment, enthusiasm, grateful, love, proud, willing, willingness, affection, devotion, friendly, like, passion, trust, understand

invention, and novelty) and word groupings commonly used to indicate innovativeness (e.g., dream up, next generation, and technologically advanced).

For *social impact*, we use the "social value orientation" wordlist as systematically developed and validated by Moss et al. (2018). The word list, which contains 66 keywords (e.g., equality, humankind, and wisdom) and word stems (e.g., empower*, beneficiar*, and societ*), is particularly suited for our context because it was specifically developed and validated to infer language consistent with social impact values as opposed to language consistent with economic values.

For *market culture*, we referred to the words and synonyms suggested by Cameron et al. (2006) to identify words that would allow us to encode the natural language of those involved in writing the book.

For *emotional impact*, we referred to the Harvard-IV-4 Psycho-Social Dictionary, which is a commonly used source for word classification, partly because its composition is out of the researcher's control and the possible impact of the researcher's subjectivity is significantly reduced. Using the freely available Inquiry tool, we identified a subset of 84 words labeled as indicating affiliation or support ("Affil" label) and emotions ("Emot" label).

11.4 Findings and Discussion

In this section, we present the results of our analysis of the stories collected in the book *Pop Chronicle of Widiba* in which, voluntarily, board members, consultants, managers, and employees have responded to the invitation to "*telling what Widiba was for them, even describing a moment, an experience they consider particularly memorable*". Our analysis focuses on 33 stories placed in the book in the years 2013, 2014, and 2015 and will highlight the following themes:

- the cultural resonance with the entrepreneurial story;
- the construction of collective sense-making;
- a proposal for the expansion of the Theory of Cultural Entrepreneurship, focusing on the role of workers and how those who participate in the creative process can strengthen corporate storytelling in a logic of cultural intrapreneurship.

11.4.1 Cultural Resonance: From Entrepreneurial Story to Collective Story

"Change and adaptation to a new world do not transform needs but the way of knowing how to meet and grasp them. W. is the bank of all times that has embraced with passion, dedication and study all the tools of today to become effective, efficient, and ready to be competitive" (the founder).

The initial message contained in the book *Pop Chronicle of Widiba* summarizes all the elements of the entrepreneurial story. The founder recounts the distinctive element of the new venture: namely, the orientation toward innovation that makes technology a means and not an end. He then takes up established concepts in the industry, recalling the goals of effectiveness, efficiency, and competitiveness. Finally, he emphasizes the passion and commitment of those who have participated in its birth and growth.

For collective storytelling, there must be cognitive alignment and/or emotional impact in the audience's stories. There does not necessarily have to be both. Our analysis of the selected stories reveals a collective coherence, that is, shared storytelling in line with the themes highlighted by the founder, albeit with distinctions between individuals.

Concerning resonance based on cognitive alignment, the main differences are found in the completeness of the themes embedded in the stories of individuals, which depends on their functional role in the organization, as exemplified below in some particularly significant excerpts (see Example 11.1).

For board members, the cognitive alignment is comprehensive in all aspects outlined in the framework of analysis. Conversely, it is primarily innovation-oriented if the role of the individual is that of a specialist one, such as manager or employee involved in information technology or the digital web development.

Example 11.1

Cognitive alignment resonance

Innovativeness
When I was attending team meetings, I was dwelling on a new piece each time: people, systems, ideas and new applications (Board member)
Social Impact
In W. there is passion that stems from the idea that services are necessary for people, and we have a very high responsibility; enabling customers to experience them in a new and positive way was (and is) the engine that drove the people of W. to dream and realise this dream (Board member)
Market culture
There was a need and a new way of listening to and serving customers (Board member)
Innovativeness
We nicknamed ourselves "incrediBOL"[BOL stands for Bank On Line] because no one believed us that we would succeed in bringing the most modern bank to life inside the oldest bank in the world (IT manager)

As far as the emotional impact is concerned, the intensity and characteristics of the response differ according to the actual involvement in the creative process of the new venture and the stage in which the individual was involved (i.e., seed, launch or early growth), as evidenced by the excerpts in the following example (see Example 11.2).

Example 11.2

Emotional resonance

W. It is one of the most extraordinary and exciting things of my long professional life (Board member involved since the seed phase)
for me it was love at first sight (Board member involved since the seed phase)
I saw the birth of W. experiencing excitement, enthusiasm and pride with the founder .... It is a daily challenge where winning is a must and at the same time a great reward (Employer involved since the seed phase)

11.4.2 Unlocking the Collective Sense-Making of the Theme of Innovativeness

In our analysis of the text, we found that the collective sense-making for the theme of innovativeness confirms the meaning attributed by the WordNet lexical database (see Table 11.4):

Table 11.4 Collective sense-making of the theme Innovativeness

Theme	Collective meaning	Excerpts
Innovativeness	#1 originality through the introduction of new ideas	"dwelling on a new piece each time: people, systems, ideas, and new applications (BM2)" "technology, systems, and behaviors would make their thinking possible (PF3)" "He gave me a blank sheet and asked me to invent the bank's systems (EF4)" "A large white box (BM6)" "The only context was that of the dream (MF7)" "So much white paper (MF9)" "From comparison, insights were born, from insights ideas (PF13)" "Laboratory of new ideas (BM33)" "When you were just a pioneering idea, I was there (EF24)"
	#2 being or producing something like nothing previously done or experienced or created	"building a bank from scratch (BM1)" "in the cosmic void, nothing could suggest that a new bank factory would be born there (MF7)" "we had to change the entire paradigm of approach (EF10)" "great professionalism and a desire to act, imagination and concreteness, the two ingredients without which there is no true innovation (BM11)" "the brand name was chosen with an online vote worthy of a talent show (EF15)" "A 'social digital platform' project aimed at designing the bank that did not exist (PF17)" "How old and outdated the [banking] world I came from seemed (MF20)" "Materializing something concrete, new, beautiful (EF22)" "… something completely unprecedented in such an ancient sector (EF23)" "W. is the ability to interpret the future, the search for the no ordinary (EF27)" "Our revolution (EF30)"
	#3 ahead of its time	"The idea was powerful (PF3)" "We nicknamed ourselves 'incrediBOL' because no one believed we could create the most modern bank within the world's oldest bank (MF8)" "What are they doing, StarTrek? (EF12)" "A unique decision in our banking experience (BM14)"

Legend: *BM* holding Board Member and venture Board Member, *PF* professionals, *MF* managers, *EF* employees

1. originality through the introduction of new ideas
2. being or producing something similar to nothing previously done or experienced or created
3. ahead of its time

11.4.2.1 Advancing Research: The Relevance of Cultural Value in the Innovative and Creative Processes of New Ventures

However, it is worthy of attention to point out that from the integral reading of the texts also other recurrent words and meanings emerged, which will be the subject of future in-depth analysis through open coding.

In particular, we highlight the words "beautiful", "beauty" which, in the units of analysis, is mainly associated with the meaning of innovation as the ability to concretely create something new (#2) through an approach that combines tradition with innovation, but also with attention to design and aesthetics (see Example 11.3).

While this does not come as much of a surprise, considering that W. has won several design awards over time, we believe that it is peculiar for the fintech sector to recall dimensions that mainly relate to the concept of cultural value understood in its artistic and aesthetic dimensions (Throsby, 2001; Del Baldo & Demartini, 2021, pp. 297–300).

To elaborate on this statement, which highlights another perspective on the relevance of culture even in a highly technological sector, let us briefly recall the concept of cultural value. Throsby (2003, pp. 279–280) states that cultural value is made up of several facets and attributes that also emerge in the words of the stories we analyzed, such as aesthetic value, which refers to properties of beauty, harmony, form, and other aesthetic characteristics; social value, which is linked to a sense of connection with others, present and past generations; symbolic value, which is linked to the artwork's ability to evoke, for example, a sense of belonging, identity, and self-awareness.

On the basis of the evidence that has emerged and the thoughts that have been expressed, we believe that it may be interesting to explore, through future research, the role that the cultural dimension can play within the innovative and creative processes that characterize the new ventures.

Example 11.3

Beauty, algorithms, and artistic sensibility

It is technology and the search for beauty in design; algorithms and artistic sensibility; virtual world and focus on personal relationships, a combination of new and old (BM6)
Beauty and banking can find a meeting point (MF21)
Something concrete, something new, something beautiful materialised (EF22)
The launch of W. was the desire to move forward to see what beautiful could be (EF28)

11.4.3 Advancing Cultural Entrepreneurship Theory Research: From Collective Story to Intrapreneurial Story

Analyzing the text based on the keywords identified to capture the most emotion-related features, two main impacts emerge.

For individuals not directly involved in the company's operations (board members and professionals), the recurring words to describe their experience express a strongly positive sentiment (i.e., "fantastic world", "love at first sight", and "a captivating bank"), as codified by the wordlists of the Harvard-IV-4 Psycho-Social Dictionary.

For workers directly involved in the creative process, recurring words such as "pride", "enthusiasm", and "passion", "friendship", and "trust" can be found, emphasizing the active involvement of those who participated in the creation and launch of the new venture (see Example 11.4).

Example 11.4

Workers' enthusiasm and passion

I saw W. come to life by sharing excitement, enthusiasm and pride with the founder .... It is a daily challenge where winning is a must and at the same time a great gratification
I talked about the enthusiasm and passion we put into it. Feelings that have allowed us to never feel tired, to overcome difficult moments, to feel part of a team and protagonists of a success story

Furthermore, a comprehensive analysis of the workers' narratives has led to the identification of new keywords that pertain to the emotional impact of the creative process, including terms such as "dream" and "achievement". These keywords illustrate the personal transformation and growth that often accompany creative endeavors. Additionally, the analysis has revealed keywords, such as "goals", "challenges", and "no fear", that reflect a determination to achieve ambitious results without fear of failure (see Example 11.5).

These words recall passion, need for achievement, responsibility, and risk taking, all of which are recognized in the literature as the main motivational factors for entrepreneurial activity and which, when expressed by employees, recall the concept of intrapreneurship (Antoncic & Hisrich, 2001), paving the way for future research on intrapreneurial storytelling.

Example 11.5

Intrapreneurial storytelling

it would be impossible to go back ... not to chase one's dreams ... I realised that the real revolution ... has to be made within ourselves, first with the heart and then with the head that's what W. is for me: the chance to grow together to reach new goals and overcome ambitious challenges. Here you must never be afraid to take a penalty kick!

11.5 Conclusions

Our research unfolds around the following Research Question: Why and how does culture matter for a fintech new venture?

To answer the question: Why does culture matter for a fintech new venture? we decided to use the lens of cultural entrepreneurship theory.

Innovation and entrepreneurship are fundamental to the modern economy. While much research has focused on the economic factors driving these areas, the cultural influences shaping them are less understood. Lounsbury and Glynn (2001, 2019) emphasize the critical role of culture in entrepreneurial and innovative practices and argue for a broader perspective on culture, highlighting the symbolic meaning systems entrepreneurs use as tools to pursue novelty and to create the firm identity.

Our analysis underpins the idea that entrepreneurs must be skilled cultural operators (Lounsbury & Glynn, 2001, p. 549) who construct entrepreneurial stories to influence the audiences who possess the relevant resources for their companies' survival. Their narrative should produce cultural resonance, that is to say, effectively engage and align with the values, beliefs, and emotions of an audience, leading to greater acceptance, support, and legitimacy (Lounsbury & Glynn, 2019).

Operationalizing the construct of cultural resonance highlights the fruitfulness of understanding cultural entrepreneurship as an interactive, negotiated process, compared to the dominant entrepreneur-centric focus in much entrepreneurship research, as well as how these processes may differ in time and across different entrepreneurial contexts. This study applies the theoretical lens of cultural entrepreneurship to a specific entrepreneurial context, that of a digital bank, named Widiba, that needed to legitimize itself, having been launched and financed by a large Italian bank that was going through a reputational crisis.

By focusing on collective storytelling embedded in a book titled *Pop Chronicle of Widiba*, we could address the research question "How does culture matter for a fintech new venture?" and conduct a thorough analysis of how a target audience, consisting of board members, start-up team members, professionals, managers, and employees, engaged with the founder narrative during the early stages of the venture.

The results of our study confirm that cultural resonance is a complex construct that encompasses cognitive alignment and emotional impact, thereby reinforcing the sense of participation and commitment of qualified human resources in a critical and delicate period for the survival of a company. Furthermore, they provide a foundation for advancing research in the field of collective storytelling as a tool to enhance intrapreneurship.

Limitations and Future Research

The first aspect of debate concerns the role that one of the authors had inside the digital bank as an independent board member from the seed phase until 2019. This involvement, as we have already pointed out, can be an enrichment for the research, but also a source of bias, which the researchers mitigated through the content analysis protocol. It is also emphasized that the time elapsed since the end of the assignment allowed the insider researcher to mature into a reflective discourse, also supported by the comparison with the co-author who analyzed the information in the role of an external researcher.

The case study methodology and manual coding employed in this research offer both strengths and limitations.

A key strength lies in the depth and richness of the insights derived from the participants' voluntary contributions to the collective story. This qualitative approach allows for a nuanced understanding of the different roles highlighted in the study. As highlighted by Lounsbury and Glynn (2001, pp. 549–550), one of the key benefits of storytelling is its ability to reduce uncertainty, which is critical to the success of emerging entrepreneurial ventures, by simplifying and organizing complex, ambiguous, and contradictory actions into a more coherent narrative. They provide structure and a sense of coherent social reality, which we were able to effectively identify in relation to an audience of individuals involved in the creation of the venture.

However, a significant limitation of our research is the partial audience, which does not fully represent the diversity of both internal and external audiences. This limits the completeness of the findings, as the sample may not capture the full range of perspectives relevant to assessing whether the founding story of Widiba was successful. Therefore, future research could analyze the customer-user perspective through the collective storytelling that emerges, for example, on social media, and this could be fruitful in exploring whether and how competing stories told by different audiences might exist and how they might affect the company's identity and image.

Future research could also employ open coding to map new constructs that emerge from the data. Open coding, as proposed by Strauss and Corbin (1990), would enable researchers to remain receptive to data that fall outside predefined constructs, potentially uncovering novel insights from individuals' unique experiences and stories. This approach could enhance the comprehensiveness and flexibility of the coding process, leading to a more robust analysis.

Additionally, future studies could utilize computer-assisted text analysis to examine the semantic network between words. Analyzing co-occurrence data can help develop a semantic network analysis, providing a deeper understanding of the relationships and patterns within the textual data. This method would complement the manual coding process by offering a more systematic and quantitative approach to data analysis.

Open coding and computer-assisted text analysis will help to explore new themes that emerge from the whole reading of individual stories. At this stage, we have identified two promising new lines of research.

The first concerns the relevance of cultural value (as defined in the literature by Throsby, 1999, 2003) within the innovative and creative processes that characterize the new ventures, and which are particularly important in high-tech sectors that provide services to end consumers, as in the case study examined.

Second, future research should delve deeper into the role and construct of intrapreneurship in new ventures. Investigating how intrapreneurial activities influence the development and success of new ventures can provide valuable insights into this critical aspect of cultural entrepreneurship. By exploring these areas, future studies can build on the current research and contribute to a more comprehensive understanding of the dynamics at play in collective storytelling and entrepreneurial contexts.

Annex: Our Database Structure

Phase	Individuals story no	Role of individuals	Innovativeness excerpts	Social impact excerpts	Market culture excerpts	Emotional impact excerpts

(info available on request)

References

Aldrich, H. E., & Fiol, C. M. (1994). Fools rush in? The institutional context of industry creation. *Academy of Management Review, 19*(4), 645–670.

Anne, V. N. (2014). *Journal of Emerging Trends in Educational Research and Policy Studies (JETERAPS), 5*(2), 272–281.

Antoncic, B., & Hisrich, R. D. (2001). Intrapreneurship: Construct refinement and cross-cultural validation. *Journal of Business Venturing, 16*(5), 495–527.

Ansari, S., Garud, R., & Kumaraswamy, A. (2016). The disruptor's dilemma: TiVo and the US television ecosystem. *Strategic Management Journal, 37*(9), 1829–1853.

Aguinis, H., & Solarino, A. M. (2019). Transparency and replicability in qualitative research: The case of interviews with elite informants. *Strategic Management Journal, 40*(8), 1291–1315.

Arner, D. W., Barberis, J. N., & Buckley, R. P. (2017). FinTech, RegTech, and the reconceptualization of financial regulation. *Northwestern Journal of International Law and Business, 37*(3), 371–413.

Barney, J. (1991). Firm resources and sustained competitive advantage. *Journal of Management, 17*(1), 99–120.

Cameron, K. S., Quinn, R. E., DeGraff, J., & Thakor, A. V. (2006). Competing values leadership: Creating value in organizations. In *Competing Values Leadership*. Edward Elgar.

Czarniawska, B. (1997). *Narrating the organization: Dramas of institutional identity*. University of Chicago Press.

Del Baldo, M., & Demartini, P. (2021). Cultural Heritage through the "youth eyes": Towards participatory governance and management of UNESCO sites. In P. Demartini, L. Marchegiani, M. Marchiori, & G. Schiuma (Eds.), *Cultural initiatives for sustainable development: Management, participation and entrepreneurship in the cultural and creative sector* (pp. 293–319). Springer.

DiMaggio, P. J., & Powell, W. W. (1983). The iron cage revisited: Institutional isomorphism and collective rationality in organizational fields. *American Sociological Review, 48*(2), 147–160.

Elsbach, K. D., & Kramer, R. M. (1996). Members' responses to organizational identity threats: Encountering and countering the Business Week rankings. *Administrative Science Quarterly, 41*(3), 442–476.

Fisher, G., Kuratko, D. F., Bloodgood, J. M., & Hornsby, J. S. (2017). Legitimate to whom? The challenge of audience diversity and new venture legitimacy. *Journal of Business Venturing, 32*(1), 52–71.

Gabriel, Y. (2000). *Storytelling in organizations: Facts, fictions, and fantasies*. OUP Oxford.

Gehman, J., & Soublière, J.-F. (2017). Cultural entrepreneurship: From making culture to cultural making. *Innovation, 19*(1), 61–73.

Gioia, D. A., Patvardhan, S. D., Hamilton, A. L., & Corley, K. G. (2013). Organizational identity formation and change. *Academy of Management Annals, 7*(1), 123–193.

Giorgi, S. (2017). The mind and heart of resonance: The role of cognition and emotions in frame effectiveness. *Journal of Management Studies, 54*(5), 711–738.

Glaser, V. L., & Lounsbury, M. (2021). Designing legitimacy: Expanding the scope of cultural entrepreneurship. *Journal of Business Venturing Design, 1*(1–2), 100007.

Glynn, M. A. (2000). When cymbals become symbols: Conflict over organizational identity within a symphony orchestra. *Organization Science, 11*(3), 285–298.

Glynn, M. A., & Lounsbury, M. (2022). Two decades of the theory of cultural entrepreneurship: Recollection, elaboration, and reflection. In *Advances in cultural entrepreneurship* (pp. 241–251). Emerald Publishing.

Glynn, M. A., & Lounsbury, M. (2005). From the critics' corner: Logic blending, discursive change and authenticity in a cultural production system. *Journal of Management Studies, 42*(5), 1031–1055.

Golant, B. D., & Sillince, J. A. (2007). The constitution of organizational legitimacy: A narrative perspective. *Organization Studies, 28*(8), 1149–1167.

Grimes, M. (2018). The pivot: How founders respond to feedback through idea and identity work. *Academy of Management Journal, 61*(5), 1692–1717.

Guba, E. G. (1981). Criteria for assessing the trustworthiness of naturalistic inquiries. *Educational Technology Research and Development, 29*(2), 75–91.

Lee, I., & Shin, Y. J. (2018). Fintech: Ecosystem, business models, investment decisions, and challenges. *Business Horizons, 61*(1), 35–46.

Lee, M., & Huang, L. (2018). Gender bias, social impact framing, and evaluation of entrepreneurial ventures. *Organization Science, 29*(1), 1–16.

Levinson, S. C. (2003). *Space in language and cognition: Explorations in cognitive diversity* (Vol. 5). Cambridge University Press.

Lockwood, C., Giorgi, S., & Glynn, M. A. (2019). "How to do things with words": Mechanisms bridging language and action in management research. *Journal of Management, 45*(1), 7–34.

Lounsbury, M., & Glynn, M. A. (2001). Cultural entrepreneurship: Stories, legitimacy, and the acquisition of resources. *Strategic Management Journal, 22*(6–7), 545–564.

Lounsbury, M., Gehman, J., & Ann Glynn, M. (2019). Beyond homo entrepreneurs: Judgment and the theory of cultural entrepreneurship. *Journal of Management Studies, 56*(6), 1214–1236.

Lounsbury, M., & Glynn, M. A. (2019). *Cultural entrepreneurship: A new agenda for the study of entrepreneurial processes and possibilities*. Cambridge University Press.

McKenny, A. F., Aguinis, H., Short, J. C., & Anglin, A. H. (2018). What doesn't get measured does exist: Improving the accuracy of computer-aided text analysis. *Journal of Management, 44*(7), 2909–2933.

Meyer, R. E., & Höllerer, M. A. (2010). Meaning structures in a contested issue field: A topographic map of shareholder value in Austria. *Academy of Management Journal, 53*(6), 1241–1262.
Milian, E. Z., Spinola, M. D. M., & de Carvalho, M. M. (2019). Fintechs: A literature review and research agenda. *Electronic Commerce Research and Applications, 34*, 100833.
Miller, G. A. (1995). WordNet: A lexical database for English. *Communications of the ACM, 38*(11), 39–41.
Morse, J. M., Barrett, M., Mayan, M., Olson, K., & Spiers, J. (2002). Verification strategies for establishing reliability and validity in qualitative research. *International Journal of Qualitative Methods, 1*(2), 13–22.
Moss, T. W., Renko, M., Block, E., & Meyskens, M. (2018). Funding the story of hybrid ventures: Crowdfunder lending preferences and linguistic hybridity. *Journal of Business Venturing, 33*(5), 643–659.
Navis, C., & Glynn, M. A. (2011). Legitimate distinctiveness and the entrepreneurial identity: Influence on investor judgments of new venture plausibility. *Academy of Management Review, 36*(3), 479–499.
Pan, L., Li, X., Chen, J., & Chen, T. (2020). Sounds novel or familiar? Entrepreneurs' framing strategy in the venture capital market. *Journal of Business Venturing, 35*(2), 105930.
Penrose, E. (1959). *The theory of the growth of the firm*. Oxford University Press.
Schueffel, P. (2016). Taming the beast: A scientific definition of Fintech. *Journal of Innovation Management, 4*(4), 32–54.
Scott, W. R. (1995). *Institutions and organizations. Ideas, interests and identities*. Sage.
Snihur, Y., Thomas, L. D., & Burgelman, R. A. (2018). An ecosystem-level process model of business model disruption: The disruptor's gambit. *Journal of Management Studies, 55*(7), 1278–1316.
Stone, P. J., Dunphy, D. C., Smith, M. S., & Ogilvie, D. M. (1966). *The general inquirer: A computer approach to content analysis*. M.I.T. Press.
Strauss, A., & Corbin, J. (1990). *Basics of qualitative research: Grounded theory procedures and techniques*. Sage.
Teece, D. J., Pisano, G., & Shuen, A. (1997). Dynamic capabilities and strategic management. *Strategic Management Journal, 18*(7), 509–533.
Throsby, D. (1999). Cultural capital. *Journal of Cultural Economics, 23*(1–2), 3–12.
Throsby, C. D. (2001). *Economics and culture*. Cambridge university press.
Throsby, D. (2003). Determining the value of cultural goods: How much (or how little) does contingent valuation tell us? *Journal of Cultural Economics, 27*(3–4), 275–285.
Überbacher, F. (2014). Legitimation of new ventures: A review and research programme. *Journal of Management Studies, 51*(4), 667–698.
Unluer, S. (2012). Being an insider researcher while conducting case study research. *Qualitative Report, 17*, 58.
Vaara, E., Sonenshein, S., & Boje, D. (2016). Narratives as sources of stability and change in organizations: Approaches and directions for future research. *Academy of Management Annals, 10*(1), 495–560.
Van Werven, R., Bouwmeester, O., & Cornelissen, J. P. (2015). The power of arguments: How entrepreneurs convince stakeholders of the legitimate distinctiveness of their ventures. *Journal of Business Venturing, 30*(4), 616–631.
Wegener, F. E., & Lorino, P. (2021). Capturing the experience of living forward from within the flow. In J. Reinecke, R. Suddaby, & A. Langley (Eds.), *Time, temporality, and history in process organization studies* (pp. 138–168). Oxford University Press.
Weick, K. E. (1995). *Sensemaking in organizations*. Sage.
Widiba Cronanca Pop. (2018). (title translated as Pop Chronicle of Widiba). Gribaudo, Feltrinelli, Milan.
Widiba Website. https://www.widiba.it
Wry, T., Lounsbury, M., & Glynn, M. A. (2011). Legitimating nascent collective identities: Coordinating cultural entrepreneurship. *Organization Science, 22*(2), 449–463.

The manufacturer's authorised representative in the EU is Springer
Nature Customer Service Centre GmbH, Europaplatz 3, 69115 Heidelberg,
Germany. If you have any concerns regarding our products, please
contact ProductSafety@springernature.com

Printed and bound by CPI Group (UK) Ltd, Croydon, CR0 4YY
01/10/2026
02225966-0013